CCNA Self-Study:
Introduction to Cisco Networking Technologies (INTRO)

Steve McQuerry, Editor

Cisco Press

Cisco Press
800 East 96th Street
Indianapolis, Indiana 46240 USA

CCNA Self-Study:

Introduction to Cisco Networking Technologies (INTRO)

Steve McQuerry, Editor

Copyright© 2004 Cisco Systems, Inc.

Published by:
Cisco Press
800 East 96th Street
Indianapolis, IN 46240 USA

ISBN: 1587051613

Library of Congress Cataloging-in-Publication Number: 2003108306

Printed in the United States of America 2 3 4 5 6 7 8 9 0

Second Printing May 2004

Warning and Disclaimer

This book is designed to provide information about Cisco networking. Every effort has been made to make this book as complete and as accurate as possible, but no warranty or fitness is implied.

The information is provided on an "as is" basis. The author, Cisco Press, and Cisco Systems, Inc., shall have neither liability nor responsibility to any person or entity with respect to any loss or damages arising from the information contained in this book or from the use of the discs or programs that may accompany it.

The opinions expressed in this book belong to the author and are not necessarily those of Cisco Systems, Inc.

The Cisco Press self-study book series is as described, intended for self-study. It has not been designed for use in a classroom environment. Only Cisco Learning Partners displaying the following logos are authorized providers of Cisco curriculum. If you are using this book within the classroom of a training company that does not carry one of these logos, then you are not preparing with a Cisco trained and authorized provider. For information on Cisco Learning Partners please visit:www.cisco.com/go/authorizedtraining. To provide Cisco with any information about what you may believe is unauthorized use of Cisco trademarks or copyrighted training material, please visit: http://www.cisco.com/logo/infringement.html.

Trademark Acknowledgments

All terms mentioned in this book that are known to be trademarks or service marks have been appropriately capitalized. Cisco Press or Cisco Systems, Inc., cannot attest to the accuracy of this information. Use of a term in this book should not be regarded as affecting the validity of any trademark or service mark.

Corporate and Government Sales

Cisco Press offers excellent discounts on this book when ordered in quantity for bulk purchases or special sales.

For more information please contact: **U.S. Corporate and Government Sales** 1-800-382-3419
corpsales@pearsontechgroup.com

For sales outside the U.S. please contact: **International Sales** international@pearsoned.com

Feedback Information

At Cisco Press, our goal is to create in-depth technical books of the highest quality and value. Each book is crafted with care and precision, undergoing rigorous development that involves the unique expertise of members from the professional technical community.

Readers' feedback is a natural continuation of this process. If you have any comments regarding how we could improve the quality of this book, or otherwise alter it to better suit your needs, you can contact us through e-mail at feedback@ciscopress.com. Please make sure to include the book title and ISBN in your message.

We greatly appreciate your assistance.

Publisher	John Wait
Editor-in-Chief	John Kane
Executive Editor	Brett Bartow
Cisco Representative	Anthony Wolfenden
Cisco Press Program Manager	Nannette M. Noble
Production Manager	Patrick Kanouse
Development Editor	Dayna Isley
Senior Project Editor	Sheri Cain
Copy Editor	Kevin Kent
Technical Editors	Don Johnston, Steve Kalman, Jay Swan
Team Coordinator	Tammi Barnett
Cover Designer	Louisa Adair
Composition	Tolman Creek Design
Indexer	Tim Wright

CISCO SYSTEMS

Corporate Headquarters
Cisco Systems, Inc.
170 West Tasman Drive
San Jose, CA 95134-1706
USA
www.cisco.com
Tel: 408 526-4000
      800 553-NETS (6387)
Fax: 408 526-4100

European Headquarters
Cisco Systems International BV
Haarlerbergpark
Haarlerbergweg 13-19
1101 CH Amsterdam
The Netherlands
www-europe.cisco.com
Tel: 31 0 20 357 1000
Fax: 31 0 20 357 1100

Americas Headquarters
Cisco Systems, Inc.
170 West Tasman Drive
San Jose, CA 95134-1706
USA
www.cisco.com
Tel: 408 526-7660
Fax: 408 527-0883

Asia Pacific Headquarters
Cisco Systems, Inc.
Capital Tower
168 Robinson Road
#22-01 to #29-01
Singapore 068912
www.cisco.com
Tel: +65 6317 7777
Fax: +65 6317 7799

Cisco Systems has more than 200 offices in the following countries and regions. Addresses, phone numbers, and fax numbers are listed on the
Cisco.com Web site at www.cisco.com/go/offices.

Argentina • Australia • Austria • Belgium • Brazil • Bulgaria • Canada • Chile • China PRC • Colombia • Costa Rica • Croatia • Czech Republic
Denmark • Dubai, UAE • Finland • France • Germany • Greece • Hong Kong SAR • Hungary • India • Indonesia • Ireland • Israel • Italy
Japan • Korea • Luxembourg • Malaysia • Mexico • The Netherlands • New Zealand • Norway • Peru • Philippines • Poland • Portugal
Puerto Rico • Romania • Russia • Saudi Arabia • Scotland • Singapore • Slovakia • Slovenia • South Africa • Spain • Sweden
Switzerland • Taiwan • Thailand • Turkey • Ukraine • United Kingdom • United States • Venezuela • Vietnam • Zimbabwe

About the Editor

Steve McQuerry, CCIE No. 6108, is an instructor, technical writer, and internetworking consultant with more than 10 years of networking industry experience. He is a certified Cisco Systems instructor teaching routing and switching concepts to internetworking professionals throughout the world and has been teaching CCNA and CCNP candidates since 1998. Steve is also a consultant with Intrellix, LLC, an internetworking consulting company specializing in post sales consulting services.

About the Technical Reviewers

Don Johnston is a certified Cisco Systems instructor and consultant with 20 years of experience teaching computing and networking. He is currently teaching CCNP courses with Global Knowledge as a contract instructor and consults with clients on routing and switching design, implementation, and diagnosis of existing problems.

Steve Kalman is the principal officer at Esquire Micro Consultants, which offers lecturing, writing, and consulting services. He has more than 30 years of experience in data processing, with strengths in network design and implementation. Kalman is a freelance instructor and author. He has written and reviewed many networking-related titles and, most recently, authored *Web Security Field Guide* with Cisco Press. In addition to being an attorney, he holds CISSP, CCNA, CCDA, ECNE, A+, Security+, and Network+ certifications.

Jay Swan, CCNP, CCSP, teaches Cisco courses with Global Knowledge. He is a certified Cisco Systems instructor with bachelor's and master's degrees from Stanford University. Prior to joining Global Knowledge, he worked in the ISP and higher education fields. He lives in southwest Colorado, where he is an active trail runner, search and rescue volunteer, and martial arts practitioner.

Dedications

I would like to dedicate this work to my loving wife Becky. As long as I can remember, you have always been there for me. I could not have asked for a more perfect partner in life. I would also like to dedicate this work to my children. Katie, you show a great spirit, work ethic, and determination. I am confident you will achieve all of your goals in life. Logan, your sense of responsibility and fair play will give you the leadership skills to be successful in anything you want to do. Cameron, you have energy and drive that gives you the ability to do great things; I know that you will be able to do anything you desire. It is said that children learn from their parents, I only wish I could take the credit for the roles you are growing into. The truth is that I learn from you, everyday, and it is my wish that you will continue to teach me all the wonder that life holds.

Acknowledgments

If you are reading this, you have probably been involved in some type of publishing process or know someone who has. If you do not fall into one of these categories, let met thank you for taking the time to find out about all the wonderful people behind this book. For anyone who has worked anywhere in the publishing community, it is common knowledge that regardless of whose name is on the cover, there are dozens of people behind a successful project, and this one is no exception. As a matter of fact, the people here deserve more credit for this project than I do. So as insignificant as these acknowledgments seem, to me, they are among the most important words I can write in the entire work.

I would like to thank the technical editors: Steve Kalman, Don Johnston, and Jay Swan. Without their keen eyesight and insight, my work would be much less polished.

I would like to thank all the wonderful people at Cisco Press. This is my sixth writing project in the past five years and the second of this summer. I cannot begin to express in this paragraph how great it has been to work with these fine professionals. I would not begin to think about writing without this fine group. Thanks to Dayna Isley for keeping me on track and focused. It has been a joy to work with you on this project, and I hope we get to work together again. Thanks to Brett Bartow, the acquisitions editor, who back in 1998 gave me the opportunity to start in the technical-writing field. You have been a guiding force in my writing career and I truly appreciate that. Thanks to Tammi Barnett, who puts up with my relentless requests and keeps everything in the proper queues. Also, thanks to John Kane, Sheri Cain, and Tim Wright—you are the best in the industry!

I would be remiss if I didn't mention all the students and instructors I have had the pleasure of teaching and working with over the past several years. Your questions, comments, and challenges offered many of the tips, cautions, and questions for this book.

I would like to thank my family for their patience and understanding during this project and all of my projects.

Most important, I would like to thank God for giving me the skills, talents, and opportunity to work in such a challenging and exciting profession.

Contents at a Glance

Contents

Icons Used in This Book

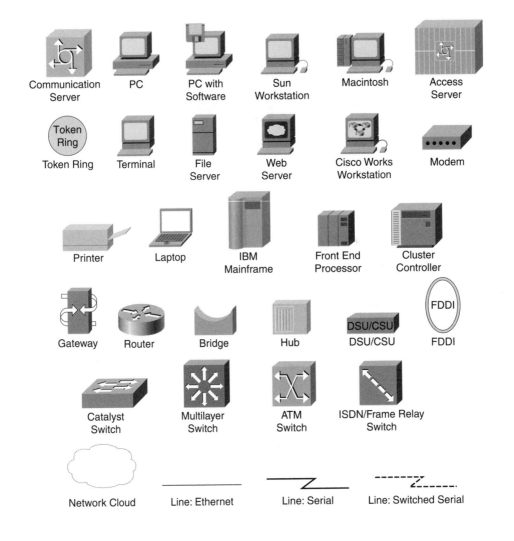

Command Syntax Conventions

The conventions used to present command syntax in this book are the same conventions used in the *Cisco IOS Command Reference*, as follows:

- **Boldface** indicates commands and keywords that are entered literally as shown. In examples (not syntax), boldface indicates user input (for example, a **show** command).

- *Italics* indicate arguments for which you supply values.

- Square brackets ([and]) indicate optional elements.

- Braces ({ and }) contain a choice of required keywords.

- Vertical bars (|) separate alternative, mutually exclusive elements.

- Braces and vertical bars within square brackets—for example, [x {y | z}]—indicate a required choice within an optional element. You do not need to enter what is in the brackets, but if you do, you have some required choices in the braces.

Foreword

CCNA Self-Study: Introduction to Cisco Networking Technologies (INTRO) is a Cisco authorized, self-paced learning tool that helps you understand foundation concepts covered on the Cisco Certified Network Associate (CCNA) exams. This book was developed in cooperation with the Cisco Internet Learning Solutions Group, the team within Cisco responsible for the development of the CCNA exams. As an early stage exam preparation product, this book presents detailed and comprehensive coverage of the tasks that network engineers need to perform to build and support small- to medium-sized networks. Whether you are studying to become CCNA certified or are simply seeking to gain a better understanding of networking fundamentals using the Open System Interconnection (OSI) seven-layer model concepts, you will benefit from the information presented in this book.

Cisco Systems and Cisco Press present this material in text-based format to provide another learning vehicle for our customers and the broader user community in general. Although a publication does not duplicate the instructor-led or e-learning environment, we acknowledge that not everyone responds in the same way to the same delivery mechanism. It is our intent that presenting this material via a Cisco Press publication will enhance the transfer of knowledge to a broad audience of networking professionals.

Cisco Press will present other books in the certification self-study series on existing and future exams to help achieve Cisco Internet Learning Solutions Group's principal objectives: to educate the Cisco community of networking professionals and to enable that community to build and maintain reliable, scalable networks. The Cisco Career Certifications and classes that support these certifications are directed at meeting these objectives through a disciplined approach to progressive learning.

To succeed with Cisco Career Certifications and in your daily job as a Cisco certified professional, we recommend a blended learning solution that combines instructor-led training with hands-on experience, e-learning, and self-study training. Cisco Systems has authorized Cisco Learning Partners worldwide, which can provide you with the most highly qualified instruction and invaluable hands-on experience in lab and simulation environments. To learn more about Cisco Learning Partner programs available in your area, visit www.cisco.com/go/authorizedtraining.

The books Cisco Press creates in partnership with Cisco Systems meets the same standards for content quality demanded of our courses and certifications. It is our intent that you will find this and subsequent Cisco Press certification self-study publications of value as you build your networking knowledge base.

Thomas M. Kelly
Vice President, Internet Learning Solutions Group
Cisco Systems, Inc.
January 2004

Introduction

Since the introduction of the personal computer in the early 1970s, businesses have found more uses and applications for technology in the workplace. With the introduction of LANs, file sharing, and print sharing in the 1980s, it became obvious that distributed computing was no longer a passing fad. By the 1990s, computers became less expensive, and innovations such as the Internet allowed everyone to connect to computer services worldwide. Computing services have become large and distributed. The days of punch cards and greenbar paper are behind us, and a new generation of computing experts is being asked to keep this distributed technology operational. These experts are destined to have a new set of issues and problems to deal with, the most complex of them being connectivity and compatibility between differing systems and devices.

The primary challenge with data networking today is to link multiple devices' protocols and sites with maximum effectiveness and ease of use for the end users. Of course, this must all be accomplished in a cost-effective way. Cisco Systems offers a variety of products to give network managers and analysts the ability to face and solve the challenges of internetworking.

In an effort to ensure that these networking professionals have the knowledge to perform these arduous tasks, Cisco Systems has developed a series of courses and certifications that act as benchmarks for internetworking professionals. These courses help internetworking professionals learn the fundamentals of internetworking technologies along with skills in configuring and installing Cisco products. The certification exams are designed to be a litmus test for the skills required to perform at various levels of internetworking. The Cisco certifications range from the associate level, CCNA (Cisco Certified Network Associate), through the professional level, CCNP (Cisco Certified Network Professional), to the expert level, CCIE (Cisco Certified Internetwork Expert). This book is a self-study product based on the Cisco course "Introduction to Networking," one of the two courses, the second being "Interconnecting Cisco Network Devices," used to ground individuals in the fundamentals of switched and routed internetworks.

This book presents the foundation concepts and basic interface commands required to configure Cisco switches and routers to operate in corporate internetworks. You are introduced to all the basic concepts and configuration procedures required to build a multiswitch, multirouter, and multigroup internetwork that uses LAN and WAN interfaces for the most commonly used routing and routed protocols.

INTRO is the first of a two-part introductory level series and is recommended for individuals who have one to three years of internetworking experience and want to become familiar with basic internetworking concepts and the TCP/IP protocol. This book also provides a working knowledge of the Cisco IOS operating system.

Although the self-study book is designed for those who are pursuing the CCNA certification, it is also useful for network administrators responsible for implementing and managing small and medium-sized business networks. Network support staff who performs a help desk role in a medium- or enterprise-sized company will find this a valuable resource. Finally, Cisco customers or channel resellers and network technicians entering the internetworking industry who are new to Cisco products can benefit from the contents of this book.

Goal of This Book

This book is intended as a self-study book for the INTRO exam, which is required for the CCNA certification. Like the certification itself, this book helps readers become literate in the basics of internetworking, TCP/IP, and the use of Cisco IOS on switches and routers. By using these skills, someone who completes this book and/or the INTRO course should be able to pass the INTRO exam and be adequately prepared to continue on to the ICND materials.

Readers interested in more information about the CCNA certification should consult the Cisco website at http://www.cisco.com and navigate to the CCNA page through the Learning & Events/Career Certifications and Paths link. To schedule a Cisco certification test, contact Pearson Vue on the web at http://www.vue.com/cisco or Prometric on the web at www.2test.com.

Chapter Organization

This book is broken up into four parts. This book is designed to be read in order because many chapters build on content from a previous chapter.

Part I, "Internetworking Basics," includes chapters that explain the basic networking computing concepts:

- Chapter 1, "Introduction to Internetworking," reviews the components that make up a computer network and some common numbering systems used in computing.

- Chapter 2, "Internetworking Devices," explores the different components used to interconnect various computer networks.

- Chapter 3, "Common Types of Networks," describes many of the common network topologies and media used in today's network environments.

Part II, "The Internetworking Layers," describes how internetworking devices provide services at the lower three layers of the OSI model:

- Chapter 4, "Network Media (The Physical Layer)," looks at the different media used to connect network devices and describes where each should be deployed in an internetwork.

- Chapter 5, "Layer 2 Switching Fundamentals (The Data Link Layer)," discusses the process used to forward frames in a Layer 2 environment. This chapter also discusses the problems caused by Layer 2 forwarding and the solutions that contain these problems.

- Chapter 6, "TCP/IP (The Transport and Internetworking Layer Protocol)," describes the basics of the TCP/IP protocol, including the use of ICMP, ARP, UDP, and TCP in internetwork environments.

- Chapter 7, "IP Addressing and Routing (The Internetworking Layer)," describes the how IP addresses are assigned and how Layer 3 devices use these address structures for the delivery of packets throughout the internetwork.

Part III, "Administering Cisco Devices," looks beyond the LAN and discusses connecting devices across wide geographic locations and also discusses the Cisco IOS and management functions used in configuring and managing internetworking devices:

- Chapter 8, "Using WAN Technologies," provides an overview of WAN connectivity. This chapter discusses methods of connecting to remote sites using leased lines, circuit-switching, and frame-switching services.

- Chapter 9, "Operating and Configuring Cisco IOS Devices," describes how a router and switch boots and how to use the command-line interpreter to configure a Cisco IOS switch or router.

- In Chapter 10, "Managing Your Network Environment," you learn how to use tools like CDP, ping, and traceroute to discover, map, and troubleshoot devices in the internetwork.

Part IV of this book includes the following:

- Appendix A, "Answers to the Chapter Review Questions and Quizzes," provides answers to the review questions at the end of each chapter and the quizzes throughout each chapter.

- The Glossary contains the definitions to commonly used internetworking terms throughout this book.

Features

This book features actual router and switch output to aid in the discussion of the configuration of these devices. Many notes, tips, and cautions are spread throughout the text. In addition, you can find many references to standards, documents, books, and websites that help you understand networking concepts. At the end of each chapter, your comprehension and knowledge are tested by questions reviewed by a certified Cisco Systems instructor.

NOTE   The operating systems used in this book are Cisco IOS version 12.2 for the routers, and Cisco Catalyst 2950 is based on Cisco IOS version 12.1.13.EA1b.

Internetworking Basics

Upon completion of this chapter, you will be able to perform the following tasks:

- Identify the major components of a computer system
- Understand the binary and hexadecimal numbering system used in computer and networking systems and be able to convert between these numbering systems and decimal numbers
- Define basic networking terminology
- Describe the benefits and functions of the OSI reference model and the TCP/IP protocol stack
- Describe the basic process of communications between the layers of the OSI reference model

CHAPTER 1

Introduction to Internetworking

This chapter provides a baseline of knowledge for the understanding of computer internetworking. It addresses the components of a computer and the role of computers in an internetworking system. This chapter begins with the most basic component of the internetwork, the computer. It also covers the numbering systems used by computers along with a comparison to the decimal numbering system.

This chapter also explains how standards ensure greater compatibility and interoperability between various types of networking technologies by discussing the basic functions that occur at each layer of the Open System Interconnection (OSI) reference model. It also discusses how information (or data) makes its way from application programs (such as spreadsheets or e-mail) through a network medium (such as copper wiring) to other application programs located on other computers in a network.

Network devices are products used to interconnect computer networks into what are known as internetworks. Understanding, building, and managing internetworks are the jobs of a networking professional. As computer internetworks grow in size and complexity, so do the network devices used to connect them. This chapter also discusses how different network devices interconnect computer networks by operating at different layers of the OSI model to appropriately separate and organize traffic patterns. In addition to looking at the OSI module, the chapter references the TCP/IP standard used throughout the world for network communications.

Network Computing Basics

Networks have become a fundamental component of almost every business throughout the world, but the network exists only to provide a medium for the computer. Much like roads and highways provide a medium for cars, the network allows computers to move information from one system to another. The computer is the reason that the data network exists. Before exploring the many fascinating aspects of data networks, it is vital that you have a thorough understanding of the components in a computer and how they relate to the data network.

In particular, you should be familiar with the system components like the processor, bus, storage units, and expansion cards. You should also have a basic understanding of how the personal computer or desktop differs from a laptop computer. You also need to understand how an expansion card known as the *network interface card (NIC)* interacts with applications and network media to provide communications between devices. It is this communication that defines a data network.

Personal Computer Components

The computer is the reason that the data network exists. Almost every device that attaches to a data network could be classified as a computer. Some of these computers are specialized devices such as servers, print servers, and even network devices like routers, whereas other computers are general-purpose devices like a personal computer. Regardless of the type of device, the computer is made up of several components such as the central processing unit (CPU), memory, storage device, input devices, output devices, and communications components. The CPU and memory are the two primary components that drive a computing device.

CPU and Memory

A *CPU*, like the one shown in Figure 1-1, is the brain of a computing device and is where most of the calculations and operations take place. For a personal computer, the CPU is where software instructions, like those used by an operating system, are carried out. This CPU also enables the user to provide input via a keyboard or mouse and the CPU sends output to the monitor, speaker, or printer.

Figure 1-1   *CPU*

The CPU is a silicon-based microprocessor. The speed at which a computer can operate depends on the type and speed of CPU that is installed. A CPU's speed is typically measured in gigahertz (GHz) or megahertz (MHz), which relates to the clock speed in cycles per second (hertz). The faster the CPU's clock speed, the faster it can carry out instructions and calculations from software.

Like a brain connects to the rest of the systems in the body, the CPU is connected to several other components in a computer to create a whole unit known as the *personal computer (PC)*. The foundation that the CPU resides on is called the *motherboard*. Figure 1-2 shows a typical motherboard.

Figure 1-2   *Motherboard*

The motherboard houses the base components of the computer system like the CPU. The motherboard also provides connectors between the primary components and devices that provide storage, input, output, and communications. The motherboard is built on what is known as a *printed circuit board (PCB)*. A PCB is a thin plate on which chips (integrated circuits) and other electronic components are placed.

The motherboard also houses the key memory components of the system. Memory stores applications and data for use by the CPU. Two main types of memory exist on the system board: random-access memory (RAM) and read-only memory (ROM).

RAM is typically used by the CPU to write data from an application into its memory locations as well as read that data out of the memory locations. These read-writes are performed to allow an application to manipulate data. RAM is also known as read-write memory. One of the major drawbacks of RAM is that it requires electrical power to maintain data storage. If the computer is turned off or loses power, all data stored in RAM is lost unless the data was saved to a storage location like a disk. Because of this, RAM is considered volatile memory whose data is lost when the power is removed.

ROM is a memory device that contains information needed by the computer for operation. ROM is maintained even when the computer does not have power. ROM usually contains instructions used by the system during startup or can contain information that identifies a system. Memory in ROM is considered permanent because it is not lost during power down.

Because RAM loses information during power down and because only limited amounts of memory exist in a system, computers need storage devices so that the data can be saved and recalled as needed. There are two main types of storage for computers: removable storage and permanent storage. A floppy disk drive and compact disc read-only memory (CD-ROM) are examples of removable storage devices. A hard disk drive is an example of a permanent storage device.

Storage Devices

A floppy disk drive, like the one shown in Figure 1-3, can hold a limited amount of data on a thin removable disk. The drive can read and write to a disk. The disk, and the information on it, can then be inserted into a drive on another computer and be read by that device as well.

Figure 1-3   *Floppy Disk Drive*

A CD-ROM drive can read information from a compact disc. A compact disc can hold large amounts of memory, but a CD-ROM drive can only read data and cannot write to the disc.

NOTE   Many PCs also offer a derivative of the CD-ROM called a *CD-R/W*, or compact disc read/write, which allows a user to read and write to the compact disc. The advantage of the CD is that it stores more data than a floppy disk.

The hard disk drive is a read-write storage device typically located inside the computer. This device is capable of holding very large amounts of data, but the device cannot be removed easily and attached to another system so that the data can be used in another device. The hard drive is also the common location for the PC's operating system and removal of the drive could prevent the computer from working.

The CPU, memory, and storage are the key components in any computer system, but they must be tied together to operate properly. On the motherboard is a collection of wires that connects all the internal computer components to the CPU. This collection of conductors through which data is transmitted from one part of the computer to another is called a *bus.*

Expansion Bus

A computer contains several types of buses, such as address, data, and control buses. Also, some buses add components. These are called *expansion buses*. The Industry Standard Architecture (ISA) and the Peripheral Component Interface (PCI) are two common types of expansion buses.

The expansion bus also connects to openings called *expansion slots* on the motherboard. (See Figure 1-4). You can install a printed circuit board called an *expansion card* in an expansion slot to add new capabilities to the computer. Expansion cards typically add input/output or communications capabilities to a computer. A modem and a NIC are two examples of expansion cards.

Figure 1-4   *Expansion Slot*

The final component that a computer requires is power. The computer contains a power supply that supplies all the power to the devices within the computer.

When all of these components are placed together it is called the *system unit*. The system unit is the main part of a PC. It includes the chassis or case, microprocessor, main memory, bus, and ports. The system unit does not include the keyboard, monitor, or any other external devices connected to the computer.

Input and Output Devices

However, this system unit would be useless without the components that attach to the device. In particular, you need to attach input devices (mouse and keyboard), an output device (monitor), power, and a network connection to the PC for use within a data network.

The cards and services that provide these attachments are sometimes called *backplane components* because they attach to the PC bus. A *backplane* is a large circuit board that contains sockets for expansion cards and is another name for the motherboard and bus. The cards or components of the backplane contain *interfaces* or *ports*. An interface is a piece of hardware, such as a modem connecter, that allows two devices to be connected together. A port is a socket or opening on the PC that allows a device to be connected to the PC for input/output of data.

Several ports exist on a system unit, such as the keyboard port, mouse port, parallel port, and serial port. The *keyboard* and *mouse ports* are designed to connect these devices to the PC for input from a user. The *parallel port* is a port capable of transferring more than one bit of data simultaneously across parallel paths. The parallel port connects to external devices like a printer. The *serial port* is a port that transfers one bit at a time across the port. This type of transfer is known as serial communications because the bits are transferred one after another. Serial ports can be used to attach devices like modems or other asynchronous devices.

The backplane also contains devices for output such as the video card and sound card. The video card can plug into an expansion slot or be built into the motherboard and gives the PC its display capabilities. The sound card can also be an expansion card or a built-in card that provides sound functions. Video and sound allow the user to get responses from the PC about its operation.

To communicate with external devices, you have to attach your computer to a network using a network interface card (NIC). A NIC is an expansion board inserted into a computer so that the computer can be connected to a data network.

Once all these components have been powered and connected, a computer is ready for use. All the items described here are critical to the operation of the PC and therefore required for the computer to be networked.

Laptop Versus PC

Laptop and notebook computers have become increasingly popular devices within computer networks because of their mobility. The components in a PC are also present in a laptop computer. The main difference between PCs and laptops is that the laptop components are smaller than those found in a PC. Also in a laptop, the expansion slots are Personal Computer Memory Card International Association (PCMCIA) slots or PC card slots, through which a NIC, modem, hard drive, or other useful device can be connected to the system. A PCMCIA card is about the size of a credit card, but thicker. Figure 1-5 shows a PCMCIA network interface card.

Figure 1-5 *PCMCIA Card*

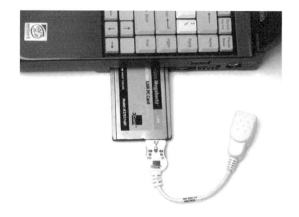

Network Interface Cards

As previously discussed in the chapter, the network interface card (NIC) is a printed circuit board that installs into an expansion slot to provide the PC or laptop with network communication capabilities. Figure 1-6 shows a typical NIC.

Figure 1-6 *Network Interface Card*

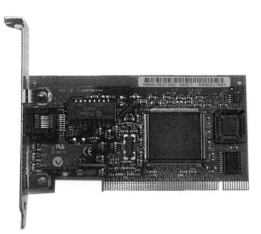

Also called a LAN adapter, a NIC plugs into a motherboard and provides a port for connecting to the network. The NIC constitutes the computer interface with the local-area network (LAN).

The NIC communicates with the network through a serial connection and with the computer through a parallel connection. When a NIC is installed in a computer, it requires an interrupt request line (IRQ), an input/output (I/O) address, a memory space for the operating system (such as Windows or Linux), and drivers to communicate between the operating system and hardware.

An IRQ is a signal that informs a CPU that an event needing the CPU's attention has occurred. An IRQ is sent over a hardware line to the microprocessor. An example of an interrupt being issued is when a key is pressed on a keyboard. The CPU must move the character from the keyboard to RAM. An I/O address is a location in memory used to enter or retrieve data from a computer by an auxiliary device.

When selecting a NIC for a network, you should consider the following items:

- **Type of network**—A 10/100 Ethernet NIC can be used for Ethernet LANs operating at 10 or 100 Mbps. A 10-Mbps Ethernet NIC can be used only for an Ethernet segment operating a 10 Mbps.

- **Type of media**—The type of port or connector used by the NIC for network connection is specific to media type, such as twisted pair, fiber, and so on.

- **Type of system bus**—PCs can have PCI or ISA expansion slots. The Ethernet card must match the expansion slot type the PC contains. Because ISA slots are slower than PCI, many manufacturers are phasing out ISA slots in their computers.

The NIC enables hosts to connect to the network. The NIC is considered a key component to the data network. To install a NIC into a computer, you need the following resources:

- Knowledge of how the network card is configured, including jumpers, "plug-and-play" software, and erasable programmable read-only memory (EPROM), which is similar to ROM. This information should be in the documentation related to the NIC.

- Use of network card diagnostics, including the vendor-supplied diagnostics and loopback tests, which allow you to test the send and receive components of the card. This information should also be contained in the documentation for the card.

- The ability to resolve hardware resource conflicts, including IRQ, I/O base address, and direct memory access (DMA) conflicts. DMA transfers data from the RAM to a device without going through the CPU, which improves performance.

NOTE   The plug-and-play features of most computers today automate the assignment of IRQ, I/O, and DMA addresses so that you should have no conflicts. However, it is still important to be able to recognize and possibly override these setting to correct possible conflicts.

Figure 1-7 shows the installation of a NIC.

WARNING	You should always be careful to use a static strap to avoid damage to the circuits when handling PCBs.

Figure 1-7   *Installing a NIC*

Network Computing Basics Section Quiz

Use the practice questions here to review what you learned in this section.

1 Match each of the following definitions with the appropriate word. (Choose the best answer.)

___ A silicon based CPU

___ Read-write memory that is lost when the power turned off

___ The main part of a PC, including the chassis, microprocessor, main memory, bus and ports

___ A printed circuit board that adds capabilities to a computer

A Motherboard

B Microprocessor

C ROM

D   PCB

E   Chassis

F   System unit

G   RAM

H   NIC

I   Expansion card

2   A laptop has the same main components as a PC, but they are typically smaller in size.

A   True

B   False

3   Which of the following are true statements about a NIC?

A   A NIC is an expansion card.

B   NIC communicates with the network media using parallel communications.

C   NIC requires an IRQ to request CPU services.

D   All NICs have PCI bus connections.

E   A NIC can use DMA architecture to directly access the system memory without using the CPU.

Computer Numbering Systems

Computers are electronic devices made up of electronic switches. At the lowest levels of computation, computers depend on these electronic switches to make decisions. As such, computers react only to electrical impulses. These electrical impulses are understood by the computer as either "on" or "off" states.

Computers can understand and process only data that is in the binary format. *Binary* is a numbering system that is represented by 0s and 1s, which are referred to as binary digits (bits). 0s represent the off state and 1s represent the on state of an electronic component. The binary number system is also closely related to the hexadecimal numbering system, which is used in programming and addressing. Understanding the numbering systems used by computers and being able to relate these systems to the decimal numbering system used by humans is an important tool in internetworking. Many of the addresses used by NICs and network protocols are based on the binary and hexadecimal numbering systems.

Computing Measurement Terms

This section describes the common networking numbers and the measurements of data. In this section, you learn how to count using these numbering systems. You also learn how to convert between binary, decimal, and hexadecimal.

Most computer coding schemes use 8 bits to represent each number, letter, or symbol. A series of 8 bits in memory is referred to as a *byte*. A byte also represents a single addressable storage location in memory or a hard drive.

The following are commonly used computer measurement terms:

- **Bit**—The bit is smallest unit of storage in memory or on a storage device. A bit equals 1 or 0 and is the binary format in which data is processed by computers.

- **Byte**—A byte is equal to 8 bits of data and is the smallest storage unit in memory or on a hard drive. A byte is the unit of measure used to describe the size of a data file, the amount of space on a disk or other storage medium, or the amount of data being sent over a network.

- **kb (kilobit)**—A kilobit is approximately 1000 bits.

- **kB (kilobyte)**—A kilobyte is approximately 1000 bytes (1024 bytes exactly).

- **kbps (kilobits per second)**—This is a standard measurement of the amount of data in bits transferred over a network connection.

- **kBps (kilobytes per second)**—This is a standard measurement of the amount of data in bytes transferred over a network connection.

- **Mb (megabit)**—A megabit is approximately 1 million bits.

- **MB (megabyte)**—A megabyte is approximately 1 million bytes (1,048,576 bytes exactly). A megabyte is sometimes referred to as a "meg."

- **Mbps (megabits per second)**—This is a standard measurement of the amount of data transferred in bits over a network connection.

- **MBps (megabytes per second)**—This is a standard measurement of the amount of data transferred in bytes over a network connection.

WARNING   It is a common error to confuse kB with kb and MB with Mb. A capital B (byte) represents 8 lowercase b's (bits). Remember to do the proper calculations when comparing transmission speeds that are measured in bytes with those measured in bits. For example, modem software usually shows the connection speed in kilobits per second, but popular browsers display file-download speeds in kilobytes per second. This means that for a modem with a 45 kbps connection, the download speed would be a maximum of 5.76 kBps. In reality, this download speed would not be achieved because of other factors like error checking that consume the bandwidth at the same time as the transfer.

Table 1-1 compares the common units of measurement.

Table 1-1   *Units of Measurement for Data*

Unit	Bytes	Bits
bit (b)		1 bit
byte (B)	1 byte	8 bits
kilobyte(kB)	1000 bytes	8000 bits
megabyte (MB)	1 million bytes	8 million bits
gigabyte (GB)	1 billion bytes	8 billion bits

Another common set of measurements for computers relates to the frequency in time that a clock state changes or the cycle of a waveform. These rates often describe CPU speeds and also relate to how fast data can be transferred between the CPU and the expansion cards. The following describe these clock rates:

- **Hz (hertz)**—A hertz is a unit of frequency. It is the rate of change in the state or cycle in a sound wave, alternating current, or other cyclical waveform. It represents one cycle per second.

- **MHz (megahertz)**—A megahertz is one million cycles per second. This is a common measurement of the speed of a processing chip such as a computer microprocessor.

- **GHz (gigahertz)**—A gigahertz is one thousand million, or 1 billion (1,000,000,000), cycles per second. This is a common measurement of the speed of a processing chip, such as a computer microprocessor.

NOTE   PC processors continue to get faster. The microprocessor used on PCs in the 1980s typically ran under 10 MHz. (The original IBM PC was 4.77 MHz.) By 2000, PC processors were approaching the speed of 1 GHz and have now passed that number.

Converting numbers between binary, decimal, and hexadecimal is an important aspect of computer networking. The next sections discuss conversion techniques.

Decimal-to-Binary Conversion

Computers recognize and process data using the binary, or base 2, numbering system. The binary number system uses only 2 symbols (0 and 1) instead of the 10 symbols used in the decimal numbering system. The position or place of each digit represents the number 2 (the base number) raised to a power (exponent) based on its position (2^0, 2^1, 2^2, 2^3, 2^4, 2^5, and so on).

Converting a decimal number to a binary number is one of the most common procedures performed while working with network addresses such as IP addresses. IP addresses identify a device on a network and the network to which it is attached. An IP address is a binary number that is 32 bits long. To make them easy to remember, IP addresses are usually written in dotted-decimal notation. This is accomplished by breaking the 32 bit binary IP address into four 8 bit sections, expressing them as decimals and separating each number by a dot. An example is the address 192.168.255.1. Keep in mind that a decimal number is a base 10 number.

To convert the decimal number to binary you must first find the biggest power of 2 that fits into the decimal number. Consider the number 35. Look at Figure 1-8 and determine which is the greatest power of 2 that is less than or equal to 35. This would be 2^5 (decimal 32). Place a 1 in that position of the decimal number and calculate how much is left over by subtracting 32 from 35. The remainder is 3.

Figure 1-8   *Values of Positions in a Decimal Number*

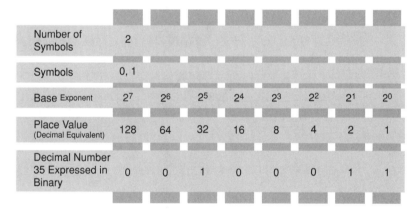

Number of Symbols	2							
Symbols	0, 1							
Base Exponent	2^7	2^6	2^5	2^4	2^3	2^2	2^1	2^0
Place Value (Decimal Equivalent)	128	64	32	16	8	4	2	1
Decimal Number 35 Expressed in Binary	0	0	1	0	0	0	1	1

Next, check to see if the next lowest power 2^4 (decimal 16) fits into 3. Since it does not, place a 0 in that column. Continue this process for each next lowest power until you find a value that the remainder fits into. Because the values 2^3 and 2^2 (decimal 8 and 4) are both larger than 3, you place 0s in those positions. The next lowest power of 2, 2^1 (decimal 2), fits so you place a 1 in this position and subtract 2 from 3. The remainder is 1 so you move to the next lowest power of 2, 2^0 (decimal 1), which is equal to the remainder and place a 1 in that position. Because nothing is left over and this is the last position, you have completed the task. Your result should be 100011 or if you put 0s in the leading positions 00100011.

Figure 1-9 shows a flow chart that can be used to convert decimal numbers less than or equal to 255 into binary numbers.

When working with binary numbers, you also need to be able to reverse the process to convert them back to decimal numbers.

Figure 1-9 *Converting Decimal to Binary Number*

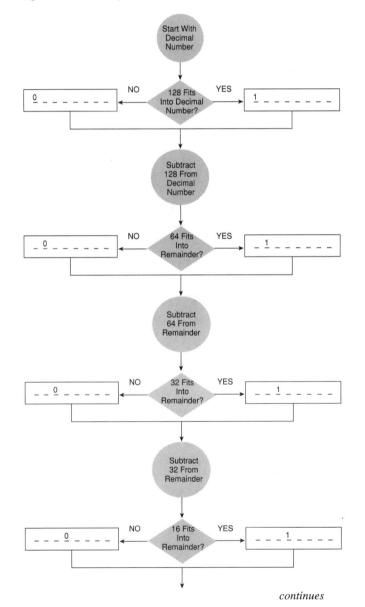

continues

Figure 1-9   *Converting Decimal to Binary Number (Continued)*

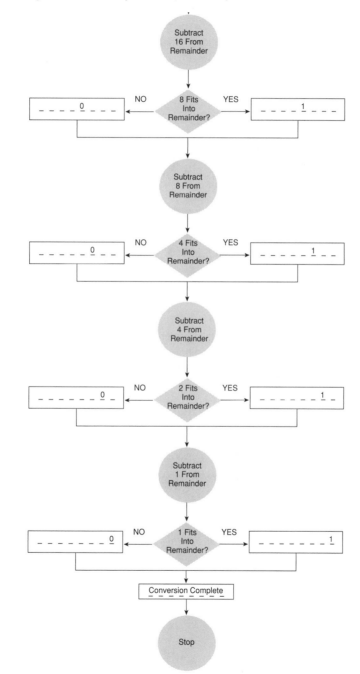

Binary-to-Decimal Conversion

As with decimal-to-binary conversion, you usually have more than one way to solve the conversion problem. You should use the method that is easiest for you. Perhaps one of the easiest methods is to add the values of each place (or position) in the binary number. For example, to convert the binary number 10111001 to a decimal number, you look to see which power of 2 positions have 1s in them. (Recall that 1s indicate an on state.) Figure 1-10 shows the values of the positions in the on state for this decimal number.

Figure 1-10   *Values of Positions in a Binary Number*

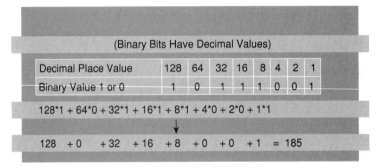

Figure 1-10 shows that this binary number has the values 128, 32, 16, 8, and 1 in the on position. This means that you would need to add these values up to get the decimal number (128 + 32 + 16 + 8 + 1) = 185. Figure 1-11 shows a flowchart that can be used for binary-to-decimal conversions.

Figure 1-11   *Converting Binary to Decimal Numbers*

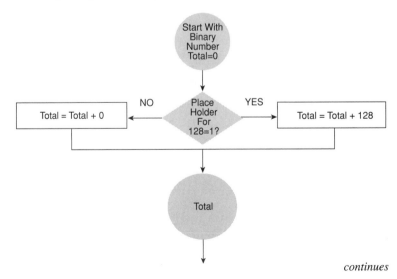

continues

Figure 1-11 *Converting Binary to Decimal Numbers (Continued)*

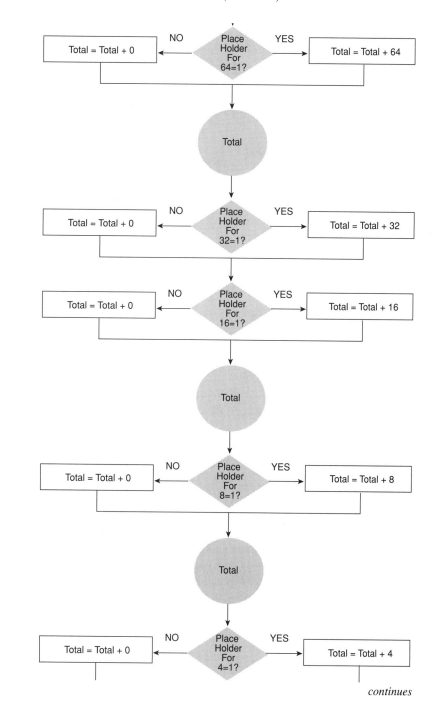

continues

Figure 1-11   *Converting Binary to Decimal Numbers (Continued)*

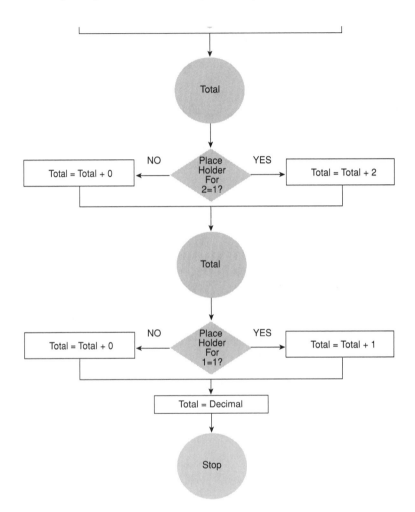

Another numbering system that is used frequently when working with computers is the base 16, or hexadecimal (hex) numbering system, which you learn about in the next section. This system is used because it can represent binary numbers in a more readable form. The computer performs computations in binary, but in several instances, the binary output of a computer is expressed in hexadecimal to make it easier to read. For example, the binary values 11110011 and 11110111 are hard to distinguish, but the hexadecimal counterparts F3 and F7 are much easier to tell apart.

Hexadecimal Conversions

Hexadecimal is referred to as base 16 because it uses 16 symbols. Combinations of these symbols represent all possible numbers. Because only 10 symbols represent digits (0, 1, 2, 3, 4, 5, 6, 7, 8, 9) and base 16 requires 6 more symbols, the extra symbols are the letters A, B, C, D, E, and F. These numbers represent the values shown in Table 1-2.

Table 1-2   *Values for Hexadecimal Symbols*

Hexadecimal Symbol	Decimal Value
0	0
1	1
2	2
3	3
4	4
5	5
6	6
7	7
8	8
9	9
A	10
B	11
C	12
D	13
E	14
F	15

The position of each symbol (digit) in hex number represents that number multiplied by the base number 16 raised to a power (exponent) based on its position. Moving from right to left, the first position represents 16^0 (or 1), the second position represents 16^1 (or 16), the third position represents 16^2 (or 256), and so on. So the hex number 0x12A would be [(1 x 256) + (2 x 16) + (10 x 1)] = 298.

Converting a hexadecimal (commonly referred to as hex) number to binary, and vice versa, is a common task when dealing with the configuration register in Cisco routers and switches. A Cisco router has a configuration register that is 16 bits long. That 16-bit binary number can be represented as a four digit hexadecimal number. For example, 00100000100000010 in binary equals 2102 in hex.

Layer 2 Media Access Control (MAC) addresses, which identify the individual NIC, are typically written in hex also. For Ethernet and Token Ring, these addresses are 48 bits, or 6 octets (1 octet is 1 byte, or 8 bits). Because these addresses consist of 6 distinct octets, they can be expressed as 12 hex numbers. For example, instead of writing 10101010.11110000.11000001.11100010.01110111.01010001, the much shorter hex equivalent can be written AA.F0.C1.E2.77.51. To make handling hex versions of MAC addresses even easier, the dots are placed only after each four hex digits, as in AAF0.C1E2.7751.

The most common way for computers and software to express hexadecimal output is by using 0x in front of the number. So when you see 0x, you know that the number that follows is a hexadecimal number. For example, 0x1234 means 1234 in base 16.

While converting hex to decimal is somewhat cumbersome, converting binary to hex is easy because base 16 (hexadecimal) is a power of base 2 (binary). Every four binary digits (bits) are equal to one hexadecimal digit, as shown in Table 1-3.

Table 1-3   *Values for Hexadecimal Symbols*

Binary Value	Hexadecimal Value
0000	0
0001	1
0010	2
0011	3
0100	4
0101	5
0110	6
0111	7
1000	8
1001	9
1010	A
1011	B
1100	C
1101	D
1110	E
1111	F

So, if you have a binary number that looks like 01011011, it can be broken into 2 groups of 4 bits and then converted. For the given number, the two groups would look like the following: 0101 and 1011. When converting these two groups to hex the value of the first 4 bits is a 5 and the value of the second four bits is a B. So the hexadecimal equivalent to 01011011 is 5B. The decimal equivalent would be (64 + 16 + 8 + 2 + 1) or [(5 x 16) + (11 x 1)], which is 91.

No matter how large the binary number, you can always apply the same conversion. Start from the right of the binary number and break the digits into groups of four. If the number of digits is not divisible by four, add zeros to the left end until four digits (bits) remain in every group. Then, convert each group of four to its hexadecimal equivalent as shown in the following conversion example:

> 1001001000101111101111110111001001
> Converts to:
> 0001 0010 0100 0101 1111 0111 1101 1100 1001
> Converts to:
> 1   2   4   5   F   7   D   C   9
> Therefore:
> 1001001000101111101111110111001001 binary = 1245F7DC9 hexadecimal

The conversion from hexadecimal to binary is the reverse process, as discussed in the next section.

Hexadecimal-to-Binary Conversion

To convert from hexadecimal to binary, convert every hex digit into 4 binary digits (bits). For example, to convert hex AC (0xAC) to binary, you first convert hexadecimal A, which is 1010 binary, and then convert hexadecimal C, which is 1100 binary. Refer to Table 1-3 for the conversion values. Next, you need to place the binary digits in the proper order, A (1010) followed by C (1100), so the conversion of hex AC is 10101100 binary.

The following example converts a hexadecimal number to a binary number, where 0x2102 = 0010 0001 0000 0010 in binary.

> 0x2102
> Converts to:
> 2   1   0   2
> 0010 0001 0000 0010
> Therefore:
> 2102 hexadecimal converts to 0010 0001 0000 0010 binary

Be especially careful to include 4 binary digits for each hexadecimal character, adding zeros to the left of the number when necessary.

The basics of computer architecture and computer numbering systems are important to internetworking. The more you know about these topics, the easier it is to understand networks and internetworking devices. It is important to be familiar with the components of a computer and to understand the functions of a network interface card. Because computers can recognize and process data only by using the binary number system, it is important to understand the relationship between the binary, hexadecimal, and decimal numbering systems. After you have an understanding of these fundamentals, it is time to apply that understanding to computer networks and internetworks.

Computer Numbering Systems Section Quiz

Use the practice questions here to review what you learned in this section.

1 Which of the following value expressions are true? (Choose all that apply.)

A 2000 kBps > 2 Mbps

B 9000 kbps > 1 kBps

C 8000 kBps = 8 MBps

D 200 kbps < 2000 kBps

E 1 GHz > 1000 MHz

2 Which of the following characters express hexadecimal values?

A A

B G

C H

D F

E C

3 Given the binary number 11110100111010101010010101, which of the following would be the hexadecimal equivalent?

A 0x59AE8F

B 0xF1A595

C 0xF81F85

D 0xE1FC2A

E 0xF4EA95

F 0x58F18F

Internetworking Fundamentals

The process of providing communications between data devices like computers is called *computer networking*. A group of multiple computer networks connected together is called an *internetwork*. The goal of the CCNA program is to make individuals proficient in basic computer networking and internetworking technologies.

Many types of computer networks exist, and these networks vary based on media, protocol, and topologies. However different these networks might be, some very common elements bind them. These elements are the fundamentals that make up network communications. These fundamentals include concepts like layered protocol stacks, addressing schemes, and address mappings. The foundations of networking have changed little since the earliest data networks, but the networks and protocols themselves have changed dramatically. To better understand networking and be able to keep up with changes in technologies, a network professional must have a solid grounding in the basic concepts of computer networks and internetworks.

To achieve a foundation in internetworking concepts, you need to have a firm grasp of basic networking terminology, understand the difference between computer applications and networking applications, and understand the reasons for networking computers.

Basic Internetworking Terminology

Working with computer networks requires you to learn the language of the industry. It is not uncommon to listen in on a conversation between two internetworking technicians that contains more acronyms, abbreviations, or technical terms than it does actual words. If you don't have a good grasp of this terminology, it is difficult to understand the concepts and processes contained in this book. This section covers some of the terminology used throughout this book. Note that this is not intended to be a comprehensive glossary of networking terms, but is intended to be a quick reference that defines and briefly discusses some of the most important and most basic words, phrases, and acronyms that will enable you to navigate through most of this book.

NOTE   For a complete list of networking terms, refer to the Cisco Press title *Dictionary of Internetworking Terms and Acronyms* (ISBN: 1587200457).

You should have a thorough understanding of the following terms:

- **Network interface card (NIC)**—Pronounced "nick," NIC refers to the network interface card, also called the LAN adapter, or just the network interface. This expansion card typically goes into an ISA, PCI, or PCMCIA slot in a computer and connects to the network medium, which, in turn, is connected to other computers on the network.

- **Media**—Media refers to the various physical environments through which transmission signals pass. Common network media include twisted-pair, coaxial, fiber-optic cable, and the atmosphere through which wireless transmission occurs.

- **Protocol**—A network protocol is a set of rules by which computers communicate. Protocols are like the syntax of a language, which is the order in which processes occur. Many different types of computer protocols exist. The term *protocol suite* describes a set of several protocols that perform different functions related to different aspects of the communications process.

- **Cisco IOS Software**—The Cisco Internetwork Operation System (IOS) Software runs on Cisco devices and is one of the most widely deployed network systems software suites. It delivers intelligent network services on a flexible networking infrastructure for enabling the rapid deployment of internetworking applications.

- **Network operating system (NOS)**—NOS refers to server software such as Windows NT, Windows 2000 Server, Novell NetWare, UNIX, or Linux.

- **Connectivity devices**—This term refers to several different device types, all of which connect cable segments, connect two or more smaller networks (or subnets) into a larger network, or divide a large network into smaller ones. The term encompasses repeaters, hubs, switches, bridges, and routers.

- **Local-area network (LAN)**—A LAN is a network that is confined to a limited geographic area. This area can be a room, a floor, a building, or even an entire campus.

- **Metropolitan-area network (MAN)**—A MAN is a network that is larger in size than a LAN and smaller in size than a WAN. This is a network that covers approximately the area of a large city or metropolitan area.

- **Wide-area network (WAN)**—A WAN is made up of interconnected LANs. It spans wide geographic areas by using WAN links such as telephone lines or satellite technology to connect computers in different cities, countries, or even different continents.

- **Physical topology**—The physical topology refers to the layout or physical shape of the network, and includes these topologies:

  - **Bus**—Computers and devices arranged so that cabling goes from one to another in a linear fashion.

  - **Ring**—No clear beginning points or endpoints exist within this topology, forming a circle.

  - **Star**—Systems "meet in the middle" by connecting to a central hub.

  - **Mesh**—Multiple redundant connections make pathways to some or all of the endpoints.

- **Logical topology**—The logical topology is the path that the signals take from one computer to another. The logical topology might or might not correspond to the physical topology. For example, a network can be a physical "star," in which each computer connects to a central hub, but inside the hub the data can travel in a circle, making it a logical "ring."

Networking Applications

Network applications are software programs that run between different computers connected together on a network. Networking applications require a connection to a networking service before these applications function.

Some of the more common uses of network applications include using a web browser program to find content from the World Wide Web or using an e-mail program to send e-mails over the Internet, as shown in Figure 1-12.

Figure 1-12   *Using Networking Applications on the Internet*

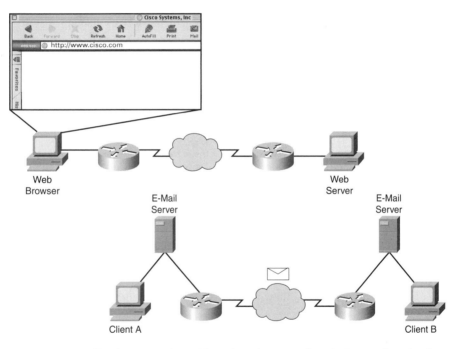

Network applications are selected based on the type of work that needs to be done. A complete set of programs is available to interface with the Internet. Each application program type is associated with its own application protocol, including the following:

- **Hypertext Transfer Protocol (HTTP)**—The World Wide Web uses HTTP, which is the communications protocol used to connect to web servers. Its primary function is to establish a connection with a web server and transmit HTML pages to the client browser.

- **Post Office Protocol 3 (POP3)**—E-mail programs support the POP3 application-layer protocol for electronic mail. POP3 is a standard e-mail server commonly used on the Internet. It provides a message storage container that holds incoming e-mail until users log on and download it.

- **File Transfer Protocol (FTP)**—FTP is a simple file utility program for transferring files between remote computers, which also provides for basic user authentication.

- **Telnet**—Telnet is a remote access application and protocol for connecting to remote computer consoles, which also provides for basic user authentication. Telnet is not a graphical user interface, but it is command-line driven or character mode only.

- **Simple Network Management Protocol (SNMP)**—Network management programs use SNMP for monitoring the network device status and activities.

NOTE   It is important to understand that the application layer is just another protocol layer in the OSI model or TCP/IP protocol stack. The programs interface with application layer protocols.

E-mail client applications (such as Eudora, Microsoft Mail, Pegasus, and Netscape Mail) all work with the POP3 protocol. The same principle is true with web browsers. The two most popular web browsers are Microsoft Internet Explorer and Netscape Communicator.

E-mail enables you to send messages between connected computers. The procedure for sending an e-mail document involves two separate processes: sending the e-mail to the user's post office, which is a computer running the POP3 server software, and delivering the e-mail from that post office to the user's e-mail client computer, which is the recipient.

Internetworking Fundamentals Section Quiz

Use these practice questions to review what you learned in this section.

1 Match each of the following definitions with the appropriate word. (Choose the best answer.)

___ A set of rules by which computers communicate

___ A high-speed network confined to a limited geographic region

___ Devices used to connect cable segments, or subnets, into a larger internetwork

___ The layout or physical shape of a network

A   NOS

B   Connectivity devices

C   MAN

D   WAN

E LAN

F Logical topology

G Protocol

H NIC

I Physical topology

J NIC

2 Which of the following are network applications?

A Spreadsheet

B E-mail

C FTP

D Word processor

E Calculator

F Web browser

G PowerPoint

3 All corporate internetworks use the same components regardless of their business structure.

A True

B False

Principles of Data Communications

No matter what type of connectivity, operating system, or network services interconnect computers and computer networks, the fact still remains that for these devices to communicate, some rules must exist. Like any system of communication, rules govern how the communication must take place. Also, some medium for the communication to take place over exists. For example, a language has rules for the formation of sentences using basic words. This language can be used to communicate verbally, using air as the medium, or written, using paper as the medium.

Most languages have rules that specify how words are put together and then how they are spoken or written. In many western languages, words are written from left to right, but in some eastern languages words are written from right to left or even top to bottom. To be able to effectively communicate, you must understand how to read the words and in what order to read them.

Many of the computers and operating systems within an organization are manufactured by different companies and use different types of programs to operate; however, if these systems are going to communicate with one another, they must use a common set of rules for data communications. The rules that define how systems talk to one another are called *protocols.*

Many internetworking protocols can be used to establish communications paths between systems, and each of these protocols provides very similar functions. To provide a way to establish some common and open rules for building a data communications protocol, the International Organization for Standardization (ISO) created the Open System Interconnection (OSI) reference model.

The next sections describe the purpose of the OSI model and the TCP/IP protocol stack. You also learn how the OSI model facilitates data communication.

OSI Model

The OSI reference model is the primary model for network communications. The early development of LANs, MANs, and WANs was chaotic in many ways. The early 1980s saw tremendous increases in the number and sizes of networks. As companies realized that they could save money and gain productivity by using networking technology, they added networks and expanded existing networks as rapidly as new network technologies and products were introduced.

By the mid-1980s, companies began to experience difficulties from all the expansions they had made. It became more difficult for networks using different specifications and implementations to communicate with each other. The companies realized that they needed to move away from proprietary networking systems, those systems that are privately developed, owned, and controlled.

NOTE   In the computer industry, proprietary is the opposite of open. Proprietary means that one company or a small group of companies control(s) all usage of the technology. Open means that free usage of the technology is available to the public.

To address the problem of networks being incompatible and unable to communicate with each other, the ISO researched different network schemes. As a result of this research, the ISO created a model that would help vendors create networks that would be compatible with, and operate with, other networks.

The OSI reference model, released in 1984, was the descriptive scheme that the ISO had created. It provided vendors with a set of standards that ensured greater compatibility and interoperability between the various types of network technologies produced by companies around the world. Although other models exist, most network vendors today relate their products to the OSI reference model, especially when they want to educate customers on the use of their products. The OSI model is considered the best tool available for teaching people about sending and receiving data on a network.

The OSI reference model has seven layers, as shown in Figure 1-13, each illustrating a particular network function. This separation of networking functions is called *layering*. The OSI reference model defines the network functions that occur at each layer. More important, the OSI reference model facilitates an understanding of how information travels throughout a network. In addition, the OSI reference model describes how data travels from application programs (for example, spreadsheets), through a network medium, to an application program located in another computer, even if the sender and receiver are connected using different network media.

Figure 1-13   *OSI Reference Model*

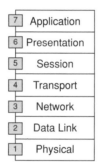

Dividing the network into these seven layers provides these advantages:

- **Reduces complexity**—It breaks network communication into smaller, simpler parts.
- **Standardizes interfaces**—It standardizes network components to allow multiple vendor development and support.
- **Facilitates modular engineering**—It allows different types of network hardware and software to communicate with each other.
- **Ensures interoperable technology**—It prevents changes in one layer from affecting the other layers, allowing for quicker development.
- **Accelerates evolution**—It provides for effective updates and improvements to individual components without affecting other components or having to rewrite the entire protocol.
- **Simplifies teaching and learning**—It breaks network communication into smaller components to make learning easier.

The practice of moving information between computers is divided into seven techniques in the OSI reference model. Each of the seven techniques is represented by its own layer in the model. The seven layers of the OSI reference model are as follows:

- Layer 7: Application layer
- Layer 6: Presentation layer
- Layer 5: Session layer
- Layer 4: Transport layer
- Layer 3: Network layer
- Layer 2: Data link layer
- Layer 1: Physical layer

Each OSI layer contains a set of functions performed by programs to enable data to travel from a source to a destination on a network. Following is a brief description of each layer in the OSI reference model.

Layer 7: The Application Layer

The application layer is the OSI layer that is closest to the user. This layer provides network services to the user's applications. It differs from the other layers in that it does not provide services to any other OSI layer, but rather only to applications outside the OSI model. The application layer establishes the availability of intended communication partners and synchronizes and establishes agreement on procedures for error recovery and control of data integrity.

Layer 6: The Presentation Layer

The presentation layer ensures the information that the application layer of one system sends out is readable by the application layer of another system. For example, a PC program communicates with another computer, one using Extended Binary Coded Decimal Interchange Code (EBCDIC) and the other using ASCII to represent the same characters. If necessary, the presentation layer might be able to translate between multiple data formats by using a common format.

Layer 5: The Session Layer

The session layer establishes, manages, and terminates sessions between two communicating hosts. It provides its services to the presentation layer. The session layer also synchronizes dialogue between the presentation layers of the two hosts and manages their data exchange. For example, web servers have many users, so many communication processes are open at a given time. It is important, therefore, to keep track of which user communicates on which path. In addition to session regulation, the session layer offers provisions for efficient data transfer, class of service, and exception reporting of session layer, presentation layer, and application layer problems.

Layer 4: The Transport Layer

The transport layer segments data from the sending host's system and reassembles the data into a data stream on the receiving host's system. For example, business users in large corporations often transfer large files from field locations to a corporate site. Reliable delivery of the files is important, so the transport layer breaks down large files into smaller segments that are less likely to incur transmission problems.

The boundary between the transport layer and the session layer can be thought of as the boundary between application protocols and data-flow protocols. Whereas the application, presentation, and session layers are concerned with application issues, the lower four layers are concerned with data transport issues.

The transport layer attempts to provide a data-transport service that shields the upper layers from transport implementation details. Specifically, issues such as reliability of transport between two hosts are the concern of the transport layer. In providing communication service, the transport layer establishes, maintains, and properly terminates virtual circuits. Transport error detection and recovery and information flow control provide reliable service.

Layer 3: The Network Layer

The network layer provides connectivity and path selection between two host systems that might be located on geographically separated networks. The growth of the Internet has increased the number of users accessing information from sites around the world, and it is the network layer that manages this connectivity.

Layer 2: The Data Link Layer

The data link layer defines how data is formatted for transmission and how access to the network is controlled. This layer is responsible for defining how devices on a common media communicate with one another including addressing and control signaling between devices.

Layer 1: The Physical Layer

The physical layer defines the electrical, mechanical, procedural, and functional specifications for activating, maintaining, and deactivating the physical link between end systems. Characteristics such as voltage levels, timing of voltage changes, physical data rates, maximum transmission distances, physical connectors, and other similar attributes are defined by physical layer specifications.

Data Communications Process

All communications on a network originate at a source and are sent to a destination. A networking protocol using all or some of the layers listed in the OSI reference model move data between devices. Recall that Layer 7 is the part of the protocol that communicates with the application, and Layer 1 is the part of a protocol that communicates with the media. A data frame is able to travel across a computer network because of the layers of the protocol. The process of moving data from one device in a network is accomplished by passing information from applications down the protocol stack adding an appropriate header at each layer of the model.

This method of passing data down the stack and adding headers and trailers is called *encapsulation*. After the data is encapsulated and passed across the network, the receiving device removes the information added, using the messages in the header as directions on how to pass the data up the stack to the appropriate application.

Data encapsulation is an important concept to networks. It is the function of like layers on each device, called *peer* layers, to communicate critical parameters such as addressing and control information.

Although encapsulation seems like an abstract concept, it is actually quite simple. Imagine that you want to send a coffee mug to a friend in another city. How will the mug get there? Basically, it will be transported on the road or through the air. You can't go outside and set the mug on the road or throw it up in the air and expect it to get there. You need a service to pick it up and deliver it. So, you call your favorite parcel carrier and give them the mug. But, that's not all. Here's the complete process:

Step 1   Pack the mug in a box.

Step 2   Place an address label on the box so the carrier knows where to deliver it.

Step 3   Give the box to a parcel carrier.

Step 4   The carrier drives it down the road toward its final destination.

This process is similar to the encapsulation method that protocol stacks use to send data across networks. After the package arrives, your friend has to reverse the process. He takes the package from the carrier, reads the label to see who it's from, and finally opens the box and removes the mug. The reverse of the encapsulation process is known as de-encapsulation. The next sections describe the encapsulation and de-encapsulation processes.

Encapsulation

Encapsulation on a data network is very similar. Instead of sending a coffee mug, however, you send information from an application. The information sent on a network is referred to as *data* or *data packets*.

Encapsulation wraps data with the necessary protocol information before network transit. Therefore, as the data moves down through the layers of the OSI model, each OSI layer adds a header (and a trailer, if applicable) to the data before passing it down to a lower layer. The headers and trailers contain control information for the network devices and receiver to ensure proper delivery of the data and to ensure that the receiver can correctly interpret the data.

Figure 1-14 illustrates how encapsulation occurs. It shows the manner in which data travels through the layers. These steps occur to encapsulate data:

Step 1 The user data is sent from an application to the application layer.

Step 2 The application layer adds the application layer header (Layer 7 header) to the user data. The Layer 7 header and the original user data become the data that is passed down to the presentation layer.

Step 3 The presentation layer adds the presentation layer header (Layer 6 header) to the data. This then becomes the data that is passed down to the session layer.

Step 4 The session layer adds the session layer header (Layer 5 header) to the data. This then becomes the data that is passed down to the transport layer.

Step 5 The transport layer adds the transport layer header (Layer 4 header) to the data. This then becomes the data that is passed down to the network layer.

Step 6 The network layer adds the network layer header (Layer 3 header) to the data. This then becomes the data that is passed down to the data link layer.

Step 7 The data link layer adds the data link layer header and trailer (Layer 2 header and trailer) to the data. A Layer 2 trailer is usually the frame check sequence (FCS), which is used by the receiver to detect whether the data is in error. This then becomes the data that is passed down to the physical layer. The physical layer then transmits the bits onto the network media.

Figure 1-14   *Data Encapsulation*

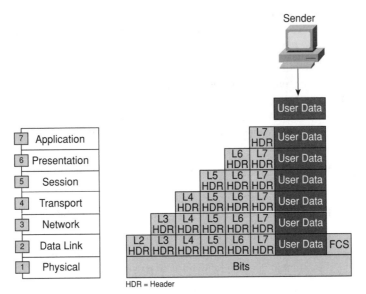

De-Encapsulation

When the remote device receives a sequence of bits, the physical layer at the remote device passes the bits to the data link layer for manipulation. The data link layer performs the following process, referred to as de-encapsulation:

Step 1   It checks the data-link trailer (the FCS) to see if the data is in error.

Step 2   If the data is in error, it is discarded.

Step 3   If the data is not in error, the data-link layer reads and interprets the control information in the data-link header.

Step 4   It strips the data link header and trailer and then passes the remaining data up to the network layer based on the control information in the data-link header.

Each subsequent layer performs a similar de-encapsulation process, as shown in Figure 1-15.

Figure 1-15   *De-Encapsulation*

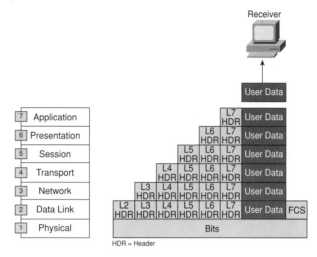

HDR = Header

Think of de-encapsulation as the process of reading the address on a package to see whether it is for you, and then opening and removing the contents of the package if it is addressed to you.

Peer-to-Peer Communication

For data to travel from the source to the destination, each layer of the OSI model at the source must communicate with its peer layer at the destination. This form of communication is referred to as *peer-to-peer communication*. During this process, the protocols at each layer exchange information, called *protocol data units (PDUs)*, between peer layers, as shown in Figure 1-16.

Figure 1-16   *Peer-to-Peer Communication*

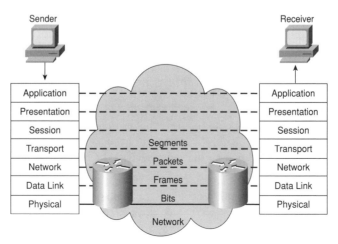

Data packets on a network originate at a source and then travel to a destination. Each layer depends on the service function of the OSI layer below it. To provide this service, the lower layer uses encapsulation to put the PDU from the upper layer into its data field. It then adds whatever headers the layer needs to perform its function. As the data moves down through Layers 7 through 5 of the OSI model, additional headers are added. The grouping of data at the Layer 4 PDU is called a *segment*.

The network layer provides a service to the transport layer, and the transport layer presents data to the internetwork subsystem. The network layer moves the data through the internetwork by encapsulating the data and attaching a header to create a datagram (the Layer 3 PDU). The header contains information required to complete the transfer, such as source and destination logical addresses.

The data link layer provides a service to the network layer by encapsulating the network layer datagram in a frame (the Layer 2 PDU). The frame header contains the physical addresses required to complete the data-link functions, and the frame trailer contains the FCS.

The physical layer provides a service to the data link layer, encoding the data-link frame into a pattern of 1s and 0s (bits) for transmission on the medium (usually a wire) at Layer 1.

Network devices such as hubs, switches, and routers work at the lower three layers. Hubs are at Layer 1, switches are at Layer 2, and routers are at Layer 3.

TCP/IP Protocol Stack

Although the OSI reference model is universally recognized, the historical and technical open standard of the Internet is the TCP/IP protocol stack. The TCP/IP protocol stack, shown in Figure 1-17, varies slightly from the OSI reference model.

Figure 1-17 *TCP/IP Protocol Stack*

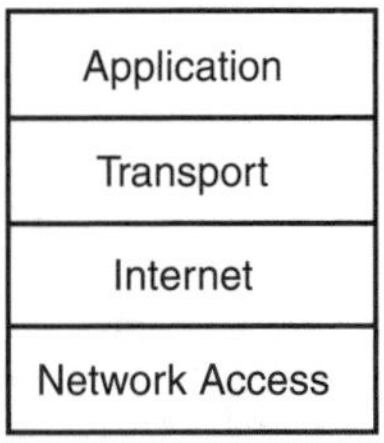

| Application |
| Transport |
| Internet |
| Network Access |

The TCP/IP protocol stack has four layers. It is important to note that although some of the layers in the TCP/IP protocol stack have the same names as layers in the OSI model, the layers have different functions in each model, as is described in the following list:

- **Application layer**—The application layer handles high-level protocols, including issues of representation, encoding, and dialog control. The TCP/IP model combines all application-related issues into one layer and ensures that this data is properly packaged for the next layer.

- **Transport layer**—The transport layer deals with quality of service (QoS) issues of reliability, flow control, and error correction. One of its protocols, Transmission Control Protocol (TCP), provides for reliable network communications.

- **Internet layer**—The purpose of the Internet layer is to send source datagrams from any network on the internetwork and have them arrive at the destination, regardless of the path they took to get there.

- **Network access layer**—The name of this layer is broad and somewhat confusing. It is also called the host-to-network layer. It includes the LAN and WAN protocols, and all the details in the OSI physical and data link layers.

OSI Model Versus TCP/IP Stack

Both similarities and differences exist between the TCP/IP protocol stack and the OSI reference model. Figure 1-18 offers a side-by-side comparison of the two models.

Figure 1-18   *OSI Model Versus TCP/IP*

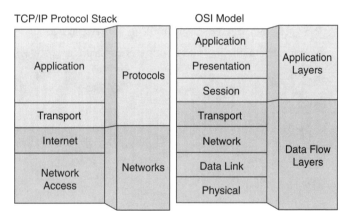

Similarities between the TCP/IP protocol stack and the OSI model include the following:

- Both have application layers, though they include different services.

- Both have comparable transport and network layers.

- Both assume packet-switched technology, not circuit-switched. (Analog telephone calls are an example of circuit-switched.)

Some differences also exist between the TCP/IP protocol stack and the OSI model, such as the following:

- TCP/IP combines the presentation and session layers into its application layer.
- TCP/IP combines the OSI data link and physical layers into the network access layer.

TCP/IP protocols are the standards around which the Internet developed, so the TCP/IP protocol stack gains credibility just because of its protocols. In contrast, networks are not typically built on the OSI model, even though the OSI model is used as a guide.

Principles of Data Communication Section Quiz

Use these practice questions to review what you learned in this section.

1 Match the layer of the OSI model with the appropriate function.

____ Synchronizes dialogue between the presentation layers of the two hosts and manages their data exchange.

____ Defines the maximum transmission distance and data rates for a network.

____ Provides connectivity and path selection between two host systems.

____ Establishes, maintains, and terminates connectivity between devices.

A Layer 1

B Layer 2

C Layer 3

D Layer 4

E Layer 5

F Layer 6

G Layer 7

2 For peer-to-peer communications, which of the following statements are true?

A Between systems, the headers at each layer communicate information from peer-to-peer.

B Communications are verified at every layer using a FCS.

C The name of the encapsulated information at a particular layer of the OSI model is called a PDU.

D Network devices operate at the upper three layers of the OSI model.

E The physical address of a device is located in the Layer 2 PDU.

Chapter Summary

Computer networks are a vital part of almost every business organization today. Before you can administer a company's internetwork, you must first understand the basic components of a computer and a computer network. You must also understand the language that is spoken by computers and computer professionals. This chapter covered the basic components of a computer and the numbering systems used in computers and in computer networks. This chapter also discussed many key terms used by internetworking professionals to describe internetworking systems.

The OSI reference model was discussed to explain how a network protocol is used for data communications. The chapter also covered the basic way that a computer uses a protocol to communicate with other systems describing the process of data encapsulation and de-encapsulation. Finally the chapter discussed how the TCP/IP protocol compares to the OSI reference model.

Chapter Review Questions

Use these review questions to test your knowledge of the concepts discussed in this chapter.

1 The _____ is a signal that informs a CPU that an event that needs its attention has occurred.

   A   Fiber-optic pulse

   B   Frequency

   C   I/O address

   D   IRQ

2 What computer component allows the computer to communicate with the network?

   A   Sound card

   B   NIC

   C   Video card

   D   Port adapter

3 Today, what are the common measurements for the speed of a computer microprocessor? (Choose two.)

A Hz

B Kbps

C MHz

D Mbps

E GHz

4 Convert the decimal number 240 into binary.

A 11110000

B 11101110

C 11111000

D 11101111

5 What is the binary number 10111001 in decimal?

A 180

B 185

C 157

D 179

E 178

6 Which of the following is an application layer protocol?

A HTTP

B FTP

C Telnet

D SMNP

E All of the above

7 What organization created the OSI reference model?

A IEEE

B ISO

C DEC

D DIX

8 An e-mail message is sent from Host A to Host B on a LAN. To send this message, the data must be encapsulated. Which of the following best describes the first step of data encapsulation?

A Alphanumeric characters are converted into data.

B The message is segmented into easily transportable chunks.

C A network header is added to the message (source and destination addresses).

D The message is converted into binary format.

E The user data is sent from an application to the application layer.

Upon completion of this chapter, you will be able to perform the following tasks:

- Define network components
- Map network devices to a hierarchy
- Explain how internetworking devices operate at different layers of the OSI model
- Describe the different types of networking topologies and the features and benefits of each topology
- Understand the functions of services devices like firewalls and AAA servers

CHAPTER 2

Internetworking Devices

Every internetwork exists because of the devices used to provide connectivity between individual networked systems. Cisco Systems manufactures devices and operating systems that are used in the integration and management of these internetworks. To effectively build, manage, and troubleshoot an internetwork, you need to understand the roles that each of these devices play.

You need to understand many concepts in internetworking. These include the differences between a logical and physical network; how devices function at the physical, data link, and network layers of the OSI model; and how internetworking devices are interconnected to provide services that are beneficial to the organization that they serve. This chapter provides you with a base knowledge of these fundamental internetworking concepts. After the concepts are introduced, the remaining chapters provide more detail on how internetworking devices function within the OSI model.

Defining Network Components

The purpose of an internetwork is to help an organization increase productivity by linking all the computers and computer networks so that people have access to the information regardless of differences in time, location, or type of computer equipment.

Internetworks have changed how companies and employees are viewed. It is no longer necessary to have everyone in the same location to access the information needed to do the job. Because of this, many companies have changed their business strategy to utilize these networks in the way that mirrors how the business operates. With a corporate internetwork, a company optimizes its resources by grouping employees (users) in the following ways, as illustrated in Figure 2-1:

- **Main office**—The main office is where everyone is connected to a LAN and where the majority of the corporate information is located. A main office could have hundreds or thousands of users who depend on the network to do their jobs. The main office might be a building with many LANs or might be a campus of such buildings. Because everyone needs access to central resources and information, it is common to see a high-speed backbone LAN and a centralized data center with mainframe computers and application servers.

- **Remote-access locations**—The other users include a variety of remote-access locations that need to connect to the resources at the main offices and/or each other, including the following:

  - **Branch offices**—These are remote locations where smaller groups of people work. These users connect to each other via a LAN. To access the main office, these users access wide-area network (WAN) services. Although some information might be stored at the branch office, it is likely that users have to access much of the data from the main office. How often the main office network is accessed determines whether the WAN connection is a permanent or dialup connection.

  - **Telecommuters**—These employees work out of their homes. These users typically require a dialup connection to the main office and/or the branch office to access network resources.

  - **Mobile users**—These individuals work from various locations and rely on different services to connect to the network. While at the main or branch offices, these users connect to the LAN. When they are out of the office, these users usually rely on dialup services to connect to the corporate network.

Figure 2-1   *Corporate Networking Strategy*

To understand what types of equipment and services to deploy in your network and when, it is important to understand business and user needs. You can then subdivide the network into a hierarchical model that spans from the end user's machine to the core (backbone) of the network. Figure 2-2 shows how the different employee groups interconnect.

Figure 2-2   *Group Interconnection*

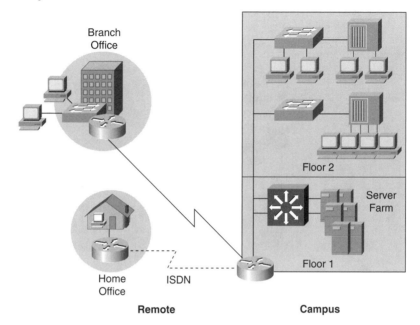

Mapping Business Needs to a Hierarchical Model

To simplify network designs, implementation, and management, Cisco uses a hierarchical model to describe the network. Although using this model is typically associated with designing a network, it is important to understand the model to know what equipment and features are needed in your network.

Campus networks have traditionally placed basic network-level intelligence and services at the center of the network and shared bandwidth at the user level. As businesses continue to place more emphasis on the network as a productivity tool, distributed network services like voice/video and switching continue to migrate to the desktop level.

User demands and network applications have forced networking professionals to use the traffic patterns in the network as the criteria for building an internetwork. Networks cannot be divided into smaller networks or subnetworks based only on the number of users, but should also consider the types of traffic involved. The emergence of servers that run global applications also has a direct impact on the load across the network. A higher traffic load across the entire network results in the need for more efficient routing and switching techniques.

Traffic patterns now dictate the type of services needed by end users in networks. To properly build an internetwork that can effectively address a user's needs, a three-layer hierarchical model organizes traffic flow. (See Figure 2-3.)

Figure 2-3   *Three-Layer Hierarchical Network Model*

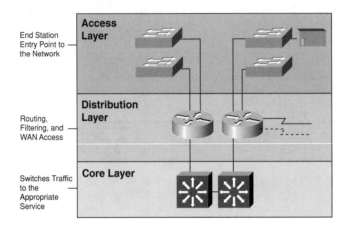

The model consists of three layers:

- Access

- Distribution

- Core

Each of these layers serves a function in delivering network services, as described in the following sections.

Access Layer

The access layer of the network is the point at which end users are connected to the network. This is why the access layer is sometimes referred to as the desktop layer. Users, and the resources they need to access most, are locally available. Traffic to and from local resources is confined between the resources, switches, and end users. Multiple groups of users and their resources exist at the access layer.

In many networks, it is not possible to provide users with local access to all services, such as database files, centralized storage, or dial-out access to the web. In these cases, user traffic for these services is directed to the next layer in the model, the distribution layer.

Distribution Layer

The distribution layer of the network (also referred to as the workgroup layer) marks the point between the access layer and the core services of the network. This layer's primary function is to perform functions such as routing, filtering, and WAN access. In a campus environment, the distribution layer represents a multitude of functions, including the following:

- Serving as an aggregation point for access layer devices
- Routing traffic to provide departmental or workgroup access
- Segmenting the network into multiple broadcast/multicast domains
- Translating between different media types, such as Token Ring and Ethernet
- Providing security and filtering services

The distribution layer can be summarized as the layer that provides policy-based connectivity because it determines if and how packets can access the core services of the network. The distribution layer determines the fastest way for a user request (such as file server access) to be forwarded to the server. After the distribution layer chooses the path, it forwards the request to the core layer. The core layer then quickly transports the request to the appropriate service.

Core Layer

The core layer (also called the backbone layer) switches traffic as fast as possible to the appropriate service. Typically, the traffic being transported is to and from services common to all users. These services are referred to as global or enterprise services. Examples of these services are e-mail, Internet access, and videoconferencing.

When a user needs access to enterprise services, the request is processed at the distribution layer. The distribution layer device then forwards the user's request to the backbone. The backbone simply provides quick transport to the desired enterprise service. The distribution layer device provides controlled access to the core.

To properly build a network, you must first understand how your internetwork is used, your business needs, and your user needs. Those needs can then be mapped into a model that can be used to build your internetwork. One of the best ways to understand how to build an internetwork is to first understand the way in which traffic is passed across the data network. The following sections describe how networks are interconnected using different types of internetworking devices.

Physical Network Versus Logical Network

The topology of a network describes the layout of the wire and devices as well as the paths used by data transmissions. The physical topology of a network refers to the physical layout of the devices and media.

The logical topology of a network refers to the logical paths that signals travel from one point on the network to another (that is, the way in which data accesses media and transmits packets across it).

The physical and logical topologies of a network can be the same. For example, in a network physically shaped as a linear bus, the data travels along the length of the cable. Therefore, it has both a physical bus topology and a logical bus topology.

A network can also have physical and logical topologies that are different. For example, a physical topology in the shape of a star, where cable segments can connect all computers to a central hub, can have a logical ring topology. Remember from Chapter 1, "Introduction to Internetworking," that in a ring the data travels from one computer to the next, and inside the hub, the wiring connections are such that the signal actually travels around in a circle from one port to the next, creating a logical ring. Therefore, you cannot always predict how data travels in a network by simply observing its physical layout.

Token Ring uses a logical ring topology in either a physical ring or a physical star, whereas Ethernet uses a logical bus topology in either a physical bus or a physical star. Star topology is by far the most common implementation of LANs today. Token Ring is used in some places; however, most LANs use Ethernet.

The following sections describe each topology in more detail.

Bus

Commonly referred to as a linear bus, all the devices on a bus topology are connected by one single cable. As illustrated in Figure 2-4, in a bus topology a cable proceeds from one computer to the next, like a bus line going through a city.

Figure 2-4   *Bus Topology*

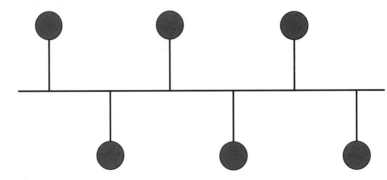

With a physical bus topology, the main cable segment must end with a terminator that absorbs the signal when it reaches the end of the line or wire. If no terminator exists, the electrical signal representing the data bounces back at the end of the wire, causing errors in the network.

Star and Extended Star

The star topology is the most common physical topology in Ethernet LANs. This section describes both the star topology and the extended star topology.

When installed, the star topology resembles spokes in a bicycle wheel. It is made up of a central connection point that is a device such as a hub, switch, or router, where all the cabling segments meet. Each host in the network is connected to the central device with its own cable.

Although a physical star topology might require more materials and labor to implement than the physical bus topology, the advantages of a star topology make it worth the additional cost. Each host is connected to the central device with its own wire, so that when that cable has a problem, only that host is affected, and the rest of the network remains operational. This benefit is extremely important and is the reason why almost every newly designed Ethernet LAN has a star topology.

When a star network is expanded to include an additional networking device that is connected to the main networking device, it is called an extended or distributed star topology. Figure 2-5 shows a star and extended star topology.

Figure 2-5   *Star and Extended Star Topology*

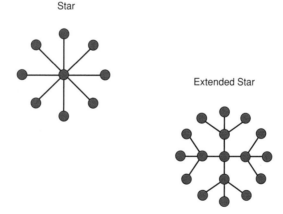

Ring

The logical ring topology is another important topology in LAN connectivity. This section describes both types of ring topology, single-ring and dual-ring, which are shown in Figure 2-6.

Figure 2-6   *Ring Topology*

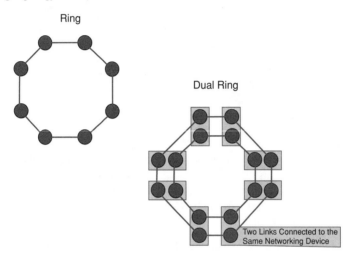

As the name implies, hosts are connected in the form of a ring. Unlike the physical bus topology, it has no beginning or end that needs to be terminated. Data is transmitted in a way unlike the logical bus topology. A token, which is a series of bits in a frame required to send data, travels around the ring, stopping at each node. If a node wants to transmit data, it adds that data and the destination address to the token. The data and token then continue around the ring through each device until it arrives at the destination node, which takes the data out of the token and sends the token back onto the ring. The advantage of using this type of method is that no collisions of data packets occur.

In a single-ring topology, all the devices on the network share a single cable, and the data travels in one direction only. Each device waits its turn to send data over the network.

In a dual-ring topology, two counter-rotating rings allow data to be sent in both directions. This setup creates redundancy (fault tolerance), meaning that if one ring fails, data can be transmitted in the other direction on the other ring. Dual rings are used in FDDI or CDDI.

Mesh and Partial Mesh

Mesh topology is yet another type of network topology. This section describes both full-mesh and partial-mesh topologies.

The full-mesh topology connects all devices (nodes) to each other for redundancy and fault tolerance. Implementing the full-mesh topology is expensive and difficult.

In a partial-mesh topology, at least one device maintains multiple connections to others, without being fully meshed. Figure 2-7 illustrates both mesh topologies.

Figure 2-7   *Partial Mesh and Full Mesh Topology*

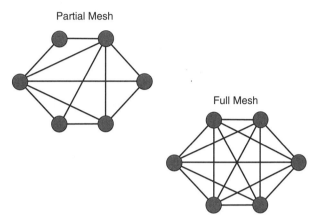

The technology and devices used at the lower two layers of the OSI model define a network topology. In particular, physical and logical topologies are defined by the physical and data link layer.

Network Topology Section Quiz

Use the practice questions here to review what you learned in this section.

1   Which of the following correctly describes networking topology?

   A   The network topology defines the way in which the computers, printers, network devices, and other devices are connected.

   B   Networks can have either a physical or a logical topology.

   C   A physical topology describes the paths that signals travel from one point on the network to another.

   D   A logical topology defines the layout of the device and media.

2   Which of the following statements best describes the bus topology?

   A   All of its nodes connect directly to a central point.

   B   All of its nodes connect directly to one physical link.

   C   All of its nodes connect directly to each other.

   D   All of its nodes connect to exactly two other nodes.

3 Which topology has all its nodes connected directly to one center point and has no other connections between nodes?

   A Bus

   B Ring

   C Star

   D Mesh

4 What is the primary purpose of the second ring in a dual-ring network?

   A Duplex

   B Signaling

   C Redundancy

   D None of the above

5 In a complete, full-mesh topology, every node

   A Is linked directly to every other node.

   B Is connected to two central nodes.

   C Is linked wirelessly to a central node.

   D None of the above.

Functions of Internetworking Devices

Networking devices interconnect individual computer networks to create a functional internetwork. The devices in a computer internetwork define a physical topology and a logical topology. These devices typically function at the lower three layers of the OSI reference model to define the ways in which computers function.

This section describes the functions of each layer and how each device works to provide internetwork services.

Physical Layer Functions

To fully understand how these devices provide services, you must first closely examine each of the lower layers. You can start with the physical layer, shown in Figure 2-8. Ethernet is defined at the physical layer.

Figure 2-8   *Physical Layer*

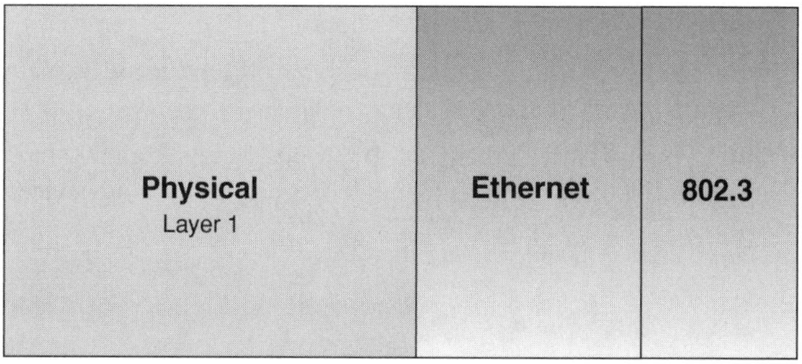

The physical layer defines the media type, connector type, and signaling type. It specifies the electrical, mechanical, procedural, and functional requirements for activating, maintaining, and deactivating the physical link between end systems. The physical layer also specifies characteristics such as voltage levels, data rates, maximum transmission distances, and physical connectors. In the mug analogy used in Chapter 1, the physical layer is the road on which the mug is carried. The roadway is a physical connection between different cities that allows you to go from one place to another. Different roads have different rules, such as speed limits or weight limits, just as different network media have different bandwidths or maximum transmission units (MTUs).

Physical Media and Connectors

The physical media and the connectors used to connect devices into the media are defined by standards at the physical layer. In this book, the primary focus is on the standards that are associated with Ethernet implementations.

The Ethernet and IEEE 802.3 (CSMA/CD) standards define a bus topology LAN that operates at a baseband signaling rate of 10 megabits per second (Mbps), 100 Mbps, and 1000 Mbps. Figure 2-9 shows five defined physical layer wiring standards, defined as follows:

- **10BASE2**—Known as Thinnet. Allows network segments up to 185 meters at the data rate of 10 Mbps on coaxial cable by interconnecting or chaining devices together.

- **10BASE5**—Known as Thicknet. Allows network segments up to 500 meters at the data rate of 10 Mbps on large coaxial cable with devices tapping into the cable to receive signals.

- **10BASE-T**—Carries Ethernet signals at 10 Mbps up to 100 meters on inexpensive twisted-pair wiring from stations to a centralized concentrator called a *hub* and between hubs and other network devices.

- **100BASE-T**—Carries Ethernet signals at 100 Mbps up to 100 meters on inexpensive twisted-pair wiring back to a centralized *hub*.

- **100BASE-F**—Carries Ethernet at 100 Mbps signals from 2000 to 10,000 meters using multimode or single-mode fiber between networking devices.

Figure 2-9   *Defined Physical Layer Ethernet Wiring Standards*

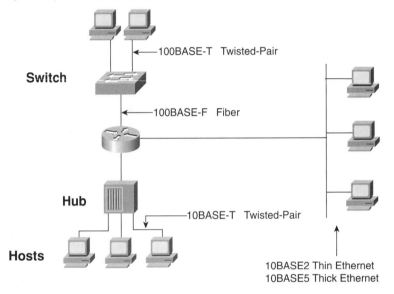

The 10BASE5 and 10BASE2 standards provide access for multiple stations on the same segment by physically connecting each device to a common Ethernet segment. 10BASE5 cables attach to the bus using a cable and an attachment unit interface (AUI). 10BASE2 networks chain devices together using coaxial cable and T-connectors to connect the stations to the common bus.

Because the 10BASE-T standard provides access for a single station at a time, each station must attach to a common bus structure to interconnect all the devices. The hub becomes the bus of the Ethernet devices and is analogous to the segment.

100BASE-T segments can also be connected to a hub so that the hub becomes the bus. 100BASE-T is physically similar to 10BASE-T except it operates 10 times faster. It is becoming more common to interconnect 100BASE-T or 100BASE-F devices using a switch. With a switch, each segment becomes a separate collision domain off a star topology.

NOTE   10BASE5 and 10BASE2 Ethernet standards are typically no longer used in corporate networks. They are listed here for educational value to help explain the differences between physical network types.

Collision and Broadcast Domains

Because all stations on an Ethernet segment are connected to the same physical media, signals sent out across that wire are received by all devices. This situation also means that if any two devices send out a signal at the same time, those signals will collide. Therefore, the structure of Ethernet must have rules that allow only one station to access the media at a time. There must also be a way to detect and correct errors known as *collisions* (when two or more stations try to transmit at the same time).

When discussing networks, you must understand two important concepts:

- **Collision domain**—A group of devices connected to the same physical media such that if two devices access the media at the same time, the result is a collision of the two signals

- **Broadcast domain**—A group of devices in the network that receive one another's broadcast messages

These terms help you understand the basic structure of traffic patterns and help define the need for devices such as switches and routers.

Layer 1 Devices

Layer 1 devices are the most basic internetworking devices. They support physical layer connectivity between networking devices. Several types of Layer 1 devices exist, but the most common devices are the following:

- Repeaters
- Hubs

A repeater is a networking device that exists at Layer 1, the physical layer, of the OSI reference model. As data leaves a source and goes out over a network, it is transformed into either electrical or light pulses that pass along the networking media. These pulses are referred to as signals. When signals leave a transmitting station, they are clean and easily recognizable. However, the longer the cable length, the more the signals deteriorate. The purpose of a repeater is to regenerate and retime network signals at the bit level, allowing them to travel a longer distance on the media.

The term *repeater* originally referred to a device with a single "in" port and a single "out" port. Today, multiport repeaters also exist. Repeaters are classified as Layer 1 devices in the OSI model because they act only at the bit level and look at no other information.

The purpose of a hub is to regenerate and retime network signals. Because a hub performs the same basic function as a repeater, it is also known as a multiport repeater. The difference between a repeater and a hub is the number of cables that connect to the device. A repeater typically has only 2 ports, whereas a hub generally has from 4 to 24 or more ports. A repeater receives on one port and repeats on the other, whereas a hub receives on one port and transmits on all other ports.

Hubs have these properties:

- Hubs amplify signals.

- Hubs propagate signals through the network.

- Hubs do not perform filtering.

- Hubs do not perform path determination or switching.

- Hubs are used as network concentration points.

Hubs are commonly used in Ethernet 10BASE-T or 100BASE-T networks. Hubs create a central connection point for the wiring media and increase the reliability of the network, because the failure of any single cable does not disrupt the entire network. This feature differs from the bus topology, where failure of one cable disrupts the entire network. Hubs are considered Layer 1 devices because they only regenerate the physical signal and repeat it out all of their ports (network connections).

Many Ethernet segments today are devices interconnected with switches and occasionally hubs. These devices allow the concentration of many Ethernet devices into a centralized device that connects all the devices to the same physical bus structure in the hub or backplane in a switch. This means that all the devices connected to a hub share the same media and, consequently, share the same collision domain, broadcast domain, and bandwidth. With a switch, the collision domain and bandwidth are separate for each connected device; the broadcast domain is typically the same by default, but can be configured otherwise. The resulting physical connection is that of a star topology as opposed to a linear topology. Figure 2-10 shows a common connection to the hub.

Figure 2-10 *Ethernet Hub*

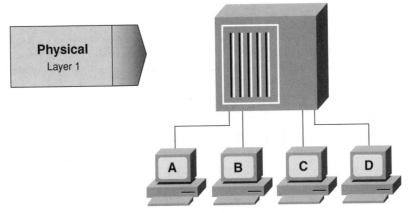

A hub does not manipulate or view the traffic that crosses that bus; it is used only to extend the physical media by repeating the signal it receives in one port out all the other ports. This means that a hub is a physical layer device. It is concerned only with propagation of the physical signaling, without any regard for upper-layer functions. This does not change the rules of Ethernet, however. Stations still share the bus of the hub, which means that contention still occurs.

Because all devices are connected to the same physical media, a hub is a single collision domain. If one station sends out a broadcast, the hub propagates it to all other stations, so it is also a single broadcast domain.

The Ethernet technology is known as carrier sense multiple access collision detect (CSMA/CD). It means that multiple stations have access to the media, and before one station can access that media, it must first "listen" (carrier sense) to make sure that no other station is using the same media. If the media is in use, the station must wait before sending out any data. If two stations both listen and hear no other traffic, and then they both try to transmit at the same time, the result is a collision.

For example, in Figure 2-11, both cars try to occupy the same road at the same time, and they collide. In a network, as with cars, the resulting collision causes damage. In fact, the damaged frames become error frames, which the transmitting stations detect as a collision, forcing both stations to retransmit their respective frames. A backoff algorithm determines when the stations retransmit to minimize the chance of another collision. The more stations that exist on an Ethernet segment, the greater the chance that collisions will occur. These excessive collisions are the reason that networks are segmented (broken up) into smaller collision domains using switches and bridges.

Figure 2-11   *Ethernet Collisions*

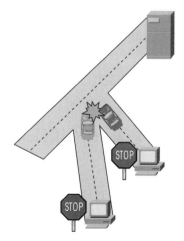

Data Link Layer Functions

Before traffic can be placed on the network, it must be given some details about where to go and what to do when it gets there. The data link layer provides this function. The data link layer is Layer 2 of the OSI reference model, and it differs depending on the topology. Figure 2-12 shows the various physical topologies and some corresponding data link encapsulation methods.

Figure 2-12 *Data Link Layer*

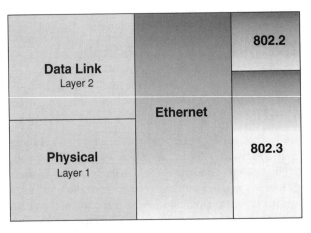

This layer provides the communications between workstations at the first logical layer above the bits on the wire. As a result, many functions are provided by the data link layer. The physical addressing of the end stations is done at the data link layer. To help the network devices determine whether they should pass a message up the protocol stack, fields exist in this layer to identify which upper-layer stack to pass the data to (such as IP, IPX, AppleTalk, and so on). The data link layer provides support for connection-oriented and connectionless services and provides for sequencing and flow control. With the addition of 802.1Q as a data link protocol, frames can now be marked with priority for classification of services. All the Layer 2 fields are used by data link layer devices to control the flow of traffic between devices.

To provide these functions, the Institute of Electrical and Electronic Engineers (IEEE) data link layer is defined by two sublayers:

- **Media Access Control (MAC) sublayer (802.3)**— The MAC sublayer is responsible for how the data is transported over the physical wire. This is the part of the data link layer that communicates downward to the physical layer. It defines such functions as physical addressing, network topology, line discipline, and error notification.

- **Logical Link Control (LLC) sublayer (802.2)**— The LLC sublayer is responsible for logically identifying different protocol types and then encapsulating them to be transmitted across the network. A type code or service access point (SAP) identifier does the logical identification. The type of LLC frame used by an end station depends on what identifier the upper-layer protocol expects. Additional LLC options include support for connections between applications running on the LAN, flow control to the upper layer, and sequence control bits. For some protocols, LLC defines reliable or unreliable services for data transfer instead of the transport layer. (Reliable and unreliable services are discussed further in the section, "Transport Layer Functions.")

MAC Sublayer Frames

Figure 2-13 illustrates the basic frame structure for the MAC IEEE 802.3 frames.

Figure 2-13 *Data Link Layer*

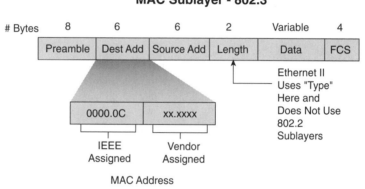

Figure 2-13 shows the standard frame structure to provide an example of how control information transmits information at this layer. The definitions of the MAC sublayer fields are as follows:

- **Preamble**—The IEEE 802.3 frame begins with an alternating pattern of 1s and 0s ending with three consecutive 1s, called a *preamble*. The preamble tells receiving stations that a frame is coming.

- **Destination address and source address**—Immediately following the preamble are the *destination* and *source physical address* fields. These addresses are referred to as *MAC layer addresses*. They are unique to each device in the internetwork. On most LAN interface cards, the MAC address is burned into ROM, thus explaining the term burned-in address (BIA). When the network interface card initializes, this address is copied into RAM to identify the device on the network.

The MAC address is a 48-bit address expressed as 12 hexadecimal digits. The first 24 bits or 6 hexadecimal digits of the MAC address contain a manufacturer identification or vendor code. Another name for this part of the address is the organizational unique identifier (OUI). To ensure vendor uniqueness, the IEEE administers OUIs. The last 24 bits or 6 hexadecimal digits are administered by each vendor and often represent the interface serial number.

The source address is always a unicast (single node) address, and the destination address might be unicast, multicast (group of nodes), or broadcast (all nodes). In addition to the Layer 2 addressing, the Layer 2 fields in the frame include the following:

- **Length**—In IEEE 802.3 frames, the 2-byte field following the source address is a *length* field, which indicates the number of bytes of data that follow this field and precede the frame check sequence (FCS) field.

- **Type**—For Ethernet Type II, the 2-byte field following the source address identifies the EtherType. The EtherType is a hexadecimal field that identifies the upper-layer protocol. For example, 0x0800 would be an EtherType of IP.

- **Data**—Following the length field is the *data* field, which includes the LLC control information, other upper-layer control information, and the user data, such as a Layer 3 datagram.

- **FCS**—A 4-byte *FCS* field containing a cyclic redundancy check (CRC) value follows the data field. The CRC is created by the sending device and recalculated by the receiving device to check for damage that might have occurred to the frame in transit.

LLC Sublayer Frames

Two LLC frame types exist: service access point (SAP) and Subnetwork Access Protocol (SNAP). Which frame type your system uses depends on the protocols that you have running on your system. Some protocols are defined by a SAP ID, and others defined using a type code. Figure 2-14 shows the format of the SAP and SNAP frame types.

For IEEE 802.3 frames, the sublayer fields provide additional services and identify the upper-layer protocol. The LLC and SNAP sublayers are used in IEEE 802.3 frames.

- **LLC header**— The LLC header contains service access points that indicate the upper-layer protocol. The destination SAP (DSAP) and source SAP (SSAP) fields are 1 byte each and act as pointers to the upper-layer protocols in a station. For example, a frame with a SAP of 06 hex is destined for IP, and a frame with a SAP of E0 hex is destined for IPX. From the perspective of these lower MAC sublayers, the SAP process provides a convenient interface to the upper layers of the protocol stack. These SAP entries allow the physical and data link connections to provide services for many upper-layer protocols.

  If a frame uses the SNAP fields, the SSAP and DSAP addresses are both set to AA hex, and the control field is set to 03 hex. In addition to the SAP fields, a SNAP header has a type code field that allows for the inclusion of the EtherType field. The EtherType field defines which upper-layer protocol receives the data using the same hexadecimal types used by Ethernet II.

- **SNAP header**—In a SNAP frame, the first 3 bytes of the SNAP header after the control field are the OUI vendor code. Following the OUI vendor code is a 2-byte field containing the EtherType for the frame. Here is where the backward compatibility with Ethernet Version II is implemented. As with the 802.3 frame, a 4-byte FCS field follows the data field and contains a CRC value.

Figure 2-14 *SAP and SNAP LLC Sublayer Frames*

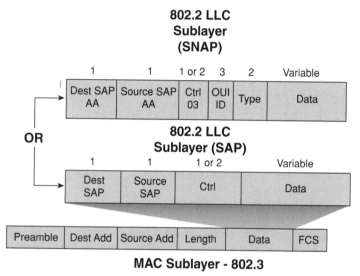

Layer 2 Class of Services

Another important feature at Layer 2 is the ability to identify important frames to devices within the network. Being able to mark certain frames enables devices to process these frames more expediently than others that might be waiting. This type of classification is very important for applications like voice and video. The IEEE 802.1p standard defines a method for classification of frames. 802.1p frames include a 4-byte tag that helps identify 8 different levels of service for Layer 2 frames. Figure 2-15 shows an IEEE 802.1p frame, the 3 priority bits provide CoS services.

Figure 2-15 *Layer 2 CoS Using 802.1p*

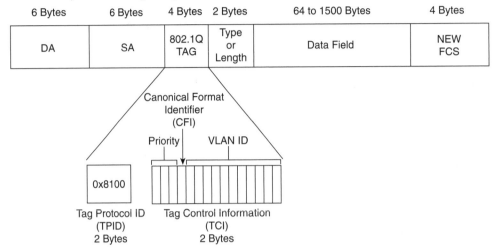

Data Link Layer Devices

Bridges, network interface cards (NICs), and Layer 2 switches are devices that function at the data link layer of the protocol stack. Figure 2-16 shows the devices typically encountered at Layer 2. Layer 2 switching is hardware-based bridging. In a switch, frame forwarding is handled by specialized hardware called application-specific integrated circuits (ASICs). ASIC technology allows a silicon chip to be programmed to perform a specific function as it is built. This technology allows functions to be performed at much higher rates of speed than that of a chip that is programmed by software. Because of ASIC technology, switches provide scalability to gigabit speeds with low latency.

Figure 2-16 *Data Link Devices*

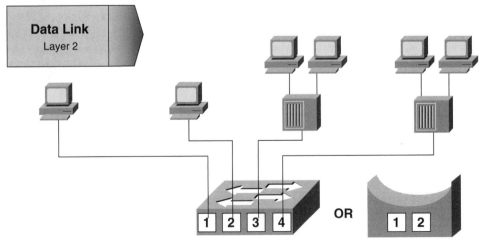

NOTE	Although some Layer 3 and Layer 4 switches perform routing, this book uses the term *switch* to refer to a Layer 2 device.

A bridge is a Layer 2 device designed to create two or more LAN segments, where each segment is a separate collision domain. Therefore, by filtering traffic on a LAN to keep local traffic local, yet allowing connectivity to other segments for traffic specifically directed there, bridges make more bandwidth available for valid data exchange.

Every networking device has a unique MAC address on the NIC. The bridge keeps track of which MAC addresses are on each side of the bridge and makes forwarding decisions based on this MAC address list. Because bridges filter network traffic by looking only at the MAC address, they are not concerned with the network layer protocol and can rapidly forward frames regardless of their payload. The following are the important properties of bridges:

- Bridges are more "intelligent" than hubs. That is, they can analyze incoming frames and forward (or drop) them based on address information.

- Bridges collect and pass packets between two or more LAN segments.

- Bridges create multiple collision domains, allowing more than one device to transmit simultaneously without causing a collision.

- Bridges maintain MAC address tables.

When a bridge or switch receives a frame, it uses the data link information to process the frame. In a transparent bridge environment, the bridge processes the frame by determining whether it needs to be copied to other connected segments. A transparent bridge hears every frame that crosses a segment and views each frame and source address field to determine on what segment the source station resides. The transparent bridge stores this information in memory in a *forwarding table*. The forwarding table lists each end station (from which the bridge has heard a frame within a particular time period) and the segment on which it resides. When a bridge hears a frame on the network, it views the destination address and compares it to the forwarding table to determine whether to filter, flood, or copy the frame onto another segment.

This decision process occurs as follows:

- If the destination device is on the same segment as the frame, the bridge blocks the frame from going on to other segments. This process is known as *filtering*.

- If the destination device is on a different segment, the bridge forwards the frame to the appropriate segment. This process is knows as *forwarding*.

- If the destination address is unknown to the bridge, the bridge forwards the frame to all segments except the one on which it was received. This process is known as *flooding*.

Because a bridge learns all the station destinations by listening to source addresses, it never learns the broadcast address. Therefore, all broadcasts are always flooded to all the segments on the bridge or switch. Therefore, all segments in a bridged or switched environment are considered to be in the same broadcast domain.

Like repeaters and hubs, another device, called a switch, is used as a concentrator for multiple network devices. A switch, however, defines different physical connections for each device using multiple bridge connections. A switch, also called a LAN switch, often replaces hubs and works with existing cable infrastructures to provide minimal disruption to existing networks.

Switches are data link layer devices that, like bridges, enable multiple physical LAN segments to be interconnected into single larger networks. Like bridges, switches forward traffic based on MAC addresses. Because switching is performed in hardware instead of software, it is significantly faster. Think of each switch port as a microbridge. The process of dividing large network segments into smaller network segments is called *micro-segmentation*. Thus, each switch port acts as a separate bridge and, when connected to an individual host, gives the full bandwidth of the medium to that host.

NOTE   This book focuses on transparent bridging because this is the function performed by the Cisco Catalyst series of switches. This is also the most common form of bridging/switching in Ethernet environments. It should also be noted that other types of bridges exist, such as source-route bridging, in which the source determines the route to be taken through the network, and translational bridging, which allows the frame to move from a source route to a transparent environment between Ethernet and Token Ring.

A bridged/switched network provides excellent traffic management. The purpose of the Layer 2 device is to reduce collisions, which waste bandwidth and prevent packets from reaching their destinations. Part A of Figure 2-17 shows how a switch reduces collisions by comparing frames to cars. With a switch, each segment is given its own collision domain. Part B of Figure 2-17, using a car analogy, shows that when two or more packets need to get onto the same segment, the traffic is stored in memory until the segment is available for use.

Bridged/switched networks have the following characteristics:

- Each port on a switch is its own collision domain.
- All devices connected to the same bridge or switch are part of the same broadcast domain, by default.
- All segments must use the same data link layer implementation, such as all Ethernet or all Token Ring. If an end station must communicate with another end station on different media, then some device, such as a router or translational bridge, must translate between the different media types.

Figure 2-17   *Bridging Reduces Collisions*

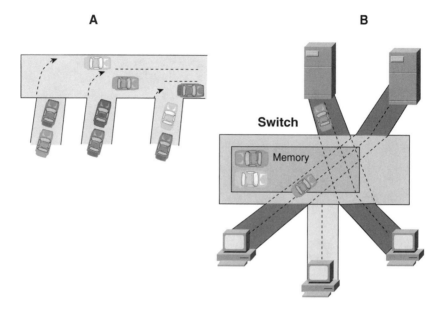

In a switched environment, there can be one device per segment, and each device can send frames at the same time, thus allowing the primary pathway to be shared.

Network Layer Functions

The network layer defines how to transport traffic between devices that are not locally attached in the same broadcast domain. Two pieces of information are required to achieve this:

- A logical address associated with the source and destination stations
- A path through the network to reach the desired destination

Figure 2-18 shows the location of the network layer in relation to the data link layer. The network layer is independent of the data link and can therefore be used to connect devices residing on different physical media. The logical addressing structure provides this connectivity.

Figure 2-18 *Location of the Network Layer in the Protocol Model*

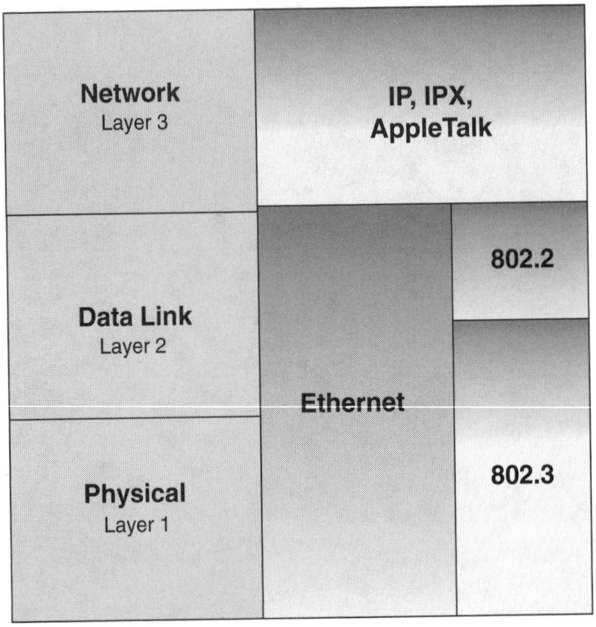

Logical addressing schemes identify networks in an internetwork and the location of the devices within the context of those networks. These schemes vary based on the network layer protocol in use. This book discusses the network layer operation for the TCP/IP protocol stack.

Network Layer Addresses

Network layer addresses (also called *virtual* or *logical addresses*) exist at Layer 3 of the OSI reference model. Unlike data link layer addresses, which usually exist within a flat address space, network layer addresses are usually hierarchical in that they define networks first and then devices or nodes on each of those networks. In other words, network layer addresses are like postal addresses, which describe a person's location by providing a ZIP code and a street address. The ZIP code defines the city and state, and the street address is a particular location in that city. This is in contrast to the MAC layer address, which is flat in nature. Once assigned, MAC addresses remain with the device no matter where it is located. A good example of a flat address space is the U.S. Social

Security numbering system, in which each person has a single, unique Social Security number that they keep regardless of where they live. Figure 2-19 shows a sample network layer address as defined within a network layer packet. In addition to addressing, the Layer 3 protocol also defines fields which can identify the importance of a frame. All Layer 3 fields are used by Layer 3 internetworking devices for the delivery of frames.

Figure 2-19   *Network Layer Addressing*

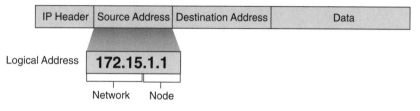

Network Layer End-Station Packet

The logical address consists of two portions. One part uniquely identifies each network within the internetwork, and the other part uniquely identifies the hosts on each of those networks. Combining both portions results in a unique network address for each device. This unique network address has two functions:

- The network portion identifies individual networks, allowing the routers to identify paths through the network cloud. The router uses this address to determine where to send network packets in the same manner that the ZIP code on a letter determines the state and city that a package should be delivered to.

- The host portion identifies a particular device or a device's port on the network in the same manner that a street address on a letter identifies a location within that city.

Many network layer protocols exist, and they all share the function of identifying networks and hosts throughout the internetwork structure. Most of these protocols have different schemes for accomplishing this task. TCP/IP is a common protocol that is used in routed networks. An IP address has the following components to identify networks and hosts:

- A 32-bit address, divided into four 8-bit sections called *octets*. This address identifies a specific network and a specific host on that network by subdividing the bits into network and host portions.

- A 32-bit subnet mask that is also divided into four 8-bit octets. The subnet mask determines which bits represent the network and which represent the host. The bit pattern for a subnet mask is a string of consecutive 1s followed by the remaining bits, which are 0s. Figure 2-20 shows that the boundary between the 1s and the 0s marks the boundary for the network and host portions of the address, the two components necessary to define an IP address on an end device.

Figure 2-20 *IP Address Components*

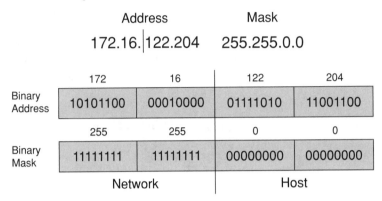

NOTE   IP addresses are represented by taking the 8-bit octets, converting them to decimal, and then separating the octets with dots or periods. This format is known as *dotted decimal* and is done to simplify addressing for those of us who count in base 10.

Layer 3 Quality of Service Marking

Because internetworking devices operate at different layers of the OSI model, you need to be able to identify important frames to each internetworking device. At the internetworking layer of IP, this identification is accomplished using bits from the type of service (TOS) field in the IP header. Using these bits, applications can identify a frame's importance using IP Precedence or Differential Services. Figure 2-21 shows the TOS field in the IP header.

Figure 2-21 *Layer 3 QoS Marking*

Network Layer End-Station Packet

IP Header	Source Address	Destination Address	Data

TOS Field

Router Operation at the Network Layer

Routers operate at the network layer by tracking and recording the different networks and choosing the best path to those networks. The routers place this information in a routing table, which includes the following items (see Figure 2-22):

- **Network addresses**—Represent known networks to the router. A network address is protocol-specific. If a router supports more than one protocol, it has a unique table for each protocol.

- **Interface**—Refers to the interface used by the router to reach a given network. This is the interface that forwards packets destined for the listed network.

- **Metric**—Refers to the cost or distance to the target network. This is a value that helps the router choose the best path to a given network. This metric changes depending on how the router chooses paths. Common metrics include the number of networks that must be crossed to get to a destination (also known as *hops*), the time it takes to cross all the interfaces to a given network (also known as *delay*), or a value associated with the speed of a link (also known as *bandwidth*).

Figure 2-22 *Routing Tables*

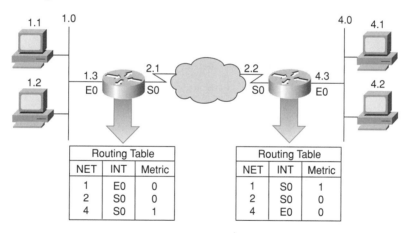

Because routers function at the network layer of the OSI model, they separate segments into unique collision and broadcast domains. Each segment is referred to as a *network* and must be identified by a network address to be reached by end stations. In addition to identifying each segment as a network, each station on that network must also be uniquely identified by the logical address. This addressing structure allows for hierarchical network configuration but is defined by the network it is on as well as a host identifier (that is, a station is not known merely by a host identifier). For routers to operate on a network, it is required that each interface be configured on the unique network it represents. The router must also have a host address on that network. The router uses the interface's configuration information to determine the network portion of the address to build a routing table.

In addition to identifying networks and providing connectivity, routers also perform other functions:

- Routers filter Layer 2 broadcast and Layer 2 multicast frames.

- Routers attempt to determine the optimal path through a routed network based on routing algorithms.

- Routers strip Layer 2 frames and forward packets based on Layer 3 destination addresses.

- Routers map a single Layer 3 logical address to a single network device; therefore, routers can limit or secure network traffic based on identifiable attributes within each packet. These options, controlled via access lists, can be applied to inbound or outbound packets.

- Routers can be configured to perform both bridging and routing functions.

- Routers provide connectivity between different virtual LANs (VLANs) in a switched environment.

- Routers can be used to deploy quality of service parameters for specified types of network traffic.

In addition to the benefits in the between Ethernet networks, routers can be used to connect remote locations to the main office using WAN services, as illustrated in Figure 2-23.

Figure 2-23   *Routers Connect Remote Locations to the Main Office*

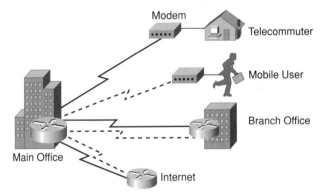

Routers support a variety of physical layer connectivity standards that allow you to build WANs. In addition, they can provide the security and access controls that are needed when interconnecting remote locations.

Transport Layer Functions

To connect two devices in the fabric of the network, a connection or session must be established. The transport layer defines the end-to-end station establishment guidelines between two end stations. A session constitutes a logical connection between the peer transport layers in source and destination end stations. Figure 2-24 shows the relationship of some transport layer protocols to their respective network layer protocols. Different transport layer functions are provided by these protocols.

Figure 2-24   *Transport Layer Protocols*

Transport	TCP	UDP	SPX
Network	IP		IPX

Specifically, the transport layer defines the following functions:

- Allows end stations to assemble and disassemble multiple upper-layer segments into the same transport layer data stream. This is accomplished by assigning upper-layer application identifiers. Within the TCP/IP protocol suite, these identifiers are known as *port numbers*. The OSI reference model refers to these identifiers as service access points (SAPs). The transport layer uses these port numbers to identify application layer entities such as FTP and Telnet. An example of a port number is 23, which identifies the Telnet server application. Data with a destination transport port number of 23 would be going to the Telnet application.

- Allows applications to request reliable data transport between communicating end systems. Reliable transport uses a connection-oriented relationship between the communicating end systems to accomplish the following:

  — Ensure that segments delivered are acknowledged back to the sender

  — Provide for retransmission of any segments that are not acknowledged

  — Put segments back into their correct sequence order at the receiving station

  — Provide congestion avoidance and control

At the transport layer, data can be transmitted reliably or unreliably. For IP, TCP is reliable or connection-oriented and UDP is unreliable or connectionless. A good analogy to connection-oriented versus connectionless is a phone call versus a postcard. With a phone call, you establish a dialogue that lets you know how well you are communicating. A postcard offers no real-time feedback.

For a connection-oriented transport layer protocol to provide functions like basic communications and reliability, a connection is established between the end stations, data is transmitted, and then the session is disconnected.

Like a phone call, to communicate with a connection-oriented service, you must first establish the connection. To do this within the TCP/IP protocol suite, the sending and receiving stations perform an operation known as a three-way handshake.

After the connection is established, the transfer of information begins. During the transfer, the two end stations continue to communicate with their transport layer PDUs (headers) to verify that the data is received correctly. If the receiving station does not acknowledge a packet within a predefined amount of time, the sender retransmits the package. This ensures reliable delivery of all traffic. After the data transfer is complete, the session is disconnected.

Multilayer Devices

A multilayer switch works much like a Layer 2 switch. In addition to switching using Layer 2 MAC addresses, a multilayer switch can also use Layer 3 network addresses (IP).

Traditionally, Layer 3 functions have occurred only within routers. However, over the past few years, improved hardware has allowed many Layer 3 routing functions to occur in hardware. Layer 3 routing has traditionally been a software-bound process that creates network bottlenecks. With the advent of high-speed, hardware-based multilayer switches, Layer 3 functions can be performed as quickly as Layer 2 functions. Layer 3 no longer is a bottleneck.

Layer 3 functions include added capability for quality of service (QoS) and for security. Packets can be prioritized based on the network (IP) that they are coming from or the network to which they are being sent. Traffic can also be prioritized based on the kind of traffic, for example Voice over IP traffic could be given a higher priority than normal user traffic. Traffic from specific networks can be barred from entering the network.

A multilayer switch can also examine Layer 4 information, including TCP headers that can help identify the type of application from which the protocol data unit (PDU) came, or to which the PDU is directed. Some examples of a multilayer switch would be the Cisco Catalyst 3550, 4500, and 6500 series switches.

Mapping Devices to Layers and the Hierarchical Model

Earlier in this chapter, you learned about the hierarchical model used to design and implement networks. Given a particular function of networking and what you have learned about the service performed at each layer, you should be able to match Cisco products to your internetworking needs.

The following list summarizes the factors for selecting internetworking devices:

- Device provides desired functionality and features.
- Device has required capacity and performance.
- Device is easy to install and offers centralized management.
- Device provides network resiliency.
- Device provides investment protection in existing infrastructure.
- Device provides migration path for change and growth.

The most important task is to understand the needs and then identify the device functions and features that meet those needs. To accomplish this, obtain information about where in the internetworking hierarchy the device needs to operate and then consider factors such as ease of installation, capacity requirements, and so forth.

Other factors, such as remote access, also play a role in product selection. When supporting remote access requirements, you must first determine the kind of WAN services that meet your needs. Then, you can select the appropriate device.

Services Devices

Recent networking trends have resulted in the development of new internetworking devices. This section describes those devices.

Some of the newer internetworking devices include the following:

- Voice gateways for handling converged packetized voice and data traffic
- Digital subscriber line access multiplexers (DSLAMs) used at the service provider's central office for concentrating DSL modem connections from hundreds of homes
- Optical platforms for sending and receiving data over fiber-optic cable, providing high-speed connection

A voice gateway is a special-purpose device that performs an application layer conversion of information from one protocol stack to another. The Cisco AS5400 Series Universal Access Server provides cost-effective platforms that combine routing, remote access, voice gateway, firewall, and digital modem functionality. The Cisco AS5400 Series Universal Gateway offers high capacity in only two rack units. The Cisco AS5400 offers data, voice, wireless, and fax services on any port at any time.

A DSLAM is a device used in a variety of digital subscriber line (DSL) technologies. A DSLAM serves as the point of interface between a number of subscriber premises and the carrier network.

Several optical platforms are available on the market for the optical network. The Cisco ONS 15454 is a dense wavelength-division multiplexing (DWDM) optical network system. The Cisco ONS 15454 provides the functions of multiple network elements in a single platform. Part of the Cisco IP+Optical product line, the Cisco ONS 15454 combines the capacity of optical transport with the intelligence of IP to cost-effectively deliver next-generation voice and data services.

DWDM increases bandwidth by using multiple discrete wavelengths, each carrying its own data stream to share a single fiber. Coupled with the increased distance between repeaters (amplifiers), this offers a huge cost benefit to WAN and MAN service providers.

Other common network devices that work at more than only the lower three layers include firewalls and AAA servers. Figure 2-25 shows how firewalls and authentication, authorization, and accounting (AAA) servers are used in internetwork connections.

Figure 2-25 *Firewalls and AAA Servers in Internetworks*

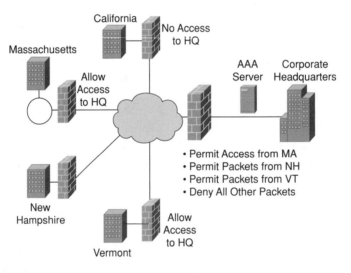

The term *firewall* refers to either a firewall program(s) running on a router or server, or a special standalone hardware component of a network. A firewall protects the resources of a private network from users in other networks.

Working closely with a router program, a firewall examines each network packet to determine whether or not to forward it to its destination. Using a firewall·is like using a traffic cop to ensure that only valid traffic can enter or leave certain networks.

An AAA server is a program that handles user requests for access to computer and network resources. It provides AAA services for an enterprise. The AAA server ensures that only authenticated users can get into the network (authentication), that the users are allowed access only to the resources they need (authorization), and that records are kept of everything they do after they are allowed entry (accounting).

An AAA server is like the credit card system. To put charges on a credit card, the merchant must verify the credit card actually belongs to the person using it (authentication). The merchant must also check to see if the credit card has enough credit left for the requested charge amount (authorization) and then record the charge to the user's account (accounting).

Each device discussed in this chapter provides particular network services. All these devices allow network administrators to build networks based on the needs of an organization's connectivity requirements.

Functions of Internetwork Devices Section Quiz

Use these practice questions to review what you learned in this section.

1 Multiport repeaters can provide a simple solution for which of the following problems?

A Too many types of incompatible equipment on the network

B Too much traffic on a WAN network

C Too slow data transmission rates

D No single cable connecting all devices

2 What is one disadvantage of using a hub?

A A hub cannot extend the network operating distance.

B A hub cannot filter network traffic.

C A hub does not allow a star topology.

D A hub cannot regenerate signals.

3 Which of the following is true concerning bridges and their forwarding decisions?

A Bridges operate at OSI Layer 2 and use IP addresses to make decisions.

B Bridges operate at OSI Layer 3 and use IP addresses to make decisions.

C Bridges operate at OSI Layer 2 and use MAC addresses to make decisions.

D Bridges operate at OSI Layer 3 and use MAC addresses to make decisions.

4 Which of the following is true concerning the function of switches?

   A Switches increase the sizes of collision domains.

   B Switches combine the connectivity of a hub with the traffic regulation of a bridge.

   C Switches combine the connectivity of a hub with the traffic direction of a router.

   D Switches perform Layer 4 path selection.

5 What does a router do?

   A A router matches information in the routing table with the destination IP address of the data and sends incoming data to the correct next hop device or host.

   B A router matches information in the routing table with the destination MAC address of the data and sends incoming data to the correct subnetwork.

   C A router matches information in the ARP table with the destination IP address of the data and sends incoming data to the correct network address.

   D A router matches information in the routing table with the source IP address of the data and sends incoming data to the correct subnet.

6 Which of the following statements is true?

   A A gateway is a special-purpose device that performs an application layer conversion of information from one protocol stack to another.

   B The Cisco AS5400 Series Universal Gateway offers high capacity in only two rack units, with universal port data, voice, wireless, and fax services on any port at any time.

   C A DSLAM serves as the point of interface between a number of subscriber premises and the carrier network.

   D All of the above.

7 What are the functions of AAA servers?

   A Ensure that only authenticated users can get in the network

   B Ensure that the users are allowed access only to the resources they need

   C Record everything the users do after they are allowed entry

   D All of the above

Chapter Summary

This chapter reviewed the core concepts of network devices. This chapter discussed the roles of network devices in relation to business needs and how a network hierarchy can be used to provide network services. This chapter also discussed the difference between a physical and logical network and reviewed some basic network topologies. Next, you read about how the different layers of the OSI model function in providing these services and which devices operate at each layer. After you understand why and how these internetworking devices operate, you can better understand the tasks associated in configuring and maintaining an internetwork.

This chapter laid the groundwork for an in-depth look at each of the lower three layers of the OSI model and how Cisco internetworking devices provide the services for an organizations internetwork.

Chapter Review Questions

Use these review questions to test your knowledge of the concepts discussed in this chapter.

1 In a star topology, what happens when a cable between a device and the central device fails?

   A The entire network becomes disconnected.

   B The network resets itself.

   C The device at the end of the cable becomes disconnected.

   D Nothing, the devices remain online.

2 The rings in a dual-ring topology operate in different directions.

   A True

   B False

3 Which three functions are defined by the Cisco hierarchical model?

   A Access zone

   B Distribution layer

   C Core layer

   D User layer

   E Distribution zone

   F Access layer

4 Which of the following is a characteristic of a hub?

   A They do Layer 2 filtering.

   B They do Layer 2 path determination.

   C They are used as network concentration points.

   D They cannot amplify signals.

5 What universally unique identifier does each network device have at Layer 2?

   A IP address

   B Subnet address

   C MAC address

   D Layer 2 address

6 Which of the following does a router forward?

   A Layer 1 bits

   B Layer 2 frames

   C Layer 3 datagrams

   D Layer 4 segments

7 What does DSLAM stand for?

   A Device for segments, links, and multiplexers

   B Digital subscriber line access multiplexer

   C Device for segments, links, and multilayer switches

   D Digital subscriber link access multiplexer

8 Which of the following characteristics do firewalls have? (Select all that apply.)

   A Software-based

   B Hardware-based

   C Filter traffic

   D Layer 2 device

9 Which OSI layer defines an address that consists of a network portion and a node portion?

A Layer 1

B Layer 2

C Layer 3

D Layer 4

E Layer 5

F Layer 6

G Layer 7

10 Which OSI layer defines a flat address space?

A Layer 1

B Layer 2

C Layer 3

D Layer 4

E Layer 5

F Layer 6

G Layer 7

Upon completion of this chapter, you will be able to perform the following tasks:

- Describe the functions and operation of important LAN technologies, including Ethernet, Fast Ethernet, and Gigabit Ethernet

- Describe the functions, operation, and primary components of a WAN

- Describe the functions, operations, and primary components of a MAN, a SAN, a CN, and a VPN

CHAPTER 3

Common Types of Networks

An internetwork is made up of multiple computer networks interconnected by networking devices. Many types of computer networks exist, including LANs, WANs, MANs, storage-area networks (SANs), content networks (CNs), virtual private networks (VPNs), and the global Internet.

LANs are high-speed data networks within a limited geographic area. The LAN is the most common computer network because most user devices connect to a LAN. WANs are networks that cover large geographic areas. Although the Internet is one of the most familiar examples, a WAN can also be private, connecting the worldwide locations of a corporation, an educational system, or government offices. WANs employ a number of special devices, physical and data link protocols, and connections obtained from service providers. A MAN is a type of high-speed WAN in a smaller geographic region, like a single city or metropolitan area. SANs, CNs, and VPNs are all service networks that provide some end service to the user or the organization.

This chapter provides you with an overview of these different types of networks and their functions in a corporate internetwork. Learning about these networks and how they function expands your understanding of how internetworks operate and how they meet different data communication needs.

LANs Overview

Ethernet LANs are the most common local-area networks, and this term is often used to refer to all types of LANs. Since Ethernet was first developed more than 20 years ago, it has been upgraded several times to meet evolving technology demands. Therefore, different types of Ethernet LAN technologies exist, including Ethernet, Fast Ethernet, and Gigabit Ethernet.

Ethernet networks are found in most business environments. Learning about their standards and functions gives you a working perspective about LAN components and technologies and how internetworking devices provide services for these networks.

LANs are high-speed, low-error data networks that cover a relatively small geographic area, up to a few thousand meters, or a few miles. LANs connect workstations, peripherals, terminals, and other devices in a single building or other geographically limited area. This section describes the standards that apply to LANs in relation to the OSI reference model.

LAN standards specify cabling and signaling at both the physical and data link layers of the Open System Interconnection (OSI) model. Figure 3-1 shows how LAN protocols map to the OSI reference model.

Figure 3-1 *LAN Standards and the OSI Model*

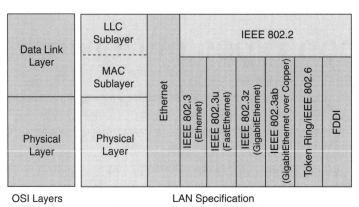

Ethernet, the most common type of LAN, was originally developed at Xerox. As it became used in business communications, Digital Equipment Corporation, Intel, and Xerox agreed upon some standards for interconnectivity. This agreed-upon type of Ethernet was called *DIX Ethernet* after these three companies. Later, this came to be called *thick Ethernet* because of the thickness of the cable used in this type of network. Thick Ethernet ran at 10 Mbps. The standard for Ethernet was updated in the 1980s to add more capability, and the new version of Ethernet was referred to as Ethernet II, or *thin Ethernet*. The Type II frame identifies the upper-layer protocol using an Ethertype field in the frame header.

As the technology became more widely used, it began to attract the attention of the computing and communications industry. In 1980, the Institute of Electrical and Electronic Engineers (IEEE), a professional organization that defines electronics and communication standards, formed a working group to write industry wide standards for Ethernet. The IEEE standards are the predominant and best-known LAN standards in the world today. When the work group (referred to as IEEE 802.3) defined standards for Ethernet, the standard was called Ethernet 802.3. The standard is based on a process called *carrier sense multiple access collision detect (CSMA/CD)*, which specifies the physical layer (Layer 1) and the Media Access Control (MAC) portion of the data link layer (Layer 2). Today, this standard is most often referred to as simply Ethernet.

The IEEE divides the OSI data link layer into these two separate sublayers:

- Logical Link Control (LLC) (transitions up to the network layer)
- MAC (transitions down to the physical layer)

The IEEE created the LLC sublayer to allow part of the data link layer to function independently from existing technologies. This layer provides versatility in services to network layer protocols that are above it, while communicating effectively with the variety of MAC and Layer 1 technologies below it. The LLC, as a sublayer, participates in the encapsulation process.

The LLC header tells the data link layer what to do with a packet when it receives a frame. For example, a host receives a frame and then looks in the LLC header to understand that the packet is destined for the IP protocol at the network layer.

The original Ethernet header (prior to IEEE 802.2 and 802.3) did not use an LLC header. Instead, it used a Type field in the Ethernet header to identify the Layer 3 protocol being carried in the Ethernet frame.

The MAC sublayer deals with the physical media access. The IEEE 802.3 MAC specification defines MAC addresses, which uniquely identify multiple devices at the data link layer. Each device must have a unique MAC address to participate on the network.

Ethernet

Ethernet signals, or frames, are transmitted to every station connected to the LAN, using a special set of rules to determine which station can talk at any particular time. Ethernet LANs manage the signals on a network by CSMA/CD.

In an Ethernet LAN, before transmitting, a computer first listens to the media. If the media is idle, the computer sends its data. After a transmission is sent, the computers on the network once again compete for the next available idle time in order to send another frame. Because each computer waits for idle time before transmitting, no one station has an advantage over another station on the network, but this also guarantees that no station in particular gains access to the media. It is more or less first come, first serve.

Figure 3-2 shows the interaction of a CSMA/CD network. Stations on a CSMA/CD LAN can access the network at any time. Before sending data, CSMA/CD stations listen to the network to determine whether it is already in use. If it is, then they wait. If the network is not in use, the stations transmit. A collision occurs when two stations listen for network traffic, hear none, and transmit simultaneously. In this case, both transmissions are damaged, and the stations must retransmit at some later time. CSMA/CD stations must be able to detect collisions so that they know when they must retransmit.

Figure 3-2   *CSMA/CD Network Interaction*

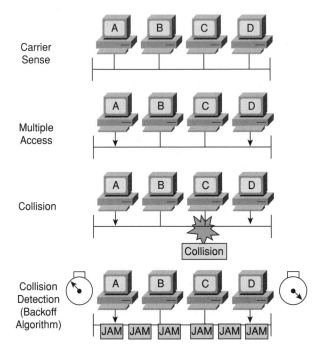

When a station transmits, the signal is referred to as a carrier. The network interface card (NIC) of the devices on the network "senses" the carrier and consequently restrains itself from broadcasting a signal. If no carrier exists, a waiting station knows that it is free to transmit. This is the carrier sense part of the protocol.

In the CSMA/CD process, priorities are not assigned to particular stations. Therefore, all stations on the network have equal access. This is the multiple access part of the protocol. If two or more stations attempt a transmission simultaneously, a collision occurs. The stations are alerted of the collision by a JAM signal, and they execute a backoff algorithm that randomly schedules retransmission of the frame. The JAM signal is generated by the transmitting stations once the collision is detected. The primary purpose of the JAM signal is to "reinforce" the collision to the other transmitting station. This scenario prevents the machines from repeatedly attempting to transmit at the same time. Collisions are normally resolved in microseconds. This is the collision detect part of the protocol. Figure 3-3 shows the flow of the CSMA/CD process.

Figure 3-3   *CSMA/CD Process*

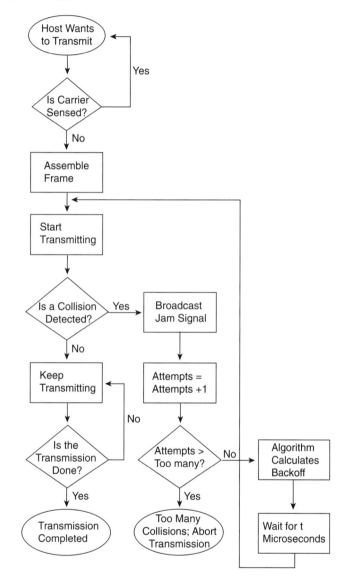

Ethernet refers to the family of LAN protocols that includes these four popular implementations:

- **10-Mbps Ethernet**—These LAN specifications (IEEE 802.3 and Ethernet II) operate at 10 megabits per second (Mbps) over coaxial or twisted-pair cable.

- **100-Mbps Ethernet**—This single LAN specification (IEEE 802.3u), also known as Fast Ethernet, operates at 100 Mbps over twisted-pair cable.

- **Gigabit Ethernet**—An extension of the IEEE 802.3 Ethernet standard, Gigabit Ethernet increases speed tenfold over Fast Ethernet, to 1000 Mbps, or 1 gigabit per second (Gbps). Two IEEE 802.3 standards, IEEE 802.3z and IEEE 802.3ab, define Gigabit Ethernet operations over fiber optics and twisted-pair cable.

- **10000-Mbps (10-Gbps) Ethernet**—Another extension of the IEEE 802.3 Ethernet standard, 10-Gbps Ethernet (also called 10GigEthernet) increases the speed 1000 times of that of Ethernet, adding another factor of 10 to the speed. Gigabit Ethernet is being defined under the IEEE 802.3ae standard for operation over fiber-optic cable.

Each of these protocols has a different naming convention. Ethernet protocols are usually described as a function of data rate, maximum segment length, and medium as shown in Figure 3-4. As faster types of Ethernet are used, more users can be added to the network without degrading network performance.

Figure 3-4 *Ethernet Protocol Naming Convention*

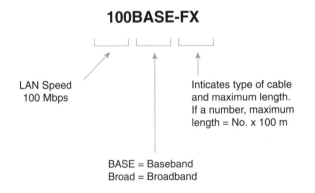

Fast Ethernet

The Fast Ethernet standard (IEEE 802.3u) raises the Ethernet speed from 10 Mbps to 100 Mbps with only minimal changes to the existing cable structure. Data can move from 10 Mbps to 100 Mbps without protocol translation or changes to application and networking software and hardware. As mentioned in Chapter 1, "Introduction to Internetworking," this modular engineering is one of the advantages to a layered protocol. Because Ethernet is defined at the lower two layers of the OSI model, a change to these layers does not require a change to the protocol or application layers on the device. Table 3-1 shows the physical specifications for the Fast Ethernet protocol.

Table 3-1   *Fast Ethernet Specifications*

Protocol	Maximum Segment Length (Meters)	Transmission Medium
100BASE-T		Unshielded twisted-pair (UTP) or shielded twisted-pair (STP) copper cabling
100BASE-F		Single mode or multimode fiber
100BASE-X		Refers to two strands of copper or fiber
100BASE-FX	1000 (full duplex) 400 (half duplex)	Two strands of multimode fiber
100BASE-T4	100	UTP using 4 pairs Category 3–5 UTP
100BASE-TX	100	Two Pairs UTP or STP Category 5 cabling

Gigabit Ethernet

Gigabit Ethernet is an extension of the IEEE 802.3 Ethernet standard. IEEE 802.3z specifies operations over fiber optics, and IEEE 802.3ab specifies operations over twisted-pair copper cable. Gigabit Ethernet builds on the Ethernet protocol but increases speed tenfold over Fast Ethernet, to 1000 Mbps, or 1 Gbps. It has become a dominant player in high-speed LAN backbones and server connectivity. Gigabit Ethernet uses Ethernet as its basis, and network managers have been able to take advantage of their existing knowledge to manage and maintain gigabit networks.

Gigabit Ethernet is often used for connecting buildings on the campus to a central multi-layer gigabit switch located at the campus data center. Servers located at the campus data center would also be connected to the same gigabit multilayer switch that provides connectivity to the entire campus. Table 3-2 outlines the physical specifications for Gigabit Ethernet.

Table 3-2   *Gigabit Ethernet Specifications*

Protocol	Maximum Segment Length (Meters)	Transmission Medium
1000BASE-LX	3000 (single mode) 500 (multimode)	Long-wave laser over single-mode and multimode fiber
1000BASE-SX	500	Short-wave laser over multimode fiber
1000BASE-CX	25	Balanced shielded 150-ohm two-pair STP copper cable
1000BASE-T	100	Category 5 UTP copper wiring

Because Gigabit ports are so expensive, it is beneficial to have a way to change the medium without having to special order a card or device. The industry-standard Cisco Gigabit Interface Converter (GBIC) is a hot-swappable input/output device that plugs into a Gigabit Ethernet port (slot), linking the port with the physical media used by the network. GBICs can be used and interchanged on a wide variety of Cisco products and can be intermixed in combinations of IEEE 802.3z-compliant 1000BASE-SX, 1000BASE-LX/LH, or 1000BASE-ZX interfaces on a port-by-port basis.

Cisco offers a 1000BASE-LX/LH interface that is fully compliant with the IEEE 802.3z 1000BASE-LX standard, but has the ability to go up to 10 kilometers (6.2 miles) over single-mode fiber, which is 5 km (3.1 miles) farther than generic 1000BASE-LX interfaces.

As additional capabilities are developed, these modules make it easy to upgrade to the latest interface technology, without buying new hardware. Figure 3-5 shows Cisco GBICs.

Figure 3-5   *Gigabit Interface Converter*

LANs are the most common networks in most internetworks. Ethernet has become the de-facto standard for most corporate and private LANs. Understanding the physical and logical components of these networks is the first step to building an internetwork.

LANs Overview Section Quiz

Use these practice questions to review what you learned in this section.

1 Which of the following is *not* one of the recognized IEEE sublayers?

   A   Media Access Control

   B   Data Link Control

   C   Logical Link Control

   D   None of the above

2 What is the name of the access control method used by Ethernet?

   A   TCP/IP

   B   CSMA/CD

   C   CMDA/CS

   D   CSMA/CA

3 Fast Ethernet supports up to what transfer rate?

   A   5 Mbps

   B   10 Mbps

   C   100 Mbps

   D   1000 Mbps

4 Identify two Gigabit Ethernet cable specifications.

   A   1000BASE-TX

   B   1000BASE-FX

   C   1000BASE-CX

   D   1000BASE-LX

   E   1000BASE-X

WANs Overview

WANs are networks that cover large geographic areas. Although the Internet is one of the most familiar examples of a WAN, this type of network can also be private, connecting the worldwide locations of a corporation, an educational system, or government offices. WANs employ a number of special devices, physical and data link protocols, and connections obtained from service providers.

Understanding how a WAN operates enables you to understand how networks can connect users and services beyond the physical limitations of LANs. This section provides an overview of how a WAN functions and how WAN technologies relate to the OSI reference model.

The main way that a WAN differs from a LAN is that WAN members must subscribe to an outside WAN service provider—such as a Regional Bell Operating Company (RBOC); Post, Telephone, and Telegraph (PTT); or other service provider—to use WAN carrier network services. A WAN uses data link layer protocols, such as Integrated Services Digital Network (ISDN) and Frame Relay, that are provided by carriers to transmit data over wide areas.

When you connect to the service provider network, you must be familiar with a number of terms and equipment. The following are the most commonly used terms associated with WAN services:

- **Customer premises equipment (CPE)**—Devices physically located on the subscriber's premises. Includes devices owned by the subscriber and devices leased to the subscriber by the service provider.

- **Demarcation (or demarc)**—The point at which the CPE ends and the local loop portion of the service begins. This often occurs at the point of presence (POP) of a building.

- **Local loop (or "last mile")**—Cabling (usually copper wiring) that extends from the demarcation into the WAN service provider's central office.

- **Central office (CO) switch**—A switching facility that provides the nearest POP for the provider's WAN service.

- **Point of presence**—A place where the service provider's equipment is installed.

- **Toll network**—The collective switches and facilities (called trunks) inside the WAN provider's cloud. The traffic might cross a trunk to a primary center, then to a sectional center, and then to a regional, or international, carrier center as the call travels the long distance to its destination.

A WAN connects the locations of an organization to each other, to locations of other organizations, to external services (such as databases), and to remote users over a varied type of media and a diverse geographic area. WANs generally carry a variety of traffic types, such as voice, data, and video.

WAN technologies function at the three lowest layers of the OSI reference model: the physical layer, the data link layer, and the network layer. Figure 3-6 illustrates the relationship between the common WAN technologies and the OSI reference model.

Figure 3-6   *WANs Operate at the Lower Three Layers of the OSI Model*

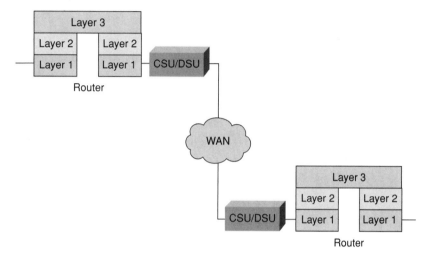

Telephone and data services are the most commonly used WAN services, connected from the building demarcation point (demarc) to the WAN provider's central office (CO) or point of presence (POP). The CO or POP is the local telephone company or service provider location to which local loops, or connections between the user and CO, in a given area connect, and in which circuit switching of subscriber lines occurs. Figure 3-7 shows different service provider services between two data sites.

Figure 3-7   *Service Provider Service Types*

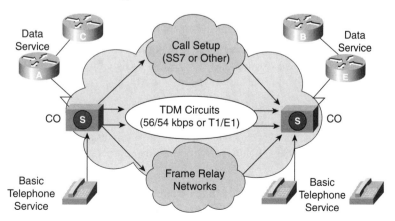

Three main types of WAN provider services exist:

- **Circuit switching**—This access method gives each user a dedicated path to the network. To operate, there is a call setup phase. This feature sets up and clears calls between telephone users. Also called *signaling*, call setup uses a separate channel not used for other traffic. The most commonly used call setup is Signaling System 7 (SS7), which uses call control messages and signals between the transfer points along the way to the called destination. Most telephone calls are circuit switched.

- **Time-division multiplexing (TDM)**—Data from many sources has bandwidth allocated on a single medium. Circuit switching uses signaling to determine the call route, which is a dedicated path between the sender and the receiver. By multiplexing traffic into fixed time slots, TDM avoids congested facilities and variable delays. A T1 or E1 is an example of a TDM link.

- **Frame Relay**—Information contained in frames shares bandwidth with other WAN Frame Relay subscribers. Frame Relay is a statistical multiplexed service. Unlike TDM, Frame Relay uses Layer 2 identifiers and permanent virtual circuits (PVCs).

WAN Devices

A variety of devices are involved in a WAN operation. Each device performs a particular function in relationship to the internetwork and the layers of the OSI model. The devices discussed in this book are as follows:

- Routers, which offer many services, including LAN and WAN interface ports

- WAN switches, such as an ATM switch, used for voice, data, and video communication

- Modems and channel service units/data service units (CSUs/DSUs), which are used as interfaces between the end-user devices (such as PCs or routers) and the service provider switches

- Access servers, which concentrate modem connections (for example, an ISP needs access servers so that its dialup customers can call in and connect to its services. Access servers usually contain many built-in modems)

Routers are devices that implement the network layer services. They provide a wide range of interfaces, such as Ethernet, Fast Ethernet, and Gigabit Ethernet, and Token Ring for LAN connections, and serial and Asynchronous Transfer Mode (ATM) interfaces for WAN connections.

The Internet is a special WAN that contains many thousands of routers used to interconnect users from around the world. Routers are like post offices and traffic cops in the Internet that direct how a packet should travel to reach its destination.

A WAN switch is a multiport networking device that switches traffic such as Frame Relay, X.25, and ATM. WAN switches usually operate at the data link layer of the OSI reference model. Figure 3-8 illustrates two routers at remote ends of a WAN that are connected by ATM WAN switches.

Figure 3-8   *ATM Switches Connect Network Devices*

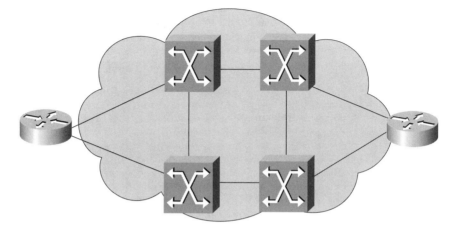

A virtual circuit is used by the WAN switches to logically connect the two routers. It is called a virtual circuit because the routers do not have a physical connection to each other. Each router has only one physical connection to the ATM switch that it connects to directly. The ATM switches in the ATM network establish a virtual circuit to logically connect the two routers. ATM is one of the service types used to connect various networks, but before you can connect to these services, you must have the appropriate equipment to interface with the provider networks. To use WAN services, you need a device like a modem or CSU/DSU to connect to the provider network.

A modem, as shown in Figure 3-9, is a device that interprets digital and analog signals by modulating and demodulating the signals, enabling data to be transmitted over voice-grade telephone lines. At the source, digital signals are converted to a form that is suitable for transmission over analog communication facilities. At the destination, these analog signals are returned to digital form. Figure 3-9 illustrates a simple modem-to-modem connection through the Public Switched Telephone Network (PSTN).

Figure 3-9   *Modem Connection*

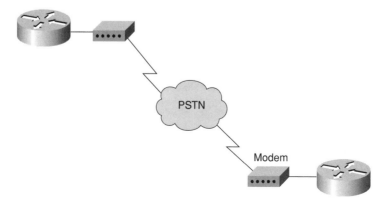

A CSU/DSU, as shown in Figure 3-10, is a digital interface device (or sometimes two separate digital devices) that adapts the physical interface on a data terminal equipment (DTE) device (such as a terminal) to the interface of a data circuit-terminating equipment (DCE) device (such as a switch) in a switched-carrier network. Figure 3-10 illustrates the placement of the CSU/DSU in a WAN implementation. Sometimes, CSUs/DSUs are integrated in the router interface. CSU/DSUs connect to services like Frame Relay or leased lines.

Figure 3-10   *CSU/DSU Connection*

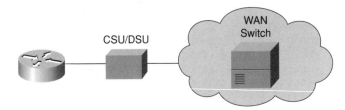

After the signal leaves the WAN interface, it uses the modem or CSU/DSU to send the appropriate Layer 1 signals to the service provider network.

WAN Service Providers and Signaling Standards

Advances in technology over the past decade have made many WAN solutions available to network designers. When selecting an appropriate WAN solution, you should discuss the costs and benefits of each with the service providers. To select these services, you need an understanding of these WAN services, as well as WAN signaling standards.

When an organization subscribes to an outside WAN service provider for network resources, the provider specifies connection requirements to the subscriber, such as the type of equipment to be used to receive services. Two routers, like those shown in Figure 3-11, can be connected by the service provider, using either a dialup (circuit-switched) connection or a permanent leased-line (point-to-point) connection. Choosing which type of connection to use most often depends on the cost, availability of the service, and the traffic requirements.

A key interface in the customer's site occurs between the DTE and the DCE. Typically, the DTE is the router, and the DCE is the device used to convert the user data from the DTE into a form acceptable to the facility providing WAN services. As shown in Figure 3-12, the DCE is the attached modem or CSU/DSU.

Figure 3-11 *WAN Service Provider Connections*

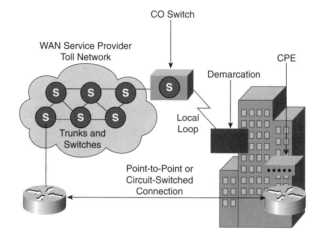

Figure 3-12 *DTE and DCE Devices*

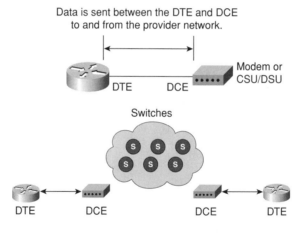

The WAN path between the DTE and the DCE is called the link, circuit, channel, or line. The DCE primarily provides an interface for the DTE into the communication link in the WAN cloud. The DTE/DCE interface acts as a boundary where responsibility for the traffic passes between the WAN subscriber and the WAN provider.

WAN links can be ordered from the WAN provider at various speeds, which are stated in bits per second (bps). This bps capacity determines how fast data can be moved across the WAN link. Table 3-3 lists WAN link types and bandwidth.

Table 3-3   *WAN Link Types and Bandwidth*

Link Type	Signal Standard	Bit Rate Capacity
56	DS0	56 kbps
64	DS0	64 kbps
T1	DS1	1.544 Mbps
E1	ZM	2.048 Mbps
E3	M3	34.064 Mbps
J1	Y1	2.048 Mbps
T3	DS3	44.736 Mbps
OC-1	SONET	51.84 Mbps
OC-3	SONET	155.54 Mbps
OC-9	SONET	466.56 Mbps
OC-12	SONET	622.08 Mbps
OC-18	SONET	933.12 Mbps
OC-24	SONET	1244.16 Mbps
OC-36	SONET	1866.24 Mbps
OC-48	SONET	2488.32 Mbps

WAN Physical Layer Protocols

The WAN physical layer protocols describe how to provide electrical, mechanical, operational, and functional connections for WAN services. Most WANs require an interconnection that is provided by a communications service provider (such as an RBOC); an alternative carrier (such as an Internet service provider); or a Post, Telephone, and Telegraph (PTT) agency.

The WAN physical layer also describes the interface between the DTE and the DCE. Typically, the DCE is the connection to the service provider and the DTE is the attached network device. In Figure 3-13, the services offered to the DTE are made available through a modem or a CSU/DSU.

Figure 3-13   *Physical Layer Standards*

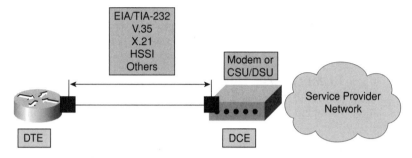

Several physical layer standards define the rules governing the interface between the DTE and the DCE:

- **EIA/TIA-232**—This common physical layer interface standard, developed by the Electronic Industries Alliance (EIA) and the Telecommunications Industry Alliance (TIA), supports signal speeds of up to 64 kbps. It was formerly known as RS-232. This standard has been in place for many years.

- **EIA/TIA-449**—This popular physical layer interface, developed by the EIA and TIA, is essentially a faster (up to 2 Mbps) version of the EIA/TIA-232, capable of longer cable runs.

- **EIA/TIA-612/613**—This standard describes High-Speed Serial Interface (HSSI), which provides access to services at T3 (45 Mbps), E3 (34 Mbps), and Synchronous Optical Network (SONET) STS-1 (51.84 Mbps) rates. The actual rate of the interface depends on the external DSU and the type of service to which it is connected.

- **V.24**—This is an International Telecommunications Union-Telecommunication Standardization Sector (ITU-T) standard for a physical layer interface between DTE and DCE.

- **V.35**—This ITU-T standard describes a synchronous, physical layer protocol used for communications between a network access device and a packet network. V.35 is most commonly used in the United States and in Europe.

- **X.21**—This ITU-T standard for serial communications over synchronous digital lines is used primarily in Europe and Japan.

- **G.703**—This ITU-T electrical and mechanical specification for connections between telephone company equipment and DTE uses Bayonett Neill Concelman connectors (BNCs) and operates at E1 data rates.

The physical layer offers the connection to the service provider network. However, many data-link protocols that can be used to communicate across the service provider network.

WAN Data Link Layer Protocols

Data link layer protocols describe how frames are carried between systems on a data link. They are designed to operate over dedicated point-to-point, multipoint, and multiaccess switched services such as Frame Relay. The common data link layer encapsulations associated with synchronous serial lines on Cisco devices include the following:

- **Cisco High-Level Data Link Control (HDLC)**—This Cisco standard is not compatible with the industry-standard HDLC protocol. Cisco HDLC contains a protocol field to identify the network layer protocol being carried in a Cisco HDLC frame.

- **Point-to-Point Protocol (PPP)**—This protocol is described by RFC 1661. PPP contains a protocol field to identify the network layer protocol being carried in the PPP frame.

- **Synchronous Data Link Control (SDLC) Protocol**—This protocol is an IBM-designed WAN data link protocol for Systems Network Architecture (SNA) environments. It is largely being replaced by the more versatile HDLC.

- **Serial Line Internet Protocol (SLIP)**—This is a WAN data link protocol for carrying IP packets. It has largely been replaced by the more versatile PPP.

- **Link Access Procedure, Balanced (LAPB)**—This data link protocol is used by X.25 and ISDN. It has extensive error-checking capabilities.

- **Link Access Procedure on the D channel (LAPD)**—This WAN data link protocol is used for signaling and call setup on an ISDN D channel. Data transmissions take place on the ISDN B channels.

- **Link Access Procedure for Frame Relay (LAPF)**—This protocol specifies the frame structure, format of fields, and access procedures for frame mode bearer services. This WAN data link protocol is based on LAPD but is used with Frame Relay technologies.

NOTE   The working groups of the Internet Engineering Task Force (IETF) develop standards called Request for Comments (RFCs) that deal with the architecture and operation of the Internet. You can find all RFCs online at http://www.ietf.org/rfc.html.

WAN data link protocols must be the same between two communicating systems and might vary depending on the service provider connection. If two remote sites are connected via a point-to-point leased line connection, the only requirement for the data-link protocol is that both end devices (DTEs) understand the protocol. For two Cisco routers this protocol is commonly Cisco HDLC, but can also be PPP or LABP, as shown in Figure 3-14.

Figure 3-14   *Point-to-Point Data Link Protocols*

Cisco HDLC, PPP, LAPB

If you are connecting to a multiaccess service like X.25 or Frame Relay, as shown in Figure 3-15, you need to configure the DTE to communicate with the service provider switch using the appropriate data link layer encapsulation.

Figure 3-15   *Data Link Protocols for Multiaccess WAN Link*

X.25, Frame Relay

Frame Relay is a WAN service that has become popular because of its flexibility. With Frame Relay, you connect to a provider network and the provider can establish virtual circuits between multiple sites. The benefit of this type of service is that like a LAN, a device needs only one connection to the network to communicate with everyone.

The downside to WANs is speed. For the most part, WANs lack the speed and throughput that is offered by a LAN. Although some services, like OC circuits, can operate at LAN speeds, they are expensive. A high-speed alternative to the WAN is the MAN.

MANs Overview

A MAN is a network that spans a metropolitan area such as a city or suburban area. A MAN usually consists of two or more LANs in a common geographic area, as shown in Figure 3-16. For example, a bank with multiple branches might use a MAN. Typically, a service provider connects two or more LAN sites using optical services or T3 connections. A MAN can also be created using wireless bridge technology by transmitting signals across public areas. The higher optical bandwidths that are currently available make MANs a more functional and economically feasible option than it has been in the past.

Traditionally, most MANs have been designed using either SONET or a similar technology known as Synchronous Digital Hierarchy (SDH). SONET and SDH are self-healing network architectures that prevent interruption in service by rerouting traffic almost instantaneously if a fiber is cut. A ring topology, however, requires provisioning for the maximum bandwidth required in the network on every segment, regardless of the actual load on the segment.

Figure 3-16 *Metropolitan-Area Network*

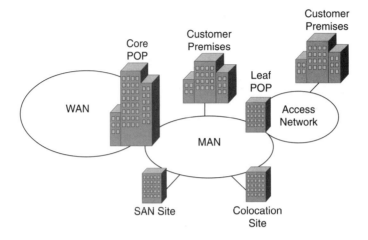

WANs and MANs make it possible for a business to provide interconnections between remote locations. This capability allows a business to provide the critical information between employees regardless of their locations.

Global Internet

Another specialized network service is the global Internet. By definition, an internet, which is short for internetwork, is a network of networks, and the Internet is the interconnection of thousands of large and small networks all over the world. The Internet is essentially the world's largest WAN.

Using the analogy of the telephone system to explain the concept of the Internet, the telephone system is really a collection of interconnected local phone service providers. The Internet is practically the same thing: It is a collection of local network providers of IP connectivity.

A hierarchy exists in the Internet, and the way it is deployed. The largest component of the Internet is commonly referred to as the Internet backbone. No one entity can be pointed to as the Internet backbone; it is a collection of large transit networks operated by many different network service providers. This is the highest level of connectivity in the Internet. From there, the Internet branches down to individual Internet service providers (ISPs), which sell Internet access to businesses and individual consumers.

WANs Overview Section Quiz

Use these practice questions to review what you learned in this section.

1 Which of the following statements best describes a WAN?

   A Connects LANs that are separated by a large geographic area

   B Connects workstations, terminals, and other devices in a metropolitan area

   C Connects LANs within a large building

   D Connects workstations, terminals, and other devices within a building

2 What is a group of networks that are networked to each other called?

   A An internetwork

   B A WAN

   C A LAN

   D A workgroup

3 A CSU/DSU is generally used as what type of equipment?

   A Router

   B DTE

   C Switch

   D DCE

4 DCE and DTE equipment is found at which layer of the OSI reference model?

   A Network

   B Data link

   C Physical

   D Transport

5 Which physical layer standard is used primarily in Europe and Japan?

   A EIA/TIA-232

   B V.35

   C X.21

   D G.703

6 Which data link layer has been replaced by PPP?

   A HDLC

   B SLIP

   C SDLS

   D LAPF

Services Networks

Many types of networks besides LANs and WANs exist, each with its own purpose and functions. Some of those other types of networks include the following:

- **Storage-area networks (SANs)**—Provide connectivity to storage locations
- **Content networks (CNs)**—Provide connectivity to network content
- **Virtual private networks (VPNs)**—Provide secure connections across a public network

Each of these service networks has been created out of a need to provide secure high-speed services for end users.

SANs

A SAN, as shown in Figure 3-17, is a dedicated, high-performance network used to move data between heterogeneous servers and storage resources. By building a separate dedicated network, a SAN avoids any traffic conflict between clients and servers. Adopting SAN technology through the use of Fibre Channel, hubs, and switches allows high-speed server-to-storage, storage-to-storage, or server-to-server connectivity. The method of providing a storage-area network uses a separate network infrastructure that relieves any problems associated with existing network connectivity.

Figure 3-17   *Storage-Area Networks*

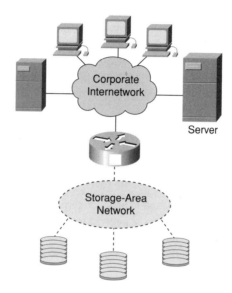

NOTE   *Fibre Channel* is a technology for transmitting data between computer devices at a data rate of up to 1 billion bits per second (Gbps). Fibre Channel is especially suited for connecting computer servers to shared storage devices and for interconnecting storage controllers and drives.

SANs also have the potential to allow cable lengths up to 500 meters (1640.4 feet) today, and up to 10 kilometers (6.2 miles) in the future, so that servers in different buildings can share external storage devices.

SANs offer the following features:

- **Performance**—SANs enable concurrent access of disk or tape arrays by two or more servers at high speeds across Fibre Channel, providing enhanced system performance.

- **Availability**—SANs have disaster tolerance built in because data can be copied using a Fibre Channel SAN up to 10 km away.

- **Cost**—Because a SAN is an independent network, initial costs to set up the infrastructure are higher, but the potential exists for rapid unit cost erosion as the SAN installed base increases.

- **Scalability**—Scalability is natural to SAN architecture, depending on the SAN network management tools used. Like a LAN or WAN, a SAN can use a variety of technologies, which allows easy relocation of backup data, restore operations, file migration, and data replication between heterogeneous environments.

- **Manageability**—SANs are data-centric, meaning the technology is specifically designed for data services as opposed to voice or other services. SANs implement a stripped-down communications protocol that is limited in functionality but provides low latency.

The Cisco SN 5420 Storage Router is based on both IP and SAN standards. It provides interoperability with existing LAN, WAN, optical, and SAN equipment. Network administrators familiar with IP networking will be instantly familiar with the Cisco SN 5420 Storage Router and its management interfaces.

The Cisco SN 5420 Storage Router enables Internet Small Computer System Interface over IP (iSCSI), which is the first storage networking implementation based on IP standards and interoperability. It has the ability to automatically discover the storage devices on the attached Fibre Channel and iSCSI networks. It also allows easy mapping of servers to storage devices.

CNs

A content network (CN) is a globally coordinated network of devices designed to accelerate the delivery of information over the Internet infrastructure. Figure 3-18 shows the components involved in a CN.

Figure 3-18 *Content Network Services*

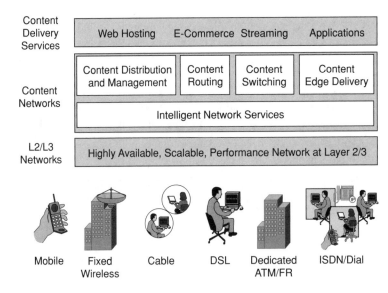

By taking advantage of content-aware services in the core IP network and OSI Layers 4 through 7, enterprises and service providers are able to accelerate and improve the use of rich content such as streaming multimedia, which also improves network performance and eliminates the stream of rich media on the infrastructure.

CNs bypass potential sources of congestion by distributing the load across a collection of content engines, which are located close to the viewing audience. Rich web and multimedia content is replicated to the content engines, and users are routed to an optimally located content engine. For example, when you download a large movie from an ISP, if the ISP is using the CN technology, the movie might take only minutes to download rather than hours, because a CN can accelerate the delivery of information.

The Cisco content networking solution is a tiered solution that starts with highly reliable Layer 2 and Layer 3 networks delivered by the Cisco IOS Software core network. The Cisco content networking solution is defined in five major technology categories:

- **Content distribution and management**—Distributes content to the network edge and provides the business/operations support system (BSS/OSS) for the content network service

- **Content routing**—Locates the optimum site to serve a specific content request based on network topology, network latency, server load, and policy

- **Content switching**—Selects the best server within that site to deliver the content request based not only on server availability and load, but also on verification of content and application availability; provides content services based on end-user session and the specific content requested

- **Content edge delivery**—Delivers static and streaming content at the network edge and keeps the content continuously fresh

- **Intelligent network services**—Augments the content networks with IP core services such as Layer 3 quality of service (QoS), VPNs, security, and multicast

VPNs

A VPN is a private network that is constructed within a public network infrastructure, such as the Internet, as shown in Figure 3-19. In a VPN, access is controlled to permit peer connections only within a defined community of interest.

A VPN is constructed through portioning of a common underlying communications medium. This communications medium provides services to the network on a nonexclusive basis. For example, using a VPN, a telecommuter can access the company headquarters network through the Internet by building a secured tunnel between the telecommuter's PC and a VPN router in the headquarters.

Figure 3-19 *VPNs Use Public Networks*

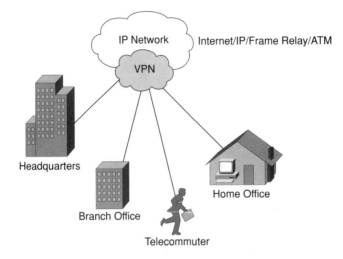

VPNs offer secure, reliable connectivity over a shared public network infrastructure such as the Internet, maintaining the same security and management policies as a private network. They are the most cost-effective method for establishing a point-to-point connection between remote users and an enterprise customer's network.

Several types of VPNs exist, each designed to satisfy certain requirements. These are the three main types of VPNs:

- **Access VPNs**—Access VPNs provide remote access to a mobile worker, and a small office/home office (SOHO) to the headquarters intranet or extranet over a shared infrastructure. Access VPNs use analog, dialup, ISDN, digital subscriber line (DSL), mobile IP, and cable technologies to securely connect mobile users, telecommuters, and branch offices.

- **Intranet VPNs**—Intranet VPNs link regional and remote offices to the headquarter's internal network over a shared infrastructure using dedicated connections. Intranet VPNs differ from extranet VPNs in that they allow access only to the enterprise customer's employees.

- **Extranet VPNs**—Extranet VPNs link business partners to the headquarters network over a shared infrastructure using dedicated connections. Extranet VPNs differ from intranet VPNs in that they allow access to users outside the enterprise.

Figure 3-20 shows how these VPNs can be used for connectivity between locations.

VPNs can be used to create secure private networks between devices that are both local to the corporate network or members of a remote network.

Figure 3-20   *VPN Technologies*

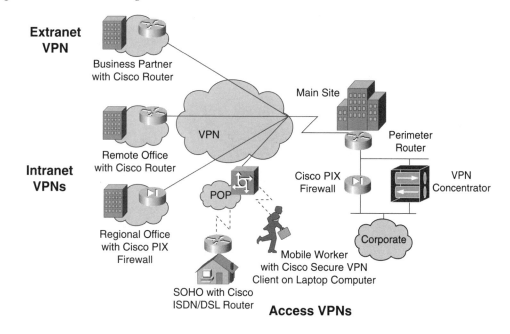

Intranets and Extranets

Intranet VPNs allow access only to the members of an enterprise, while extranet VPNs allow access to a wider range. One common configuration of a LAN is an intranet, or the corporate internetwork. Intranet web servers differ from public web servers in that the public does not have access to an organization's intranet without the proper permissions and passwords. Intranets are designed to be accessed by users who have access privileges to an organization's internal LAN. Within an intranet, web and file servers are installed in the network, and browser technology is used as the common front end to access graphical or text-based data stored on those servers.

The addition of an intranet VPN on a network is just one of many features that can cause an increase in the amount of bandwidth needed. New desktops and servers should be outfitted with 100/1000-Mbps Ethernet NICs to provide the most configuration flexibility, thus enabling network administrators to dedicate bandwidth to individual end stations as needed. Some high-traffic servers might need to be outfitted with Gigabit Ethernet NICs.

Extranet VPNs refer to applications and services that are intranet based, but that provide extended, secured access to external users or enterprises. This access is usually accomplished through passwords, user IDs, and other application-level security mechanisms. Therefore, an extranet is the extension of two or more intranet strategies with a secure interaction between participant enterprises and their respective intranets.

The extranet maintains control of access to those intranets within each enterprise in the deployment. Extranets link customers, suppliers, partners, or communities of interest to a corporate intranet over a shared infrastructure using dedicated connections. Businesses use the same policies as a private network, including security, QoS, manageability, and reliability. Figure 3-21 shows how intranet and extranet VPNs can be deployed in an internetworking structure.

Figure 3-21 *Intranet and Extranet VPNs*

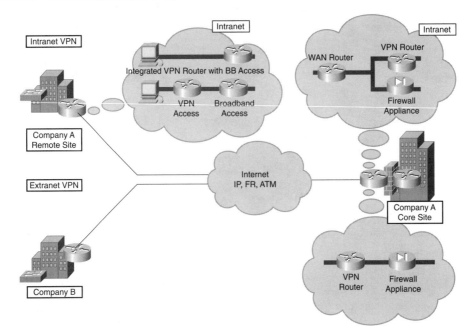

Each of these service networks provides additional connectivity and features that are useful for many corporate networks.

Services Networks Section Quiz

Use these practice questions to review what you learned in this section.

1 Which of the following is *not* one of the features of a SAN?

    A SANs enable concurrent access of disk or tape arrays, providing enhanced system performance.

    B SANs provide a reliable disaster recover solution.

    C SANs are scalable.

    D SANs minimize the system and data availability.

2 Which of the following does *not* correctly describe the features of CNs?

A CNs accelerate and improve the use of rich content and eliminate the stream of rich content on the infrastructure.

B CNs utilize a collection of content engines, located close to the audience, to distribute the content.

C The CN was designed to accelerate the delivery of information over the MAN infrastructure.

D Cisco CNs are tiered.

3 What service offers secure, reliable connectivity over a shared public network infrastructure?

A Internet

B Virtual private network

C Virtual public network

D Wide-area network

4 What links enterprise customer headquarters, remote offices, and branch offices to an internal network over a shared infrastructure?

A Access VPNs

B Intranet VPNs

C Extranet VPNs

D Internet VPNs

5 What is the name for the part of the company's LAN that is made available to select parties such as employees, customers, or partners?

A The internet

B The extranet

C The intranet

D The LAN

Chapter Summary

This chapter reviewed the common types of networks and how they relate to internet-working technologies. The majority of the networks you encounter as a network administrator are LANs. LAN technologies operate at Layers 1 and 2 of the OSI reference model. To interconnect LAN services you use a service provider's WAN or MAN network. Like LANs, WANs operate at Layers 1 and 2 of the OSI model and require special equipment, such as modems or CSU/DSUs, to connect to provider services.

Finally, this chapter reviewed some of the service networks that have been created to enhance network performance. SANs provide high-speed storage locations for servers and clients within a network structure. CNs provide a load-balancing technique to alleviate the congestion associated with many users accessing the same content or device. VPNs provide a method for securing connections within an internal or external network structure. Each of these functions is important to understand because these are the services that are interconnected to provide a corporate internetwork.

Chapter Review Questions

Use these review questions to test your knowledge of the concepts discussed in this chapter.

1 Why did the IEEE create LLC?

   A To allow for data encryption before transmission

   B To replace an older IBM protocol

   C To create a protocol that would not be controlled by the U.S. government

   D To meet the need to have part of the data link layer function independently of existing technologies

2 What happens in the event of a collision on an Ethernet segment?

   A Transmission with higher priority is unaffected, and lower-priority transmissions are lost.

   B Initially, the data is lost but is resent using a backoff algorithm.

   C Transmissions are lost and not resent.

   D Nothing, the Ethernet is immune to collisions.

3 Which is the IEEE standard for Fast Ethernet?

   A 802.3z

   B 802.10

   C 802.3u

   D 802.5

4 What is the transmission medium for 1000BASE-SX?

   A Long-wave laser over single-mode and multimode fiber

   B Category 5 UTP copper wiring

   C Balanced, shielded, 150-ohm, two-pair STP copper cable

   D Short-wave laser over multimode fiber

5 Which statement is *not* true about a Cisco GBIC?

   A A 1000BASE-LX/LH interface has the ability to go up to 20 kilometers over single-mode fiber.

   B A Cisco GBIC is hot swappable.

   C Cisco GBIC has been accepted as an industry standard.

   D Cisco GBIC can be intermixed in different combinations on a port-by-port basis.

6 What is the largest component of the Internet commonly referred to as?

   A Structured hierarchy

   B The Internet backbone

   C Global carrier

   D LANs

7 Select all correct attributes of a WAN.

   A It operates at the same geographical level as a LAN.

   B WAN users must subscribe to services.

   C It uses only Layers 1–4 (physical through transport) of the OSI model.

   D It can transport data, voice, and video.

8 The WAN path between DTEs is known as what?

  A The link

  B The circuit

  C The channel

  D All of the above

9 Which two aspects of CNs make them better than traditional transmission over the Internet? (Choose two.)

  A They bypass potential sources of congestion by distributing the load across a collection of content engines.

  B They take advantage of Layers 1–3 to optimize WAN communication.

  C They locate content engines near the audience.

  D They run over Gigabit Ethernet.

10 What is the name given to a private network that is constructed within a public network infrastructure?

  A The Internet

  B ISDN

  C Frame Relay

  D VPN

11 What type of VPN links regional and remote offices to the headquarter's internal network?

  A Access VPN

  B Intranet VPN

  C Dialup VPN

  D Extranet VPN

12 An extranet is the extension of two or more intranet strategies with a secure interaction between participant enterprises and their respective intranets.

  A True

  B False

The Internetworking Layers

Upon completion of this chapter, you will be able to perform the following tasks:

- Describe the primary types of network cabling, including shielded and unshielded twisted-pair, coaxial, fiber optics (multimode and single-mode), and wireless communications

- Describe types and characteristics of cabling and connectors used in an Ethernet LAN

- Describe the necessary components for enabling WAN connectivity over serial or ISDN BRI, local loop using DSL, and a cable connection for a Cisco router

CHAPTER 4

Network Media
(The Physical Layer)

This chapter examines several types of network media, including twisted-pair cable, coaxial cable, fiber-optic cable, and wireless. It highlights the concepts and procedures for assembling and cabling Cisco routers. This chapter also covers cabling and connectors used to interconnect switches and routers in a LAN or WAN. Finally, it presents factors that you should consider when selecting network devices.

Cabling and Infrastructure

Media is the actual physical environment through which data travels as it moves from one component to another, and it connects network devices. The most common types of network media are twisted-pair cable, coaxial cable, fiber-optic cable, and wireless. Each media type has specific capabilities and serves specific purposes.

Understanding the types of connections that can be used within a network provides a better understanding of how networks function in transmitting data from one point to another.

Twisted-Pair Cable

Twisted-pair is a copper wire-based cable that can be either shielded or unshielded. Twisted-pair is the most common media for network connectivity.

Unshielded twisted-pair (UTP) cable, as shown in Figure 4-1, is a four-pair wire. Each of the eight individual copper wires in UTP cable is covered by an insulating material. In addition, the wires in each pair are twisted around each other. The advantage of UTP cable is its ability to cancel interference, because the twisted-wire pairs limit signal degradation from electromagnetic interference (EMI) and radio frequency interference (RFI). To further reduce crosstalk between the pairs in UTP cable, the number of twists in the wire pairs varies. UTP, as well as shielded twisted-pair (STP) cable, must follow precise specifications as to how many twists or braids are permitted per meter.

Figure 4-1 *Unshielded Twisted-Pair Cable*

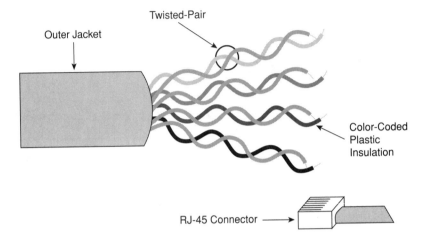

UTP cable is used in a variety of networks. When used as a networking medium, UTP cable has four pairs of either 22- or 24-gauge copper wire. UTP used as a networking medium has an impedance of 100 ohms, differentiating it from other types of twisted-pair wiring such as that used for telephone wiring. Because UTP cable has an external diameter of approximately 0.43 cm (0.17 inches), its small size can be advantageous during installation. Also, because UTP can be used with most of the major networking architectures, it continues to grow in popularity.

Several categories of UTP cable exist:

- **Category 1**—Used for telephone communications; not suitable for transmitting data

- **Category 2**—Capable of transmitting data at speeds of up to 4 Mbps

- **Category 3**—Used in 10BASE-T networks; can transmit data at speeds up to 10 Mbps

- **Category 4**—Used in Token Ring networks; can transmit data at speeds up to 16 Mbps

- **Category 5**—Capable of transmitting data at speeds up to 100 Mbps

- **Category 5e**—Used in networks running at speeds up to 1000 Mbps (1 Gbps)

- **Category 6**—Consists of four pairs of 24-gauge copper wires that can transmit data at speeds up to 1000 Mbps

Shielded twisted-pair (STP) cable, as shown in Figure 4-2, combines the techniques of shielding and the twisting of wires to further protect against signal degradation. Each pair of wires is wrapped in a metallic foil. The four pairs of wires are then wrapped in an overall metallic braid or foil, usually 150-ohm cable. Specified for use in Ethernet network installations, STP reduces electrical noise both within the cable (pair-to-pair coupling, or crosstalk) and from outside the cable (EMI and RFI). Token Ring network topology uses STP.

Figure 4-2   *Shielded Twisted-Pair Cable*

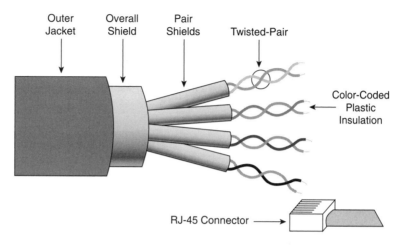

When you consider using UTP and STP for your network media, consider the following:

- Speed of either media type is usually satisfactory for local-area distances.

- Both are the least-expensive media for data communication. UTP is less expensive than STP.

- Because most buildings are already wired with UTP, many transmission standards are adapted to use it to avoid costly rewiring with an alternative cable type.

Twisted-pair cabling is the most common networking cabling in use today; however, some networks still use older technologies like coaxial cable, as discussed in the next section.

Coaxial Cable

Coaxial cable consists of a hollow outer cylindrical conductor that surrounds a single inner wire conducting element. This section describes the characteristics and uses of coaxial cable.

As shown in Figure 4-3, the single inner wire located in the center of a coaxial cable is a copper conductor, surrounded by a layer of flexible insulation. Over this insulating material is a woven copper braid or metallic foil that acts both as the second wire in the circuit and as a shield for the inner conductor. This second layer, or shield, can help reduce the amount of outside interference. An outer jacket covers this shield. The BNC connector shown looks much like a cable-television connector and connects to an older NIC with a BNC interface.

Figure 4-3 *Coaxial Cable*

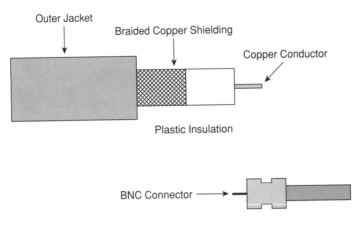

Coaxial cable supports 10 to 100 Mbps and is relatively inexpensive, although more costly than UTP. Coaxial cable can be laid over longer distances than twisted-pair cable. For example, Ethernet can run approximately 100 meters using twisted-pair cable, but 500 meters using coaxial cable.

Coaxial cable offers several advantages for use in LANs. It can be run with fewer boosts from repeaters, which regenerate the signals in a network so that they can cover greater distances between network nodes than either STP or UTP cable. Coaxial cable is less expensive than fiber-optic cable, and the technology is well known. It has been used for many years for all types of data communication.

When you work with cable, consider its size. As the thickness, or diameter, of the cable increases, so does the difficulty in working with it. Cable must often be pulled through existing conduits and troughs that are limited in size. Coaxial cable comes in a variety of sizes. The largest diameter, frequently referred to as *Thicknet*, was specified for use as Ethernet backbone cable because historically it had greater transmission length and noise rejection characteristics. However, Thicknet cable can be too rigid to install easily in some environments because of its thickness. Generally, the more difficult the network media is to install, the more expensive it is to install. Coaxial cable is more expensive to install than twisted-pair cable, and Thicknet cable is almost never used except for special-purpose installations, where shielding from EMI or distance requires the use of such cables.

In the past, coaxial cable with an outside diameter of only 0.35 cm, sometimes referred to as *Thinnet*, was used in Ethernet networks. It was especially useful for cable installations that required the cable to make many twists and turns. Because Thinnet was easier to install, it was also cheaper to install. Thus, it was also referred to as *Cheapernet*. However, because the outer copper or metallic braid in coaxial cable comprised half the electrical circuit, special care needed to be taken to ground it properly, by ensuring that a solid electrical connection existed at both ends of the cable. Installers frequently failed to make a good connection. Connection problems resulted in electrical noise, which interfered with signal transmission. For this reason, despite its small diameter, Thinnet is no longer commonly used in Ethernet networks.

Although coaxial cable offers some distance advantages over twisted-pair, the disadvantages far outweigh the benefits. If a communications signal needs to travel a greater distance at high rates of speed, it is more common to use fiber-optic cable.

Fiber-Optic Cable

Fiber-optic cable is a networking medium capable of conducting modulated light transmission. This section describes the types, characteristics, and uses of fiber-optic cable.

Fiber-optic cable used for networking consists of two fibers encased in separate sheaths. Viewing it in cross section in Figure 4-4, you can see that each optical fiber is surrounded by layers of protective buffer material: usually a plastic shield, then a plastic such as Kevlar, and finally, an outer jacket that provides protection for the entire cable. The plastic conforms to appropriate fire and building codes. The purpose of the Kevlar is to furnish additional cushioning and protection for the fragile, hair-thin glass fibers. Where buried fiber-optic cables are required by codes, a stainless steel wire is sometimes included for added strength. Several connectors can connect fiber to the networking device; the most common is a SC connector, which has two optics, one connecting to transmit and the other connecting to receive.

Figure 4-4   *Fiber-Optic Cable*

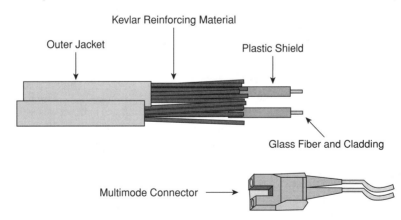

The light-guiding parts of an optical fiber are called the *core* and the *cladding*. The core is usually very pure glass with a high index of refraction. When a cladding layer of glass or plastic with a low index of refraction surrounds the core glass, light can be trapped in the fiber core. This process is called *total internal reflection*, and it allows the optical fiber to act like a light pipe, guiding light for long distances, even around bends. Fiber-optic cable is the most expensive of the three types discussed in this lesson, but it supports higher rate line speeds.

Fiber-optic cable does not carry electrical impulses as copper wire does. Instead, signals that represent bits are converted into pulses of light. Two types of fiber-optic cable exist:

- **Single-mode**—Single-mode fiber-optic cable allows only one mode (or wavelength) of light to propagate through the fiber. This type of cable is capable of higher bandwidth and greater distances than multimode and is often used for campus backbones. Single-mode cable uses lasers as the light-generating method and is more expensive than multimode cable. The maximum cable length of single-mode cable is 60+ km (37+ miles).

- **Multimode**—Multimode fiber-optic cable allows multiple modes of light to propagate through the fiber. Multimode cable is often used for workgroup applications, using light emitting diodes (LEDs) as light-generating devices. The maximum length of multimode cable is 2 km (1.2 miles).

The characteristics of the different media have a significant impact on the speed of data transfer. Although fiber-optic cable is more expensive, it is not susceptible to EMI and is capable of higher data rates than any of the other types of networking media discussed here. Fiber-optic cable is also more secure because it does not emit electrical signals that could be received by external devices.

NOTE   Even though light is an electromagnetic wave, light in fibers is not considered wireless because the electromagnetic waves are guided in the optical fiber. The term *wireless* is reserved for radiated, or unguided, electromagnetic waves.

In some instances, it might not be possible to run any type of cable for network communications. This situation might be the case in a rented facility or in a location where you do not have the ability to install the appropriate infrastructure. In these cases, it might be useful to install a wireless network, as discussed in the next section.

Wireless Communications

Wireless networks are becoming increasingly popular, and they utilize a different type of technology. Wireless communication uses radio frequencies (RFs) or infrared waves to transmit data between devices on a LAN. For wireless LANs, a key component is the wireless hub, or access point, used for signal distribution. To receive the signals from the access point, a PC or laptop needs to install a wireless adapter card, or wireless network interface card (NIC). Figure 4-5 shows a number of wireless access points connected to an Ethernet backbone to provide access to the Internet.

Figure 4-5   *Wireless Access Points*

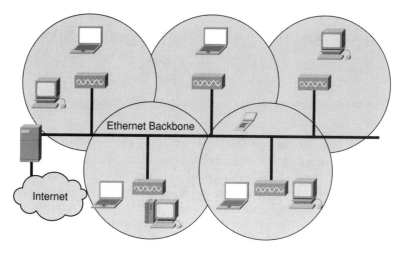

Wireless signals are electromagnetic waves that can travel through the vacuum of outer space and through a medium such as air. No physical medium is necessary for wireless signals, making them a versatile way to build a network. They use portions of the RF spectrum to transmit voice, video, and data. Wireless frequencies range from 3 kHz to 300 GHz. The data-transmission rates range from 9 kbps to 54 Mbps. Figure 4-6 shows the electromagnetic spectrum chart.

Figure 4-6   *Electromagnetic Spectrum*

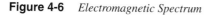
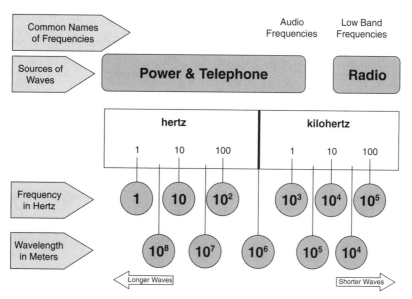

You can differentiate electromagnetic waves by their frequency. Low-frequency electromagnetic waves have a long wavelength (the distance from one peak to the next on the sine wave), while high-frequency electromagnetic waves have a short wavelength.

Some common applications of wireless data communication include the following:

- Accessing the Internet using a cellular phone
- Home or business Internet connection over satellite
- Beaming data between two handheld computing devices
- Wireless keyboard and mouse for the PC

Another common application of wireless data communication is the wireless LAN (WLAN), which is built in accordance with Institute of Electrical and Electronic Engineers (IEEE) 802.11 standards. WLANs typically use radio waves (for example, 902 MHz), microwaves (for example, 2.4 GHz), and infrared (IR) waves (for example, 820 nm) for communication. Wireless technologies are a crucial part of the future of networking.

Comparing Media Types

The choice of media type affects the type of network interface cards installed, the speed of the network, and the ability of the network to meet future needs. Table 4-1 compares the features of the common network media, including UTP, STP, coaxial cable, fiber-optic, and wireless connections.

Table 4-1   *Comparing Media Types*

Media Type	Maximum Segment Length	Speed	Comparative Cost	Advantages	Disadvantages
UTP	100 meters	10 Mbps 100 Mbps	Least expensive	Easy to install, widely available, widely used	Susceptible to interference; can cover only a limited distance
STP	100 meters	10–100 Mbps	More expensive than UTP	Reduced crosstalk, less susceptible to EMI than UTP or Thinnet	Difficult to work with; can cover only a limited distance
Coaxial	500 meters (Thicknet) 185 meters (Thinnet)	10–100 Mbps	Relatively inexpensive, but more costly than UTP	Less susceptible to EMI than other types of copper media	Difficult to work with (Thicknet); limited bandwidth; limited application (Thinnet); damage to cable can bring down entire network

Table 4-1   *Comparing Media Types (Continued)*

Media Type	Maximum Segment Length	Speed	Comparative Cost	Advantages	Disadvantages
Coaxial	500 meters (Thicknet) 185 meters (Thinnet)	10–100 Mbps	Relatively inexpensive, but more costly than UTP	Less susceptible to EMI than other types of copper media	Difficult to work with (Thicknet); limited bandwidth; limited application (Thinnet); damage to cable can bring down entire network
Fiber-optic	3 km and further (single-mode) 2 km and further (multimode)	10–1000 Mbps (single-mode) 100 Mbps–9.92 Gbps (multimode)	Expensive	Cannot be tapped easily, so security is better; can be used over great distances; not susceptible to EMI; higher data rate than coaxial and twisted-pair	Difficult to terminate
Wireless	50 km—global	1–54 Mbps	Expensive	Does not require installation of media	Susceptible to atmospheric conditions

The media you choose has an important impact on the network's capabilities. You should consider all the factors before making your final selection.

Cabling and Infrastructure Section Quiz

Use these practice questions to review what you learned in this section.

1 What is the maximum cable length for STP?

   A 100 ft

   B 150 ft

   C 100 m

   D 1000 m

2 What is an advantage that coaxial cable has over STP or UTP?

    A It is capable of achieving 10 to 100 Mbps.

    B It is inexpensive.

    C It can run for a longer distance unboosted.

    D All of the above.

3 A _____ fiber-optic cable transmits multiple streams of LED-generated light.

    A Multimode

    B Multichannel

    C Multiphase

4 Wireless communication uses which of the following to transmit data between devices on a LAN?

    A Radio frequencies

    B LED-generated light

    C Fiber optics

    D None of the above

5 What is one advantage of using fiber-optic cable in networks?

    A It is inexpensive.

    B It is easy to install.

    C It is an industry standard and is available at any electronics store.

    D It is capable of higher data rates than either coaxial or twisted-pair cable.

Choosing LAN Cabling Options

Several types of cables and connectors can be used in LANs, depending on the requirements for the network and the type of Ethernet to be implemented. These connectors also vary depending on the type of media that you have installed.

Learning about the different types of cables and connectors in an Ethernet LAN and their various functions can help you understand more about how a LAN works.

LAN Physical Layer

Ethernet is the most widely used LAN technology. Since its initial implementation, Ethernet has been extended to four new types:

- 802.3u (Fast Ethernet)
- 802.3z (Gigabit Ethernet over Fiber)
- 802.3ab (Gigabit Ethernet over UTP)
- 802.3ae (10 Gigabit Ethernet)

The cabling aspects of the LAN exist at Layer 1 of the Open System Interconnection (OSI) reference model. Figure 4-7 shows a subset of physical layer implementations that can be deployed to support Ethernet.

Figure 4-7   *Ethernet at the Physical Layer*

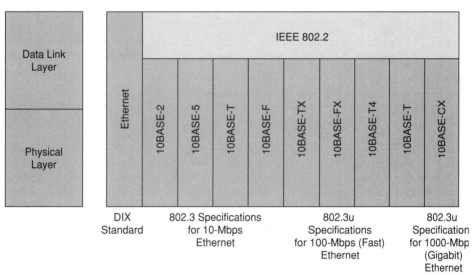

Ethernet in the Campus

Before implementing a network, you need to determine the requirements for the network. You can remember a few common recommendations on how various Ethernet technologies can be used in a campus network environment.

In many modern installations, infrastructure costs for cabling and adapters can be high. Using the appropriate Ethernet connectivity provides the necessary speed for the parts of the network that require it while controlling costs.

In general, you can use Ethernet technologies in a campus network in several different ways:

- An Ethernet speed of 10 Mbps can be used at the access layer to provide adequate performance for most users. In addition, 100-Mbps Fast Ethernet can be used for high-bandwidth-consuming clients or servers.

- Gigabit Ethernet is typically used as the link between the access layer and network devices, supporting the aggregate traffic from each Ethernet segment on the access link.

- To enhance client-server performance across the campus network and avoid bottlenecks at the server, Fast Ethernet or Gigabit Ethernet links can be used to connect enterprise servers. Gigabit Ethernet, in combination with switched Fast Ethernet, creates an effective solution for avoiding slow networks.

- Gigabit Ethernet links can provide the connection between the distribution layer and the core. Because the campus network model supports dual links between each distribution layer router and core switch, you can load balance the aggregate traffic from multiple-access switches across the links.

- Gigabit Ethernet (or 10 Gigabit Ethernet) should be used between switches and the backbone. The fastest affordable media should be implemented between backbone switches.

Table 4-2 outlines the recommendations for Ethernet deployment.

Table 4-2 *Ethernet Connectivity Recommendations*

Network Hierarchy Layer	Ethernet 10 Mbps	Fast Ethernet 100 Mbps	Gigabit Ethernet 1000 Mbps	10 Gigabit Ethernet 10000 Mbps
Access layer	Connects users with low to moderate bandwidth requirements	Connects users with high-speed requirements or servers with low to moderate usage	Connects servers with high usage	Not currently recommended at this layer
Distribution layer	Not recommended at this layer	Connects routers and switches with moderate usage	Interconnects access switches with Fast Ethernet users and used to connect distribution switches to core layer	Not currently recommended at this layer
Core layer	Not recommended at this layer	Not recommended at this layer	Interconnects core switches in networks with moderate use	Interconnects core switches with high usage

NOTE	Currently, some organizations are considering providing Gigabit Ethernet to the end user; however, not many applications can take full advantage of this infrastructure, and providing Gigabit Ethernet to the end user can potentially create a bottleneck between network devices. You should consider this carefully before installing gigabit technology to the end users.

Ethernet Media and Connector Requirements

In addition to considering the requirements for the Ethernet LAN, the media and connector requirements for each implementation must be considered. This topic outlines the cable and connector specifications used to support Ethernet implementations.

The cable and connector specifications used to support Ethernet implementations are derived from the Electronic Industries Alliance and (newer) Telecommunications Industry Alliance (EIA/TIA) standards body. The categories of cabling defined for Ethernet are derived from the EIA/TIA-568 (SP-2840) Commercial Building Telecommunications Wiring Standards. EIA/TIA specifies an RJ-45 connector for UTP cable. The letters *RJ* stand for *registered jack*, and the number *45* refers to a specific physical connector that has eight conductors.

Table 4-3 compares the cable and connector specifications for the most popular Ethernet implementations.

The important difference to note is the media used for 10-Mbps Ethernet versus 100-Mbps Ethernet. In today's networks, in which you see a mix of 10- and 100-Mbps requirements, you must be aware of the need to change over to UTP Category 5 to support Fast Ethernet.

Connection Media

Several connection media can be used in an Ethernet LAN implementation. Figure 4-8 illustrates different connection types—attachment unit interface (AUI), RJ-45, and gigabit—used by each physical layer implementation. The RJ-45 connector and jack are the most prevalent. RJ-45 connectors are discussed in more detail later in this chapter.

In some cases, the type of connector on a NIC does not match the type of media that it needs to connect to. As shown in Figure 4-8, an interface exists for the AUI connector on many Cisco devices. The AUI is the 15-pin physical connector interface between a computer's NIC and coaxial Ethernet cable.

Table 4-3 *TCable and Connector Specifications*

	10BASE-2	10BASE-5	10BASE-T	100BASE-TX	100BASE-FX	1000BASE-CX	1000BASE-T	1000BASE-SX	1000BASE-LX
Media	50-ohm coaxial (Thinnet) RG-58 coaxial cable	50-ohm coaxial (Thicknet) RG-50 coaxial cable	EIA/TIA Category 3, 4, 5 UTP 2 pair	EIA/TIA Category 5 UTP 2 pair	62.5/125 micro multimode fiber	STP	EIA/TIA Category 5 UTP 4 pair	62.5/50 micro multimode fiber	9 micro single-mode fiber
Maximum Segment Length	185 m (606.94 ft)	500 m (1640.4 ft)	100 m (328 ft)	100 m (328 ft)	400 m (1312.3 ft)	25 m (82 ft)	100 m (328 ft)	260 m (853 ft)	3-10 km (1.86-6.2 miles)
Topology	Bus	Bus	Star	Star	Point-to-point	Star or point-to-point	Star or point-to-point	Point-to-point	Point-to-point
Connector	AUI or BNC connector	AUI	ISO 8877 (RJ-45)	ISO 8877 (RJ-45)	MT-RJ or SC connector	ISO 8877 (RJ-45)	ISO 8877 (RJ-45)	SC	SC

Figure 4-8   *Ethernet Connection Types*

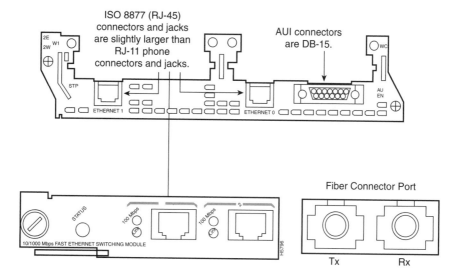

A Gigabit Interface Converter (GBIC), like the one shown in Figure 4-9, is a hot-swappable input/output device that plugs into a Gigabit Ethernet port. A key benefit of using a GBIC is that GBICs are interchangeable. This allows users the flexibility to deploy other 1000BASE-X technology without needing to change the physical interface/model on the router or switch. GBICs support UTP (copper) and fiber-optic media for Gigabit Ethernet transmission.

Figure 4-9   *GBIC*

Typically, GBICs are used in the LAN for aggregation and in the backbone. You also see GBICs in SANs and MANs.

The fiber-optic GBIC is a transceiver that converts serial electric currents to optical signals and optical signals to digital electric currents. Some of the optical GBICs include the following:

- Short wavelength (1000BASE-SX)

- Long wavelength/long haul (1000BASE-LX/LH)

- Extended distance (1000BASE-ZX)

UTP Implementation

In a UTP implementation, you must determine the EIA/TIA type of cable and whether to use a straight-through or crossover cable. This section describes the types of connectors used in a UTP implementation and the characteristics and uses of straight-through and crossover cables.

If you look at an RJ-45 transparent end connector, like the one in Figure 4-10, you can see eight colored wires, twisted into four pairs. Four of the wires (two pairs) carry the positive or true voltage and are considered *tip* (T1 through T4); the other four wires carry the inverse of false voltage grounded and are called *ring* (R1 through R4). Tip and ring are terms that originated in the early days of the telephone. Today, these terms refer to the positive and the negative wires in a pair. The wires in the first pair in a cable or a connector are designated as T1 and R1, the second pair is T2 and R2, and so on.

Figure 4-10   *RJ-45 Connector*

The RJ-45 plug is the male component, crimped at the end of the cable. As you look at the male connector from the front (the side with the metal pins exposed), the pin locations are numbered from 8 on the left to 1 on the right.

The RJ-45 jack, shown in Figure 4-11, is the female component in a network device, wall, cubicle partition outlet, or patch panel.

Figure 4-11   *RJ-45 Jack*

In addition to identifying the correct EIA/TIA category of cable to use for a connecting device (depending on what standard is being used by the jack on the network device), you need to determine which of the following to use:

- A straight-through cable

- A crossover cable

The RJ-45 connectors on both ends show all the wires in the same order. If the two RJ-45 ends of a cable are held side by side in the same orientation, the colored wires (or strips or pins) are seen at each connector end. If the order of the colored wires is the same at each end, the cable is straight-through. Figure 4-12 shows the wiring for a straight-through cable.

Figure 4-12   *Straight-Through Cable Wiring*

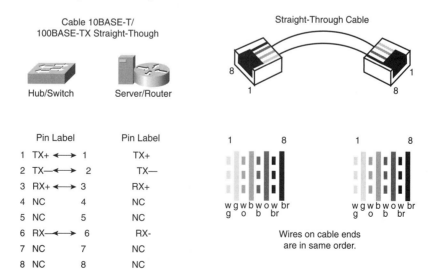

With crossover, the RJ-45 connectors on both ends show that some of the wires on one side of the cable are crossed to a different pin on the other side of the cable. Specifically, for Ethernet, pin 1 at one RJ-45 end should be connected to pin 3 at the other end. Pin 2 at one end should be connected to pin 6 at the other end, as shown in Figure 4-13.

Figure 4-13 *Crossover Cable Wiring*

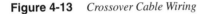

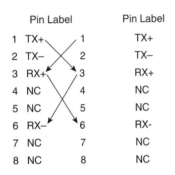

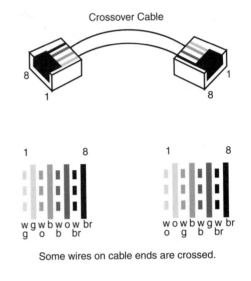

Each device using RJ-45 connectors transmits or receives on particular pins depending on the device type. A PC or router typically transmits on pins 1 and 2 while a switch or hub receives on pins 1 and 2. You must follow certain guidelines when connecting these devices.

Use straight-through cables for the following cabling:

- Switch to router
- Switch to PC or server
- Hub to PC or server

Use crossover cables for the following cabling:

- Switch to switch
- Switch to hub
- Hub to hub
- Router to router
- PC to PC
- Router to PC

Occasionally, ports on network devices are marked with an X, like those in Figure 4-14. This marking means that these devices receive on pins 1 and 2, or that they are crossed. When connecting devices in a network, you might be required to use a variety of cable types.

NOTE   Most hubs and some switches have a port that can be changed from X to not-X by moving a switch or pressing a button. This feature enables you to use straight-through cables where crossovers would ordinarily be required.

Figure 4-14   *RJ-45 Port Designations*

UTP Implementation Straight-Through Versus Crossover

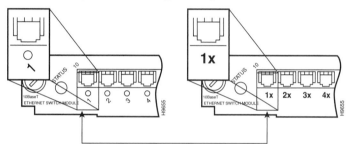

Use straight-through when only one port is designated with an x.

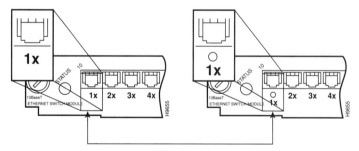

Use crossover cable when *both* ports are designated with an x
or neither port is designated with an x.

Being aware of the different cabling media types, specifications, and connectors is an important step to interconnecting network devices.

LAN Cabling Options Section Quiz

Use these practice questions to review what you learned in this section.

1 Which of the following is an 802.3u specification?

A 10BASE-F

B 10BASE-T

C 100BASE-TX

D 1000BASE-CX

2 Which of the following is a more appropriate choice for Ethernet connectivity?

A 10-Mbps Ethernet as a connection between server and LAN

B Gigabit Ethernet as the link at the access layer to provide good performance

C Fast Ethernet as a link between the access layer and distribution layer devices to support the aggregate traffic from each Ethernet segment on the access link

D 100-Mbps between core switches to provide greater bandwidth.

3 Which standard body created the cables and connector specification used to support Ethernet implementation?

A ISO

B NSI

C EIA/TIA

D IETF

4 Which of the following statements does *not* correctly describe a media connector?

A RJ-45 connectors are 8-pin connectors that resemble telephone jacks.

B An AUI is a 15-pin connector used between an NIC and an Ethernet cable.

C The GBIC is a transceiver that converts serial electric currents to optical signals and vice versa.

D None of the above is correct.

5 For which of the following would you *not* need to provide a crossover cable?

A Connecting uplinks between switches

B Connecting routers to switches

C Connecting hubs to switches

D Connecting to a console port

Understanding WAN Cabling

Just as several types of physical layer implementations for LANs exist, various kinds of serial and router connections can also be used in a WAN environment, depending on the network requirements.

Learning about the different types of WAN serial and router connections and their functions can help you understand more about how a WAN works.

WAN Physical Layer

Many physical implementations carry traffic across the WAN. Needs vary, depending on the distance of the equipment from the services, the speed, and the actual service itself. Figure 4-15 shows a subset of physical implementations that support some of the more prominent WAN solutions today.

Figure 4-15 *WAN at the Physical Layer*

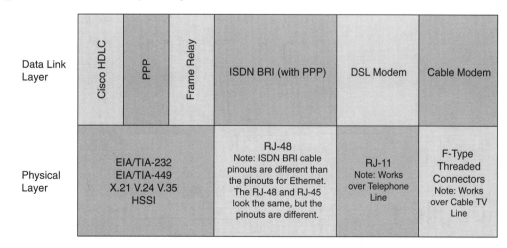

Serial connections support WAN services such as dedicated leased lines that run the Point-to-Point Protocol (PPP) or Frame Relay. The speed of these connections ranges up to E1 (2.048 Mbps).

Other WAN services, such as ISDN, offer dial-on-demand connections or dial backup services. An ISDN BRI is composed of two 64-kbps bearer channels (B channels) for data, and one 16-kbps data channel (D channel) for signaling and other link-management tasks. PPP is typically used to carry data over the B channels.

With the increasing demand for residential broadband high-speed services, DSL and cable modem connections are beginning to dominate. For example, typical residential DSL service can offer a speed of up to 1.5 Mbps over the existing telephone line. Cable services, which work over the existing coaxial cable TV line, also offer high-speed connectivity matching or surpassing that of DSL.

WAN Serial Connections

For long-distance communication, WANs use serial transmission. Serial transmission is a method of data transmission in which bits of data are transmitted sequentially over a single channel. This one-at-a-time transmission contrasts with parallel data transmission, which transmits several bits at a time. To carry the bits, serial channels use a specific electro-magnetic or optical frequency range.

Figure 4-16 shows all the different serial connector options available for Cisco routers.

Figure 4-16 *Serial Connectors*

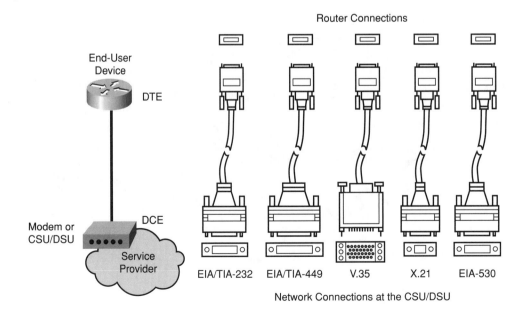

Serial ports on Cisco routers use a proprietary 60-pin connector or smaller "smart serial" connector. The type of connector on the other end of the cable is dependent on the service provider or end-device requirements.

Frequencies, described in terms of their cycles per second (Hz), function as a band or spectrum for communication. For example, the signals transmitted over voice-grade telephone lines use up to 3 kHz. The size of this frequency range is called the *bandwidth*. Another way to express bandwidth is to specify the amount of data in bits per second that can be carried using two of the physical layer implementations (EIA/TIA-232 and EIA/TIA-449). Table 4-4 compares physical standards for these two WAN serial connection options.

Table 4-3   *Comparison of Physical Serial Standards*

Data Rates in bps	EIA/TIA-232 Distance in Meters	EIA/TIA-449 Distance in Meters
2400	60	1250
4800	30	625
9600	15	312
19,200	15	156
38,400	15	78
115,200	3.7	N/A
1,544,000 (T1)	N/A	15

Several types of physical connections allow you to connect to serial WAN services. Depending on the physical implementation that you choose or the physical implementation that your service provider imposes, you need to select the correct serial cable type to use with the router.

Serial Connections

In addition to determining the cable type, you need to determine whether you need data terminal equipment (DTE) or data circuit-terminating equipment (DCE) connectors for your WAN equipment. The DTE is the endpoint of the user's device on the WAN link. The DCE is typically the point where responsibility for delivering data passes into the hands of the service provider.

As shown in Figure 4-17, if you are connecting directly to a service provider, or to a device (like a channel/data service unit [CSU/DSU]) that performs signal clocking, the router is a DTE and needs a DTE serial cable. This situation is typically the case for routers.

Figure 4-17   *DTE and DCE Connections*

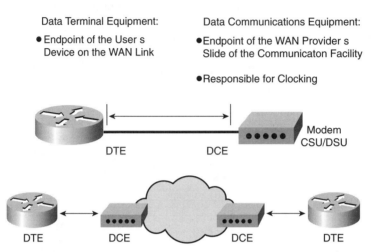

In some cases, the router needs to be the DCE. For example, if you are performing a back-to-back router scenario in a test environment, one of the routers is a DTE, and the other is a DCE. Figure 4-18 shows a back-to-back router configuration. To implement this, you need a DTE cable for one router, and a DCE cable for another router. You might also be able to buy a special back-to-back cable, which is wired with a DTE side and DCE side.

Figure 4-18   *Back-to-Back Router Connections*

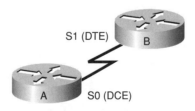

When you are cabling routers for serial connectivity, the routers have either fixed or modular ports. The type of port being used affects the syntax that you use later to configure each interface.

Figure 4-19 shows an example of a router with fixed serial ports (interfaces). Each port is given a label of port type and port number, for example, Serial 0. To configure a fixed interface, specify the interface using this convention.

Figure 4-19 *Fixed Serial Ports*

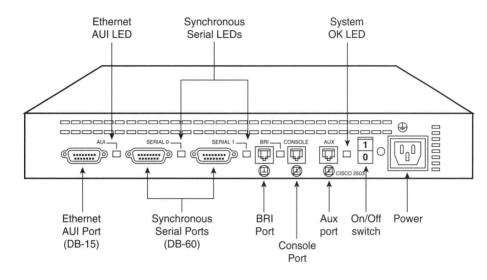

Figure 4-20 shows examples of routers with modular serial ports. Usually, each port is given a label of port type, slot (the location of the module), and port number. To configure a port on a modular card, it is necessary to specify the interface using the convention "port type slot number/port number." For example, given serial 1/0, the type of interface is a serial interface, the slot number where the interface module is installed is slot 1, and the port referenced on that serial interface module is port 0.

Figure 4-20 *Modular Serial Portsts*

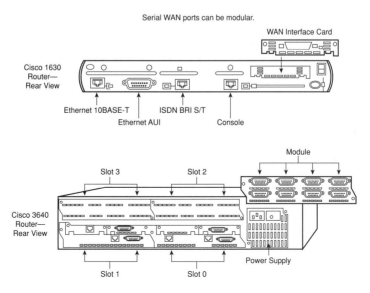

ISDN BRI Connections

With ISDN BRI, you can use two types of interfaces: BRI S/T and BRI U, which are reference points for user connectivity. To determine the appropriate interface, you need to verify whether you or the service provider provides a Network Termination 1 (NT1) device.

An *NT1 device* is an intermediate device between the router and the service provider ISDN switch (cloud) that connects four-wire subscriber wiring to the conventional two-wire local loop. In North America, the customer typically provides the NT1, while in the rest of the world, the service provider provides the NT1 device.

You might find it necessary to provide an external NT1 if an NT1 is not integrated into the router. Looking at the labeling on the router interface is the easiest way to determine if the router has an integrated NT1. A BRI interface with an integrated NT1 is labeled *BRI U*, and a BRI interface without an integrated NT1 is labeled *BRI S/T*. Because routers can have multiple ISDN interface types, you must determine the interface needed when the router is purchased. You can determine the type of ISDN connector that the router has by looking at the port label.

Figure 4-21 shows the different port types for the ISDN interface. To interconnect the ISDN BRI port to the service-provider device, use a UTP Category 5 straight-through cable.

Figure 4-21   *ISDN Interface Types*

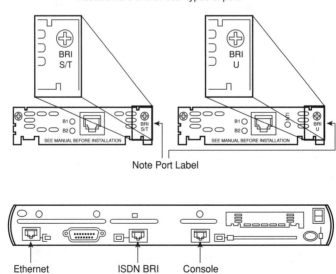

WARNING   It is important to insert a cable running from an ISDN BRI port only to an ISDN jack or an ISDN switch. ISDN BRI uses voltages that can seriously damage non-ISDN devices.

DSL Connections

Routers can also be connected to an asymmetric digital subscriber line (ADSL). The Cisco 827 ADSL router has one ADSL interface. To connect an ADSL to the ADSL port on a router, one end of the phone cable is connected to the ADSL port on the router. The other end of the phone cable is connected to the external wall phone jack.

To connect a router for DSL service, you need a phone cable with RJ-11 connectors. The RJ-11 connector is the same one used on a traditional telephone connection and is slightly smaller than a RJ-45 connector. Figure 4-22 shows a connection to a phone jack with DSL services. DSL works over standard telephone lines. It uses only two pins on the RJ-11 connector.

Figure 4-22   *DSL Connection*

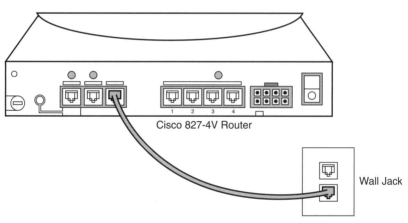

Cable Connections

The Cisco uBR905 cable access router provides high-speed network access on the cable television system to residential and small office/home office (SOHO) subscribers. The uBR905 router has an F-connector coaxial cable interface that can be connected to a cable system.

To connect the Cisco uBR905 cable access router to the cable system, a cable splitter/ directional coupler can be installed, if needed, to separate signals for TV and computer use. If necessary, you can also install a high-pass filter to prevent interference between TV and computer signals.

The coaxial cable is connected to the F connector of the router, as shown in Figure 4-23.

Figure 4-23 *Cable Connection*

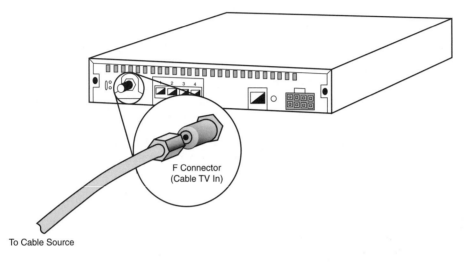

To Cable Source

Asynchronous Router Connections

All Cisco devices also have at least one asynchronous connection that is used for management purposes. In some cases, these devices might also have an auxiliary asynchronous device that can be used for management or dialup network connections. When configuring and managing Cisco devices, you must be aware of how to connect to these ports.

Console Port Connections

To initially configure the Cisco device, you must provide a management connection, also known as a *console connection*, directly to the device. For Cisco equipment, this management attachment is called a *console port*. The console port allows monitoring and configuring of a Cisco hub, switch, or router.

The cable used between a terminal and a console port is a rollover cable, with RJ-45 connectors as illustrated in Figure 4-24.

Figure 4-24 *Connecting a Device with a Console Cable*

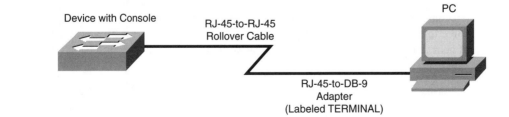

The rollover cable, also known as a console cable, has a different pinout than the straight-through or crossover RJ-45 cables used with Ethernet or the ISDN BRI. The pinout for a rollover cable is as follows:

1–8
2–7
3–6
4–5
5–4
6–3
7–2
8–1

To set up the connection between your terminal and the Cisco console port, you must perform the following:

Step 1 Cable the device to the PC using a rollover cable. You might need an RJ-45-to-DB-9 or and RJ-45-to-DB25 adapter for your PC or terminal.

Step 2 Configure terminal emulation software for the PC with the following COM port settings: 9600 bps, 8 data bits, no parity, 1 stop bit, and no flow control.

This connection to the console port provides you with access to the device's executive process command-line interface (CLI). From there, you can configure the device.

NOTE Many PCs and laptops are no longer manufactured with a 25- or 9-pin (legacy) serial connector. Instead, most devices now ship with USB connectors. If you are working with a USB connector, you need to obtain a USB-to-DB-9 converter cable to connect to the console.

Auxiliary Connections

The auxiliary (AUX) port is another asynchronous connection that can provide out-of-band management—management not using the network bandwidth—through a modem. To provide out-of-band management, you can connect a modem directly to the AUX port. When you dial the modem, you are connected to the AUX port and the executive process CLI. The AUX port must be configured using the console port before it can be used in this manner.

The AUX port can also be used as a dial-on-demand WAN port for passing user traffic.

Understanding WAN Cabling Section Review

Use these practice questions to review what you learned in this section.

1 Which of the following is *not* a physical WAN implementation?

   A DSL

   B ISDN

   C Frame Relay

   D Gigabit Ethernet

2 What type of data transmission method is used by a WAN?

   A Parallel

   B Serial

   C Single

   D Multimode

3 Which of the following media interconnects the ISDN BRI port to the service provider device?

   A UTP straight-through

   B UTP crossover

   C Coaxial

   D Fiber-optic

4 What type of connector is used for DSL connection?

   A RJ-45

   B RJ-11

   C BNC

   D DB-9

5 What type of connector connects a router and cable system?

A RJ-45

B RJ-11

C F-Type

D AUI

6 What type of cable connects a terminal and a console port?

A Straight-through

B Rollover

C Crossover

D Coaxial

Chapter Summary

As you begin to build an internetwork, the first thing you have to consider is the physical implementation of the LAN and WAN connections. These considerations include speed of services, infrastructure, and physical interfaces. This chapter discussed how Ethernet physical layer standards correlate to the infrastructure that you have to install to use the services. This chapter also reviewed the connection differences for WAN connections and how to connect to a console or AUX port for management of the device.

Chapter Review Questions

Use these review questions to test your knowledge of the concepts discussed in this chapter.

1 What is the maximum cable length for Thinnet coaxial cable?

A 100 meters

B 185 meters

C 500 meters

D 1600 meters

2 What are the transmission rates of wireless communication?

   A 9–11 Mbps

   B 9 kbps–54 Mbps

   C 1–9 Mbps

   D 1 kbps–9 Mbps

3 At which layer of the OSI model do the cabling aspects of a LAN exist?

   A Transport

   B Network

   C Data link

   D Physical

4 Which of the following are *not* optical GBICs?

   A Short wavelength (1000BASE-SX)

   B High-frequency wavelength (1000BASE-FX/HX)

   C Long wavelength/long haul (1000BASE-LX/LH)

   D Extended distance (1000BASE-ZX)

5 How is serial transmission different from parallel transmission? (Select two.)

   A Serial transmission is faster than parallel transmission.

   B They use different connectors.

   C Serial transmission sends data 1 bit at a time, and parallel transmission sends several bits at one time.

   D Parallel transmission is used over WAN links.

6 Typically, a router is _____.

   A A DTE device

   B A DCE device

   C Both a DTE and a DCE device

   D Neither a DTE nor a DCE device

7 If you are using an ISDN device that has an interface marked *BRI S/T*, what does this imply?

A The BRI interface is capable of supertransmission.

B The device has an NT1 built in.

C The device does not have an NT1 built in.

D The ISDN send/transmit interface.

Upon completion of this chapter, you will be able to perform the following tasks:

- Describe how technology can extend Ethernet LANs
- Describe how LAN switching satisfies demand for network access
- Describe how virtual networks meet the demand for extending LANs

CHAPTER 5

Layer 2 Switching Fundamentals (The Data Link Layer)

Today's LANs are becoming increasingly congested and overburdened. In addition to an ever-growing population of network users, several factors have combined to stress the capabilities of traditional LANs. Workstations with 50 to 75 million instructions per second of processing power are common, and several of these more modern workstations on the same LAN can easily saturate the LAN. Faster operating systems allow PC users to increase their demands for network resources. All this network demand requires faster interconnections.

Switching is a technology that alleviates congestion in Ethernet LANs by reducing traffic on a segment, which increases a device's available bandwidth. Layer 2 switches, known as LAN switches, are designed to work with existing cable infrastructures so that they can be installed with minimal disruption to existing networks. They often replace shared hubs. This chapter describes how LAN switching works, what the different types of LAN switches are, and how virtual LANs (VLANs) can expand the traditional LAN.

Understanding Shared Ethernet Technologies

LANs were introduced as a low-cost, timesaving technology that evolved along with the PC revolution. LANs allow multiple users in a relatively small geographical area to exchange files and messages, and to access shared resources such as file servers. Today, LANs have rapidly evolved into support systems that are critical to communications within organizations. However, some limitations of a shared LAN require solutions. This section examines the properties of Ethernet segments, how communications take place within these segments, and finally, some of the limitations of traditional shared segments.

Properties of Ethernet Segments

Segment length is an important consideration when using Ethernet technology in a LAN. A *segment* is a network connection made by a single unbroken network cable. Ethernet cables and segments can span only a limited physical distance, after which transmissions likely fail because of line noise, reduced signal strength, and failure to follow the carrier sense multiple access collision detect (CSMA/CD) specifications for collision detection. This means that when you connect users, you must consider how far they are located from the network connection point, as shown in Figure 5-1.

Figure 5-1   *Maximum Segment Length*

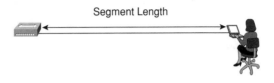

Many organizations have buildings that span large distances vertically and horizontally. When connecting devices to the network, you need to know where the users are located in relation to the network devices. Table 5-1 shows the maximum segment length for some of the common Ethernet standards.

Table 5-1   *Ethernet Segment Distances*

Ethernet Specification	Segment Length
10BASE5	500 meters
10BASE2	185 meters
10BASE-T	100 meters
10BASE-FL	2000 meters
100BASE-TX	100 meters
100BASE-FX	400 meters
100BASE-T4	100 meters
100BASE-T2	100 meters
1000BASE-LX	550 meters if 62.5 μ or 50 μ multimode fiber; 10 km if 10 μ single-mode fiber
1000BASE-SX	250 meters if 62.5 μ multimode fiber; 550 meters if 50 μ multimode fiber
1000BASE-CX	25 meters

Chapter 4 discussed segment length when considering physical media. One method of extending the segment length is to install a hub, or repeater.

A hub, or repeater, is a device that joins multiple Ethernet segments to extend the length. Technology limits the distance a frame can travel on a segment before the signal degrades. Adding a hub can overcome distance issues, as illustrated in Figure 5-2.

Figure 5-2   *Extending Segment Lengths*

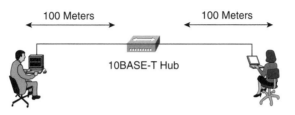

However, a timing issue regarding collision detection exists that hub technology cannot improve, so hubs cannot be cascaded infinitely.

A hub extends the Ethernet LAN, but the bandwidth limitation of a shared technology remains. Although each device has its own cable that connects into the hub, all users of a given Ethernet segment compete for the same amount of bandwidth.

Hubs operate at Layer 1 in the Open System Interconnection (OSI) model. At the physical layer, hubs support little in the way of sophisticated networking. Hubs do not read any of the data passing through them and are not aware of the source or destination of the frame. Essentially, a hub simply receives incoming bits, regenerates the electrical signal, and transmits these bits out all ports except the incoming port to the other devices on the network.

Communications Within the Segment

Within a LAN, devices can communicate in different ways. The different types of communication are based on which device or devices a networking component is communicating with. The communication takes place using addressing. Because all devices on a LAN segment receive every frame, addressing allows a device to determine if a particular frame is of interest. The type of addressing used dictates the type of communication that takes place.

Communication between devices in a LAN network occurs in three ways, as illustrated in Figure 5-3:

- **Unicast**—Communication where a frame is sent from one host addressed to a specific destination. In this case, you have just one sender and one receiver. Unicast transmission is still the predominant form of transmission on LANs and within the Internet.

- **Broadcast**—Communication where a frame is sent from one address to all other devices. In this case, you have just one sender, but the information is sent to all connected receivers by using a universal broadcast address. Broadcast transmission is essential when sending the same message to all devices on the LAN.

- **Multicast**—Communication where a destination addresses a specific group of devices, or clients. Unlike broadcast transmission, multicast clients must join the multicast group to receive the information.

Figure 5-3   *LAN Communications Methods*

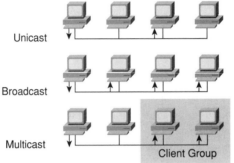

Unicast

Broadcast

Multicast

Client Group

Because all devices on a segment have access at the same time, as the number of devices increase, it is likely that two or more stations might try to communicate simultaneously. The next sections discuss the potential effects of simultaneous transmission.

Collision Domains

A *collision domain* is a group of Ethernet devices that are directly connected by hubs. A collision occurs when two stations transmit bits at the same time on the same Ethernet segment. Ethernet device are in a collision domain within an Ethernet LAN. Figure 5-4 shows how collisions occur.

Figure 5-4   *Collision Domain*

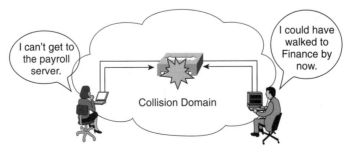

I can't get to the payroll server.

I could have walked to Finance by now.

Collision Domain

On a cable, like coaxial media, when you interconnect all the devices on a LAN, the possibility of conflict, or more than one user sending data at the same time, is high. The same is true if a nonfiltering device, such as a hub, interconnects segments of a LAN.

Within a single collision domain, only one device can transmit at any one time. When a device is transmitting, all other devices in the collision domain listen or receive the frame. If two or more stations on a shared media try to transmit at the same time, a collision results. The more stations you have attempting to transmit data, the more collisions occur. The more collisions that occur, the worse the congestion becomes, and network accessibility can become slow or nonexistent. Although collisions are a natural part of the way Ethernet works, they still create congestion and latency within a segment.

Hubs extend collision domains. Extending a run of cable with a hub results in a larger collision domain.

Consuming Bandwidth

Bandwidth is an important consideration in the function of Ethernet LANs. This section identifies several examples of bandwidth consumption.

Shared LAN segments have a fixed amount of bandwidth. As users are added, the amount of bandwidth per user decreases. This reduction results in collisions, and collisions reduce performance.

In early PC applications, workstations delivered limited amounts of traffic to the network. With faster CPUs, buses, peripherals, and more data-intensive applications, a single workstation can saturate a network segment. Bandwidth-intensive applications, such as desktop publishing, engineering applications, imaging applications, and multimedia applications, quickly deplete available bandwidth.

Table 5-2 lists the bandwidth consumption differences between text and graphics files.

Table 5-2   *Bandwidth Consumption*

Item	File Size	Network Utilization
700-page novel (only text)	1 MB	3 seconds
Complete works of Shakespeare	5 MB	13 seconds
1 large GIF image (uncompressed)	5 MB	13 seconds
1 large GIF image (compressed)	1 MB	3 seconds
DVD movie trailer	68 MB	180 seconds

Limitations of Shared Networks

Shared networks are somewhat effective at providing user connections; however, they have several limitations, such as distance limitations, maximum number of cascaded devices, shared bandwidth, and collisions. As networks have grown, these limitations have been the driving force for technologies that can alleviate the problems with large Ethernet segments. Bridges and switches provide a solution for many of these problems.

Understanding Shared Ethernet Technologies Section Quiz

Use these practice questions to review what you learned in this section.

1 What is the maximum distance for thin Ethernet without using a repeater?

A 185 meters

B 250 meters

C 500 meters

D 800 meters

2 Which statements describe a feature of a hub? (Choose three.)

A All resources are shared.

B A hub filters traffic based on a MAC address.

C A hub implements physical layer functionality.

D A hub implements data link layer functionality.

E A hub reduces the size of the collision domain.

F A hub transmits all bits to all devices on a segment.

3 Which behavior best describes a unicast transmission?

A A frame is filtered through a single bridge.

B A frame is sent from one point to another point.

C A frame is passed but not filtered through a hub.

D A frame is sent from one point to all other points.

E A frame is sent simultaneously to a specific group of devices.

4 Which behavior best describes a broadcast transmission?

   A A frame is filtered through a single bridge.

   B A frame is sent from one point to another point.

   C A frame is passed but not filtered through a hub.

   D A frame is sent from one point to all other points.

   E A frame is sent simultaneously to a specific group of devices.

5 Which behavior best describes a multicast transmission?

   A A frame is filtered through a single bridge.

   B A frame is sent from one point to another point.

   C A frame is passed but not filtered through a hub.

   D A frame is sent from one point to all other points.

   E A frame is sent simultaneously to a specific group of devices.

6 What term describes the results of two or more stations on a network trying to transmit simultaneously on a shared network segment?

   A Filtering

   B Collision

   C Switching

   D Propagation

   E Broadcasting

7 Which condition is a likely cause of network congestion?

   A Short cables

   B Too many collision domains

   C Multiple segments on a bridge

   D Bandwidth-intensive applications

Bridged and Switched Ethernet

Hub-connected networks previously worked well for end-user stations that could drive traffic only at a fraction of the carrying capacity of the network. Today, end-user stations are so fast and complex that a single end-user station can exceed the entire capacity of 10- and 100-Mbps Ethernet. This section describes how bridging and switching technology contributes to the efficiency of a network by providing dedicated bandwidth in the LAN. Understanding how this technology functions increases your understanding of how LANs function in high-speed networking environments.

Bridges in LANs

Ethernet uses collision detection. As a result, a single collision domain with a large number of users leads to excessive frame collisions. A Layer 2 device can reduce the size of collision domains in an Ethernet LAN.

The potential for frame collision in an Ethernet LAN limits the effective size of a network. The section, "Consuming Bandwidth," earlier in this chapter illustrated how high-bandwidth applications consume bandwidth. Layer 2 networking devices, such as bridges and switches, reduce the size of collision domains as well provide dedicated bandwidth to users through a process called *segmentation*.

When using Layer 2 devices, each device builds a frame-forwarding table, also referred to as a Media Access Control (MAC) or content-addressable memory (CAM) table. When a frame is transmitted from a node, the switch then compares the destination MAC address against the MAC table and forwards the frame, without modification, to the appropriate LAN segment.

Filtering is also performed based on the destination MAC address of the frame. The frame is not forwarded if the destination is a station on the same segment where the frame originated. If the frame is destined for a station on another LAN segment, the frame is forwarded to the port that connects to the segment on which the node with that address resides. This function creates a separate collision domain for each LAN segment, as shown in Figure 5-5. Frame collisions are reduced when frames destined for MAC addresses known to the switch are forwarded to only the port that leads to that device.

| NOTE | A special rule controls the interconnection of bridges or switches. Only *one active path* exists between any two computers in a LAN containing bridges and switches. If more than one parallel path exists, a loop is formed, and the bridges or switches continually transmit frames over the loop. This action soon results in overload of the network. This situation is discussed further in the section, "Preventing Loops," later in this chapter. |

Figure 5-5   *Switches Create Multiple Collision Domains*

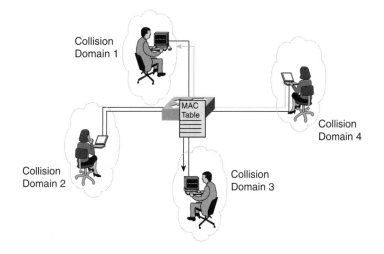

A good analogy for the need for segmentation is a bike path that has too many bikers. A single bike path has become saturated with the maximum number of bikes and traffic has slowed down to a standstill. You widen the bike path to provide a total of 10 lanes. This widening enables bikes to travel at maximum speed, each in their own lane. However, if traffic continues to increase, even these lanes fill up, causing the bikes to slow down again.

Layer 2 Switches

LAN switching, sometimes referred to as Layer 2 switching, operates at the data link layer of the OSI model, as shown in Figure 5-6.

Figure 5-6   *LAN Switches Operate at Layer 2 of the OSI Model*

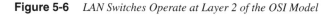
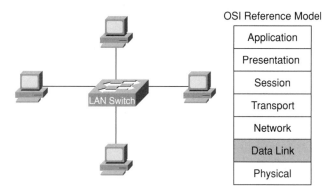

Functionally, LAN switches are virtually identical to bridges. Like bridges, switches connect LAN segments, reduce traffic, and use a table of MAC addresses to determine the segment on which a frame needs to be transmitted.

The difference between LAN switches and multiport bridges is in the internal hardware and cost. LAN switches use either proprietary or third-party application-specific integrated circuits (ASICs), which have the switching code optimized and embedded in hardware, resulting in faster execution time. Switches operate at much higher speeds than bridges and can support new functionality such as virtual LANs. Also, LAN switches provide much higher port density at a lower cost than traditional bridges do.

Identifying Switching Features

Although LAN switches have some similarities to bridges, switches also have some additional features beyond speed that set them apart from bridges. LAN switches are similar to bridges in the basic functions, such as learning the topology, forwarding, and filtering. However, LAN switches additionally support these features:

- **Dedicated communication between devices**—This increases file-transfer throughput. Creating private or dedicated segments with one user per segment is called *microsegmentation*. In this type of configuration, each user receives access to the full bandwidth and does not have to contend for available bandwidth with other users. As a result, collisions do not occur.

- **Multiple simultaneous conversations**—Multiple simultaneous conversations can occur by forwarding, or switching, several packets at the same time, thereby increasing network capacity by the number of conversations supported.

- **Full-duplex communication**—This theoretically doubles the capacity of a link. For example, point-to-point 100-Mbps connections have 100 Mbps of transmit capacity and 100 Mbps of receive capacity, for a total 200-Mbps capacity, if you are sending and receiving simultaneously on a single connection. Full duplex can occur only on dedicated connections.

- **Media-rate allocation**—The LAN switch can translate between 10 and 100 Mbps, allowing bandwidth to be allocated as needed.

With each feature, the user device is able to achieve better communication access without the consequences of collisions on shared media.

Because the switch is receiving multiple frames at the same time, it must schedule the delivery or forwarding of the frames between the different ports. Some Cisco switches use the following two methodologies, as illustrated in Figure 5-7:

- **Store-and-forward**—In the store-and-forward switching method, error checking is performed and erroneous frames are discarded. The LAN switch copies the entire frame into its onboard buffers and computes the cyclic redundancy check (CRC). The frame is discarded if it contains a CRC error. The frame is also discarded if its size is less than 64 bytes (runt) or more than 1518 bytes (giant), including the CRC. If the frame does not contain any errors, the LAN switch looks up the destination address in the forwarding, or MAC, table and determines the outgoing interface. The switch then forwards the frame toward its destination.

- **Cut-through**—With cut-through switching, the LAN switch waits until it copies the destination address, which is indicated in the first 6 bytes following the preamble, into the onboard buffers of the switch. The switch then looks up the destination address in the MAC table, determines the outgoing interface, and forwards the frame toward its destination. The cut-through switching method reduces latency by eliminating error checking and forwarding the frame as soon as the switch reads the destination address and determines the outgoing interface. However, cut-through switching is not supported with most of the more advanced Cisco switches.

Figure 5-7   *Forwarding Methods*

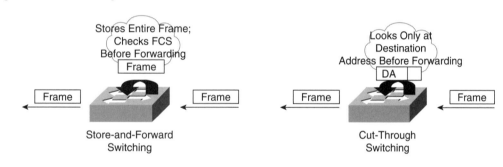

Because of the increased speed of the switching hardware and switching backplanes, most Catalyst switches use store-and-forward switching. Switches perform differently based on the types of hardware and software features that are available.

Categorizing Switches by Bandwidth

Switches can be characterized according to the proportion of bandwidth allocated to each port on the switch. LAN switches provide switched connections between ports of unlike bandwidths, such as a combination of 10BASE-T and 100BASE-T, as shown in Figure 5-8. This feature can be useful for providing the appropriate bandwidth for interconnecting the devices.

Because switches support ports of different speeds, this feature can optimize client-server traffic flows where multiple clients simultaneously communicate with a server. More bandwidth can be dedicated to a server port to prevent a bottleneck at that port.

Figure 5-8   *Switches Support Ports with Different Bandwidths*

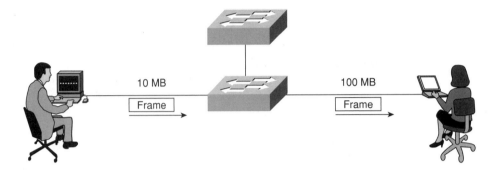

One important feature of switching is often overlooked. When you connect devices to switches, it's important to consider how many of the devices are accessing an uplink port to a server, router, or switch. If all the ports on the switch are the same speed, your switch encounters congestion because everyone is trying to access the same uplink port at the same time. When installing switches into the network, you must make sure that you have the appropriate amount of high-speed ports. Switches that are attached to end users at the access layer of the network hierarchy typically have 1 or 2 high-speed ports to connect to the distribution layer switches.

Categorizing Switches by Layer Functionality

Today, many switches are more robust than the traditional LAN switches and can provide services at multiple layers of the OSI model. Because of this, switches can also be categorized as Layer 2, Layer 2 with some Layer 3, or multilayer switches based on the OSI layer at which they filter and forward frames, as shown in Figure 5-9.

Figure 5-9   *Switches Are Categorized by OSI Layer Functionality*

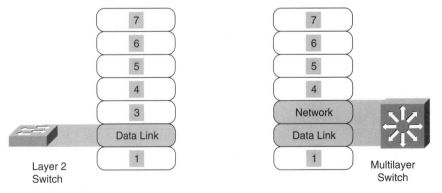

As mentioned before, a Layer 2 LAN switch is operationally similar to a bridge but has a higher capacity and supports many new features, such as full-duplex operation. A Layer 2 LAN switch performs switching and filtering using only the OSI data link layer (Layer 2) MAC address. As with bridges, the switch is completely transparent to network protocols and user applications.

A multilayer switch can make switching and filtering decisions by using more than one layer of OSI model. For example, most multilayer switches can use the data link layer (Layer 2) or OSI network layer (Layer 3) addresses to make forwarding decisions. This type of switch dynamically decides whether to switch (Layer 2) or route (Layer 3) incoming traffic. A multilayer LAN switch switches within LAN segments and routes between different networks.

Switching Frames

A Layer 2 LAN switch follows a specific procedure when forwarding frames. A switch learns the location of devices within a network topology by analyzing the source address of incoming frames from all attached networks. The following list and Figure 5-10 describe the frame switching process:

1 The switch receives a frame from a network on the incoming port of the switch.

2 The switch enters the source MAC address and the switch port that received the frame into the MAC table.

3 If the destination address is unknown, the switch floods the frame to all ports.

4 The destination device replies to the flooded frame.

5 The switch enters the MAC address and the switch port that received the frame of the destination device into the MAC table.

6 The switch can now switch frames between source and destination devices onto the network without flooding.

The rules for Layer 2 frame forwarding are explicit. If the device does not know the destination address, the frame is flooded to all ports on the network. Because addresses are learned by the source address of the sending devices, some addresses are never learned. In particular, broadcast and multicast addresses are always destination addresses and are never learned by a switch. Because of this, and without special interaction by the administrator, these frames are always flooded.

Figure 5-10 *Switching Frames*

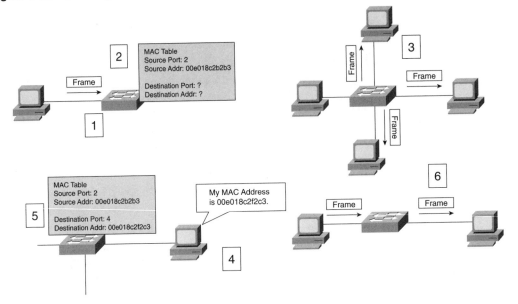

Flooding the Network

When multiple paths are connected in a Layer 2 switched or bridged network, the problem of looping can occur. Loops are created when redundant Layer 2 paths exist between a source and a destination. When this occurs, a switch allows flood traffic to be forwarded out all of the ports of the switch at the same time. If these redundant paths are both forwarding data at the same time, the frame circulates (loops) between these two paths without being removed from the network. As the frames pass through the switch, the switch looks up the source and destination addresses. The MAC table can be updated with erroneous information, resulting in inaccurate forwarding and learning in bridging environments.

In addition to basic connectivity problems, the proliferation of broadcast messages in networks with loops represents a serious network problem. Because of how switches operate, any multicast, broadcast, or unknown unicast traffic is flooded out to all ports except the incoming port. The resulting effect is a storm of traffic being looped endlessly through the network, almost instantly consuming the available bandwidth.

Loops in a Switched Network

If redundant links are active in a switched network, switch (bridge) loops occur because of the way forwarding process works. Figure 5-11 shows a typical switch (bridge) loop.

Figure 5-11   *Switch (Bridge) Loop*

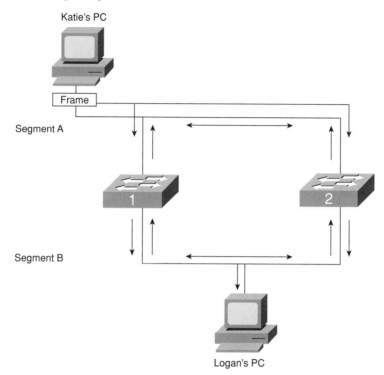

In Figure 5-11, suppose that Katie's PC sends a frame to Logan's PC. Katie's PC resides on network Segment A, and Logan's PC resides on network Segment B. Both switches have connections to network Segment A and Segment B to ensure continual operations in the case of a port or device failure. Both Switch 1 and Switch 2 receive a frame from Katie's PC and correctly learn that Katie's PC is on Segment A. Each switch forwards the frame onto Segment B.

Logan's PC then receives two copies of the frame from Katie's PC through Switch 1 and Switch 2. However, both switches also receive the frame on their Segment B interfaces. The switches now change their internal tables to indicate that Katie's PC is on Segment B. If Logan's PC replies to Katie's PC, both switches receive and subsequently drop the reply frames because the MAC table in each switch indicates that the destination (Katie's PC) is on the same network segment as the source of the frame (Logan's PC).

If the initial frame from Katie's PC were a broadcast frame, both switches would forward the frames endlessly, using all available network bandwidth and blocking the transmission of other packets on both segments. This problem would exist on all Layer 2 bridged and switched networks if there were not a method for preventing these loops.

Preventing Loops

Spanning Tree Protocol (STP) is means to resolve bridging loops in a redundant network known as the. STP allows path redundancy while preventing undesirable active loops in the network.

To allow path redundancy, STP defines a tree that spans all switches in a network. STP forces certain redundant data paths into a standby state, like the one shown in Figure 5-12.

Figure 5-12 *STP Deactivates Redundant Links*

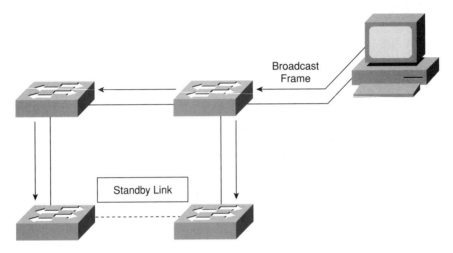

If one network segment becomes unreachable, the STP reconfigures the spanning-tree topology and reestablishes the link by activating the standby path.

STP operation is transparent to end stations, which are unaware whether they are connected to a single LAN segment or to a switched LAN of multiple segments.

Bridged and Switched Ethernet Section Quiz

Use these practice questions to review what you learned in this section.

1 Which characteristics best describe a LAN switch? (Choose two.)

   A Separates broadcast domains

   B Functionally resembles a multiport bridge

   C Connects remote and local-area networks together

   D Code is optimized and embedded in hardware

   E Forwards packets from a single source to a predefined set of client stations

2 Which statements describe a feature of a switch? (Choose three.)

A Operates at Layer 1 of OSI model

B Builds and maintains a MAC address table

C Interconnects multiple LAN segments

D Increases the size of the collision domain

E Filters frames based on the destination address

3 Which of the following functionalities of a switch differentiate it from a bridge? (Choose four.)

A Extends a collision domain

B Enables full-duplex communication

C Creates dedicated segments per user

D Connects two LAN segments together

E Uses MAC addresses to forward frames

F Handles multiple simultaneous conversations

G Translates speeds between different rate segments

4 Which statements accurately describe the two forwarding methods used by switches? (Choose two.)

A Cut-through switching increases latency.

B Store-and-forward switching performs error checking.

C Store-and-forward switching reduces latency.

D Store-and-forward switching copies only the destination address into the buffers.

E Cut-through switching does not wait to receive the whole frame before forwarding it to the destination.

F Cut-through switching discards frames of less than 64 bytes or more than 1518 bytes, including the CRC.

5 Which switch type provides switched connections between ports of unlike bandwidths?

  A Multitasking switch

  B Symmetrical switch

  C Asymmetrical switch

  D Store-and-forward switch

6 Which functionality best fits a Layer 2 switch?

  A Routes once, switches many

  B Provides security through access lists

  C Switches when it can, routes when it must

  D Forwards frames based on MAC addresses

  E Switches or routes incoming traffic dynamically

  F Switches within a collision domain and routes between collision domains

7 Number the frame-forwarding sequence in the correct order of occurrence for a switch receiving a frame that has an unknown source address.

  A The switch floods the frame to all ports.

  B The destination device replies to the request.

  C The switch forwards frames to the destination without flooding.

  D The switch receives a frame from a network on an incoming port.

  E The switch enters the source MAC address and the switch port that received the frame into the MAC table.

  F The switch receives a frame from the destination device and enters that MAC address and the switch port that received the frame into the MAC table.

8 In which of the following conditions would a bridging loop most likely occur?

  A A redundant network between two unique collision domains

  B A redundant routed network with the Spanning Tree Protocol

  C A redundant bridged network with the Spanning Tree Protocol

  D A redundant routed network without the Spanning Tree Protocol

  E A redundant bridged network without the Spanning Tree Protocol

9 The Spanning Tree Protocol performs which of the following?

  A Creates multiple broadcast domains

  B Switches when it can, routes when it must

  C Creates static routes to prevent bridging loops

  D Detects and breaks loops by placing some connections is a standby mode

  E Sends an alarm to a management station in the event of a link failure

Virtual LANs

Although switches provide separation for collisions on a network, they do not, by default, provide separation for broadcasts. As you read in the previous section, any broadcast received on a port is flooded out all other ports. This means as networks grow, the broadcasts common to all networks use valuable resources. To control these broadcasts, switch manufactures created the concept of virtual LANs (VLANs).

This section defines VLANs, discusses their benefits, and explains what devices interconnect end users and resources. Understanding how VLANs function increases your overall understanding of the operations of LANs and how they meet different requirements for networking.

Defining a VLAN

VLANs provide an important connection function in a LAN. A VLAN is defined as a group of Ethernet segments that have different physical connections but which communicate as if the LANs are connected on a single network segment.

VLAN technology allows the grouping of switch ports, and the devices connected to them, into logically defined communities of interest. These groupings can be coworkers within the same department, as is illustrated in Figure 5-13, a cross-functional product team, or diverse users sharing the same network application or software.

Figure 5-13 *VLANs by Function*

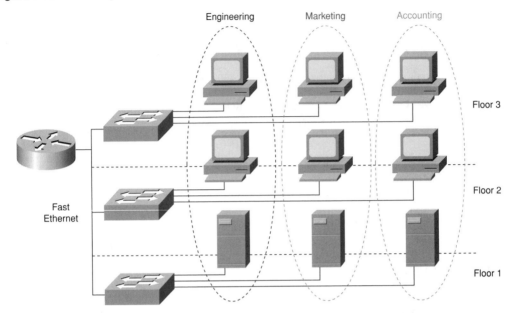

VLANs divide the network into broadcast domains. A broadcast domain is group of devices that all receive the same broadcast frames, which allows all devices within that domain to receive broadcast frames originating from any device within that VLAN.

Identifying VLAN Benefits

You gain several benefits when you use VLANs. Because the VLAN does not have any limitations to ports or locations of the ports within the internetwork, they are very flexible tools for a network administrator. VLANs provide the following advantages:

- **Reduction of administration cost**—VLANs enable logical groupings of devices that are physically dispersed on a network. When users on a VLAN move to a new physical location but continue to perform the same job function, the devices of those users do not need to be reconfigured. Similarly, if users change their job function, they need not physically move; changing the VLAN membership of the devices to that of the new team makes the users' devices local to the new team.

- **Efficient bandwidth utilization**—VLANs reduce the need to have routers deployed on a network to contain broadcast traffic. Flooding of a packet is limited to the switch ports that belong to a VLAN.

- **Enforcement of network security policies**—By confining the broadcast domains, devices on a VLAN can be isolated from listening to or receiving broadcasts not intended for them. Moreover, if a router is not connected between the VLANs, the devices of a VLAN cannot communicate with the devices of the other VLANs.

- **Reduction in network traffic**—As a result of confinement of broadcast domains on a network, traffic on the network is significantly reduced.

VLANs are created individually on each switch in the network and ports are assigned to those VLANs. As frames travel between switches, the switches can identify what VLAN a particular frame belongs to. These technologies allow a VLAN to be implemented almost anywhere within the internetwork structure. To work with VLANs, you need to be aware of the different components involved, as discussed in the next section.

Identifying VLAN Components

VLANs are made up of the following types of devices and technologies:

- **Switches**—Switches are primary components of VLAN communication. They perform critical VLAN functions by acting as the entry point for end-station devices into the network, facilitating communication across the organization, and providing the intelligence to group users, ports, or logical addresses to form common communities of interest.

- **Routers**—Routers provide the communication between logically defined work-groups. They also provide VLAN access to shared resources such as servers and hosts. Routers also connect to other parts of the network that are either logically segmented with the more traditional subnet approach or require access to remote sites across wide-area links.

- **Trunks**—A trunk is a point-to-point link between one or more switch ports and other networking devices, such as routers or switches. Trunks carry the traffic of multiple VLANs over a single link and allow you to extend VLANs across an entire network.

  Trunks require a specialized link protocol for communications. Depending on the platform, you might have one or more trunking encapsulation options, such as the following:

  — **Inter-Switch Link (ISL)**—A Cisco-proprietary trunking encapsulation, which predates the 802.1Q specification.

  — **IEEE 802.1Q**—An industry-standard frame-tagging mechanism for VLAN trunking.

Establishing VLAN Membership

Two main methods for establishing VLAN membership on a Cisco Catalyst switch exist. Each method involves assigning a port on the switch into a VLAN that also exists on that switch, as follows:

- **Port-based VLANs**—The administrator assigns each port of a switch to a VLAN. The switch determines the VLAN membership of each frame by noting the port on which the frame arrives. When a user is moved to a different port of the switch, the administrator reassigns the new port to the old VLAN of the user. The network change is completely transparent to the user, and the administrator saves a trip to the wiring closet. If a hub is attached to a port on the switch, all the users connected to that hub are members of the same VLAN.

- **MAC-based VLANs**—Membership of a frame is determined by the source MAC address. Each switch maintains a database of MAC addresses and their corresponding VLAN memberships. A key advantage of this method is that the switch does not need to be reconfigured when a user moves to a different port. However, assigning VLAN membership to each MAC address can be a time-consuming task. Also, a single MAC address cannot easily be a member of multiple VLANs, which can be a significant limitation, making it difficult to share server resources between more than one VLAN.

Figure 5-14 illustrates these two methods.

Figure 5-14   *VLAN Assignments*

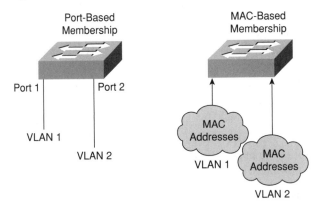

Communicating Between VLANs

As a frame is passed from one switch to another, a trunk link can maintain the information about the VLANs; however, when a device on one VLAN needs to communicate with a device on another VLAN, a router or Layer 3 switch must exist to provide communications between the VLANs. It also requires that the hosts on the VLANs be configured with a routable network address structure like TCP/IP.

When a host device connected through a VLAN sends out packets, they use the same method for connecting to other network devices as a host that is connected by a traditional Ethernet segment, as is described in the following list and illustrated in Figure 5-15:

1 The sending device recognizes the IP address of the destination is *not* on the local network.

2 The sending device then uses its IP default gateway's MAC address as the destination MAC address of the frames.

3 The default gateway (a router) forwards the packet towards the destination, which might be a directly connected network *or* it might need to go through additional routers.

Figure 5-15   *Communication Between VLANs*

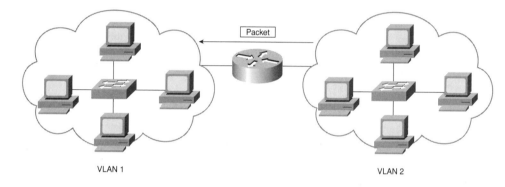

VLAN 1   VLAN 2

Virtual LAN Section Quiz

Use these practice questions to review what you learned in this section.

1 Which characteristic best describes a VLAN?

   A Devices within a VLAN are physically colocated.

   B VLANs must be interconnected with the same switch.

   C Devices within a VLAN must be interconnected with the same router.

   D Devices are geographically dispersed but are on the same physical segment.

   E Devices are geographically in the same place but communicate virtually as if they are in different broadcast domains.

2 Which statements are benefits of adding a VLAN? (Choose two.)

   A Managing broadcasts reduces traffic load.

   B Flooding of a packet is limited to the switch ports that belong to a VLAN.

   C Security is ensured by reconfiguration each time a user moves to a new VLAN.

   D Changing the VLAN membership of the devices to a new switch reduces port costs.

3 Which of these components is used as the entry point into the VLAN?

   A Trunk port

   B MAC port

   C Switch port

   D VLAN port

4 Which method can dynamically establish VLAN membership?

   A MAC address

   B Routing protocol

   C Ethernet segment

   D Layer 3 access list

5 Which device provides communication between broadcast domains?

   A Hub

   B Bridge

   C Trunk

   D Router

   E Switch

Chapter Summary

This chapter introduced you to the concept of Layer 2 networking devices including bridges and switches. This chapter reviewed how these devices use Layer 2 MAC addresses to provide a separation of user traffic into different collision domains. This chapter also discussed the need for the Spanning Tree Protocol and how it allows redundancy and prevents loops. Finally, this chapter discussed how VLANs can be used to control broadcast on a network and how routers or Layer 3 switches communicate between these VLANs.

Chapter Review Questions

Use these review questions to test your knowledge of the concepts discussed in this chapter.

1 Using a hub to interconnect devices has the same results as having the network devices on one Ethernet 10BASE2 segment.

   A True

   B False

2 Congestion causes which effects? (Choose two.)

   A Shorter segment lengths

   B Lower reliability and low traffic rates

   C Network predictability, low error rates

   D Slower response times, longer file transfers, and network delays

3 What type of traffic can cause the most overhead on an Ethernet network?

   A Unicast

   B Multicast

   C Broadcast

   D Domain Name Service

4 Which statements best describe a bridge? (Choose two.)

   A Filters data packets based on access lists

   B Routes data packets based on IP addresses

   C Forwards data packets from one network segment to another

   D Amplifies and cleans signals before passing every frame along the network

   E Addresses the problem of too much traffic on a segment or a network

5 At what layer of the OSI model do switches operate?

   A Session layer

   B Physical layer

   C Network layer

D   Data link layer

E   Transport layer

F   Presentation layer

G   Application layer

6   Which best describes a network segment?

A   A section of the network to which a group of devices share the same physical media

B   A section of network that contains Token Ring topology

C   A section of network bounded by routers, switches, or bridges

D   A section of network that is a logical grouping based on MAC addresses

7   Which statement is not a characteristic of LAN switching?

A   Operates at OSI Layer 2

B   Microsegments the network

C   Forwards packets based on IP addresses

D   Learns the location of a station by examining the source address

8   What features do store-and-forward mode allow the switch to perform? (Choose two.)

A   Broadcasting

B   Error checking

C   Cell switching

D   Full receipt of all bits before forwarding the frame

E   Forwarding of bits before entire frame is received

9 Which switching method looks at the destination address of the frame and then forwards the frame without waiting to receive the entire frame?

A Cut-through

B Cut-throat

C Fragment-free

D Store-and-forward

10 What are the functions of the Spanning Tree Protocol? (Choose two.)

A Manages the topologies within a switched or bridged network

B Switches or routes information based on the type of data packet

C Provides routing information to the connected neighboring hosts

D Transparently reconfigures bridges and switches to avoid the creation of loops

11 What is the only switching method supported by bridges?

A Cut-through

B Fast-forward

C Fragment-free

D Store-and-forward

12 What function of a Cisco switch allows a user to create separate broadcast domains?

A VLAN

B Bridging

C Cut-through

D Store-and-forward

E Transparent bridging

13 Identify the benefits of using a VLAN. (Choose two.)

A Reduced collision

B Decreased security

C Easier implementation of segmentation

D Increased number of broadcast domains

14 What device is needed to pass a packet between VLANs?

A Hub

B Bridge

C Router

D Switch

E Repeater

15 Which statement pertaining to VLANs is false for Cisco switches?

A VLANs help in distributing traffic load.

B VLANs can be defined according to port groups, users, or protocols.

C Switches form one of the core components of VLAN communications.

D VLAN benefits include tighter network security with establishment of secure user groups, and better management and control of broadcasts.

16 VLANs can be created according to which category? (Choose all that apply.)

A Ports

B Groups

C MAC addresses

D Functional teams

E Users sharing an application

17 What is the result of segmenting a switch into multiple VLANS? (Choose two.)

A Network congestion increases.

B More broadcast traffic is switched.

C The amount of broadcast traffic is limited.

D Bandwidth is more effectively allocated.

Upon completion of this chapter, you will be able to perform the following tasks:

- Identify the network layer protocols and their functions
- Identify how transport layer protocols offer guaranteed or non-guaranteed services
- Identify the IP protocol stack, its protocol layer functions, and commonly used IP protocols
- Describe the function of administrative protocols such as ICMP, ARP, and DHCP

CHAPTER 6

TCP/IP (The Transport and Internetworking Layer Protocol)

When computers communicate with one another, certain rules, or protocols, allow them to transmit and receive data in an orderly fashion. Throughout the world, one of the most routinely used sets of protocols is the Transmission Control Protocol/Internet Protocol (TCP/IP). This chapter covers the TCP/IP protocol stack with an emphasis on the Layer 3 IP routed protocol and Layer 4 end-to-end connectivity.

To understand how to configure the functions of internetworking devices, you must have a solid understanding of routed protocols and their functions. The most common protocol used in data networks today is the TCP/IP protocol stack. TCP/IP interconnects devices in corporate networks and is the protocol of the Internet.

The TCP/IP suite of protocols was developed as part of the research done by the Defense Advanced Research Projects Agency (DARPA). Later, TCP/IP was included with the Berkeley Software Distribution of UNIX.

The Internet protocols can be used to communicate across any set of interconnected networks. They are equally well-suited for both LAN and WAN communication. The Internet protocol suite includes not only Layer 3 and Layer 4 specifications (such as IP and TCP), but also specifications for such common applications as e-mail, remote login, terminal emulation, and file transfer.

The TCP/IP protocol stack maps closely to the OSI reference model in the lower layers. All standard physical and data link protocols are supported. Figure 6-1 illustrates the TCP/IP model in reference to the seven-layer OSI model.

NOTE The network interface layer of the TCP/IP stack shown in Figure 6-1 is sometimes separated and called the *physical* and *data link layers*.

To understand the protocol stack, the next sections begin by looking at the network layer and moving up.

Figure 6-1 *TCP/IP Protocol Stack*

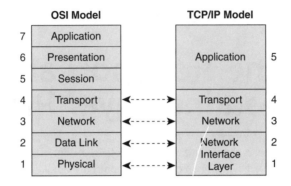

IP Internet Layer Overview

The Internet layer of the TCP/IP protocol stack is the part of the protocol that provides addressing and path selection. This is the layer that routers operate at to identify paths in the network, but many other functions are at this layer.

Several protocols operate at the IP Internet layer, which corresponds to the OSI network layer. The following list contains some of the protocols discussed in this book:

- **Internet Protocol (IP)**—Provides connectionless, best-effort delivery routing of datagrams. IP is not concerned with the content of the datagrams. Instead, it looks for a way to move the datagrams to their destination.

- **Internet Control Message Protocol (ICMP)**—Provides control and messaging capabilities.

- **Address Resolution Protocol (ARP)**—Determines the data link layer address of the destination device for known destination IP addresses.

- **Reverse Address Resolution Protocol (RARP)**—Determines source network addresses when source data link layer addresses are known.

- **Dynamic Host Configuration Protocol (DHCP)**—Provides a framework for automatic address configuration of IP hosts.

IP

IP uses packets to carry information through the network. A packet is a self-contained, independent entity of data carrying sufficient information to be routed from the source to the destination without reliance on earlier exchanges. The protocol is connectionless and unreliable.

IP is characterized as follows:

- IP packets are treated independently, with each packet carrying the addresses of the receiver and the sender.

- The IP service does not guarantee packet delivery. A packet can be misdirected, duplicated, or lost on the way to its destination.

- The IP protocol does not provide any special features that recover lost or corrupted packets. These services are instead provided by the end systems.

An analogy of IP protocol services would be mail delivery by the postal service. For example, a person lives in Lexington, Kentucky, and a friend lives in New York City. That person writes three separate letters to the friend in New York. Each letter is sealed in a separate envelope, is addressed to the friend, and has a return address in the upper-left corner of the envelope.

The three letters are placed in the out-of-town mail slot at the local post office. The postal service makes the best attempt to delivery the three letters to the friend in New York. However, the postal service does not guarantee that the letters will arrive at their destination. The postal service does not guarantee that all three letters will be handled by the same carrier or take the same route. Finally, the postal service does not guarantee that the letters will arrive in the order in which you mailed them.

This example is similar to the way the IP protocol works. IP transfers information through the network in the form of a packet. The Internet Protocol defines the packet format. The first 20 or 24 bytes of the packet are control information called the *header*.

Like the information on an envelope, the IP protocol header includes information about where the packet is going (a destination address) and where it is coming from (a source address). This information is placed in fields in the IP header, as shown in Figure 6-2.

By default, the header is five words long; the sixth word is optional. The length of the header is variable, so the header includes a field called *IP header length (IHL)* that indicates the length of the header in words.

The header contains all the information necessary to deliver the *packet* of information. Table 6-1 documents the field definitions within the IP header illustrated in Figure 6-2.

Figure 6-2   *IP Header*

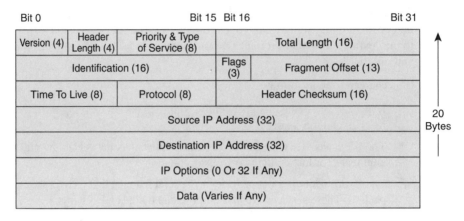

Table 6-1   *IP Header Field Descriptions*

IP Header Field	Description	Number of Bits
Version	Version number.	4 bits
Header Length	Header length in 32-bit words.	4 bits
Priority (Differential Services) or Type of Service	How the datagram should be handled. The first 3 bits are priority bits.	8 bits
Total Length	Total length (header plus data).	16 bits
Identification	Unique IP datagram value.	16 bits
Flags	Specifies whether fragmenting should occur.	3 bits
Fragment Offset	Provides fragmentation of datagrams to allow differing MTUs in the Internet.	13 bits
TTL	Time-To-Live.	8 bits
Protocol	Upper-layer (Layer 4) protocol sending the datagram.	8 bits

Table 6-1   *IP Header Field Descriptions (Continued)*

IP Header Field	Description	Number of Bits
Header Checksum	Integrity check on the header.	16 bits
Source IP Address	32-bit source IP addresses.	32 bits
Destination IP Addresses	32-bit destination IP addresses.	32 bits
IP Options	Network testing, debugging, security, and others.	0 or 32 bits, if any
Data	Upper-layer protocol data.	Varies

Figure 6-3 shows a data capture of an Ethernet frame with the IP header field expanded.

Figure 6-3   *IP Header*

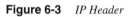

As shown in Figure 6-4, the Protocol field determines the Layer 4 protocol being carried within an IP datagram. Although most IP traffic uses TCP or User Datagram Protocol (UDP), other protocols can use IP, such as Open Shortest Path First (OSPF), generic routing encapsulation (GRE), and Enhanced Interior Gateway Routing Protocol (EIGRP).

Figure 6-4   *Protocol Field*

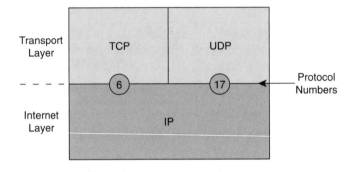

Each IP header must identify the destination Layer 4 protocol for the datagram. Transport layer protocols are numbered, similar to port numbers. IP includes the protocol number in the Protocol field. Table 6-2 lists some sample protocol numbers for the transport layer protocols.

Table 6-2   *Protocol Numbers*

Protocol	Protocol Field
Internet Control Message Protocol (ICMP)	1
Transmission Control Protocol (TCP)	6
User Datagram Protocol (UDP)	17
IP version 6 (IPv6)	41
Generic routing encapsulation (GRE)	47
ICMP for IPv6	58
Enhanced Interior Gateway Routing Protocol (EIGRP)	88

Many other Layer 4 protocols exist. The protocols presented here are not an exhaustive list. Refer to www.iana.org for a more complete list of all Protocol field numbers.

The router reads the protocol number from the header of the datagram, compares it to the entries in the transport protocol table, and then passes it to the appropriate protocol. For example, if the protocol number is 6, IP delivers the datagram to TCP. If the protocol is 17, the datagram is delivered to UDP.

Although most application traffic uses TCP or UDP, other protocols can use IP. Approximately 100 transport layer protocols are registered for other special purposes. The numbers used by TCP/IP protocols are assigned and published by a group called the Internet Assigned Numbers Authority (IANA).

Many of the protocols and applications that are implemented in TCP/IP are administrative or control protocols like ICMP or DHCP. These protocols provide basic services like addressing and messaging.

Internet Control Message Protocol

The Internet Control Message Protocol (ICMP) is implemented by all TCP/IP hosts. ICMP messages are carried in IP datagrams with a protocol type of 1 and send error and control messages.

ICMP defines a small number of messages used for diagnostic and management purposes. ICMP depends on IP to move packets around the network. These are some of the functions of ICMP:

- **Announces network errors**—ICMP announces errors such as a host or entire portion of the network being unreachable, because of some type of failure. A TCP or UDP packet directed at a port number with no receiver attached is also reported by ICMP.

- **Announces network congestion**—When a device cannot transmit packets as fast as the router receives them, the router generates ICMP Source Quench messages. Directed at the sender, these messages slow the rate of packet transmission to be slowed.

- **Assists troubleshooting**—ICMP supports an echo function, which just sends a packet on a round trip between two hosts. Ping, a common IP network management application based on this feature, transmits a series of packets, measuring average round-trip times and computing loss percentages.

- **Announces timeouts**—A router discards a packet if it has been in the network for too long a period of time. The router generates an ICMP packet announcing this fact. Traceroute is a tool that maps network routes by sending packets with small Time-To-Live values and watching the ICMP timeout announcements.

ICMP uses the following types of defined messages to provide these functions. Other types of defined messages exist that are not included in this list:

- Destination Unreachable
- Time Exceeded
- Parameter Problem
- Subnet Mask Request
- Redirect

- Echo (ping request)
- Echo Reply (ping reply)
- Timestamp
- Timestamp Reply
- Information Request
- Information Reply

The most common form of these messages are pings, ICMP echo requests, and ICMP echo replies. This testing function is not the only purpose of ICMP; it has many other functions, as well.

NOTE   The term ping describes an application that uses echo requests and echo replies to verify reachability between devices in an IP network. The word used to describe this application comes from the concept of sonar, which initially uses a unique tone (which audibly sounded like a ping) to locate objects underwater.

ICMP packet delivery is unreliable, however, so hosts cannot depend on receiving ICMP packets for any network problem.

Address Resolution Protocol

Another IP protocol is the Address Resolution Protocol (ARP). The term *address resolution* refers to the process of binding a network layer IP address of a peer computer in an Ethernet-connected network to its data link layer MAC address. The address is "resolved" using a protocol in which the known information (the destination IP address) is broadcast by the originating ARP process executing on the local computer to a target ARP process executing on the remote computer. Every station on the segment receives the broadcast.

The target recognizes itself by reading the broadcast packet and provides the required MAC address in its reply. The address resolution procedure is completed when the originator receives a response from the target containing the required MAC address and updates the table containing all the known bindings, usually called the ARP cache. This table maintains a correlation between each IP address and its corresponding MAC address. Figure 6-5 illustrates how ARP maps IP addresses to MAC sublayer addresses.

The term local ARP describes resolving an address when both the requesting host and the destination host share the same medium or wire, which is the case in Figure 6-5.

Figure 6-5   *ARP*

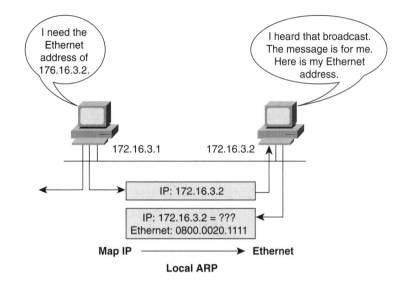

Two types of ARP messages can be sent by the ARP protocol:

- ARP request
- ARP reply

Before a device can communicate with any other device on an IP network, it must first perform the ARP so that it knows where to send the frames. Figure 6-6 and Figure 6-7 show a data capture of an ARP request and ARP reply.

Figure 6-6   *ARP Request*

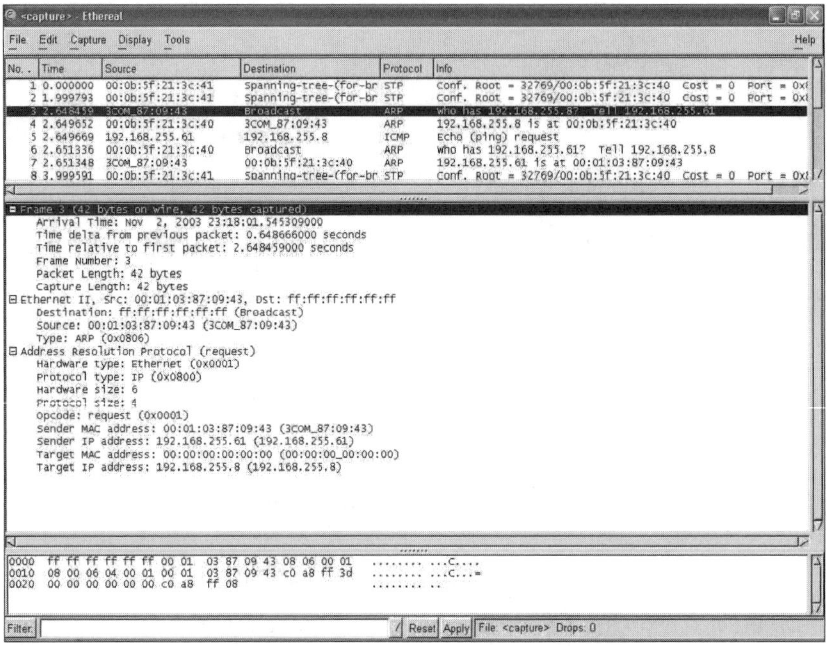

Figure 6-7   *ARP Reply*

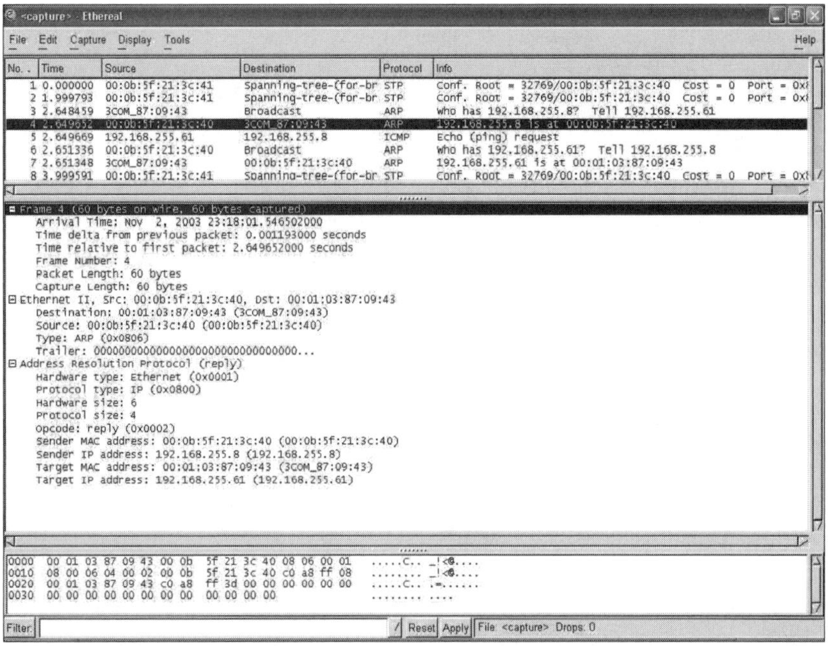

Reverse Address Resolution Protocol

Reverse Address Resolution Protocol (RARP) is another protocol defined at the IP layer. RARP is used for workstations that do not know their own IP address when they come up. RARP allows a station to send out a request for its own IP address by sending its own Layer 2 MAC address to a waiting RARP server. The RARP request is a broadcast packet. RARP relies on the presence of a RARP server with a table entry or other means on each subnet to respond to these requests. Figure 6-8 illustrates how RARP works so that workstations can identify their own IP addresses.

Figure 6-8   *RARP*

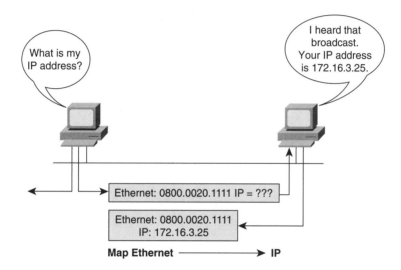

ARP and RARP are implemented directly on top of the data link layer.

NOTE   Because RARP has no port or addressing scheme at Layer 3, it requires a RARP server on each subnet. Dynamic Host Configuration Protocol (DHCP) is a modern implementation of RARP that can use a single server for all subnets.

Dynamic Host Configuration Protocol

Dynamic Host Configuration Protocol (DHCP) is an Internet protocol for automating the address configuration of computers that use TCP/IP. This protocol automatically assigns IP addresses to deliver TCP/IP stack configuration parameters, such as the subnet mask and default router, and to provide other configuration information, such as the addresses for printer, time, and news servers. DHCP consists of two components:

- A protocol for delivering host-specific configuration parameters from a DHCP server to a host
- A mechanism for allocation of network addresses to hosts

Using DHCP, a host can obtain an IP address quickly and dynamically. All that is required is a defined range of IP addresses on a DHCP server. As hosts come online, they contact the DHCP server and request an address. The DHCP server chooses an address and allocates it to that host. With DHCP, both the IP address and subnet mask of a computer can be obtained in one message. Figure 6-9 shows how the DHCP process works.

Figure 6-9   *DHCP*

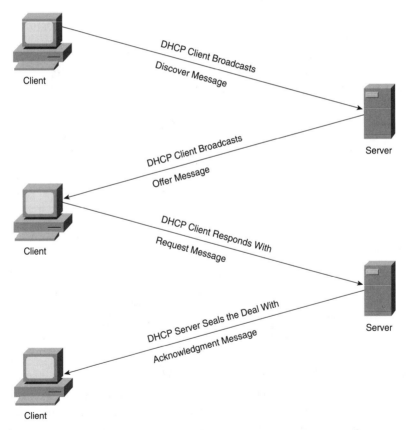

The network layer of the TCP/IP protocol stack provides the key functions for communications between devices. It also provides administrative protocols to help improve services.

IP Internet Layer Overview Section Quiz

Use these practice questions to review what you learned in this section.

1 Which of the following protocols operates at the TCP/IP network layer? (Choose two.)

A FTP

B ARP

C TFTP

D ICMP

E SMTP

2 Which statements best describe a function of IP? (Choose three.)

A Operates at the transport layer

B Is an unreliable, best-effort delivery method

C Uses datagrams to carry information through the network

D Addresses each packet with the source and destination address

E Uses a checksum technique to verify that packets are not corrupted

3 Which statements best describe a function of ICMP? (Choose three.)

A Resends unacknowledged packets

B Numbers packets for reordering at the destination

C Announces when a device is unreachable on the network

D Provides bidirectional binary file and ASCII file transfer support

E Generates messages to slow down network traffic from the source

F Uses the echo function to send a packet on a round trip between two devices

G Uses failed acknowledgments to alert the sender to slow down packet transmission

4 Which statement best describes a function of ARP?

  A Maintains an error resource table

  B Maps an IP address to a MAC address

  C Maps a given MAC address to an IP address

  D Dynamically assigns addresses across the network

  E Sends a broadcast message looking for the router address

5 Which statement best describes a function of RARP?

  A Maintains an error resource table

  B Maps an IP address to a MAC address

  C Maps a given MAC address to an IP address

  D Dynamically assigns addresses across the network

  E Sends a broadcast message looking for the router address

6 Which statement best describes a function of DHCP?

  A Maintains an error resource table

  B Maps an IP address to a MAC address

  C Maps a given MAC address to an IP address

  D Dynamically assigns addresses across the network

  E Sends a broadcast message looking for the router address

7 Which of the following are fields in the IP datagram? (Choose three.)

  A Window

  B Code bits

  C Total length

  D Time-To-Live

  E Sequence number

  F Source IP address

  G Acknowledgment number

8 Which statement best describes the function of a Protocol field in an IP diagram?

    A Identifies a link-layer protocol

    B Identifies a session layer protocol

    C Identifies a transport layer protocol

    D Identifies an application layer protocol

    E Identifies a network access layer protocol

The Transport Layer

Residing between the application and network layers, the transport layer, Layer 4, is in the core of the TCP/IP layered network architecture. The transport layer has the critical role of providing communication services directly to the application processes running on different hosts. Learning how the transport layer functions provides an understanding of how data is transmitted in a TCP/IP networking environment.

The transport layer protocol places a header on data that is received from the application layer. The purpose of this protocol is to identify the application from which the data was received and create segments to be passed down to the internetwork layer. Some transport layer protocols also perform two additional functions: flow control provided by sliding windows and reliability provided by sequence numbers and acknowledgments. Flow control is a mechanism that allows the communicating hosts to negotiate how much data is transmitted each time. Reliability provides a mechanism for guaranteeing the delivery of each packet.

Two protocols are provided at the transport layer:

- **Transmission Control Protocol (TCP)** — A connection-oriented, reliable protocol. In a connection-oriented environment, a connection is established between both ends before transfer of information can begin. TCP is responsible for breaking messages into segments, reassembling them at the destination station, resending anything that is not received, and reassembling messages from the segments. TCP supplies a virtual circuit between end user applications.

- **User Datagram Protocol (UDP)** — A connectionless and unacknowledged protocol. Although UDP is responsible for transmitting messages, no checking for segment delivery is provided at this layer. UDP depends on upper-layer protocols for reliability.

When devices communicate with one another, they exchange a series of messages. To understand and act on these messages, devices must agree on the format and the order of the messages exchanged, as well as the actions taken on the transmission or receipt of a message.

An example of a how a protocol can be used to provide this functionality is a conversation exchange between a student and a teacher in a classroom:

1 The teacher is lecturing on a particular subject. The teacher stops to ask, "Are there any questions?" This question is a broadcast message to all students.

2 You raise your hand. This action is an implicit message back to the teacher.

3 The teacher responds with "Yes, what is your question?" Here, the teacher has acknowledged your message and signals you to send your next message.

4 You ask your question. You transmit your message to the teacher.

5 The teacher hears your question and answers it. The teacher receives your message and transmits a reply back to you.

6 You nod to the teacher that you understand the answer. You acknowledge receipt of the message from the teacher.

7 The teacher asks if everything is all clear.

The transmission and receipt of messages, and a set of conventional actions taken when sending and receiving these messages, are at the heart of this question-and-answer protocol.

TCP provides transparent transfer of data between end systems using the services of the network layer below to move packets between the two communicating systems. TCP is a transport layer protocol. IP is a network layer protocol.

Similar to the OSI reference model, TCP/IP separates a full network protocol suite into a number of tasks. Each layer corresponds to a different facet of communication. Conceptually, it is useful to envision TCP/IP as a protocol stack.

The services provided by TCP run in the host computers at either end of a connection, not in the network. Therefore, TCP is a protocol for managing end-to-end connections. Because end-to-end connections can exist across a series of point-to-point connections, these end-to-end connections are called *virtual circuits*. These are the characteristics of TCP:

- **Connection-oriented**—Two computers set up a connection to exchange data. The end systems synchronize with one another to manage packet flows and adapt to congestion in the network.

- **Full-duplex operation**—A TCP connection is a pair of virtual circuits, one in each direction. Only the two synchronized end systems can use the connection.

- **Error checking**—A checksum technique verifies that packets are not corrupted.

- **Sequencing**—Packets are numbered so that the destination can reorder packets and determine if a packet is missing.

- **Acknowledgments**—Upon receipt of one or more packets, the receiver returns an acknowledgment to the sender indicating that it received the packets. If packets are not acknowledged, the sender can retransmit the packets or terminate the connection if the sender thinks the receiver is no longer on the connection.

- **Flow control**—If the sender is overflowing the buffer of the receiver by transmitting too quickly, the receiver drops packets. Failed acknowledgments alert the sender to slow down or stop sending. The receive can also lower the window size to slow the sender down.

- **Packet recovery services**—The receiver can request retransmission of a packet. If packet receipt is not acknowledged, the sender resends the packets.

TCP is a reliable transport layer protocol. Reliable data delivery services are critical for applications such as file transfers, database services, transaction processing, and other mission-critical applications in which delivery of every packet must be guaranteed.

An analogy of the TCP protocol services would be sending certified mail through the postal service. For example, someone who lives in Lexington, Kentucky, wants to send this book to a friend in New York City, but for some reason, the postal service only handles letters. The sender could rip the pages out and put each one in a separate envelope. To ensure the receiver reassembles the book correctly, the sender numbers each envelope. Then, the sender addresses the envelopes and sends the first envelope certified mail. The postal service delivers the first envelope by any truck and any route. Upon delivery of that envelope, the carrier must get a signature from the receiver and return that certificate of delivery to the sender.

The sender mails several envelopes on the same day. The postal service again delivers each envelope by any truck using any route. The sender returns to the post office each day sending several envelopes each requiring a return receipt. The receiver signs a separate receipt for each envelope in the batch as they are received. If one envelope is lost in transit, the sender would not receive a certificate of delivery for that numbered envelope. The sender might have already sent the pages that follow the missing one, but would still be able to resend the missing page. After receiving all the envelopes, the receiver puts the pages in the right order and pastes them back together to make the book. TCP provides these levels of services.

UDP is another transport layer protocol that was added to the TCP/IP protocol suite which. This transport layer protocol uses a smaller header and does not provide the reliability available with TCP.

The early IP suite consisted only of TCP and IP, although IP was not differentiated as a separate service. However, some end user applications needed timeliness rather than accuracy. In other words, speed was more important than packet recovery. In real-time voice or video transfers, a few lost packets are tolerable. Recovering packets creates excessive overhead that reduces performance.

To accommodate this type of traffic, TCP architects redesigned the protocol suite to include the UDP. The basic addressing and packet-forwarding service in the network layer was IP. TCP and UDP are in the transport layer on top of IP, and both use IP services.

UDP offers only minimal, non-guaranteed transport services and gives applications direct access to the IP layer. UDP is used by applications that do not require the level of service of TCP or that want to use communications services such as multicast or broadcast delivery, not available from TCP.

An analogy of the UDP protocol services would be using the postal service to send fliers notifying all of your neighbors of your garage sale. In this example, you make a flier advertising the day, time, and location of your garage sale. You address each flier with the specific name and address of each neighbor within a 2-mile radius of your house. The postal service delivers each flier by any truck and any route. However, it is not important if a flier is lost in transit or if a neighbor acknowledges receipt of the flier.

TCP/IP Applications

In addition to including the IP, TCP, and UDP protocols, the TCP/IP protocol suite also includes applications that support other services such as file transfer, e-mail, and remote login. This topic describes three of the TCP/IP applications.

Some of the applications that TCP/IP supports include the following:

- **File Transfer Protocol (FTP)**—FTP is a reliable, connection-oriented service that uses TCP to transfer files between systems that support FTP. FTP supports bidirectional binary and ASCII file transfers.

- **Trivial File Transfer Protocol (TFTP)**—TFTP is an application that uses UDP. Routers use TFTP to transfer configuration files and Cisco IOS images and to transfer files between systems that support TFTP.

- **Terminal Emulation (Telnet)**—Telnet provides the capability to remotely access another computer. Telnet enables a user to log on to a remote host and execute commands.

- **E-mail (SMTP)**—Simple Mail Transfer Protocol allows users to send and receive messages to e-mail applications throughout the internetwork.

Transport Layer Functionality

The transport layer hides details of any network-dependent information from the higher layers by providing transparent data transfer. Learning how the TCP/IP transport layer and the TCP and UDP protocols function provides a more complete understanding of how data is transmitted with these protocols in a TCP/IP networking environment.

Transport services allow users to segment and reassemble several upper-layer applications onto the same transport layer data stream. This transport layer data stream provides end-to-end transport services. The transport layer data stream constitutes a logical connection between the endpoints of the internetwork—the originating or sending host and the destination or receiving host.

A user of a reliable transport-layer service must establish a connection-oriented session with its peer system. For reliable data transfer to begin, both the sending and the receiving applications inform their respective operating systems that a connection is to be initiated, as shown in Figure 6-10.

Figure 6-10   *Network Connection*

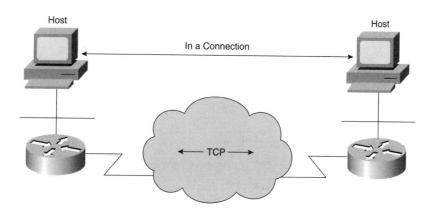

One machine initiates a connection that must be accepted by the other. Protocol software modules in the two operating systems communicate by sending messages across the network to verify that the transfer is authorized and that both sides are ready.

After successful synchronization has occurred, the two end systems have established a connection and data transfer can begin. During transfer, the two machines continue to verify that the connection is still valid.

You might recall from Chapter 1, "Introduction to Internetworking," that *encapsulation* is the process by which data is prepared for transmission in a TCP/IP network environment. This section describes the encapsulation of data in the TCP/IP stack.

The data container looks different at each layer, and at each layer the container goes by a different name, as shown in Figure 6-11.

Figure 6-11 *Names for Encapsulated Data by Layer*

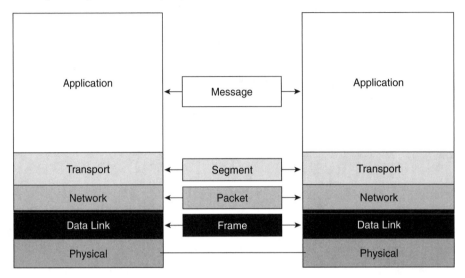

The names for the data containers created at each layer are as follows:

- **Message**—The data container created at the application layer is called a message.

- **Segment or packet**—The data container created at the transport layer, which encapsulates the application layer message, is called a segment if it comes from the transport layer's TCP protocol. If the data container comes from the transport layer's UDP protocol, it is called a datagram.

- **Datagram**—The data container at the network layer, which encapsulates the transport layer segment, is called a packet.

- **Frame**—The data container at the data link layer, which encapsulates the packet, is called a frame. This frame is then turned into a bit stream at the physical layer.

A segment or packet is the unit of end-to-end transmission containing a transport header and the data from the above protocols. In general, discussion about transmitting information from one node to another, the term *packet* is used loosely to refer to a piece of data. However, this book consistently refers to data formed in the transport layer as a *segment*, data at the network layer as a *datagram*, and data at the link layer as a *frame*.

To provide communications between the segments, each protocol uses a particular header, as discussed in the next section.

TCP/UDP Header Format

TCP is known as a connection-oriented protocol. This is because the end stations are aware of each other and are constantly communicating about the connection. A classic non-technical example of connection-oriented communication would be a telephone conversation between two people. First, a protocol lets the participants know that they have connected and can begin communicating. This protocol is analogous to an initial conversation of "Hello."

UDP is known as a connectionless protocol. An example of a connectionless conversation is the normal delivery of U.S. postal service. You place the letter in the mail and hope that it gets delivered. Figure 6-12 illustrates the TCP segment header format, the field definitions of which are described in Table 6-3. These fields provide the communication between end stations to control the conversation.

Figure 6-12   *TCP Header Format*

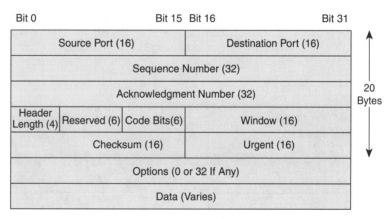

Table 6-3   *TCP Header Field Descriptions*

TCP Header Field	Description	Number of Bits
Source Port	Number of the calling port	16 bits
Destination Port	Number of the called port	16 bits
Sequence Number	Number used to ensure correct sequencing of the arriving data	32 bits
Acknowledgment Number	Next expected TCP octet	32 bits
Header Length	Number of 32-bit words in the header	4 bits

continues

Table 6-3   *TCP Header Field Descriptions (Continued)*

TCP Header Field	Description	Number of Bits
Reserved	Set to zero	6 bits
Code Bits	Control functions such as setup and termination of a session	6 bits
Window	Number of octets that the device is willing to accept	16 bits
Checksum	Calculated checksum of the header and data fields	16 bits
Urgent	Indicates the end of the urgent data	16 bits
Options	One currently defined: maximum TCP segment size	0 or 32 bits, if any
Data	Upper-layer protocol data	Varies

Figure 6-13 shows a data capture of an Ethernet frame with the TCP header field expanded.

Figure 6-13   *TCP Header*

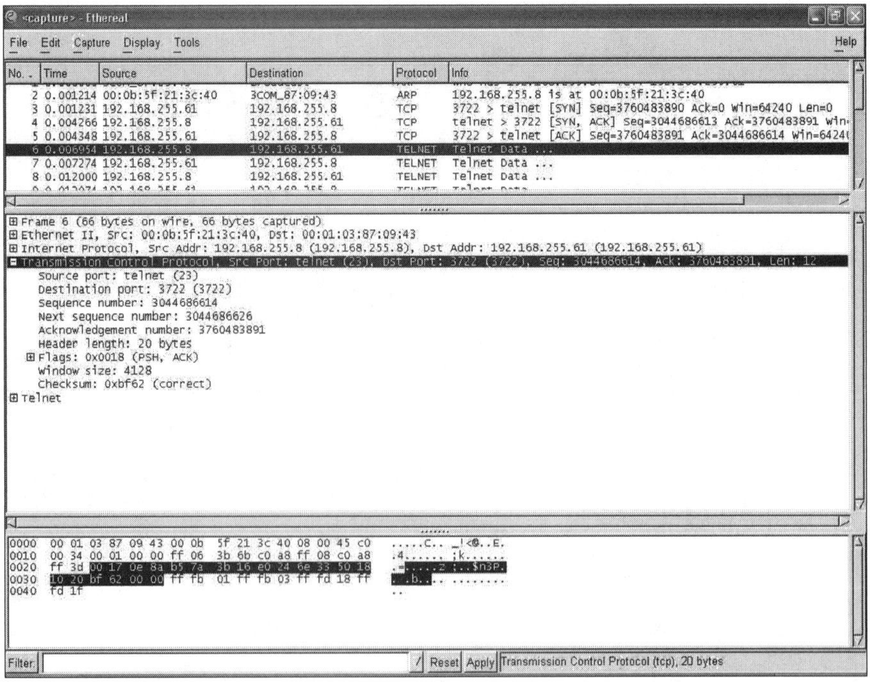

The TCP header is 20 bytes. Transporting multiple packets with small data fields results in less efficient use of available bandwidth than transporting the same amount of data with fewer, larger packets. This situation is like placing several small objects into several boxes, which could hold more than one object, and shipping each box individually instead of filling one box completely with all of the objects and sending only that box to deliver all the objects.

Figure 6-14 illustrates the UDP segment header format, the field definitions for which are described in Table 6-4. The UDP header length is always 64 bits.

Figure 6-14   *UDP Header*

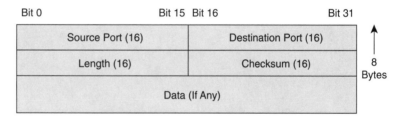

No Sequence Or Acknowledgment Fields

Table 6-4   *UDP Header Field Descriptions*

UDP Header Field	Description	Number of Bits
Source Port	Number of the calling port	16 bits
Destination Port	Number of the called port	16 bits
Length	Length of UDP header and UDP data	16 bits
Checksum	Calculated checksum of the header and data fields	16 bits
Data	Upper-layer protocol data	Varies

Figure 6-15 shows a data capture of an Ethernet frame with the UDP header field expanded.

Protocols that use UDP include TFTP, SNMP, Network File System (NFS), and Domain Name System (DNS).

Figure 6-15 *UDP Header*

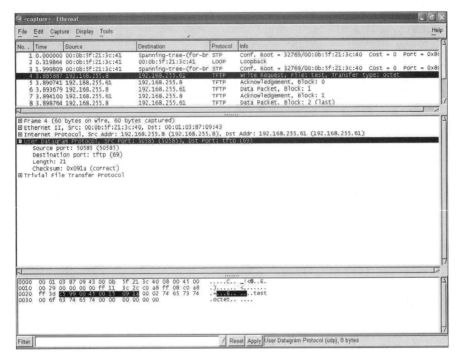

How TCP and UDP Use Port Numbers

Both TCP and UDP use port numbers to pass information to the upper layers. Port numbers keep track of different conversations crossing the network at the same time. Figure 6-16 defines some of the port numbers as used by TCP and UDP.

Figure 6-16 *Port Numbers*

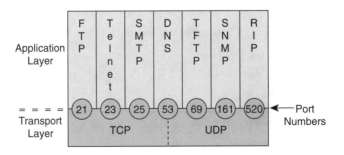

Application software developers agree to use well-known port numbers that are controlled by the IANA. For example, any conversation bound for the FTP application uses the standard port number 21. Conversations that do not involve an application with a well-known port number are assigned port numbers randomly chosen from within a specific range instead. These port numbers are used as source and destination addresses in the TCP segment.

Some ports are reserved in both TCP and UDP, but applications might not be written to support them. Port numbers have the following assigned ranges:

- Numbers below 1024 are considered well-known or assigned ports.

- Numbers above 1024 are dynamically assigned ports.

- Registered ports are those registered for vendor-specific applications. Most are above 1024.

NOTE   Some applications, such as DNS, use both transport layer protocols. DNS uses UDP for name resolution and TCP for server zone transfers.

Figure 6-17 shows how well-known port numbers are used by hosts to connect to the application on the end station. The figure also illustrates the selection of a source port so that the end station knows how to communicate with the client application.

Figure 6-17   *Port Number Example*

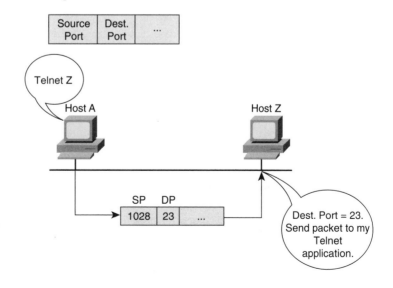

RFC 1700, "Assigned Numbers," defines all the well-known port numbers for TCP/IP. For a listing of current port numbers, refer to the IANA website at www.iana.org.

End systems use port numbers to select the proper application. Originating source port numbers are dynamically assigned by the source host—some number greater than 1023.

Establishing a TCP Connection: The Three-Way Handshake

TCP is connection-oriented, so it requires connection establishment before data transfer begins. For a connection to be established or initialized, the two hosts must synchronize on each other's initial sequence numbers (ISNs). Synchronization is done in an exchange of connection-establishing segments carrying a control bit called SYN (for synchronize) and the initial sequence numbers. As shorthand, segments carrying the SYN bit are also called "SYNs." Hence, the solution requires a suitable mechanism for picking an initial sequence number and a slightly involved handshake to exchange the ISNs.

The synchronization requires each side to send its own initial sequence number and to receive a confirmation of its successful transmission within the acknowledgment (ACK) from the other side. Here is the sequence of events:

1   **Host A→Host B SYN**—My sequence number is 100, ACK number is 0, and ACK bit is not set. SYN bit is set.

2   **Host A→Host B ACK**—I expect to see 101 next, my sequence number is 300, and ACK bit is set. Host B to Host A SYN bit is set.

3   **Host A→Host B ACK**—I expect to see 301 next, my sequence number is 101, and ACK bit is set. SYN bit is set.

NOTE   The initial sequence numbers are actually large random numbers chosen by each host.

This exchange is called the three-way handshake and is illustrated in Figure 6-18.

Figure 6-19 shows a data capture of the three-way handshake. Notice the sequence numbers in the three frames.

A three-way handshake is necessary because sequence numbers are not tied to a global clock in the network, and TCPs might have different mechanisms for picking the initial sequence number. Because the receiver of the first SYN has no way of knowing whether the segment was an old delayed one, unless it remembers the last sequence number used on the connection (which is not always possible), it must ask the sender to verify this SYN. Figure 6-20 illustrates the acknowledgment process.

Figure 6-18   *Three-Way Handshake*

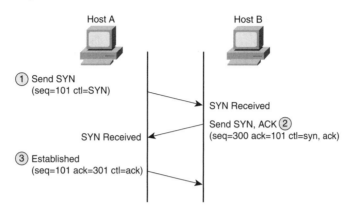

Figure 6-19   *Capture of Three-Way Handshake*

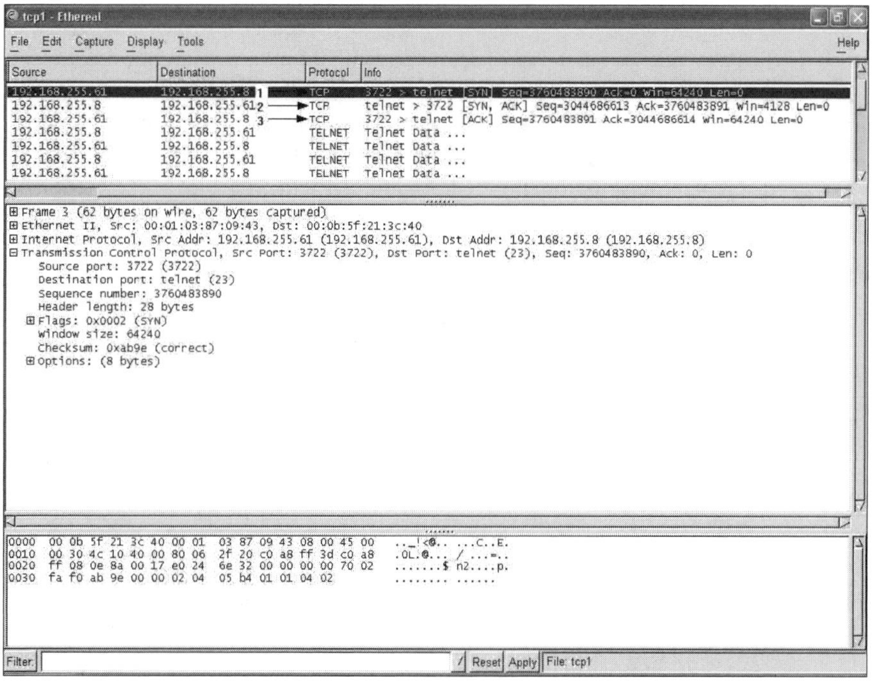

Figure 6-20 *Simple Acknowledgment*

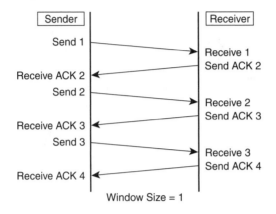

Window Size = 1

The window size determines how much data, in bytes, the receiving station accepts at one time before an acknowledgment is returned. With a window size of 1 byte (as shown in Figure 6-20), each segment must be acknowledged before another segment is transmitted. This results in inefficient use of bandwidth by the hosts.

TCP provides sequencing of segments with a forward reference acknowledgment. Each datagram is numbered before transmission. At the receiving station, TCP reassembles the segments into a complete message. If a sequence number is missing in the series, that segment is retransmitted. Segments that are not acknowledged within a given time period result in retransmission. Figure 6-21 illustrates the role that acknowledgment numbers play when datagrams are transmitted.

Figure 6-21 *Acknowledgment Numbers*

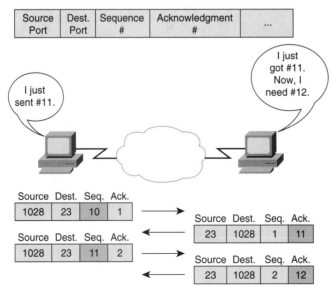

Flow Control for TCP/UDP

To govern the flow of data between devices, TCP uses a flow control mechanism. The receiving TCP reports a "window" to the sending TCP. This window specifies the number of bytes, starting with the acknowledgment number, that the receiving TCP is currently prepared to receive.

TCP window sizes are variable during the lifetime of a connection. Each acknowledgment contains a window advertisement that indicates how many bytes the receiver can accept. TCP also maintains a congestion control window that is normally the same size as the receiver's window but is cut in half when a segment is lost (for example, when you have congestion). This approach permits the window to be expanded or contracted as necessary to manage buffer space and processing. A larger window size allows more data to be processed.

NOTE   TCP window size is documented in RFC 793, "Transmission Control Protocol," and RFC 813, "Window and Acknowledgment Strategy in TCP," which you can find at http://www.ietf.org/rfc.html.

In Figure 6-22, the sender sends three 1-byte packets before expecting an ACK. The receiver can handle a window size of only 2 bytes (because of available memory). So, it drops packet 3, specifies 3 as the next byte to be received, and specifies a window size of 2. The sender resends packet 2 and also sends the next 1-byte packet, but still specifies its window size of 3. (For example, it can still accept three 1-byte packets.) The receiver acknowledges bytes 3 and 4 by requesting byte 5 and continuing to specify a window size of 2 bytes.

Figure 6-22   *TCP Windowing*

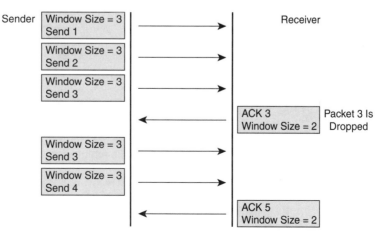

Many of the functions described in these sections, such as windowing and sequencing, have no meaning in UDP. Recall from Figure 6-14 that UDP has no fields for sequence numbers or window sizes. Application layer protocols can provide for reliability. UDP is designed for applications that provide their own error recovery process. It trades reliability for speed.

The TCP, UDP, and IP protocols and their headers are key in the communications between networks. Layer 3 devices use an internetwork protocol like TCP/IP to provide communications between remote systems.

Transport Layer Section Quiz

Use these practice questions to review what you learned in this section.

1 Which statement best describes a network protocol?

   A A tool that lets Macintosh and PC computers communicate with each other

   B A universal translator that allows different kinds of computers to share data

   C A language that all the computers on a network must use to communicate with each other

   D A standard set of rules and conventions that determine how computers communicate with each other across networks

2 Which statement best describes the TCP/IP protocol stack?

   A A suite of protocols that allows LANs to connect into WANs

   B A suite of protocols that allows for data transmission across a multitude of networks

   C A suite of protocols that defines rules for how packets of information are moved across a network

   D A suite of protocols that allows different devices to be shared by interconnected networks

3 Which statements best describe characteristics of TCP? (Choose four.)

   A TCP is a transport layer protocol.

   B TCP provides e-mail support between remote hosts.

   C Speed is more important than packet recovery.

   D TCP numbers segments so that the destination can reorder received segments.

E A checksum technique verifies that data is not corrupted.

F TCP gives applications direct access to the datagram service of the IP layer.

G TCP provides a synchronization method between end systems to manage flows and adapt to congestion in the network.

4 Which descriptions best define the differences between TCP and UDP? (Choose two.)

A TCP offers a minimal, non-guaranteed transport service.

B UDP offers accuracy rather than timeliness in packet delivery.

C TCP uses frames to carry information through the network.

D TCP uses failed acknowledgments to alert the sender of lost segments.

E UDP offers applications direct access to the datagram service of the IP layer.

F UDP uses ping to transmit packets to measure average round-trip time between devices.

5 Which applications are members of the TCP/IP protocol stack? (Choose two.)

A IP

B FTP

C ICMP

D RFTP

E TFTP

6 Place the steps for establishing a connection with a peer system in the correct order.

_____ 1. After all synchronization has occurred, a connection is established.

_____ 2. One machine initiates a connection that is accepted by the other.

_____ 3. The sending application informs the operating system that a connection is to be initiated.

_____ 4. Protocol software modules in the two operating systems communicate by sending messages across the network.

7 Which names correctly identify the encapsulation term at the transport layer? (Choose two.)

A Frame

B Packet

C Segment

D Message

E Datagram

F Bit stream

8 Which terms identify a component of the TCP header? (Choose three.)

A Priority

B Time-To-Live

C Window

D Checksum

E Identification

F Type of service

G Sequence number

9 Which terms identify a component of the UDP header? (Choose two.)

A Priority

B Length

C Window

D Checksum

E Identification

F Type of service

G Sequence number

10 Which statement best describes window size?

A   The pixel size of the monitor that must be set ahead of time so data can be viewed

B   The maximum size of the window that a software program can have and still process data rapidly

C   The size of the window opening on a monitor that is not always equal to the monitor size

D   The number of octets that can be transmitted while awaiting an acknowledgment

11 Select the statement that correctly orders the steps to establish a TCP connection.

A   SYN=0, SYN=0 ACK=1; SYN=0 ACK=1

B   SYN=1, SYN=1 ACK=0; SYN=1 ACK=0

C   SYN=1, SYN=1 ACK=1, SYN=0 ACK=1

D   SYN=0, SYN=1 ACK=1; SYN=0 ACK=1

E   SYN=1, SYN=1 ACK=0; SYN=1 ACK=1

12 Which statement best describes positive acknowledgment?

A   Positive acknowledgment is the retransmission of guaranteed and reliable data.

B   Positive acknowledgment requires a recipient to send back an acknowledgment message when the recipient receives data.

C   Positive acknowledgment ensures that if a sender does not receive a negative acknowledgment within a certain time, the sender retransmits the data.

D   Positive acknowledge guarantees that if a recipient does not receive segments, a positive acknowledgment is sent to the sender indicating the numbers of the missing segments.

13 Which statements correctly identify a characteristic of a port? (Choose two.)

A   Port numbers identify the upper-layer protocol.

B   Registered ports are assigned numbers below 1024.

C   Well-known ports are assigned numbers below 1024.

D   Well-known ports are assigned numbers above 1024.

E   Port numbers below 1024 are dynamically assigned.

Chapter Summary

This chapter introduced you to the common Layer 3 protocol TCP/IP. It introduced you to the concept of using addressing for delivery of information and showed how network services can be provided by this protocol. This chapter also defined transport layer protocols, which provide reliable and unreliable services for network traffic. This chapter discussed in detail the headers used in the provisioning of these services and how a connection-oriented protocol used handshakes and windowing to provide guaranteed delivery of packets.

Chapter Review Questions

Use these review questions to test your knowledge of the concepts discussed in this chapter.

1 Which protocols reside at the network layer? (Choose two.)

   A IP

   B NFS

   C TCP

   D ARP

   E ICMP

   F DCHP

2 Which functions are true about IP? (Choose three.)

   A Routes datagrams

   B Forwards packets

   C Guarantees delivery

   D Provides best-effort delivery

   E Acknowledges receipt

3 Which statement best describes a function of the IP protocol?

   A It adjusts its operation to maximize throughput.

   B It manages data buffers and coordinates traffic.

   C It fragments and reassembles packets transparently.

   D It automates the configuration of computers that use TCP.

   E It sequences packets to coordinate which data has been transmitted and received.

4 Identify the primary function of the ICMP protocol.

   A Edits IP packets

   B Provides IP routing

   C Discards corrupted IP packets

   D Generates IP control messages

   E Reviews IP packet headers for fast switching

5 What is the primary reason people use the ICMP protocol?

   A To test connectivity

   B To test full duplexing

   C To test VLAN initiation

   D To test collision domains

   E To provide LAN segmentation

6 What is the purpose of an ARP?

   A To start flow control

   B To multiplex packets

   C To adjust the window size

   D To associate a MAC address with an IP address

   E To associate an IP address to a MAC address

7 Which of the following statements best describes the role of RARP in an IP network?

   A RARP resolves packet-to-frame fragmentation.

   B RARP resolves an IP address to a MAC address.

   C RARP resolves a MAC address to an IP address.

   D RARP resolves physical layer to data link layer addresses.

   E RARP resolves Ethernet vendor numbers to the major IP network number.

8 Which of the following are *not* fields in an IP packet? (Choose three.)

  A Flags

  B Length

  C Protocol

  D Source address

  E Header checksum

9 What is the purpose of the Protocol field in an IP header?

  A Indicates the type of transport packet being carried

  B Detects processing errors introduced into the datagram

  C Indicates particular quality of service needs from the network

  D Identifies specific packets during reassembly of fragmented datagrams

  E Identifies the number of hops and links over which the datagram can be routed

10 Which functions best describe a communication protocol? (Choose two.)

  A Quality of devices

  B The speed of the media

  C The length of the media

  D The format a message must take

  E The way in which computers exchange messages

11 Which terms correctly correlate TCP/IP layers to OSI model layers? (Choose three.)

  A Internet; network

  B Transport; network

  C Transport; transport

  D Transport; physical-data link

  E Network access; physical-data link

  F Network access; data link-transport

12 Which of the following are primary duties of Layer 4 TCP? (Choose two.)

   A Provides end-to-end control

   B Divides segments into packets

   C Acknowledges and sequences segments

   D Ensures connectionless services to application protocols

   E Switches or routes information based on the type of data packet

   F Provides routing information to the connected neighboring hosts

13 What TCP characteristics are *not* found in UDP? (Choose three.)

   A Connections

   B Flow control

   C Data transfer

   D Multiplexing

   E Fragment-free

   F Reliable transfer

14 Which application is supported by TCP?

   A UDP

   B SAN

   C FTP

   D DHCP

   E ICMP

15 Which statement indicates the correct sequence of events in establishing a TCP connection?

   A 1) One machine initiates a connection that is to be accepted by the other.
         2) Data is transmitted.

   B 1) Synchronization has occurred.
         2) One machine initiates a connection that is to be accepted by the other.

C 1) A connection is established.
2) The sending application informs the operating system that a connection is to be initiated.

D 1) The sending application informs the operating system that a connection is to be initiated.
2) One machine initiates a connection that is to be accepted by the other.

E 1) Protocol software modules in the two operating systems communicate by sending messages across the network.
2) One machine initiates a connection that is to be accepted by the other.

16 In TCP communication, when can a data transfer begin?

A After all synchronization has occurred

B Before any synchronization has occurred

C After the hosts have an Internet connection

D Only after the connection between two hosts has been determined to be reliable

17 How is data formatted at the transport layer?

A Bits

B Frames

C Packets

D Segments

E Messages

18 Which components are found in a TCP header? (Choose three.)

A Length

B Window

C Protocol

D Checksum

E Destination port

19 Which components are found in a UDP header? (Choose two.)

  A Length

  B Window

  C Protocol

  D Checksum

  E Destination port

20 What flow control method does TCP implement?

  A ACKs

  B Sockets

  C Buffering

  D Windowing

  E Acknowledgments

21 What does the ACK refer to in a TCP acknowledgment?

  A TCP does not use acknowledgments.

  B The number of the byte expected next.

  C The number of the byte expected next, plus 1.

  D A number agreed upon at session establishment, which is then used by the receiver to indicate a successful exchange of packets.

  E A sequential number beginning with 1 and incremented by 1 with each exchange that identifies this exchange of packets as being complete.

22 What will the ACK bit of the first segment of the three-way handshake most likely be?

  A 1.

  B 0.

  C There is no ACK.

  D A randomly generated number.

  E The SEQ number of the remote host plus 1.

23 Which description best defines port numbers?

A A method to configure diskless workstations

B A numbering system to label the connections between devices

C A protocol that supports connectionless delivery

D A 32-bit number that uniquely identifies a network device

E A data structure that keeps track of the two IP addresses

F A 32-bit number that uniquely identifies a network device

24 Which statements are characteristics of port numbers? (Choose two.)

A They represent a fairly complex coupling between IP and TCP.

B They keep track of the two IP addresses in the connection.

C They allow a workstation to broadcast using its Ethernet address.

D The well-known ports cover the range of possible port numbers from 0 through 1023.

E Communicating hosts specify an assigned application number in each data transmission.

Upon completion of this chapter, you will be able to perform the following tasks:

- Describe each of the following aspects of IP addressing:
    - IP address structure (IPv4 and IPv6)
    - IP address classes
    - Reserved IP addresses
    - Public and private IP addresses
    - Classless interdomain routing (CIDR)
- Calculate valid IP subnetwork addresses and mask values so that user network requirements are met when given an IP address scheme
- Explain the basic operations of routing, including path determination, algorithms, and metrics
- Describe the features and operations of interior and exterior routing protocols, including Routing Information Protocol versions 1 and 2 (RIPv1 and RIPv2), Interior Gateway Routing Protocol (IGRP), Enhanced IGRP (EIGRP), Open Shortest Path First (OSPF), and Border Gateway Protocol (BGP)

CHAPTER 7

IP Addressing and Routing (The Internetworking Layer)

Among the protocols included in the TCP/IP protocol stack are a network layer protocol and a transport layer protocol. The internetworking layer handles the routing of packets of data by using IP addresses to identify each device on the network. Each computer, router, printer, or any other device attached to a network has its own unique IP address that routes packets of data.

Each IP address has a specific structure, and various classes of IP addresses exist. In addition, subnetworks and subnet masks play a role in IP addressing schemes, and different routing functions and protocols are involved in transmitting data from one network node to another using IP addresses. This chapter covers the major functions of IP addressing, IP subnetting, and routing protocols.

IP Network Addressing

Just as you use addresses to identify the specific locations of homes and businesses so that mail can reach them efficiently, you use IP addresses to identify the location of specific devices on a network so that data can be sent correctly to those locations. IP addressing has various aspects, including the calculations for constructing an IP address, the classes of IP addresses designated for specific routing purposes, and public versus private IP addresses.

Learning how IP addresses are structured and how they function in the operation of a network provides an understanding of how data is transmitted through Layer 3 internetworking devices using TCP/IP. To facilitate the routing of packets over a network, the TCP/IP protocol suite uses a 32-bit logical address known as an IP address. This address must be unique for each device in the internetwork.

Each IP datagram includes a source IP address and destination IP address that identify the source and destination network and host, as discussed in Chapter 6, "TCP/IP (The Transport and Internetworking Layer Protocol)."

An IP address is a hierarchical address and consists of two parts:

* The high order, or leftmost, bits specify the network address component (network ID) of the address.

* The low order, or rightmost, bits specify the host address component (host ID) of the address.

Every LAN or VLAN on the corporate internetwork is seen as a single network that must be reached before an individual host within that company can be contacted. Each LAN or VLAN has a unique network address. The hosts that populate that network share those same bits, but each host is identified by the uniqueness of the remaining bits. Like a group of houses along the same road, the street address is the same, but the house number is unique.

Figure 7-1 illustrates a sample IP addressing scheme in an internetwork.

Figure 7-1   *IP Addressing*

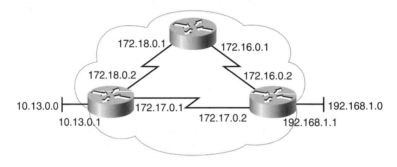

The IP address is 32 bits in length and is binary in nature, but is expressed in a format that can be easily understood by the human brain. Basically, the 32 bits are broken into 4 sections of 8 bits each, known as *octets* or *bytes*. Each of these octets is then converted into decimal numbers between 0 and 255 and each octet is separated from the following one by dots. Figure 7-2 illustrates the format of an IP address using 172.16.122.204 as an example.

Figure 7-2   *IP Address Format*

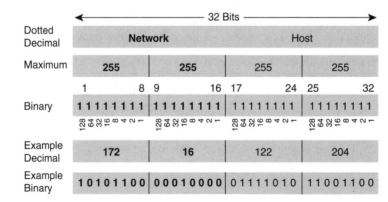

The IP address format is known as *dotted decimal* notation. Figure 7-2 shows how the dotted decimal address is derived from the 32-bit binary value:

- Sample address: 172.16.122.204.

- Each bit in the octet has a binary weight (such as 128, 64, 32, 16, 8, 4, 2, and 1), and when all the bits are on, the sum is 255.

- The minimum decimal value for an octet is 0; it contains all 0s.

- The maximum decimal value for an octet is 255; it contains all 1s.

While many computers might share the same network address, combining the network address with a host address uniquely identifies any device connected to the network.

IP Address Classes

When IP was first developed, no classes of addresses existed, because it was assumed that 254 networks would be more than enough for an internetwork of academic, military, and research computers.

As the number of networks grew, the IP addresses were broken into categories called *classes* to accommodate different sizes of networks and to aid in identifying them. These classes are illustrated in Figure 7-3.

Figure 7-3   *Address Classes*

	8 Bits	8 Bits	8 Bits	8 Bits
Class A:	Network	Host	Host	Host
Class B:	Network	Network	Host	Host
Class C:	Network	Network	Network	Host
Class D:	Multicast			
Class E:	Research			

Assigning IP addresses to classes is known as *classful addressing*. The allocation of addresses is managed by a central authority, the American Registry for Internet Numbers (ARIN), which you can go to at www.arin.net for more information about network numbers.

Five IP address classes are used, as follows:

- **Class A**—The Class A address category was designed to support extremely large networks. A Class A address uses only the first octet to indicate the network address. The remaining three octets are used for host addresses.

The first bit of a Class A address is always 0; therefore, the lowest number that can be represented is 00000000 (decimal 0), and the highest number that can be represented is 01111111 (decimal 127). However, these two network numbers, 0 and 127, are reserved and cannot be used as a network address. Any address that starts with a value between 1 and 126 in the first octet, then, is a Class A address.

NOTE   The 127.0.0.0 network is reserved for loopback testing (routers or local machines can use this address to send packets to themselves). Therefore, it cannot be assigned to a network.

- **Class B**—The Class B address category was designed to support the needs of moderate- to large-sized networks. A Class B address uses two of the four octets to indicate the network address. The other two octets specify host addresses.

  The first two bits of the first octet of a Class B address are always binary 10. The remaining 6 bits might be populated with either 1s or 0s. Therefore, the lowest number that can be represented with a Class B address is 10000000 (decimal 128), and the highest number that can be represented is 10111111 (decimal 191). Any address that starts with a value in the range of 128 to 191 in the first octet is a Class B address.

- **Class C**—The Class C address category is the most commonly used of the original address classes. This address category was intended to support a lot of small networks.

  A Class C address begins with binary 110. Therefore, the lowest number that can be represented is 11000000 (decimal 192), and the highest number that can be represented is 11011111 (decimal 223). If an address contains a number in the range of 192 to 223 in the first octet, it is a Class C address.

- **Class D**—The Class D address category was created to enable multicasting in an IP address. A multicast address is a unique network address that directs packets with that destination address to predefined groups of IP addresses. Therefore, a single station can simultaneously transmit a single stream of datagrams to multiple recipients.

  The Class D address category, much like the other address categories, is mathematically constrained. The first four bits of a Class D address must be 1110. Therefore, the first octet range for Class D addresses is 11100000 to 11101111, or 224 to 239. An IP address that starts with a value in the range of 224 to 239 in the first octet is a Class D address.

  As illustrated in Figure 7-4, Class D addresses (multicast addresses) include the following range of network numbers: 224.0.0.0 to 239.255.255.255.

- **Class E**—Although a Class E address category has been defined, the Internet Engineering Task Force (IETF) reserves the addresses in this class for its own research. Therefore, no Class E addresses have been released for use in the Internet. The first 4 bits of a Class E address are always set to 1111. Therefore, the first octet range for Class E addresses is 11110000 to 11111111, or 240 to 255.

Figure 7-4   *Multicast Addressess*

Bits: 1   8 9   16 17   24 25   32

Class D: **1110MMMM** | Multicast Group | Multicast Group | Multicast Group

Range (224—239)

Within each class the IP address is divided into a network address (or network identifier, network ID) and the host address (or host identifier, host ID). The number of networks and hosts vary by class. A bit or bit sequence at the start of each address, known as the high order bits, determines the class of the address as shown in Figure 7-5.

Figure 7-5   *Address Classification*

Bits: 1   8 9   16 17   24 25   32

Class A: **0NNNNNNN** | Host | Host | Host

Range (1–126)

Bits: 1   8 9   16 17   24 25   32

Class B: **10NNNNNN** | Network | Host | Host

Range (128–191)

Bits: 1   8 9   16 17   24 25   32

Class C: **110NNNNN** | Network | Network | Host

Range (192–223)

Figure 7-5 shows how the bits in the first octet identify the address class. The router uses the first bits to identify how many bits it must match to interpret the network portion of the address (based on the standard address class). Table 7-1 lists the characteristics of Class A, B, and C addresses that address network devices.

Table 7-1   *IP Address Classes*

Class A Address	Class B Address	Class C Address
The first bit is 0.	The first two bits are 10.	The first three bits are 110.
Range of network numbers: 1.0.0.0 to 126.0.0.0.	Range of network numbers: 128.0.0.0 to 191.255.0.0.	Range of network numbers: 192.0.0.0 to 223.255.255.0.
Number of possible networks: 127 (1 through 126 are usable; 127 is reserved).	Number of possible networks: 16,384.	Number of possible networks: 2,097,152.
Number of possible values in the host portion: 16,777,216.*	Number of possible values in the host portion: 65,536. *	Number of possible values in the host portion: 256.*

* The number of usable hosts is two less than the total number possible because the host portion must be nonzero and cannot be all 1s.

Network and Broadcast Addresses

Certain IP addresses are reserved and cannot be assigned to individual devices on a network. These reserved addresses include a network address, which identifies the network itself, and a broadcast address, which is used for broadcasting packets to all the devices on a network.

An IP address that has binary 0s in all host bit positions is reserved for the network address. Therefore, as a Class A network example, 10.0.0.0 is the IP address of the network containing the host 10.1.2.3. A router uses the network IP address when it searches its IP route table for the destination network location. As a Class B network example, the IP address 172.16.0.0 is a network address, as shown in the Figure 7-6.

Figure 7-6   *Network Address*

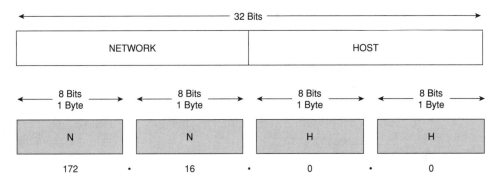

Network Address (Host Bits = All 0s)

The decimal numbers that fill the first two octets in a Class B network address are assigned. The last two octets contain 0s because those 16 bits are for host numbers and are used for devices that are attached to the network. The IP address in the example (172.16.0.0) is reserved for the network address; it is never used as an address for any device that is attached to it. An example of an IP address for a device on the 172.16.0.0 network would be 172.16.16.1. In this example, 172.16 is the network-address portion and 16.1 is the host-address portion.

If you wanted to send data to all the devices on a network, you would need to use a network broadcast address. Broadcast IP addresses end with binary 1s in the entire host part of the address (the host field), as shown in Figure 7-7.

For the network in the example (172.16.0.0), in which the last 16 bits make up the host field (or host part of the address), the broadcast that is sent out to all devices on that network includes a destination address of 172.16.255.255.

Figure 7-7   *Network Broadcast Address*

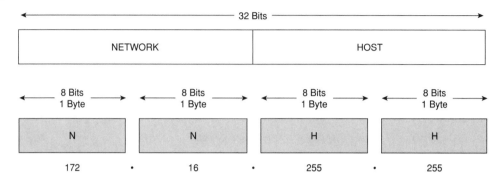

Network Address (Host Bits = All 0s)

The network broadcast is also known as a directed broadcast and is capable of being routed, because the longest match in the routing table would match the network bits. Because the host bits would not be known, the router would forward this out all the interfaces that were members of the major 172.16.0.0 network. Directed broadcast can be used to perform a denial of services attack against routed networks. This behavior is not the default for Cisco routers, however.

If an IP device wants to communicate with all devices on all networks, it sets the destination address to all 1s (255.255.255.255) and transmits the packet. This address can be used, for example, by hosts that do not know their network number and are asking some server for it as with Reverse Address Resolution Protocol (RARP) or Dynamic Host Configuration Protocol (DHCP). This form of broadcast is never capable of being routed, because RFC 1812 prohibits the forwarding of an all networks broadcast. For this reason an all networks broadcast is called a *local broadcast* because it stays local to the LAN segment or VLAN.

The network portion of an IP address is also referred to as the network ID. It is important because hosts on a network can only directly communicate with devices in the same network. If they need to communicate with devices with interfaces assigned to some other network ID, there needs to be a Layer 3 internetworking device that can route data between the networks. This is true even when the devices share the same physical media segment or VLAN.

A network ID enables a router to put a packet onto the appropriate network segment. The host ID helps the router deliver the Layer 2 frame encapsulating the packet to a specific host on the network. As a result, the IP address is mapped to the correct MAC address, which is needed by the Layer 2 process on the router to address the frame.

Specific guidelines exist for assigning IP addresses in a network. First, each device or interface must have a nonzero host number. Figure 7-8 shows devices and routers with IP addresses assigned.

Figure 7-8   *Host Addresses*

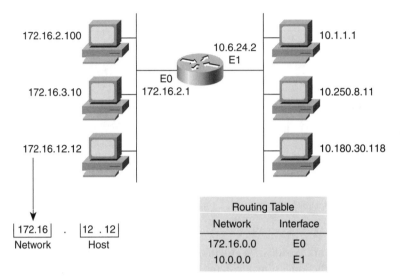

Each wire is identified with the network address. This value is not assigned, but it is assumed. A value of 0 means "this network" or "the wire itself" (for example, 172.16.0.0). This is the information used by the router to identify each network. The routing table contains entries for network or wire addresses; it usually does not contain any information about hosts.

As soon as the network portion is determined by the classification, you can determine the total number of hosts on the network by summing all available 1 and 0 combinations of the remaining address bits and subtracting 2. You must subtract 2 because an address consisting of all 0 bits specifies the network, and an address of all 1 bits is used for network broadcasts.

The same result can be derived by using the following formula:

$2^N - 2$ (where N is the number of bits in the host portion)

Figure 7-9 illustrates a Class B network, 172.16.0.0. In a Class B network, 16 bits are used for the host portion. Applying the formula $2^N - 2$ (in this case, $2^{16} - 2 = 65{,}534$) results in 65,534 usable host addresses.

All classful addresses have only a network portion and host portion, so the router(s) within the internetwork know it only as a single network, and no detailed knowledge of the internal hosts is required. All datagrams addressed to network 172.16.0.0 are treated the same, regardless of the third and fourth octets of the address.

Figure 7-9   *Determining the Available Host Addresses*

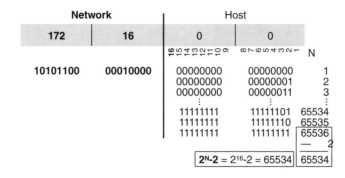

Each class of a network allows a fixed number of hosts. In a Class A network, the first octet is assigned for the network, leaving the last three octets to be assigned to hosts. The first host address in each network (all 0s) is reserved for the actual network address, and the final host address in each network (all 1s) is reserved for broadcasts. The maximum number of hosts in a Class A network is $2^{24} - 2$ (subtracting the network and broadcast reserved addresses), or 16,777,214.

In a Class B network, the first two octets are assigned for the network, leaving the final two octets to be assigned to hosts. The maximum number of hosts in a Class B network is $2^{16} - 2$, or 65,534.

In a Class C network, the first three octets are assigned for the network. This leaves the final octet to be assigned to hosts, so the maximum number of hosts is $2^8 - 2$, or 254.

Public and Private IP Addresses

Some networks connect to each other through the Internet, while others are private. Public and private IP addresses are required, therefore, for both of these network types. This topic compares the purpose and sources for both public and private IP addresses.

Internet stability depends directly on the uniqueness of publicly used network addresses. Therefore, some mechanism is needed to ensure that addresses are, in fact, unique. This responsibility originally rested within an organization known as the InterNIC (Internet Network Information Center). This organization was succeeded by the Internet Assigned Numbers Authority (IANA). IANA carefully manages the remaining supply of IP addresses to ensure that duplication of publicly used addresses does not occur. Such duplication would cause instability in the Internet and compromise its capability to deliver datagrams to networks using the duplicated addresses.

To obtain an IP address or block of addresses, you must contact an Internet service provider (ISP). The ISP allocates addresses from the range assigned by their upstream registry or their appropriate regional registry, as follows:

- APNIC (Asia Pacific Network Information Centre)
- ARIN (American Registry for Internet Numbers)
- RIPE NCC (Réseaux IP Européens Network Coordination Centre)

With the rapid growth of the Internet, public IP addresses began to run out, so new addressing schemes such as classless interdomain routing (CIDR) and IPv6 were developed to help solve the problem. CIDR and IPv6 are discussed later in this chapter in the "Address Exhaustion" section.

Although Internet hosts require a globally unique IP address, private hosts that are not connected to the Internet can use any valid address, as long as it is unique within the private network. Because many private networks exist alongside public networks, grabbing "just any address" is strongly discouraged. Therefore, the IETF defined 3 blocks of IP addresses (1 Class A network, 16 Class B networks, and 256 Class C networks) in RFC 1918 for private, internal use. Addresses in this range are not routed on the Internet backbone, as shown in Table 7-2. Internet routers are configured to discard private addresses as defined by RFC 1918.

Table 7-2   *Private IP Addresses*

Class	RFC 1918 Internal Address Range
A	10.0.0.0 to 10.255.255.255
B	172.16.0.0 to 172.31.255.255
C	192.168.0.0 to 192.168.255.255

If you are addressing a nonpublic intranet, these private addresses can be used instead of globally unique addresses. If you want to connect a network using private addresses to the Internet, however, it is necessary to translate the private addresses to public addresses. This translation process is referred to as *Network Address Translation (NAT)*. A router is often the network device that performs NAT.

Address Exhaustion

The growth of the Internet has resulted in enormous demands for IP addresses. This section describes the capabilities of IP version 4 (IPv4) in relation to that demand.

When TCP/IP was first introduced in the 1980s, it relied on a two-level addressing scheme, which at the time offered adequate scalability. The architects of TCP/IP could not have predicted that their protocol would eventually sustain a global network of information, commerce, and entertainment. Twenty years ago, IPv4 offered an addressing strategy that, although scalable for a time, eventually resulted in an inefficient allocation of addresses.

The Class A and B addresses make up 75 percent of the IPv4 address space, but a relative handful of organizations (fewer than 17,000) can be assigned a Class A or B network number. Class C network addresses are far more numerous than Class A and B addresses, although they account for only 12.5 percent of the possible 4 billion IP addresses, as shown in Figure 7-10.

Figure 7-10   *IP Address Allocation*

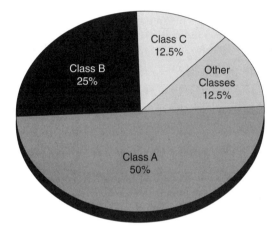

Unfortunately, Class C addresses are limited to 254 hosts, not meeting the needs of larger organizations that cannot acquire a Class A or B address.

As early as 1992, the IETF identified two specific concerns:

- The Class B address category was on the verge of depletion, and the remaining, unassigned IPv4 network addresses were nearly depleted at the time.

- As more Class C networks came online to accommodate the rapid and substantial increase in the size of the Internet, the resulting flood of new network information threatened the capability of Internet routers to cope effectively.

Over the past two decades, numerous extensions to IPv4 have been developed to improve the efficiency with which the 32-bit address space can be used.

In addition, an even more extendable and scalable version of IP, IPv6, has been defined and developed. An IPv6 address is a 128-bit binary value, which can be displayed as 32 hexadecimal digits. It provides 3.4×10^{38} IP addresses. This version of IP should provide sufficient addresses for future Internet growth needs. Table 7-3 compares IPv4 and IPv6 addresses.

Table 7-3   *IPv6 Addresses*

IPv4	IPv6
4 octets	16 octets
11000000.10101000.11001001.01110001	11010001.11011100.11001001.01110001.110100 01.11011100.110011001.01110001.11010001.110 11100.11001001.01110001.11010001.11011100.1 1001001.01110001
192.168.201.113	A524:72D3:2C80:DD02:0029:EC7A:002B:EA73
4,294,467,295 IP addresses	3.4×10^{38} IP addresses

After years of planning and development, IPv6 is slowly being implemented in select networks. Eventually, IPv6 might replace IPv4 as the dominant internetwork protocol.

Another solution to the shortage of public IP addresses is a different kind of routing. Classless interdomain routing (CIDR) is a new addressing scheme for the Internet that allows for more efficient allocation of IP addresses than the old Class A, B, and C address scheme.

First introduced in 1993 and later deployed in 1994, CIDR dramatically improved scalability and efficiency of IPv4, in the following ways:

- It replaced classful addressing with a more flexible and less wasteful scheme.
- It provided enhanced route aggregation, also known as *supernetting*. As the Internet grows, routers on the Internet require huge memory tables to store all the routing information. Supernetting helps reduce the size of router memory tables by combining and summarizing multiple routing information entries into one single entry. This reduces the size of router memory tables and also allows for faster table lookup.

A CIDR network address looks like this:

192.168.54.0/23

The 192.168.54.0 is the network address itself and the /23 means that the first 23 bits are the network part of the address, leaving the last 9 bits for specific host addresses. The effect of CIDR is to aggregate, or combine, multiple classful networks into a single larger network. This reduces the number of entries required in the IP routing tables, and allows provisioning a larger number of hosts within the network. Both are done without using a network ID from the next larger classful address group.

With the CIDR approach, if you need more than 254 host addresses, you can be assigned a /23 address instead of wasting a whole Class B address that supports 65,534 hosts.

Figure 7-11 shows an example of using CIDR. Company XYZ asks for an address block from its ISP, not a central authority. The ISP evaluates company XYZ's needs and allocates address space from its own large "CIDR block" of addresses. CIDR blocks can be, and are, assigned by the regional authorities to governments, service providers, enterprises, and organizations.

Figure 7-11   *CIDR Addressing*

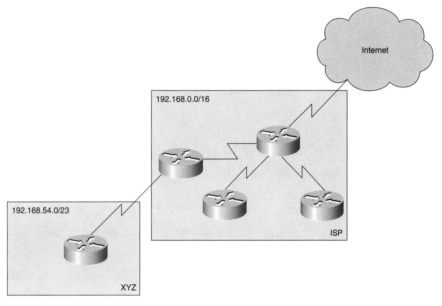

NOTE   Figure 7-11 shows an example using private IP addresses as defined in RFC 1918. These addresses would never be used by an ISP for CIDR, but are shown here merely as an illustration. Public addresses are not used in this example for security measures.

In this example, the ISP owns the 192.168.0.0/16 address block. The ISP announces only this single 192.168.0.0/16 address to the Internet (even though this address block actually consists of many Class C networks). The ISP assigns the smaller 192.168.54.0/23 address block within the larger 192.168.0.0/16 address block to the XYZ company. This allows the XYZ company to have a network that can have up to 510 hosts ($2^9 - 2 = 510$), or that network can be subdivided into multiple smaller subnets by the XYZ company. (Subnetting is discussed in the next section.)

Providers assume the burden of managing address space in a classless system. With this system, Internet routers keep only one summary route, or supernet route, to the provider's network, and only the individual provider keeps routes that are more specific to its own customer networks. This method drastically reduces the size of internetwork routing tables.

IP Network Addressing Section Quiz

Use these practice questions to review what you learned in this section.

1 The IP address consists of two parts: _____ and _____.

   A Network portion and host portion

   B Host portion and MAC portion

   C Network portion and MAC portion

   D Network portion and subnetwork portion

2 How many bits are in an IP address?

   A 16

   B 32

   C 48

   D 64

3 In a Class B address, which of the octets are the host address portion and are assigned locally?

   A The first octet is assigned locally.

   B The first and second octets are assigned locally.

   C The second and third octets are assigned locally.

   D The third and fourth octets are assigned locally.

4 The following address is of which class? 172.16.128.17

   A Class A

   B Class B

   C Class C

   D Class D

5 Which of the following is true of a broadcast address?

   A A broadcast address is an address that has all 0s in the host field.

   B Any IP address in a network can be used as a broadcast address.

   C A broadcast address is an address that has all 1s in the host field.

   D None of the above.

6 Which are private IP addresses? (Choose two.)

   A 10.215.34.124

   B 127.16.71.43

   C 172.17.10.10

   D 225.200.15.10

7 What percentage of the total IPv4 address allocation is made up of Class A addresses?

   A 25

   B 50

   C 12.5

   D 75

8 How many bits are there in an IPv6 address?

   A 32

   B 48

   C 96

   D 128

9 Which of the following is a feature of CIDR?

   A Classful addressing

   B No supernetting

   C More entries in the routing table

   D Route aggregation

IP Subnetting

As discussed in the previous section, using classful addressing limits the amount of networks and hosts available for assignment. A useful characteristic of IP addressing is the ability to divide classful networks into smaller subnets. Subnetworks are common in most internetworks, segmenting the network address space into smaller divisions that have their own addresses. To create subnet addresses, some of the bits used for the host portion of an IP address are "borrowed" to create the subnet address. Subnet masks identify which bits identify the network ID portion of the address and which portions identify the host portion.

Learning how subnet addresses and masks are created expands your understanding of IP addressing overall, as well as your understanding of how data is transmitted in a TCP/IP environment.

Figure 7-12 shows a Class B network without subnets. For this network, all devices would be in the same broadcast domain.

Figure 7-12   *Addressing Without Subnets*

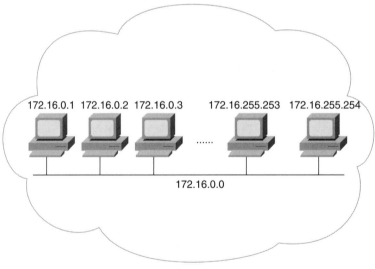

Network 172.16.0.0

With the addressing scheme in Figure 7-12, the network can be segmented into more granular segments using switches to increase the number of collision domains. However, no way of distinguishing individual segments (wires) within the network by IP addressing exists. A single large broadcast domain exists inside a network that has no subnetworks—all systems on the network encounter all the broadcasts on the network. Although you might have increased performance by segmenting with switches, you have no mechanism to control the broadcast. This type of configuration can result in relatively poor network performance, because a broadcast frame is propagated to all devices in the network.

In the extreme case, each of the 126 Class A networks would have 16,777,214 usable host addresses. The Class B address space illustrated in Figure 7-12 defines one wire with 65,534 potential workstations on it. What is needed is a way to divide this wire into segments. Subnets provide a way to address these individual segments.

Subnet Addresses

Breaking the network into smaller segments, or subnets, makes network address use more efficient. The outside world sees no change in the network, but within the organization, an additional structure exists.

In Figure 7-13, the network 172.16.0.0 is subdivided or broken into four subnets: 172.16.1.0, 172.16.2.0, 172.16.3.0, and 172.16.4.0. The third octet is being used as the subnet address in each of these addresses. Routers determine the destination network using the subnet address, limiting the amount of traffic on the other network segments.

Figure 7-13   *Addressing with Subnets*

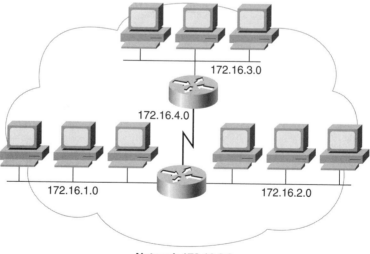

Network 172.16.0.0

Subnets are an extension of the network number. Network administrators decide the size of subnets based on organization and growth needs.

Subnet Masks

A network device uses a subnet mask to determine what part of the IP address is used for the network, the subnet, and the device (host) address, as illustrated in Figure 7-14. A *subnet mask* is a 32-bit value containing a contiguous number of 1 bits for the network and subnet ID and a contiguous number of 0 bits for the host ID. A device can also determine the class of address it has been assigned from its own IP address. The subnet mask then tells the device where the boundary is between the subnet ID and the host ID.

Figure 7-14 *Subnet Addressing on Routers*

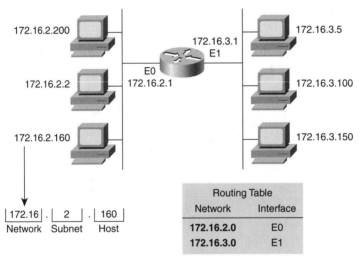

Notice that the routing table now identifies each wire by its subnet number. The router and any hosts determine what the local segment is by making a logical comparison to the subnet mask, as shown in Figure 7-15.

Figure 7-15 *Subnet Mask*

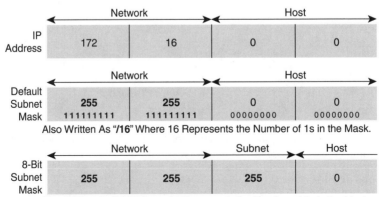

Subnet bits are taken from the host field of the address. The number of subnet bits taken from the host field is identified by a subnet mask. The subnet mask is 32 bits in size, written as four octets. Each bit in the subnet mask determines how the corresponding bit in the IP address should be interpreted, as follows:

- Binary 1 for the network bits

- Binary 1 for the subnet bits

- Binary 0 for the host bits

The subnet mask for 172.16.0.0 255.255.0.0 can be denoted in the following ways:

- **Dotted decimal**—172.16.0.0 255.255.0.0

- **Bit count**—172.16.0.0/16, where 16 is the number of 1s in the subnet mask

- **Hexadecimal**—172.16.0.0 0xFFFF0000

Only a limited number of subnet masks can be applied to an IP address. Figure 7-16 shows what values are available in an octet for subnet addresses.

Figure 7-16   *Subnet Mask Patterns*

128	64	32	16	8	4	2	1		
1	0	0	0	0	0	0	0	=	128
1	1	0	0	0	0	0	0	=	192
1	1	1	0	0	0	0	0	=	224
1	1	1	1	0	0	0	0	=	240
1	1	1	1	1	0	0	0	=	248
1	1	1	1	1	1	0	0	=	252
1	1	1	1	1	1	1	0	=	254
1	1	1	1	1	1	1	1	=	255

Subnet bits come from the high order bits of the host field. To determine a subnet mask for an address, add up the decimal values of each position that has a 1 in it. For example:

$$224 = 128 + 64 + 32$$

Because the subnet mask is not defined by the octet boundary, but by bits, you need to convert dotted decimal addresses to binary and back into dotted decimal.

An IP host, like a PC or router, uses the subnet mask to determine how to handle a datagram. The device uses the assigned IP address and subnet mask of a particular interface or NIC to determine which logical network or subnetwork that a port interface is connected to.

The IP device, which reads the IP addresses in binary format, performs a logical AND operation to obtain the network number. A *logical AND* is a Boolean algebra operation that allows for binary comparison. Table 7-4 shows the possible results for logical AND comparisons.

Table 7-4 *Logical AND*

AND	0	1
0	0	0
1	0	1

A mask of 1 returns the same value that is contained in the interface address. Because the subnet masks match high order bits, the bits that are masked with a 1 now return the network ID associated with a given interface or NIC. This network ID is used by the device to construct a table used for forwarding datagrams.

When a datagram is sent, the device examines the destination address and checks the table of network IDs to find the longest possible match, that is the match with the most bits in common starting with the high order bits. The sending device then sends the datagram out the interface with the longest match.

Prior to the creation of subnet mask, networks were defined by the high order bits. That is, if a Class B address were assigned to an interface, the device knew the network ID based on the high order bits. For this reason, each class is now associated with what is known as a default mask that specifies the network numbers that would match the class of the network. For example, a Class B network that originally only used the first 16 bits as a network ID would now have a default mask of 255.255.0.0. Figure 7-17, with no subnetting, shows that the network number "extracted" using a default mask is 172.16.0.0, which is the same as a Class B network.

Figure 7-17 *Default Subnet Mask*

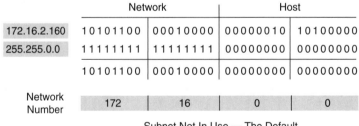

With 8 bits of subnetting, the extracted network (subnet) number is 172.16.2.0.

Figure 7-18 shows more bits turned on, extending the network portion and creating a secondary field extending from the end of the standard mask and using 8 of the host bits. This secondary field is the subnet field and represents wires (or subnetworks) inside the network.

Figure 7-18   *Extending the Mask by 8 Bits*

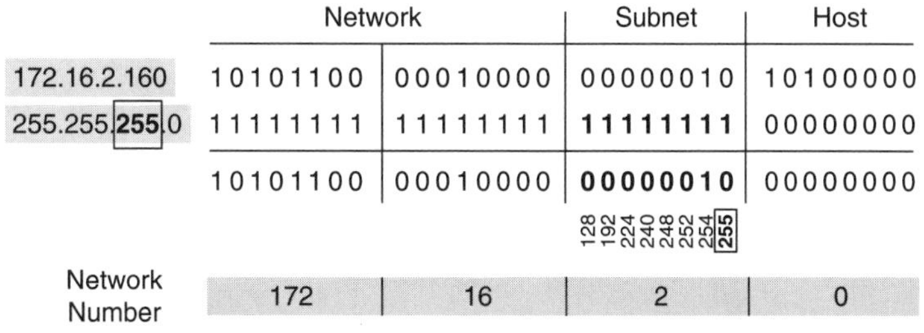

	Network		Subnet	Host
172.16.2.160	1 0 1 0 1 1 0 0	0 0 0 1 0 0 0 0	0 0 0 0 0 0 1 0	1 0 1 0 0 0 0 0
255.255.**255**.0	1 1 1 1 1 1 1 1	1 1 1 1 1 1 1 1	**1 1 1 1 1 1 1 1**	0 0 0 0 0 0 0 0
	1 0 1 0 1 1 0 0	0 0 0 1 0 0 0 0	**0 0 0 0 0 0 1 0**	0 0 0 0 0 0 0 0
			128 192 224 240 248 252 254 **255**	
Network Number	172	16	2	0

Subnetting does not have to occur between octets. An octet can be split into a subnet portion and a host portion. Figure 7-19 illustrates 10 bits of subnetting with 6 bits remaining for the host portion.

Figure 7-19   *Extending the Mask by 10 Bits*

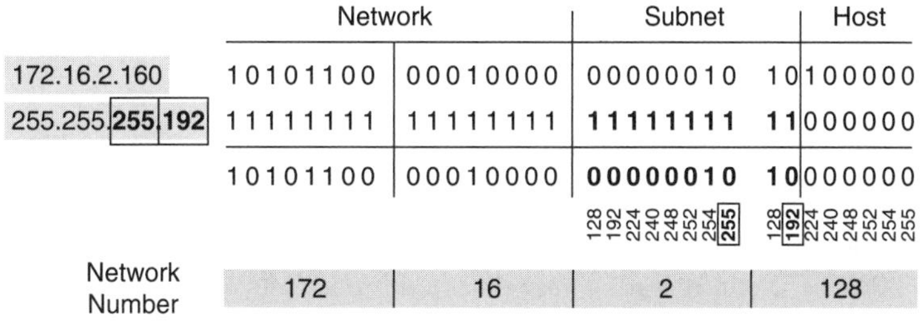

	Network		Subnet	Host
172.16.2.160	1 0 1 0 1 1 0 0	0 0 0 1 0 0 0 0	0 0 0 0 0 0 1 0	1 0 1 0 0 0 0 0
255.255.**255**.**192**	1 1 1 1 1 1 1 1	1 1 1 1 1 1 1 1	**1 1 1 1 1 1 1 1**	1 1 0 0 0 0 0 0
	1 0 1 0 1 1 0 0	0 0 0 1 0 0 0 0	**0 0 0 0 0 0 1 0**	1 0 0 0 0 0 0 0
			128 192 224 240 248 252 254 **255**	128 **192** 224 240 248 252 254 255
Network Number	172	16	2	128

A network or subnetwork defines part of an address that is common to a group of devices within the internetwork. Each device still has a unique address; however, it is sometimes useful to communicate with all of these devices or even networks at the same time. Broadcast addresses, as discussed in the next section, are special addresses used to communicate with a group of devices at the same time.

Broadcasts

Broadcasting is supported on networks. Broadcast messages are those you want every host on the network to see. The broadcast address is formed by using all 1s within all or portions of the IP address. Networks devices support three kinds of broadcasts, as illustrated in Figure 7-20:

- Flooding
- Directed broadcasts
- All subnets broadcast

Figure 7-20   *Broadcast Addresses*

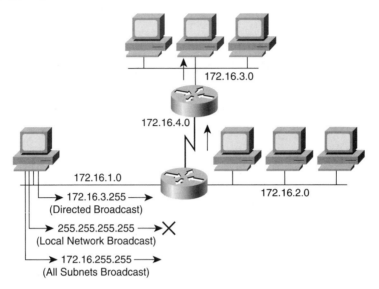

Local or flooded broadcasts (255.255.255.255) are not propagated by Layer 3 internet-working device, but are considered local broadcasts to the VLAN or LAN.

Broadcasts directed into a specific network are allowed and are forwarded by a Layer 3 device if configured. These directed broadcasts contain all 1s in the host portion of the address.

You can also broadcast messages to all hosts within a subnet and to all subnets within a network. To broadcast a message to all hosts within a single subnet, the host portion of the address contains all 1s. The following example broadcasts messages to all hosts in network 172.16, subnet 3:

   All hosts on a specific subnet = 172.16.3.255

You can also broadcast messages to all hosts on all subnets within a single network. To broadcast a message to all hosts on all subnets within a single network, the host and subnet portions of the address contain all 1s. The following example broadcasts messages to all hosts on all subnets in network 172.16:

   All hosts on all subnets in a specific network = 172.16.255.255

NOTE   In Cisco IOS Release 12.0 and later, routers by default do not forward all subnets or directed broadcast.

Identifying IP Addresses

Given an IP address and subnet mask, you can use the process illustrated in Figure 7-21 and described in the following list to identify the subnet address, the broadcast address, the first usable address, and the last usable address. (You can obtain the subnet address, the broadcast address, the first usable address, and the last usable address in many ways. This is just one method.) This method can be used to calculate the address space for your networks.

Figure 7-21   *Calculating Address Space*

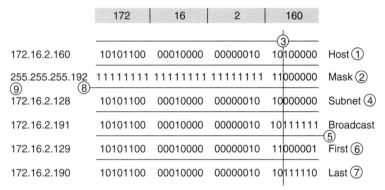

Step 1   Write the 32-bit address in binary notation.

Step 2   Write the 32-bit subnet mask in binary just below it.

Step 3   Draw a vertical line just after the last contiguous subnet mask 1 bit.

Step 4   In a row just below, place all 0s for the remaining free spaces (to the right of the line). This is the subnet address.

Step 5   In the next row, to the right of the line, place all 1s until you reach the 32-bit boundary. This is the broadcast address.

Step 6   On the right side of the line in the next row, place all 0s in the remaining free spaces until you reach the last free space. Place a 1 in that free space. This is your first usable host address.

Step 7   On the right side of the line in the next row, place all 1s in the remaining free spaces until you reach the last free space. Place a 0 in that free space. This is your last usable host address.

Step 8   Copy down all the bits you wrote in Step 1 for the bit fields to the left of the line for all four lines.

Step 9   Convert the bottom four rows back to dotted decimal.

Given this method, you can determine the subnet address, broadcast address, first, and last host addresses of the IP address 172.16.2.121 with a subnet mask of 255.255.255.0, as shown in Figure 7-22.

Figure 7-22   *Subnet Example*

IP Host Address: 172.16.2.121
Subnet Mask: 255.255.255.0

	Network	Network	Subnet	Host
172.16.2.121:	10101100	00010000	00000010	01111001
255.255.255.0:	11111111	11111111	**11111111**	00000000
Subnet:	10101100	00010000	**00000010**	00000000
Broadcast:	10101100	00010000	00000010	11111111

Subnet Address = 172.16.2.0
Host Addresses = 172.16.2.1–172.16.2.254
Broadcast Address = 172.16.2.255
Eight Bits Of Subnetting

This network has 8 bits of subnetting that provide up to 254 subnets and 254 host addresses. Table 7-5 shows how subnet masks break up IP networks and the number of subnets and hosts available when you use each mask.

Table 7-5   *Class B Subnet Table*

Number of Bits	Subnet Mask	Number of Subnets	Number of Hosts
2	255.255.192.0	2	16,382
3	255.255.224.0	6	8190
4	255.255.240.0	14	4094
5	255.255.248.0	30	2046
6	255.255.252.0	62	1022
7	255.255.254.0	126	510
8	255.255.255.0	254	254
9	255.255.255.128	510	126
10	255.255.255.192	1022	62
11	255.255.255.224	2046	30
12	255.255.255.240	4094	14
13	255.255.255.248	8190	6
14	255.255.255.252	16,382	2

With subnets, you can still use the $2^N - 2$ (where N equals the number of bits) calculation to determine the number of hosts.

Subnet Planning

The sample network shown in Figure 7-23 has been assigned a Class C address of 192.168.5.0. Assume 20 subnets are needed, with 5 hosts per subnet. Subdivide the last octet into a subnet portion and a host portion and determine what the subnet mask is.

Figure 7-23 *Subnet Planning*

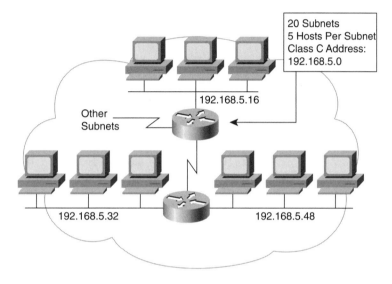

Select a subnet field size that yields enough subnetworks. In this example, choosing a 5-bit mask allows 20 subnets, each containing 32 hosts. The subnet addresses are all multiples of 8, such as 192.168.5.16, 192.168.5.32, and 192.168.5.48. This is because 8 addresses are in each network, including the network number and broadcast address; therefore, each new subnet is 8 greater than the previous one.

The remaining bits in the last octet are used for the host field. The 3 bits in our example allow enough hosts to cover the required five hosts per wire. The host numbers are 1, 2, 3, 4, 5, and 6. Address 7 is the broadcast for this network, and the next subnet is the value 8.

The final host addresses are a combination of the network/subnet "wire" starting address plus each host value. The hosts on the 192.168.5.16 subnet would be addressed as 192.168.5.17, 192.168.5.18, 192.168.5.19, 192.168.5.20, 192.168.5.21, and 192.168.5.22.

A host number of 0 is reserved for the "wire" address, and a host value of all 1s is reserved because it selects all hosts—a broadcast.

As discussed previously, when an IP device is assigned an address and subnet mask, the subnet is extracted using this information. An entry is then placed in a table on this device to identify the subnetwork associated with the given interface. The extracted subnet number should be typical of the subnets generated during this planning exercise. If you look at Figure 7-24, you can see how to determine the subnet number, broadcast address, and beginning and ending ranges of the address space for the address 192.168.5.121 with the subnet 255.255.255.248.

Figure 7-24 *Subnet Planning Example*

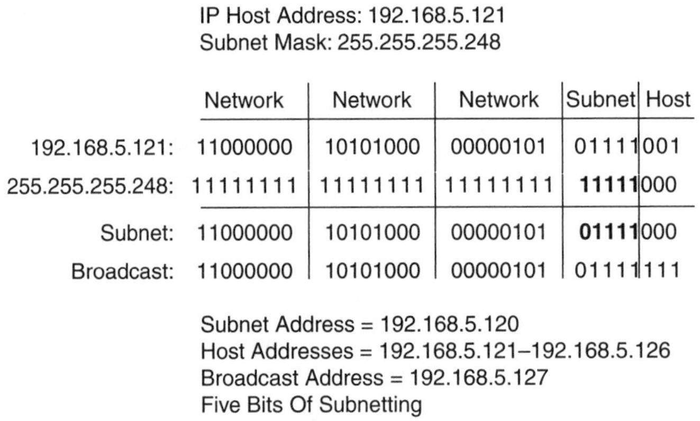

IP Host Address: 192.168.5.121
Subnet Mask: 255.255.255.248

	Network	Network	Network	Subnet	Host
192.168.5.121:	11000000	10101000	00000101	01111	001
255.255.255.248:	11111111	11111111	11111111	**11111**	000
Subnet:	11000000	10101000	00000101	**01111**	000
Broadcast:	11000000	10101000	00000101	01111	111

Subnet Address = 192.168.5.120
Host Addresses = 192.168.5.121–192.168.5.126
Broadcast Address = 192.168.5.127
Five Bits Of Subnetting

In Figure 7-24, a Class C network is subnetted to provide 6 host addresses and 30 subnets. Table 7-6 shows how subnet masks divide Class C networks and the number of subnets and hosts available with each given subnet.

Table 7-6 *Class C Subnet Table*

Number of Bits	Subnet Mask	Number of Subnets	Number of Hosts
2	255.255.255.192	2	62
3	255.255.255.224	6	30
4	255.255.255.240	14	14
5	255.255.255.248	30	6
6	255.255.255.252	62	2

IP Subnetting Section Quiz

Use the practice questions here to review what you learned in this section.

1 Originally, the Internet used how many levels of hierarchy addressing?

A Two

B Three

C Four

D Five

2 What is the function of a subnet mask?

A To determine which part of the IP address is the network or subnetwork part and which part is the host part

B To conceal outside networks from subnetworks

C To determine the numbers of subnetworks that can be created

D To determine the numbers of hosts within a subnetwork

3 What is the practical maximum number of host bits you can borrow from a Class A address for subnetting?

A 24

B 22

C 16

D 14

4 List the steps for determining a subnetwork number in order.

_____ 1. Express the subnet mask in binary form.

_____ 2. Perform a logical AND operation on the IP address and the subnet mask.

_____ 3. Express the IP address in binary form.

_____ 4. Express the subnet number as dotted-decimal notation.

5 How many octets does a Class A network have in the host field?

   A 3

   B 2

   C 1

   D 4

6 Using 6 subnet bits, how many usable subnets are created?

   A 58

   B 60

   C 62

   D 64

7 How many host addresses can be used in a Class C network?

   A 253

   B 254

   C 255

   D 256

8 What is the maximum number of bits that can be borrowed to create a usable subnet for a Class C network?

   A 2

   B 4

   C 6

   D 8

Routing Basics

Routing is the function that transmits datagrams between networks or network segments, using a router or a Layer 3 switch. The routing process uses network addressing to build network routing tables and uses routing algorithms to determine the most efficient path for transmitting a datagram from one router to another in the network until it reaches the destination device. Figure 7-25 illustrates an example of connected routers. For a host on the 10.120.2.0 subnet to communicate with a host on the 172.16.1.0 subnet, the routers between them must maintain and choose the paths to be used.

Figure 7-25   *Routing Overview*

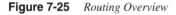
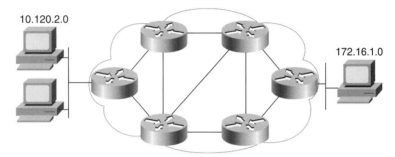

A router or Layer 3 switch is a network layer device that generally uses routing tables to determine the optimal path along which network traffic should be forwarded. (You learn more about routing tables later in this chapter.) A router has these two key functions:

- It must maintain its routing tables and make sure that other routers know of changes in the network. It does this by using a routing protocol to communicate network information from its routing table with other routers.

- It must use the routing table to determine where to forward packets. It forwards them to the appropriate interface, adds the necessary framing for the particular interface, and then sends the packet.

To be able to route packets of information, a router (or any other entity that performs routing, such as a UNIX workstation running the route daemon or a Layer 3 switch) needs to know the following key information:

- **Destination address**—What is the destination (or address) of the item that needs to be routed? This information is the responsibility of the host. (Network addressing was covered in the section, "IP Network Addressing.")

- **Information sources**—From which source (other routers) can the router learn the paths to given destinations?

- **Possible routes**—What are the initial possible routes, or paths, to the intended destinations?

- **Best routes**—What is the best path to the intended destination?

- **Routing information maintenance and verification**—A way of verifying that the known paths to destinations are valid and are the most current.

In the routing process, data is transferred through a process of encapsulation and de-encapsulation, as described in Chapter 1, "Introduction to Internetworking." The de-encapsulation and encapsulation process for a router is slightly different than the process between two hosts. This process is described in the following steps, which occur each time the packet transfers through a router:

1   The router examines the frame to determine what type of network layer data is being carried. If the router is configured to route, or forward, that protocol, it de-encapsulates the frame by discarding the (data link layer) header and trailer. The datagram is then sent to the appropriate network layer process (IP for example).

2   The network layer process examines the network layer header to determine the destination network and then references the routing table that associates networks to outgoing interfaces.

3   The packet is again encapsulated in the data link layer frame for the selected interface and sent on to the next-hop device.

At the router connected to the network containing the destination host, the packet is encapsulated in the destination LAN data-link frame type for delivery toward the destination host (or next hop). Because the de-encapsulation stops at Layer 3 on a router or Layer 3 switch, these devices are said to operate at Layer 3 of the OSI model.

The routing information that a router learns from its routing sources is placed in its routing table. The router relies on this table to determine which outgoing port to use when forwarding a packet toward its destination. The routing table is how a router knows about the networks. Figure 7-26 illustrates how a router builds a routing table using connected networks.

Figure 7-26   *Connected Routes*

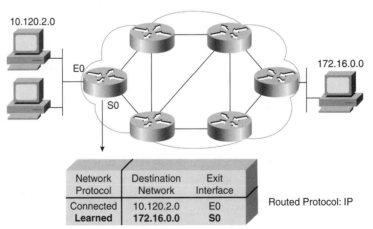

Network Protocol	Destination Network	Exit Interface
Connected	10.120.2.0	E0
Learned	**172.16.0.0**	**S0**

Routed Protocol: IP

The entry in a routing table for a directly connected network comes from the addressing and subnet mask, as is discussed in the previous sections. If the destination network is directly connected, the router already knows which port to use when forwarding packets.

If destination networks are not directly attached, the router must learn about and compute the best route to use when forwarding packets to these networks. The routing table is populated through one of the following methods:

- Manually by the network administrator
- Collected through dynamic processes running in the network

Here are two ways to tell the router where to forward packets that are not directly connected:

- **Static routes**—Routes learned by the router when an administrator manually establishes the route. The administrator must manually update this static route entry whenever an internetwork topology requires an update, such as during a link failure.
- **Dynamic routes**—Routes automatically learned by the router after an administrator configures a routing protocol that helps determine routes. Unlike static routes, as soon as the network administrator enables dynamic routing, route knowledge is automatically updated by a routing process whenever new topology information is received from routers within the internetwork.

Two types of protocols are used when discussing routing functions: routed protocols and routing protocols.

A *routed protocol* includes enough information in its network layer address to allow a router to direct user traffic. The IP protocol and Novell's IPX are examples of routed protocols.

A *routing protocol* supports a routed protocol by providing mechanisms for sharing routing information, and allows the routers to communicate with other routers to update and maintain the routing tables. Examples of routing protocols that support the IP routed protocol include the Routing Information Protocol (RIP), Interior Gateway Routing Protocol (IGRP), Open Shortest Path First (OSPF), Border Gateway Protocol (BGP), and Enhanced IGRP (EIGRP).

A routing protocol is a network layer protocol that receives packets from other participants to learn and maintain a routing table. In contrast, routed protocols, such as TCP/IP and IPX, define the format and use of the fields within a packet to provide a transport mechanism for user traffic. As soon as the routing protocol determines a valid path between routers, the router can route a routed protocol. Routing protocols also describe the following information:

- How updates are conveyed
- What knowledge is conveyed
- When to convey knowledge
- How to locate recipients of the updates

During path determination, routers evaluate the available paths to a destination and establish the preferred handling of a packet. Routing services use metrics and administrative distances when evaluating network paths. This information can be configured onto each router by the network administrator statically (static routing), or it can be learned dynamically (dynamic routing) by the routers using a routing protocol. After the router determines which path to use, it can proceed with forwarding the packet by taking the packet it accepted on one interface and forwarding it to another interface that reflects the best path toward the destination.

After a frame reaches a router connected to the target, the attached router uses the Address Resolution Protocol (ARP) to resolve the host or next hop address so that it can forward the packet to the destination host.

Before the frame can be sent to the next host, however, a router must build the routing table. The assembly and maintenance of the routing table is one of the primary functions of a router and routing protocols, as discussed in the next section.

Routing Tables

To aid in the process of path determination, routing protocols dynamically maintain the routing table, which contains route information. Route information varies, depending on the routing protocol used. Figure 7-27 shows how routers keep this table of information to aid in the traffic management and path determination.

Figure 7-27 *Routing Tables*

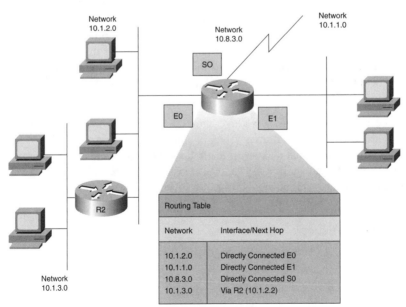

Routing tables include the following information:

- **Destination and next-hop associations**—These associations tell a router that a particular destination is either directly connected to the router or that it can be reached via another router called the "next-hop" router on the way to the final destination. When a router receives an incoming packet, it checks the destination address and attempts to associate this address with either a directly connected interface or the next-hop router.

- **Routing metric**—Different routing protocols use different routing metrics. Routing metrics determine the desirability of the route. For example, the RIP routing protocol uses hop count as its routing metric. A hop represents an intermediate router a packet must go through before reaching the destination. Therefore, a route having a lower total hop count is more desirable than another route with a higher total hop count because the lower hop count route has to go through fewer intermediate routers.

Routers communicate with one another and maintain their routing tables through the transmission of routing update messages. Depending on the particular routing protocol, routing update messages can be sent periodically or only when a change in the network topology occurs. Some of the information contained in the routing update messages includes the destination networks that the router can reach along with the routing metric to reach each destination. By analyzing the routing updates from the neighboring routers, a router can build and maintain its routing table.

Design Goals of Routing Protocols

The purpose of all routing protocols is to pick the best next hop device on the way to a destination device. The thing that differentiates routing protocols is how they choose the "best" next-hop devices. This function defines the design goal of the routing protocol. Routing protocols and algorithms often have one or more design goals to meet this objective. This section describes some of the major design goals for routing protocols.

Some of the design goals for routing protocols include the following:

- **Optimization**—Optimization describes the capability of the routing protocol or algorithm to select the best route, depending on metrics and metric weights used in the calculation. For example, one algorithm might use hop count and delay for its metric, but might weigh delay more heavily in the calculation.

- **Simplicity and low overhead**—Ideally, efficient routing algorithm functionality is achieved if the routers have minimum CPU and memory overhead so that the network can scale to large proportions.

- **Robustness and stability**—A routing algorithm should perform correctly in the face of unusual or unforeseen circumstances, such as hardware failures, high load conditions, and poor design.

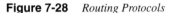

- **Rapid convergence**—Convergence occurs when all routers share the identical view or information of the network topology. When a network event causes changes in link or router availability, recalculations are needed to reestablish network connectivity. Routing algorithms that converge slowly can cause routing loops or long network outages.

Figure 7-28 illustrates that a router can populate the routing table by learning and choosing routes through dynamic routing protocols.

Figure 7-28   *Routing Protocols*

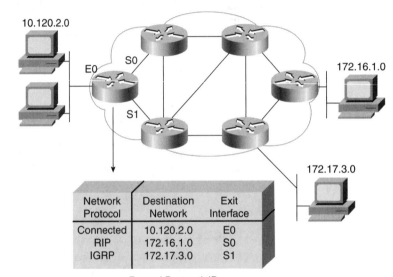

Dynamic routing relies on a routing protocol to disseminate and gather knowledge. A routing protocol defines the set of rules used by a router when it communicates with neighboring routers (that is, a routing protocol determines routing paths and maintains routing tables).

Routing Metrics

Routing protocols use many different metrics to determine the best route, each interpreting what is best in its own way. When a routing protocol updates a routing table, the primary objective of the protocol is to determine the best information to include in the table. The routing algorithm generates a number, called the metric value, for each path through the network. Sophisticated routing protocols can base route selection on multiple metrics, combining them in a single metric. Typically, the smaller the metric number is, the better the path. Figure 7-29 shows some common metrics used by routing protocols.

Figure 7-29 *Routing Metrics*

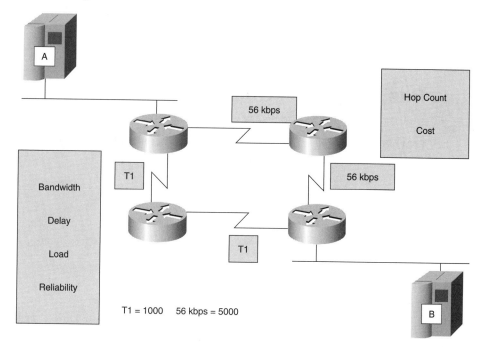

In this figure, depending on the metrics used, a datagram from Device A to Device B might take different paths. While a user might prefer to use the T1 links, because it is faster, the routing protocol might choose a different route based on its metric.

Metrics can be based on either a single characteristic or several characteristics of a path. The metrics that are most commonly used by routing protocols are as follows:

- **Bandwidth**—The data capacity of a link.

- **Delay**—The length of time required to move a packet along each link from source to destination this value could be measured based on the bandwidth of intermediate links, the status of the port queues at each router, network congestion, or physical distance between the links. For Cisco routers, the default delay of an interface is a fixed value based on the speed of the link only.

- **Load**—The amount of activity on a network resource such as a router or a link.

- **Reliability**—Usually a reference to the error rate of each network link.

- **Hop count**—The number of routers that a packet must travel through before reaching its destination.

- **Cost**—An arbitrary value, usually based on bandwidth, administrator preference, or other measurement, that is assigned by a network administrator.

Routers use addressing to identify unique networks within a routed internetwork. These routers de-encapsulate frames to examine the addresses and determine how to route frames to the appropriate destination. These destinations are determined using routing protocols to choose the best available route through the internetwork.

Routing Basics Section Quiz

Use these practice questions to review what you learned in this section.

1 Which term best describes the operation of a router in evaluating available routes to a destination and establishing the preferred handling of a packet?

   A Data linkage

   B Path determination

   C SDLC interface protocol

   D Frame Relay

2 Which best describes a routed protocol?

   A Provides enough information in its network layer address to allow a packet to be forwarded from host to host

   B Provides information necessary to translate data packets between to the next highest network layer protocols

   C Allows routers to communicate with other routers to maintain and update address tables

   D Allows routers to bind MAC and IP addresses together

3 Which of the following statements about the path determination process is *not* correct?

   A Routers evaluate the available paths to a destination.

   B Routers establish the preferred handling of a packet.

   C Dynamic routing occurs when information is configured onto each router by the network administrator.

   D Routing services use metrics and administrative distances when evaluating network paths.

4 Which of the following contains routing information that helps a router in determining the routing path?

   A IP address

   B MAC address

   C Routing table

   D Routed protocol

5 Which of the following are goals for routing protocols? (Choose three.)

   A Optimization

   B Flexibility

   C Simplicity

   D Rapid convergence

6 Which of the following is not a routing metric?

   A Delay

   B Bandwidth

   C Length

   D Load

Routing Protocols

In the routing process, protocols package data into a form that can be transmitted. Two major types of routing protocols exist, internal protocols that route information within an organization and external protocols that route information between networks. Each type of routing protocol functions differently and provides different advantages for network data transmission requirements.

Learning about the different types of routing protocols provides you with more understanding of how data is transmitted over TCP/IP and which protocol is best suited for a given environment.

The two major types of routing protocols are as follows:

- **Interior Gateway Protocols (IGP)**—Used to exchange routing information within an autonomous system. RIP and IGRP are examples of IGPs.

- **Exterior Gateway Protocols (EGP)**—Used to exchange routing information between autonomous systems. Border Gateway Protocol version 4 (BGP4) is an example of an EGP.

Figure 7-30 helps distinguish the difference between IGPs and EGPs.

Figure 7-30 *IGPs Versus EGPs*

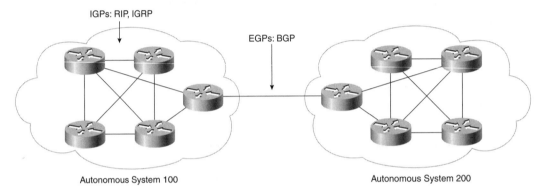

An *autonomous system* is a collection of networks under a common administrative control, consisting of routers that present a consistent view of routing to the external world. Autonomous system numbers are allocated to the regional registries by the IANA.

Autonomous system numbers can be obtained from the registry in your region. This autonomous system number is a 16-bit number. An exterior routing protocol such as Border Gateway Protocol (BGP) requires that you specify this unique, assigned autonomous system number in your configuration.

IGPs route packets within an autonomous system. Examples of IGPs include the following:

- RIP
- IGRP
- EIGRP
- OSPF
- Intermediate System-to-Intermediate System (IS-IS)

EGPs route packets between autonomous systems. BGP4 is the only currently supported EGP.

Most enterprises use IGPs to allow multiple routers to communicate information about networks to route traffic between devices within the enterprise internetwork. EGPs are used when connecting an enterprise to multiple ISPs, between ISPs, or in very large enterprise deployments.

Overview of Routing Protocol Categories

Although all routing protocols perform the function highlighted in the previous section, different ways to arrive at the end product exist. Routing protocols are divided three categories that describe how they perform these functions. These categories are as follows:

- Distance vector
- Link-state
- Hybrid

Distance Vector Routing Protocols

The distance vector routing approach determines the direction (vector) and distance (hop count) to any network in the internetwork. Distance vector-based routing algorithms (also known as Bellman-Ford algorithms) periodically (such as every 30 seconds) send all or portions of their routing table to their adjacent neighbors. While doing this, the algorithm also accumulates distance vectors. Routers running IGP distance vector routing protocols send periodic updates even if no changes in the network occur. By receiving a neighbor's routing table, a router can verify all the known routes and make changes to the local routing table based upon updated information received from the neighboring router. For example, in Figure 7-31, Router B receives information from Router A. Router B adds a distance vector metric (such as the number of hops), increasing the distance vector. It then passes the routing table to its other neighbor, Router C. This same step-by-step process occurs in all directions between direct-neighbor routers. This process is also known as *routing by rumor* because the understanding that a router has of the network is based upon the neighbors' perspective of the network topology.

Figure 7-31 *Distance Vector Algorithm*

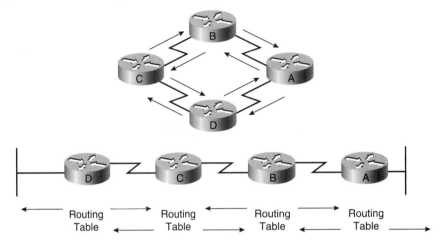

In this way, the algorithm accumulates network distances so that it can maintain a database of internetwork topology information. Distance vector algorithms do not allow a router to know the exact topology of an internetwork.

Examples of distance vector protocols include the following:

● **RIP**—A commonly used distance vector routing protocol, RIP uses hop count as its routing metric. You learn more about RIP in the section, "RIPv1 and RIPv2" later in this chapter.

● **IGRP**—IGRP was developed by Cisco to address the issues associated with routing in large, heterogeneous networks. IGRP uses bandwidth, delay, reliability, load, and maximum transmission unit (MTU) as metrics to make the overall best path determination. You learn more about this protocol in the section, "IGRP."

Link-State Routing Protocols

Link-state routing protocols use a different algorithm to respond quickly to network changes, send triggered updates only when a network change has occurred, and send periodic updates (known as link-state refreshes) at long time intervals, such as every 30 minutes.

Link-state protocols build routing tables based on a topology database. This database is built from link-state packets that are passed between all the routers to describe the state of a network. The database is used by the shortest path first algorithm to build the routing table. Figure 7-32 shows the components of a link-state protocol.

Figure 7-32   *Link-State Algorithm*

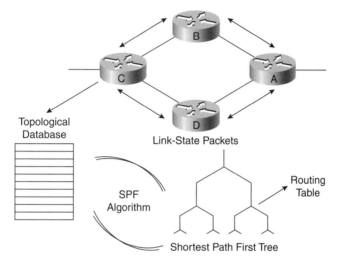

When a link changes state, the device that detected the change creates a link-state advertisement (LSA) concerning that link (route), and that LSA is propagated to all OSPF routers. Each OSPF router takes a copy of the LSA, updates its link-state (topological) database, and forwards the LSA to all neighboring OSPF routers. This flooding of the LSA is required to ensure that all OSPF routers update their databases before creating an updated routing table that reflects the new topology.

The link-state database calculates the best paths through the network, by applying the Dijkstra shortest path first (SPF) algorithm against the link-state database to build the shortest-path-first tree. The best (shortest) paths are then selected from the shortest-path-first tree and placed in the routing table. Whereas the distance vector algorithm has nonspecific information about distant networks and no knowledge of distant routers, a link-state routing algorithm maintains full knowledge of distant routers and how they interconnect.

Examples of link-state routing protocols include the following:

- **OSPF**— An IETF standard link-state routing protocol for IP. This protocol uses cost to choose the best path through the network and converges rapidly using link-state updates. You learn more about this protocol in the section "OSPF" later in this chapter.

- **IS-IS**— IS-IS is an OSI standard link-state routing protocol for multiple Layer 3 protocols like IP and DECnet Phase IV. This protocol also uses cost to choose the best path through a network and converges rapidly using link state updates. IS-IS is not covered in this book.

As networks become larger in scale, link-state routing protocols become more attractive because of the following:

- Link-state protocols send Flash updates of a topology change within the network.

- Periodic updates are more infrequent than those for distance vector protocols.

- Networks running link-state routing protocols can be segmented into area hierarchies, limiting the scope of route changes.

- Networks running link-state routing protocols support classless addressing.

- Networks running link-state routing protocols support summarization.

Engineers have implemented this link-state concept in Open Shortest Path First (OSPF) routing. RFC 2328, "OSPF Version 2," describes OSPF link-state concepts and operations (http://www.isi.edu/in-notes/rfc2328.txt).

Hybrid Routing Protocols

An emerging third type of routing protocol combines aspects of both distance vector and link-state. This third type is called *balanced hybrid* in this book.

The balanced hybrid routing protocol uses distance vectors with more accurate metrics to determine the best paths to destination networks. However, it differs from most distance vector protocols by using topology changes to trigger routing database updates as opposed to periodic updates.

The balanced hybrid routing type converges more rapidly, like the link-state protocols. However, it differs from these protocols by emphasizing economy in the use of required resources such as bandwidth, memory, and processor overhead.

An example of a hybrid algorithm is EIGRP. This protocol, developed by Cisco, is an advanced version of IGRP. It provides superior convergence properties and operating efficiency and combines the advantages of link-state protocols with those of distance vector protocols. You learn more about this protocol later in the "EIGRP" section of this chapter.

NOTE	While introductory books often refer to EIGRP as a hybrid routing protocol, it would be more accurately described as a diffused or DUAL protocol because it uses the Diffusing Update Algorithm (DUAL) to choose a route and maintains feasible successors. The DUAL routing protocol is discussed in greater detail in the Cisco Press book, *CCNP Self-Study: Building Scalable Cisco Internetworks (BSCI)*, Second Edition (Paquet and Teare, 2004).

No single best routing protocol exists for all internetworks. Network administrators must weigh technical and nontechnical aspects of their networks to determine which is best. The following sections describe some of the characteristics of the more commonly used routing protocols.

RIPv1 and RIPv2

The Routing Information Protocol (RIP) uses distance vector algorithms to determine the direction and distance to any link in the internetwork. This section describes the features and operations of both RIP version 1 (RIPv1) and RIP version 2 (RIPv2).

If multiple paths to a destination exist, RIP selects the path with the smallest number of hops. However, because hop count is the only routing metric used by RIP, it does not necessarily select the fastest path to a destination. It counts only hops.

RIP allows routers to update their routing tables at programmable intervals; the default interval is every 30 seconds. Because RIP is constantly sending routing updates to its neighboring routers, this process can cause network traffic to build. A Cisco enhancement to RIP also allows it to send triggered updates, which includes the entire routing table, when a topology change occurs.

To prevent a packet from a condition known as looping, RIP has a hop-count limitation of 15 hops. If the destination network is more than 15 routers away as shown in Figure 7-33, it is considered unreachable and the packet is dropped. This limitation creates a scalability issue when routing in large, heterogeneous networks.

RIPv1 is a classful routing protocol, which means that all devices in the same network must use the same subnet mask, because RIPv1 does not include the subnet mask information with the routing update. RIPv2 provides what is called prefix routing and does send subnet mask information with the route updates. This supports the use of classless routing. With classless routing protocols, different subnets within the same network can have different subnet masks. The use of different subnet masks within the same network is referred to as variable-length subnet masking (VLSM).

Figure 7-33 *RIP Hop-Count Limitation*

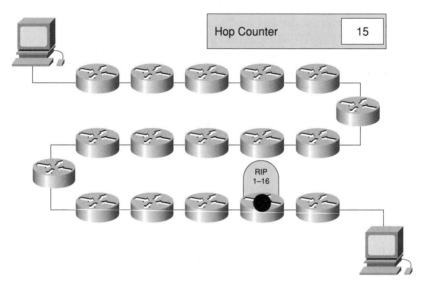

IGRP

IGRP is a distance-vector routing protocol developed by Cisco. It was developed specifically to address problems associated with routing in large networks that were beyond the scope of protocols such as RIP. While RIP selects the path with the fewest hops, IGRP can select the fastest path, based on the delay, bandwidth, load, MTU, and reliability. Network administrators can determine the importance given to any one of these metrics or allow IGRP to automatically calculate the optimal path. By default, IGRP uses bandwidth and delay metrics only. Like RIP, it supports only classful routing. IGRP also has a much higher maximum hop-count limit than RIP, to allow the network to scale.

IGRP sends routing updates at 90-second intervals or when a topology change occurs, advertising the network for a particular autonomous system. These are key design characteristics of IGRP:

- Versatility that enables it to automatically handle indefinite, complex topologies
- Flexibility for segments that have different bandwidth and delay characteristics
- Scalability for functioning in very large networks

EIGRP

EIGRP is an advanced version of IGRP and is a proprietary Cisco protocol, providing superior operating efficiency such as faster convergence and lower overhead bandwidth.

EIGRP combines the advantages of link-state protocols with those of distance vector protocols. Thus, the term hybrid describes its algorithm.

While EIGRP uses the same default and configurable metrics as IGRP, five basic components enhance its ability to route data:

- **Neighbor discovery and recovery**—This feature allows routers to learn about neighboring routers dynamically.

- **Reliable Transport Protocol**—This technology guarantees the ordered delivery of EIGRP packets to all neighbors.

- **DUAL finite-state machine**—Diffusing Update Algorithm (DUAL) tracks all routes advertised by all neighbors so that it can select a loop-free path.

- **Protocol-specific modules**—These modules are responsible for network layer, protocol-specific requirements needed to make routing decisions. EIGRP supports multiple routed protocols.

- **VLSM support**—Subnet masks are included in routing tables and updates, and EIGRP is therefore capable of classless routing and the use of different subnet masks within the network.

OSPF

The OSPF protocol is a link-state protocol that was written to address the needs of large, scalable internetworks beyond the capabilities of the RIP protocol. The IETF developed OSPF in 1988. The most recent version is known as OSPF version 2 and is an open standard. OSPF is an IGP, which means that it distributes routing information between routers belonging to the same autonomous system. The large network issues it addresses include the following:

- **Speed of convergence**—In large networks, RIP convergence can take several minutes as the routing algorithm goes through a hold-down and route-aging period. With OSPF, convergence is faster than it is with RIP because routing changes are flooded immediately and computed in parallel.

- **Support for VLSMs**—RIPv1 does not support VLSMs. OSPF is a classless routing protocol, sending subnet mask information along with the routing updates, so it supports VLSMs. (Note that RIPv2 also supports VLSMs.)

- **Network reachability**—OSPF has virtually no reachability limitations.

- **Use of bandwidth**—RIP broadcasts full routing tables to all neighbors every 30 seconds, a situation that can become especially problematic over slow WAN links. OSPF multicasts link-state updates and sends the updates only when a change in the network occurs. (Note that OSPF also sends updates every 30 minutes to ensure that all routers are synchronized.)

- **Method for path selection**—RIP has no concept of network delays and link costs. Routing decisions are based purely on hop count, a situation that could lead to suboptimal path selection in cases where a longer path (in terms of hop count) has a higher aggregate link bandwidth and shorter delays. OSPF uses a cost value, which for Cisco routers is based on the configured bandwidth of the interface.

BGP

BGP is an example of an EGP. It is the principal route advertising protocol used by major companies and ISPs on the Internet. BGP exchanges routing information between autonomous systems while guaranteeing loop-free path selection. Version 4 of BGP is the first version of BGP that supports classless interdomain routing (CIDR) and route aggregation. Unlike common IGPs such as RIP, OSPF, and EIGRP, BGP does not use metrics such as hop count, bandwidth, or delay. Instead, BGP makes routing decisions based on network policies using various BGP path attributes.

BGP updates are carried using TCP on port 179. In contrast, RIP updates use User Datagram Protocol (UDP) port 520, while OSPF uses neither TCP nor UDP (it has its own network layer protocol number of 89). Because BGP requires TCP, IP connectivity must exist between BGP peers, and TCP connections must be negotiated between them before updates can be exchanged. Therefore, BGP inherits the reliable, connection-oriented properties of TCP.

To guarantee loop-free path selection, BGP constructs a graph of autonomous systems based on the information exchanged between BGP neighbors. As far as BGP is concerned, the whole internetwork is a graph, or tree, of autonomous systems. The connection between any two autonomous systems forms a path, and the collection of path information is expressed as a sequence of autonomous system numbers (called the autonomous system path). This sequence forms a route to reach a specific destination, as shown in Figure 7-34.

BGP is used extensively in the Internet today to connect ISPs and to connect enterprises to ISPs.

Routing protocols all provide the same basic services to allow packets to be routed through an internetwork. Routing protocols have different characteristics and network administrators must choose a protocol that is best suited for their own environment.

Figure 7-34 *BGP Path Selections*

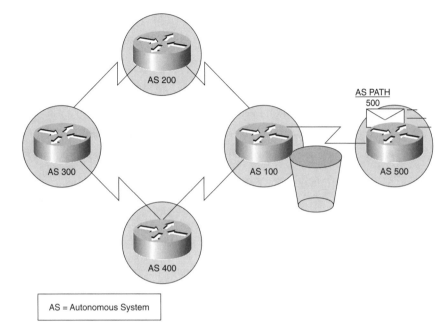

AS = Autonomous System

Routing Protocols Section Quiz

Use these practice questions to review what you learned in this section.

1 Which of the following is an example of an EGP?

  A OSPF

  B RIP

  C BGP

  D EIGRP

2 What are IGPs used for?

  A To set up a compatibility infrastructure between networks

  B To communicate between autonomous systems

  C to transmit between nodes on a network

  D To deliver routing information within a single autonomous system

3 Which best describes a distance vector protocol?

A It determines the direction and distance to any network in the internetwork.

B Each router maintains a complex database of internetwork topology information.

C It is computationally rather complex.

D It is a method of routing that prevents loops and minimizes counting to infinity.

4 Which of the following best describes link-state algorithms?

A They determine distance and direction to any link on the internetwork.

B They require minimal computation.

C They recreate the exact topology of the entire internetwork.

D They use little network overhead and reduce overall traffic.

5 In the IP RIP routing protocol, how often are periodic routing updates sent?

A Every 30 seconds

B Every 60 seconds

C Every 90 seconds

D Only when the administrator directs the router to do so

6 By default, which of the following is a routing metric used by IGRP?

A Bandwidth and delay

B MTU size and load

C Hop count and delay

D Reliability and load

7 Which of the following is *not* a basic component of EIGRP?

A Routes only for IP

B DUAL finite-state machine

C Neighbor discovery and recovery

D Rapid convergence

8 Which of the following is *not* a feature of OSPF?

   A Has fast convergence

   B Processes updates efficiently

   C Selects paths based on hop count

   D Supports VLSM

9 BGP is an example of which type of protocol?

   A Interior Gateway Protocol

   B Enhanced Interior Gateway Routing Protocol

   C Routing protocol

   D Routed protocol

Chapter Summary

The fundamental principles of building and maintaining internetworks are based on Layer 3 protocols. This chapter presented an overview of Layer 3 IP addressing and routing. In this chapter, you learned about how each IP address has a portion that identifies the network and another portion that identifies the host. You also learned how classes and subnet masks identify these portions of the address. This chapter also discussed how routing protocols determine the location of each individual network address within an internetwork to pass packets to the appropriate end device. Finally, this chapter compared and contrasted the different types of routing protocols.

Chapter Review Questions

Use these review questions to test your knowledge of the concepts discussed in this chapter.

1 Host addresses can be dynamically assigned.

   A True

   B False

2 What network address is reserved for loopback testing?

   A 0.0.0.0

   B 191.168.32.0

   C 127.0.0.0

   D 172.16.0.0

3 What is the translation of private addresses to public addresses referred to as?

   A DHCP

   B DNS

   C WINS

   D NAT

4 Which is the IP protocol that is being implemented to increase the number of network addresses available?

   A IPv2

   B IPv4

   C IPv6

   D IPv8

5 How many host addresses are available if the IP subnet address is 206.15.8.0/20?

   A 4088

   B 4098

   C 4094

   D 4096

6 Which of the following is a benefit from subnetting a network? (Choose two.)

   A Better traffic control

   B Better performance

   C Less device management

   D Increased collisions

   E Increased traffic

7 If you were going to borrow four bits to create a subnet mask for a Class B address, what would the subnet mask be?

   A 255.255.224.0

   B 255.255.255.0

   C 255.255.240.0

   D 255.255.0.0

8 How many subnets could be created if six bits are borrowed?

   A 8

   B 16

   C 32

   D 62

   E 128

9 What are the key functions of a router? (Choose all that apply.)

   A Maintain routing tables

   B Use routing tables to determine the optimal path for network traffic

   C Determine where to forward a packet of data

   D Add necessary framing for an interface

10 What happens in the third step of the encapsulation/de-encapsulation process?

   A The network layer process examines the network layer header to determine the destination network.

   B The router de-encapsulates and examines the frame to determine what type of network layer data is being carried.

   C The packet is re-encapsulated in the data link layer frame for the selected interface and transmitted.

   D The router translates the frame into the network layer protocol associated with the outgoing interface and forwards to the next hop.

11 What are some informational items contained in a routing table? (Choose two.)

   A Destination/next-hop associations

   B Routing metric

   C Segment length

   D Ticks

12 Which of the following is *not* a routing protocol?

   A RIP

   B BGP

   C IP

   D IGRP

   E OSPF

13 A router compares the destination network address to a routing table to select a path.

   A True

   B False

14 For a Cisco router, which of the following is used by the Cisco IOS to help measure delay?

   A Cost

   B Bandwidth

   C Hop

   D Load

15 What do routers use to exchange data?

   A Advanced configurations

   B Routing protocols

   C IP addresses

   D Signals

16 What do link-state protocols propagate when a network change occurs?

   A Routing tables

   B LSA

   C OSPF

   D Metrics

17 When using RIP, what is the hop-count limitation?

   A 6

   B 10

   C 15

   D No hop-count limitation

18 Which of the following are benefits of IGRP when compared to RIP? (Choose two.)

   A Higher hop-count limitation

   B Fewer metrics

   C Versatility for handling complex networks

   D More updates sent when network changes occur

19 Which of the following is *not* true about EIGRP?

   A It is a Cisco proprietary protocol.

   B It is based on the DUAL algorithm.

   C It is considered a hybrid protocol.

   D It has more overhead than IGRP.

20 Which is *not* true about OSPF?

   A It supports VLSM.

   B It has virtually no hop-count limitation.

   C It sends updates to neighbors every 30 seconds.

   D OSPF bases its metric on cost.

Administering Cisco Devices

Upon completion of this chapter, you will be able to perform the following tasks:

- Describe the functions of major WAN technologies, including point-to-point, circuit switching, packet switching, and multiplexing

- Describe the functions of WAN access technologies, including ISDN, digital subscriber line (DSL), Frame Relay, Asynchronous Transfer Mode (ATM), and SONET, and the functions of two protocols, PPP and HDLC

- Describe the functions of analog and cable modems

CHAPTER 8

Using WAN Technologies

WANs are connections between LANs across a wide geographic area. Several WAN connection technologies exist, including point-to-point, circuit switching, and packet switching, as well as physical devices to establish the connection, such as analog and cable modems. Several technologies are involved in accessing a WAN, such as Integrated Services Digital Network (ISDN), digital subscriber line (DSL), Frame Relay, Asynchronous Transfer Mode (ATM), and Synchronous Optical Network (SONET), as well as protocols such as Point-to-Point Protocol (PPP) and High-Level Data Link Control (HDLC). This chapter describes the functions of major WAN technologies, as well as WAN access technologies and provides an overview of analog and cable modems.

WAN Technology Basics

Several types of WAN connection technologies exist, including circuit switching, packet switching, and point-to-point. Bandwidth and multiplexing affect the speed at which data is transmitted over a WAN connection. Learning about WAN connections helps you understand how WANs function overall.

A WAN is a data communications network that covers a relatively broad geographic area and uses transmission facilities provided by a service provider, or carrier, such as a telephone or cable company. WAN connections connect a variety of users in different locations together, as shown in Figure 8-1.

The connection technologies in WAN environments can be classified into three major categories:

- **Circuit switched**—Using switched circuits, data connections are initiated when needed and terminated when the transmission is completed. A regular telephone line is an example of a circuit-switched connection.

- **Packet switched**—In a packet-switched environment, the carrier resources are shared among many customers who connect to the carrier's network (often referred to as a cloud). Packets of data are transmitted through the carrier's network from one customer site to another.

- **Point to point**—This technology is sometimes called a leased line because the lines are leased from a carrier (usually a telephone company) and are dedicated for use by the company leasing the lines. Companies pay for a continuous connection between two remote sites, and the line is active 24 hours a day, 7 days a week.

Figure 8-1   *WAN Connections*

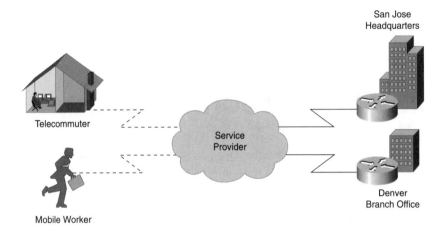

Circuit Switching

Switched circuits allow connections to be initiated when transmission is needed and terminated when the transmission is completed. With circuit switching a logical circuit is temporarily dedicated to the call. While it does not change while the call is in progress, the carrier multiplexes other customers' data onto the parts inside the cloud. Only the access path is completely dedicated to a single customer. Figure 8-2 shows an example of circuit switching using modems across the telephone company network for WAN connectivity.

Figure 8-2   *Circuit Switch Connections*

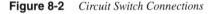

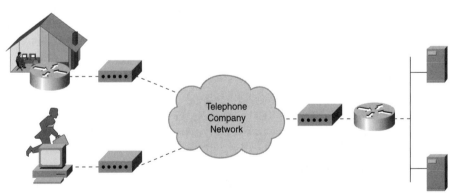

Circuit switching operates much like a normal dialup telephone call and is used extensively in telephone company networks. The Public Switched Telephone Network (PSTN) and ISDN are examples of circuit-switched WAN connection technology.

Packet Switching

Packet switching is a switching method in which users share common carrier resources for data transmission. Packet switching allows the carrier to make more efficient use of its infrastructure, so the cost to the customer is generally lower than with point-to-point leased lines.

In a packet-switching environment, many customer networks connect to the carrier's network. The carrier can then create virtual circuits between customer sites by which packets of data are delivered from one site to another through the network, as shown in Figure 8-3.

Figure 8-3 *Packet Switching Virtual Circuits*

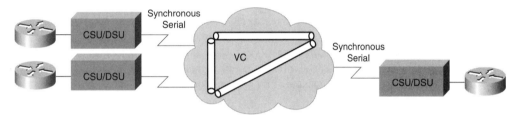

Point to Point

A point-to-point (or serial) communication link provides a single, pre-established WAN communications path from the customer premises through a carrier network, such as a telephone company, to a remote network. Point-to-point lines are usually leased from a carrier and are often called leased lines. For a point-to-point line, the carrier dedicates fixed transport capacity and facility hardware to a customer's line. The carrier still uses multiplexing technologies within the network. These circuits are generally priced based on bandwidth required, as well as the distance between the two connected points. Point-to-point links are generally more expensive than shared services such as Frame Relay. Figure 8-4 shows a leased line connection.

Figure 8-4 *Leased Line Connection*

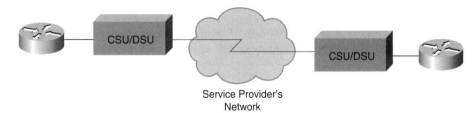

When leased line connections are made, a router interface is required for each connection. If a serial interface is used, a channel service unit/data service unit (CSU/DSU) is also required. The purpose of the CSU/DSU is to provide a clocked signal to the customer equipment interface from the DSU and terminate the carrier's channelized transport media on the CSU. It also provides diagnostic functions such as loopback. Most T1 or E1 time-division multiplexing (TDM) interfaces on current routers include approved CSU capabilities. Typically, the two devices are packaged as a single unit.

If you select a leased line connection, one of the decisions that needs to be made is how much bandwidth is needed to support the network applications.

Bandwidth

Point-to-point connections can be purchased or leased in a variety of speeds, or bandwidths. *Bandwidth* refers to the speed at which data is transferred over the communication link. It is usually expressed as a DS number (DS0, DS1, and so forth), in North America, that technically refers to the rate and format of the signal. The most fundamental line speed is 64 kbps (DS0), which is the bandwidth required for an uncompressed, digitized phone call.

Serial connection bandwidths can be incrementally increased to accommodate the need for faster transmission, as shown in Figure 8-5.

Figure 8-5   *WAN Bandwidths*

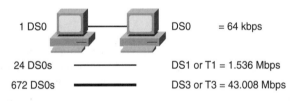

As shown, 24 DS0s can be bundled to get a DS1 line (also called a T1 line) with a speed of 1.536 Mbps (1.544 Mbps after the addition of the line signaling). Then, 28 DS1s (or 627 DS0s) can be bundled to get a DS3 (also called a T3 line) with a speed of 43.008 Mbps (44.736 Mbps after the addition of the line signaling).

NOTE   E1 (2.048 Mbps) and E3 (34.368 Mbps) are European and South American standards similar to T1 and T3, but they possess different bandwidths and frame structures.

Multiplexing

Multiplexing is a process of sharing in which multiple data channels are combined into a single data or physical channel for transmission. Multiplexing can be implemented at any of the OSI layers. After the channels are combined at the source, at the receiving end of the transmission the data is "demultiplexed" into its original, separate forms. This process allows multiple transmissions to be handled by only one line, as shown in Figure 8-6.

Figure 8-6   *Mutliplexing*

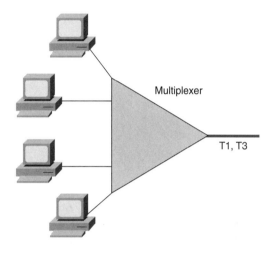

The following are the primary types of multiplexing that operate at the physical layer:

- Time-division multiplexing (TDM)
- Frequency-division multiplexing (FDM)
- Wave-division multiplexing (WDM)
- Statistical multiplexing

With time-division multiplexing (TDM), information from each data channel is allocated bandwidth based on preassigned time slots, regardless of whether there is data to transmit. As shown in Figure 8-7, bandwidth is wasted when a data channel has nothing to transmit during its assigned time slot.

Figure 8-7   *Time-Division Multiplexing*

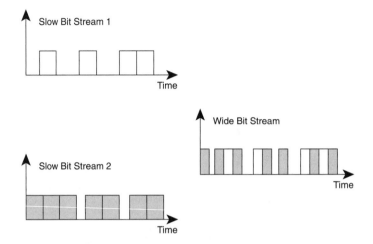

In TDM, the physical layer attribute used for sharing is based on time.

With frequency-division multiplexing (FDM), information from each data channel is allocated bandwidth based on the signal frequency of the traffic. For example, FM radio broadcast uses FDM. Each FM station is assigned a specific frequency to use for broadcasting its radio programs. Figure 8-8 shows multiplexing using two frequencies.

Figure 8-8   *Frequency-Division Multiplexing*

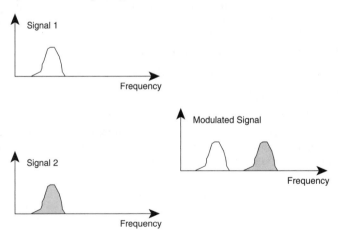

In FDM, the physical layer attribute used for sharing is based on frequency.

With wavelength-division multiplexing (WDM) and dense WDM (DWDM), the physical layer attribute used for sharing is based on wavelength (inverse of frequency).

With statistical multiplexing, a bandwidth is dynamically allocated to any data channels that have information to transmit. Figure 8-9 show an example of statistical multiplexing.

Figure 8-9   *Statistical Multiplexing*

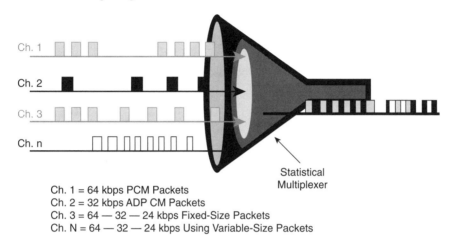

Ch. 1 = 64 kbps PCM Packets
Ch. 2 = 32 kbps ADP CM Packets
Ch. 3 = 64 — 32 — 24 kbps Fixed-Size Packets
Ch. N = 64 — 32 — 24 kbps Using Variable-Size Packets

Packets, frames, and cells could all be considered a form of statistical multiplexing because they allocate access to the link based on when a particular link needs to transmit.

Each form of WAN connectivity and the bandwidths offered provide a unique advantage for connecting sites together. With a better understanding of the advantages and disadvantages, you are able to more effectively choose a WAN service.

WAN Technology Basics Section Quiz

Use the practice questions here to review what you learned in this section.

1 Which of the following best describes a WAN?

   A Connects LANs that are separated by a large geographic area

   B Connects workstations, terminals, and other devices in a metropolitan area

   C Connects a LAN within a large building

   D Connects workstations, terminals, and other devices within a building

2 Which of the following is an example of a circuit-switching protocol?

A ISDN

B Frame Relay

C PPP

D HDLC

3 Which of the following phrases describes a packet-switching protocol?

A A switching method in which users share common carrier resources for data transmission

B Allows connections to be initiated when transmission is needed and terminated when the transmission is completed

C Operates much like a normal dialup telephone call and is used extensively in telephone company networks

D A method of using high-speed data frames to multiplex between different layers of the OSI model

4 A leased line is a _____ link that provides a single, pre-established WAN communication path from the customer to a remote network.

A Point-to-point

B Point-to-multipoint

C Analog

D Digital

5 How many DS0s can be bundled to get a DS1/T1 line?

A 24

B 28

C 48

D 64

6 Which of the following is a type of physical-layer multiplexing? (Choose all that apply.)

A TDM

B FDM

C WDM

D Frame Relay

WAN Access Technologies

Whether a WAN is connected through a circuit-switching, packet-switching, or point-to-point technology, several access technologies, including ISDN, DSL, Frame Relay, ATM, and SONET, as well the point-to-point protocols PPP and HDLC, govern the way in which data is transmitted over the WAN. Each of these access technologies serves a different purpose and provides a different type of data transmission.

After you learn the basics about how WANs function overall, learning about how the different kinds of WAN function provides you with a deeper understanding of the various methods of transmitting data over WANs.

Several protocols are used in transmitting data over point-to-point or switched communication links. Two of the most common are the Point-to-Point Protocol (PPP) and High-Level Data Link Control (HDLC).

PPP

PPP was created to solve remote Internet connectivity problems. Additionally, PPP was needed to support the dynamic assignment of IP addresses and to allow the use of multiple routed protocols over a serial link. PPP provides router-to-router and host-to-network connections over both synchronous and asynchronous circuits. An example of an asynchronous connection is a dialup connection. An example of a synchronous connection is a leased line.

PPP provides a standard method for encapsulating and transporting multiprotocol datagrams over point-to-point links, as shown in Figure 8-10.

Figure 8-10   *PPP Encapsulation*

PPP comprises these three main components:

- A method for encapsulating multiprotocol datagrams

- A link control protocol (LCP) for establishing, configuring, and testing the data-link connection

- A family of Network Control Programs (NCPs) for establishing and configuring different network layer protocols

Figure 8-11 shows the fields in the PPP frame used to carry out these services.

Figure 8-11 *PPP Frame*

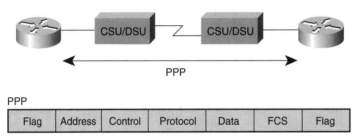

To be sufficiently versatile and portable to a wide variety of environments, PPP provides an LCP. The LCP automatically determines the encapsulation format option, to handle varying limits on sizes of packets, to detect a loopback link and other common misconfiguration errors, and to terminate the link. Other optional facilities provided are authentication of the identity of its peer on the link and determination of when a link is functioning properly or failing.

The authentication phase of a PPP session is optional. After the link has been established and the authentication protocol chosen, the peer can be authenticated. If it is used, authentication takes place before the network layer protocol configuration phase begins.

The authentication options require that the calling side of the link enter authentication information to help ensure that the user has the network administrator's permission to make the call. Peer routers exchange authentication messages.

HDLC

HDLC is a standard data link layer protocol. HDLC specifies an encapsulation method for data on synchronous serial data links using frame character and checksum. HDLC supports both point-to-point and multipoint configurations. Standard HDLC is compatible between all vendors; however, some vendors, like Cisco, might have a variant of HDLC that is not compatible with the standard form of the protocol.

Cisco has an implementation of HDLC that is proprietary and is the default encapsulation for serial lines. This implementation is very streamlined; it has no windowing or flow control, and only point-to-point connections are allowed. The Cisco HDLC implementation includes proprietary extensions in the data field, as shown in Figure 8-12.

Figure 8-12   *HDLC and Cisco HDLC Frame*

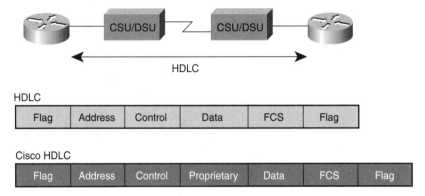

Cisco HDLC does not communicate with other HDLC implementations. HDLC encapsulations vary, however, so PPP should be used when interoperability with other vendors is required.

ISDN

ISDN is a circuit-switched connection technology. It is an efficient alternative to dialup for connecting over basic telephone service.

ISDN refers to a set of communication protocols proposed by telephone companies to permit telephone networks to carry data, voice, graphics, music, and video, as shown in Figure 8-13.

Figure 8-13   *ISDN Services*

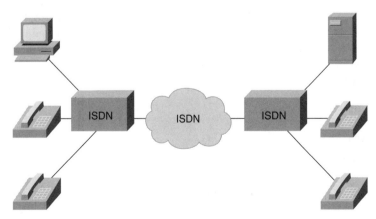

ISDN was developed to permit faster access over existing telephone systems without the additional call setup time. Because ISDN uses existing phone lines, it requires that the central office (CO) be within a certain distance, which limits service availability.

ISDN offers two types of services: Basic Rate Interface (BRI) and Primary Rate Interface (PRI). The ISDN BRI service, intended for the home and small enterprise, provides two B channels (128 kbps) and one D channel (16 kbps). The BRI B channels carry user data, while the BRI D channel carries control and signaling information.

The ISDN PRI service, intended for larger installations, delivers 23 B channels and one D channel in North America for a total bit rate of up to 1.544 Mbps (T1). In Europe, Australia, and other parts of the world, ISDN PRI provides 30 B channels and one D channel, for a total bit rate of up to 2.048 Mbps (E1). Figure 8-14 shows the bandwidth available for the different ISDN services.

Figure 8-14   *BRI and PRI Services*

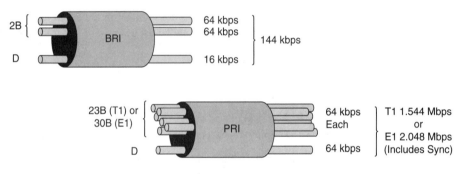

DSL

DSL technology is a circuit-switched connection technology that uses existing technology lines to transport high-bandwidth data, such as multimedia and video, to service sub-scribers. DSL uses existing phone lines, so it requires CO access equipment (digital subscriber line access multiplexer [DSLAM]) to connect the DSL line to the network and has distance restrictions that might limit service availability. Figure 8-15 shows a typical DSL connection scenario.

Figure 8-15   *DSL Services*

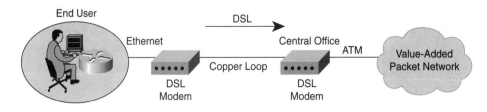

DSL provides a full-time connection. As soon as users turn on their computers connected to the DSL modem, they are connected. This setup removes the time and effort of dialing in to establish a connection.

The two primary types of DSL technologies are asymmetric (ADSL) and symmetric. All forms of DSL service are categorized as one or the other, and numerous varieties of each type exist. The term *xDSL* sometimes refers generically to any of the various forms of DSL. Figure 8-16 shows the relationship of the different DSL components and services.

Figure 8-16   *DSL Service Types*

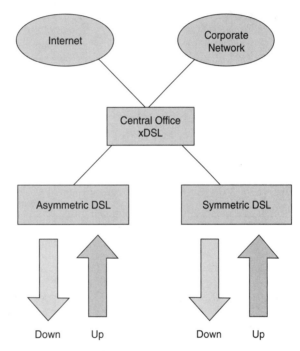

Asymmetric service provides higher download or downstream speeds than upstream speeds. Symmetric service provides the same speed in both directions.

Downstream information, such as requested web pages, comes from the internetwork to the user (from the CO to the subscriber). Upstream information is sent from the user to the internetwork (from the subscriber to the CO). Asymmetric types of DSL generally use analog transmission encoding (modulation) technology, while symmetric forms generally use digital transmission encoding techniques.

A number of standards are associated with DSL. Table 8-1 lists each DSL technology and the relevant standards organizations and standard numbers associated with those technologies.

Table 8-1   *DSL Technologies Standards*

DSL Types	Standards	Modulation/ Encoding Technique	Speed	Distance Limit
Full-Rate ADSL/ G.DMT	ANSI T1.413 issue 2	DMT or CAP	Downstream speeds of 384 kbps to 1 Mbps; upstream slower up to 1.024 Mbps	18,000 feet
G.Lite	ITU-U G.992.1 ITU-T G 992.2	DMT	Downstream speed up to 1.5 Mbps; upstream speed up to 640 kbps	18,000 feet
Very High Data Rate DSL(VDSL)	ETSI and ANSI in process	DMT/QAM	12.96 Mbps to 52.8 Mbps for both upstream and downstream	4500 feet
ISDN DSL (IDSL)	ETSI ETR 080	2B1Q	144 kbps for both upstream and downstream	18,000 feet
SDSL	None	2B1Q	768 kbps for both upstream and downstream	22,000 feet
High Data Rate DSL (HDSL)	ITU G991.1, ANSI TR 28	2B1Q	1.544 or 2.048 Mbps for both upstream and downstream	12,000 feet
G.SHDSL	ITU G.991.2	TC PAM	192 kbps to 2.3 Mbps for both upstream and downstream	28,000 feet

Not all the DSL technologies listed have a standard associated with them. Also listed is the modulation or encoding standard(s) used by the DSL modems to place digital data bits onto the wire. The most important standards listed in the table are asymmetric DSL standards G.992.1 (G.DMT) and G.992.2 (G.Lite), as well as symmetric standard G.991.2 (G.SHDSL). All vendors who are currently building DSL support these international standards.

DSL has a number of advantages over other circuit-switched technologies, as well as a few disadvantages.

DSL service can be added incrementally in any area. That means that the service provider can literally start up with a handful of clients and upgrade the bandwidth to coincide with the growth in numbers of subscribers. DSL is also backward compatible with analog voice and makes good use of the existing local loop. This means that little needs to be done to use the DSL service simultaneously with normal phone service.

However, DSL suffers from the following limitations:

* Most DSL service offerings currently require the customer to be within 18,000 feet of the provider's CO location.

* The older, longer loops present problems with line noise.

* Upstream (upload) speed is usually considerably slower than the downstream (download) speed.

Frame Relay

Frame Relay is a frame-switching connection technology and is implemented using virtual circuits. Several devices and components are involved in providing Frame Relay services.

Two classes of Frame Relay devices exist:

* **Data terminal equipment (DTE)**—Terminating equipment for a specific network that is typically located on a customer premises. An example of a Frame Relay DTE device is a router.

* **Data communications equipment (DCE)**—An internetworking device that provides clocking and switching services within a network. An example of a Frame Relay DCE device is the Frame Relay switch.

Figure 8-17 shows how this equipment relates to the WAN connections.

Figure 8-17 *Frame Relay Equipment*

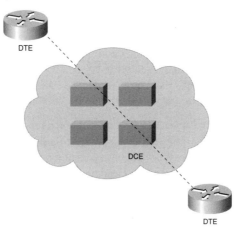

Frame Relay operates over virtual circuits, which are logical connections created to enable
communication between two remote devices across a network. Virtual circuits provide a
bidirectional communications path from one DTE device to another. A data-link connection
identifier (DLCI) within the Frame Relay address header uniquely identifies a virtual
circuit. The DLCI is specific only to the router or Frame Relay switch where it is
configured. A virtual circuit can pass through any number of intermediate DCE devices
located within the network. Numerous virtual circuits can be multiplexed into a single
physical circuit for access to and transmission across the network.

To illustrate how Frame Relay works, Figure 8-18 shows a hub-and-spoke topology used to
connect a headquarters router to three remote routers.

Figure 8-18   *Frame Relay Hub-and-Spoke Topology*

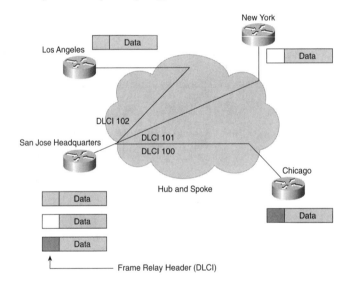

Even though the San Jose Headquarters router has only one physical connection to the
service provider, that physical connection is logically divided into three separate
connections (virtual circuits), each virtual circuit connecting to a different remote router.
The physical connection at the remote routers contains only one virtual circuit because the
remote routers need to connect to the router only at the San Jose Headquarters.

Frame Relay works at Layer 2 of the OSI reference model. An identifier, or DLCI, within
the Frame Relay header indicates which virtual circuit a frame belongs to. The Frame Relay
service provider also makes its switching decision based on the DLCI. In Figure 8-18, the
Frame Relay connection at San Jose Headquarters is provisioned with three virtual circuits.
The San Jose Headquarters router uses DLCI 102 in the Frame Relay header for sending
data to the Los Angeles router, DLCI 101 for the New York router, and DLCI 100 for the
Chicago router.

ATM and Cell Switching

Asynchronous Transfer Mode (ATM) is a type of cell-switched connection technology that is suitable of transferring voice, video, and data through private and public networks. ATM is used primarily in enterprise LAN backbones or WAN links. Like Frame Relay, ATM is implemented using virtual circuits. With ATM, the data is divided into small 53-byte cells before it is transmitted. Figure 8-19 shows how data from different devices are placed into specific time slots.

Figure 8-19   *ATM Cell Time Slots*

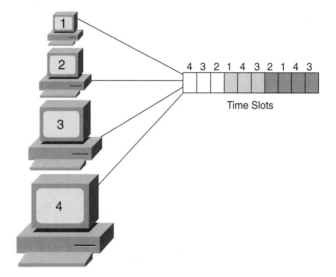

In the ATM cell header is a field called the virtual path/channel identifier (VPI/VCI) that indicates which virtual circuit an ATM cell belongs to. At the physical layer, ATM can run over a variety of physical media, including fiber optics using SONET framing and coaxial cable using digital signal level 3 (DS3).

ATM cells are always a fixed length of 53 bytes, whereas the sizes of frames and packets vary. The 53-byte ATM cell is made up of a 5-byte ATM header followed by 48 bytes of ATM payload (user data). Small, fixed-length, 53-byte cells are well suited for carrying data, voice, and video traffic because voice and video traffic are intolerant of delay that can result from having to wait for a larger data packet to be transmitted ahead of a voice or video packet.

An ATM switch is responsible for cell transit through an ATM network. It accepts the incoming cell from an ATM endpoint or another ATM switch. It then reads and updates the cell header information and quickly switches the cell to an output interface toward its destination.

An ATM virtual circuit is a logical connection created between two ATM endpoints across an ATM network. ATM virtual circuits fall into two categories:

- Permanent virtual circuit (PVC)
- Switched virtual circuit (SVC)

Virtual circuits provide a bidirectional communications path from one ATM endpoint to another. The VPI/VCI within the ATM cell header uniquely identifies the virtual circuits.

A virtual circuit can pass through any number of intermediate ATM switches in the ATM network. Numerous virtual circuits can be multiplexed into a single physical circuit for transmission across the network.

SONET

SONET is a physical layer protocol that provides for high-speed transmission using fiber-optic media. For example, ATM can run over SONET to achieve very high data transfer rates.

The term *Synchronous Digital Hierarchy (SDH)* refers to the optical technology outside the United States. The SONET signal rate is measured by optical carrier (OC) standards. Table 8-2 outlines the OC levels and their signal transmission rates.

| TIP | Each OC value is a multiple of the base rate. For example, an 0C-3 is 3 times the base rate of 51.84. $3 \times 51.84 = 155.52$. So, all you have to know is that an OC-1 is 51.84 Mbps and then multiply by the OC value to obtain the bandwidth. |

Table 8-2 *Optical Carrier Standards*

OC Level	Signal Transmission Rate
OC-1 (base rate)	51.84 Mbps
OC-3	155.52 Mbps
OC-12	622.08 Mbps
OC-24	1.244 Gbps
OC-48	2.488 Gbps
OC-192	10 Gbps
OC-256	13.271 Gbps
OC-768	40 Gbps

When you provide WAN service, it is important to understand how the technologies and encapsulations interconnect the sites. Being able to understand the issues associated with each technology enables you to choose, implement, and troubleshoot the various technologies more effectively.

WAN Access Technologies Section Quiz

Use the practice questions here to review what you learned in this section.

1 Which protocol does PPP use for establishing and maintaining point-to-point connections?

A HDLC

B LCP

C LAPD

D Cisco IETF

2 Which is the default encapsulation type for serial interfaces on a Cisco router?

A PPP

B HDLC

C Frame Relay

D X.25

3 Which of the following statements pertaining to ISDN is false?

A The ISDN BRI offers two B channels and one D channel.

B The D channel, operating at 16 kbps, is primarily the signaling channel.

C The ISDN PRI offers 23 B channels and 1 D channel in North America.

D The total bit rate of the ISDN BRI is 2.533 Mbps.

4 Which of the following media is used by DSL to transport data?

A Existing coaxial cable TV lines

B Existing twisted-pair telephone lines

C Existing Ethernet lines

D Wireless transmission

5 What are the two basic types of DSL technology?

   A Downstream DSL and upstream DSL

   B xDSL and yDSL

   C Asymmetric DSL and symmetric DSL

   D Serialized DSL and atonomized DSL

6 Which of the following standards organizations and industries have contributed to the evolution of DSL? (Choose all that apply.)

   A ANSI

   B ITU-T

   C IEEE

   D IETF

   E ETSI

7 Which of the following is *not* one of the benefits of DSL?

   A DSL service can be added incrementally in any area.

   B DSL is backward compatible with conventional analog voice.

   C ADSL stations can be up to 18,000 feet from the CO.

   D DSL is an always-on technology.

8 How does Frame Relay handle multiple conversations on the same physical connection?

   A Frame Relay multiplexes the circuits.

   B Multiple conversations are not allowed.

   C Frame Relay duplexes the conversation.

   D Frame Relay uses wavelength division multiplexing.

9 Which of the following is *not* true about ATM technology?

A It is capable of transferring voice, video, and data.

B ATM is used primarily in enterprise LAN backbones or WAN links.

C It is based on a cell-based architecture rather than on a frame-based architecture.

D ATM cells are always a fixed length of 35 bytes, whereas the sizes of frames and packets vary.

10 Name the family of very high-speed physical layer technologies that offers a series of data rates with special designations implemented at different transmission rates ranging from 51.84 Mbps to 40 Gbps.

A ADSL

B ATM

C SONET

D ISDN

Modems

To establish a WAN connection over phone lines, you must use a modem to convert digital data from a computer to analog form to travel over phone lines. Although analog modems have long been the most commonly used type of modems, cable modems have become increasingly popular as WAN users connect through cable service providers.

After you know how WANs operate and how data is transmitted over their connections, learning about the devices that enable those connections adds to your understanding of WAN operations.

Analog Modems

An *analog modem* is a device used to transmit electronic data through telephone lines. The term *modem* is derived from the function of these devices, converting (or modulating) digital signals to analog signals at the transmission source and reconverting the signals (demodulating) at the termination point. Figure 8-20 shows the operation of an analog modem.

Figure 8-20 *Modem Transmission*

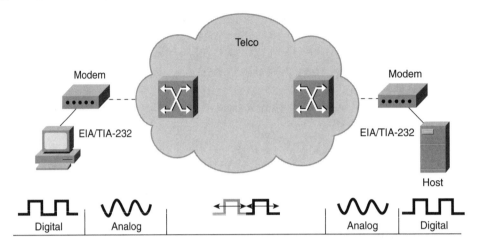

Modems can be either internal or external to the communicating devices. External modems are typically connected to the device using an EIA/TIA 232 serial line (COM port) or the Universal Serial Bus (USB). The modem then connects to the telephony network. Internal modems allow a communicating device to be connected directly to the telephony network. An internal modem can be built into the system or added with an internal expansion card or Personal Computer Memory Card International Association (PCMCIA) device.

Modems work at OSI Layer 1. At the data link layer, PPP is often used. V.22bis was the first true international standard, but is now obsolete. Starting before 1998, most new modems have supported 56 kbps rates downstream. This was standardized by V.90. The maximum upstream rate was increased to 48 kbps in ITU-T recommendation V.92.

Cable Modems

If a WAN is connected through a cable service provider, the connection is to a cable system. A different type of modem, a cable modem, is required for this connection. Cable modems enable two-way, high-speed data transmissions using the same coaxial lines that transmit cable television.

Some cable service providers are promising data speeds up to 6.5 times that of T1 leased lines. This speed makes cable an attractive medium for transferring large amounts of digital information quickly, including video clips, audio files, and large chunks of data. Information that would take 2 minutes to download using ISDN BRI can be downloaded in 2 seconds through a cable modem connection.

Cable modem access provides speeds superior to leased lines with lower costs and simpler installation. When the cable infrastructure is in place, a company can connect through installation of a modem or router. Additionally, because cable modems do not use the telephone system infrastructure, you incur no local-loop charges.

Cable modems provide a full-time connection. As soon as users turn on their computers, they are connected to the Internet. This setup removes the time and effort of dialing in to establish a connection.

How Cable Modems Work

Like analog modems, cable modems modulate and demodulate data signals. However, cable modems incorporate more functionality designed for today's high-speed Internet services. Figure 8-21 shows how users in an area connect to a cable data services.

Figure 8-21 *Cable Services Network*

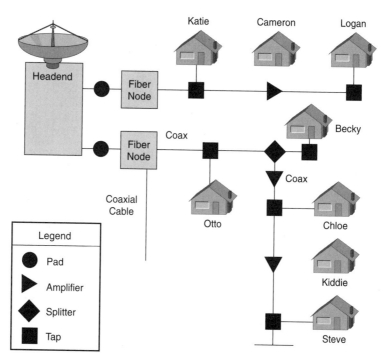

From a technical perspective, a cable modem is a Quadrature Amplitude Modulation (QAM) radio frequency (RF) receiver capable of delivering up to 30 to 40 Mbps of data in one 6-MHz cable channel. This is almost 500 times faster than a 56 kbps modem. The headend manages traffic flow from the user to the network.

NOTE   QAM is a method for encoding digital data in an analog signal in which each combination of phase and amplitude represents one of many digital bit patterns.

With a cable modem, a subscriber can continue to receive cable television service while simultaneously receiving data to be delivered to a personal computer. This is accomplished with the help of a simple one-to-two splitter, as shown in Figure 8-22.

Figure 8-22 *One-to-Two Splitter*

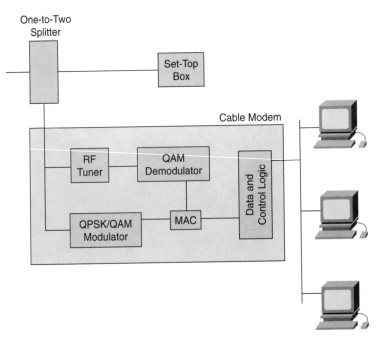

Advantages and Disadvantages of Cable Modems

Cable modems have both advantages and disadvantages, and this section describes them.

The advantage of using the high-speed access of cable modems is that coaxial cable wiring offers greater bandwidth using broadband for more applications to the home network LAN. Additionally, cable lines are already in place in most of the country because of the wide deployment of cable television in the last few decades. Therefore, cable modem high-speed Internet access is more readily available in most areas than DSL.

Unfortunately, upgrading of the cabling infrastructure that is needed to support cable modem technology has been slow, so many homes cannot use this technology. Upgrading is a big investment, particularly for small providers.

Modems provide a necessary connection between the service provider network and the local user network. Understanding where these components are placed in the network and how they function is an important part of a network administrator's job function.

Modems Section Quiz

Use these practice questions to review what you learned in this section.

1 Which of the following is true of analog modems?

   A They allow data transfer between one computer and another over the PSTN.

   B They convert analog signals to digital bit streams.

   C They convert digital data to analog signals.

   D All of the above are true.

2 Which of the following cable standards allows a 56 kbps downstream data transmission rate?

   A V.32

   B V.34

   C V.42

   D V.90

3 Which of the following media are used by a cable modem to transport data?

   A Existing coaxial cable TV lines

   B Existing twisted-pair telephone lines

   C Existing Ethernet lines

   D Existing TV antennas

4 Which of the following best describes upstream?

   A Data flowing from the user to the network

   B Data flowing from the network to the user

   C Data flowing between networks

   D Data flowing between routers

5 Which of the following is an advantage of cable modem?

A The cabling infrastructure can be upgraded.

B Because cable modems exist in a shared-media structure, the more users who come on the network, the more bandwidth is available for each user.

C Coaxial cable wiring offers greater bandwidth using broadband for more applications to the home network.

D Cable modems allow you to display data onto your cable connected television.

Chapter Summary

After completing this chapter, you should have a basic understanding of the major types of WAN services available for use in connecting remote networks. You should be able to compare and contrast dedicated, circuit-switched, and cell-switched services and the protocols and standards used by each service. Finally, you should have an understanding of how modems connect devices to provider services.

Chapter Review Questions

Use these review questions to test your knowledge of the concepts discussed in this chapter.

1 ISDN is an example of a circuit-switched WAN technology.

A True

B False

2 Which of the following are true about a point-to-point link? (Choose three.)

A It is a single, pre-established WAN communications path from the customer premises through a carrier network.

B It is usually leased from a carrier and thus is often called a leased line.

C It is generally priced based on bandwidth required and distance between the two connected points.

D The cost of leased line solutions is not significant when they connect many sites.

E Point-to-point links carry only IP traffic.

3 Which of the following statements are true about bandwidth? (Choose three.)

   A Bandwidth refers to the speed at which data is transferred over the communication link.

   B 12 DS0s can be bundled to get a DS1 line.

   C A T1 line is the same as a DS1 line.

   D 28 DS1s can be bundled to get a DS3 line.

4 Which of the following is *not* a type of multiplexing?

   A TDM

   B ATM

   c STM

   D FDM

5 Which of the following is *not* true regarding permanent virtual circuits (PVCs)?

   A PVCs use permanently established connections.

   B Data communication across a PVC requires call setup and termination states.

   C In PVCs, the DTE devices can begin transferring data whenever they are ready.

   D A PVC works like a virtual leased line connection.

6 What is the size of the ATM payload?

   A 48 bytes

   B 53 bytes

   C 32 bytes

   D 64 bytes

7 What is the aggregate speed of the B channels for ISDN BRI?

   A 16 kbps

   B 64 kbps

   C 128 kbps

   D 144 kbps

8 Which of the following is data-link encapsulation for a WAN? (Choose all that apply)

   A High-Level Data Link Control (HDLC)

   B FDDI

   C Point-to-Point Protocol (PPP)

   D IEEE 802.3 Ethernet

   E Frame Relay

9 Which of the following is *not* a symmetrical standard for DSL?

   A High Data Rate DSL (HDSL)

   B ISDN DSL (IDSL)

   C G.SHDSL

   D ADSL

   E SDSL

10 Which of the following protocols do *not* operate at Layer 2?

   A PPP

   B Ethernet

   C ATM

   D IP

11 DSL service can be added incrementally as more users subscribe.

   A True

   B False

12 Which was the first true worldwide standard for modems that allowed 2400 bits per second (bps) at 600 baud?

   A V.12

   B V.42

   C V.32

   D V.90

   E V.22bis

13 Which of the following statements about cable modems are true? (Choose three.)

   A Cable modems use the same coaxial lines that transmit cable television.

   B Cable modem access provides speeds that are superior to leased lines.

   C Cable modems provide a full-time connection.

   D Cable modem installation is more complicated than installation of analog modems.

Upon completion of this chapter, you will be able to perform the following tasks:

- Use the available configuration tools to establish connectivity to the appropriate network device to complete the initial device configuration

- Start the Cisco switch and router and describe and recognize a normal boot sequence

- Verify the default configuration of each device, given a functioning access layer switch and router

- Describe and use the command modes to interact with the Cisco IOS Software

- Use the online help facilities associated with the command-line interface to modify the configuration of a device

- Use the Cisco switch and router **show** commands to determine fundamental operational characteristics of the switch

CHAPTER 9

Operating and Configuring Cisco IOS Devices

Cisco IOS is software that operates on most Cisco network devices. Cisco IOS Software is internetwork system software that provides the features and processes necessary to interconnect networked systems.

In this chapter, you learn the process of starting and configuring a Cisco IOS switch and router. You also learn to perform tasks using the Cisco IOS Software user interfaces. To install Cisco devices in your network, you need to understand the startup of the Cisco switch and router and describe and recognize a normal boot sequence. It is also important to provide an initial configuration for the switch and apply a basic initial configuration to the router using the setup facility.

After you establish an initial setup, you need to describe and use the command modes to interact with the Cisco IOS Software. You learn to use the online help facilities associated with the command-line interface (CLI) to modify the configuration of a device. Finally, you need to use the Cisco switch and router **show** commands to determine fundamental operational characteristics of the switch.

Basic Operation of the Cisco IOS Software

The Cisco IOS Software is implemented on most Cisco hardware platforms, including switches and routers. It is the embedded software architecture in all the Cisco routers and is also the operating system common to most of the Catalyst switches. Cisco IOS Software enables network services in Cisco products, including the following:

- Features to carry the chosen network protocols and functions
- Connectivity for high-speed traffic between devices
- Security to control access and prohibit unauthorized network use
- Scalability to add interfaces and capability as needed for network growth
- Reliability to ensure dependable access to networked resources

You can access the Cisco IOS Software CLI through a console connection, a modem connection, or a Telnet session. Regardless of which connection method you use, access to the Cisco IOS Software CLI is generally referred to as an *EXEC session* because the CLI is provided by the executive process in the IOS.

The following sections discuss the initial startup of a new router and the application and/or modes used to configure the device for operation.

Cisco IOS Startup

When you start a new Cisco IOS device for the first time, it does not have an initial configuration. The Cisco IOS Software prompts you for information using a dialog called *setup*.

The setup dialog allows you to configure the device with the following information:

- Protocol addressing and parameter settings, such as configuring the IP address and subnet mask on an interface

- Options for administration and management and passwords for remote access and control of the device modes

- Network policy of the functions required, such as enabling the required routing protocol to support the network requirements

In this chapter, you set up a minimal device configuration for routers and switches. You also learn how to make changes to these minimal or default configurations to meet your particular network requirements. These tasks constitute much of the work required of a network administrator.

When a Catalyst switch or Cisco router starts up, three main operations are performed on the networking device, as follows:

1 The device performs hardware checking routines. A term often used to describe this initial set of routines is Power-On Self-Test (POST).

2 After the hardware has been shown to be in good working order, the device performs system startup routines. These initiate the switch or router operating software load.

3 After the operating system is loaded, the device tries to find and apply software configuration settings that establish the details needed for network operation.

Typically, a sequence of fallback routines provides software startup alternatives, if needed.

Configuration Sources

After the device has booted, you must initially configure a switch or router from the console port. After the initial configuration is completed, you can access a router from a remote location without a router being connected to a network by dialing directly to a modem attached to the console or auxiliary port on a device. In general, the console port is recommended because it displays router startup messages, whereas the auxiliary port does not provide this information and does not exist on most Catalyst switches. You can configure a switch and a router from the following locations:

- **Console terminal**—Upon initial installation, you can configure networking devices from the console terminal, which is connected via the console port. You need the following items to configure a Cisco device from the console port:
  - RJ-45–to–RJ-45 rollover cable
  - DB-9, DB-25, or Universal Serial Bus (USB) connector on PC and the appropriate adapter to connect a RJ-45 cable to that port
  - PC or equivalent with communications software configured with the following settings:

    Speed: 9600 bits per second

    Data bits: 8

    Parity: None

    Stop bit: 1

    Flow control: None

- **Remote terminal**—If you are supporting a remote device, a modem connection to the device's auxiliary port permits you to configure it from a remote terminal. However, you must first configure the device's auxiliary port for communication with the external modem. To connect remotely to the auxiliary port on a Cisco device, you need the following items:
  - Straight-through serial cable
  - 14.4 kbps modem
  - PC or equivalent with suitable communications software

- For selected routers and switches, a CD-ROM, such as Cisco Fast Step, can make configuration tasks easier to accomplish. Cisco Fast Step software is an easy-to-use Microsoft Windows-based software tool that simplifies the setup, monitoring, and troubleshooting of Cisco small- and home-office routers.

After initial startup, you have additional ways to access and configure the device. All of these require that TCP/IP be configured on the device. The methods are as follows:

- Establish a terminal session using Telnet.
- Download a configuration file from a Trivial File Transfer Protocol (TFTP) server on the network.
- Download a configuration file using a network management software application like CiscoWorks 2000.

NOTE   Not all network devices have all the ports options discussed. For example, most Cisco IOS switches and some Cisco small-office and home-office routers do not have an auxiliary port.

Using the Cisco IOS CLI

Cisco IOS Software uses a CLI as its traditional console environment. Although Cisco IOS Software is a core technology that extends across many products, its operation details vary on different internetworking devices. This section describes the basic console command modes used in the Cisco IOS Software.

When you access the IOS device, the software that runs on the console or a remote terminal provides an interface known as the EXEC process. The EXEC process interprets the commands you enter and carries out the corresponding operations.

To enter commands into the CLI, you type or paste your entries within one of the several console command modes. The Enter key instructs the device to parse and execute (interpret) the command. Each command mode is indicated with a distinctive prompt.

Cisco IOS Software uses a hierarchy of commands in its command-mode structure. Each command mode supports specific Cisco IOS commands related to a type of operation on the device.

For security purposes, the EXEC has the following two levels of access to commands:

- **User mode**—Typical tasks include those that check the device status.
- **Privileged mode**—Typical tasks include those that change the device configuration.

To connect to a Cisco IOS device, attach to the console and press the Enter key. If the device is configured for login options, you must log in to the device with a username and password or just a password depending on the configuration. This brings the device to a user EXEC mode prompt.

By default, a prompt appears to signify the user EXEC mode. The greater than symbol (>) in the prompt indicates that the router or switch is at the user EXEC level:

```
hostname>
```

Type **exit** or **quit** to close the session from the user EXEC mode.

In user EXEC mode, you are able to issue commands that allow you to interact with the device. EXEC commands available in user mode are a subset of the EXEC commands available in privileged mode. For the most part, these commands allow you to display information without changing device configuration settings.

To access the full set of commands, you must first enable privileged mode; by default, your EXEC prompt shows as a pound sign (#) while you are in this mode. From the privileged level, you can also access global configuration mode and the other specific configuration modes including interface, subinterface, line, router, route-map, and several others. Use the **disable** command to return to user EXEC mode from privileged EXEC mode, as demonstrated in Example 9-1.

Example 9-1 *Navigating Between User and Privileged EXEC Mode*

```
wg_ro_c con0 is now available
Press RETURN to get started.


wg_ro_c>
wg_ro_c>enable
wg_ro_c#
wg_ro_c#disable
wg_ro_c>
wg_ro_c>logout
```

Typing a question mark (**?**) at the user EXEC mode prompt or the privileged EXEC mode prompt displays a handy list of commonly used commands, as shown in Example 9-2.

Example 9-2 *Getting Help on User EXEC Mode Commands*

```
wg_ro_c>?
Exec commands:
  access-enable    Create a temporary Access-List entry
  atmsig           Execute Atm Signalling Commands
  cd               Change current device
  clear            Reset functions
  connect          Open a terminal connection
  dir              List files on given device
  disable          Turn off privileged commands
  disconnect       Disconnect an existing network connection
  enable           Turn on privileged commands
  exit             Exit from the EXEC
  help             Description of the interactive help system
  lat              Open a lat connection
  lock             Lock the terminal
  login            Log in as a particular user
  logout           Exit from the EXEC
-- More --
```

Notice the -- More -- at the bottom of Example 9-2. It indicates that multiple screens are available as output and that more commands follow. Whenever the More prompt appears, you can proceed as follows:

- Resume output of the next available screen by pressing the Spacebar.
- Display the next line by pressing the Return key (or, on some keyboards, the Enter key).
- Press any other key to return to the EXEC prompt.

NOTE   Screen output displayed varies with Cisco IOS Software level and device configuration.

Type **enable** to enter privileged mode. If the device is so configured, you might be prompted for a password.

Typing a question mark (**?**) at the user prompt or the privileged prompt displays a much longer list of EXEC commands, as illustrated in Example 9-3.

Example 9-3 *Getting Help with Privileged EXEC Mode Commands*

```
wg_ro_c#?
Exec commands:
  access-enable    Create a temporary Access-List entry
  access-profile   Apply user-profile to interface
  access-template  Create a temporary Access-List entry
  bfe              For manual emergency modes setting
  cd               Change current directory
  clear            Reset functions
  clock            Manage the system clock
  configure        Enter configuration mode
  connect          Open a terminal connection
  copy             Copy from one file to another
  debug            Debugging functions (see also 'undebug')
  delete           Delete a file
  dir              List files on a filesystem
  disable          Turn off privileged commands
  disconnect       Disconnect an existing network connection
  enable           Turn on privileged commands
  erase            Erase a filesystem
  exit             Exit from the EXEC
  help             Description of the interactive help system
-- More --
```

To return to the user EXEC level, enter **disable** at the hostname# prompt. To exit the EXEC process, use the command **quit** or **exit**.

NOTE   Screen output varies with Cisco IOS Software level and device configuration.

Keyboard Help in Device CLI

Cisco IOS Software provides you with extensive command-line input help facilities, including the following:

- **Context-sensitive help**—Provides a list of commands and the arguments associated with a specific command.

- **Console error messages**—Identifies problems with device commands entered incorrectly so that you can alter or correct them.

- **Command history buffer**—Allows recall of long or complex commands or entries for re-entry, review, or correction.

Context-Sensitive Help for Cisco IOS Devices

Cisco IOS CLI on Cisco devices offers context-sensitive word help and command syntax help:

- For word help, use the question mark (**?**) following one or more characters. This provides a list of commands that begin with a particular character sequence.

- For command syntax help, use the **?** in the place of a keyword or argument. Include a space before the **?**.

Special control and escape character combinations reduce the need to retype entire command strings. The Cisco IOS Software on Cisco devices also provides several commands and characters to recall or complete command entries from a history buffer that keeps the last several commands that you entered. You can reuse rather than retype these commands if appropriate.

TIP   You can abbreviate commands in the Cisco IOS by entering enough of the command to be unique. For example, instead of typing the command **show interface**, you could type **sh int**.

Console Error Messages for Cisco IOS Devices

Console error messages on the device help you identify problems with incorrect command entries. Interpreting the message helps you figure out how to alter your command-line entry to correct the problem.

Table 9-1 lists some of the error messages you might encounter while using the CLI on the Cisco IOS device.

Table 9-1   *Common CLI Error Messages*

Error Message	Meaning	How to Get Help
% Ambiguous command: "show con"	You did not enter enough characters for your switch to recognize the command.	Reenter the command followed by a question mark (**?**) with no space between the command and the question mark. The possible keywords that you can enter with the command are displayed.
% Incomplete command	You did not enter all the keywords or values required by this command.	Reenter the command followed by a question mark (**?**) with a space between the command and the question mark.
% Invalid input detected at '^' marker	You entered the command incorrectly. The caret (^) marks the point of the error.	Enter a question mark (**?**) to display all the commands that are available in this command mode.

Command History Buffer for Cisco IOS Devices

Reviewing the command history allows you to see a list of the contents of the device's command buffer. This is a list of commands that you have most recently entered. To see these commands, you enter the Cisco IOS Software command **show history**.

This feature is particularly useful for recalling long or complex commands or entries. With the command history feature, you can complete the following tasks:

- Set the command history buffer size
- Recall commands
- Disable the command history feature

By default, command history is enabled, and the system records 10 command lines in its history buffer. To change the number of command lines, the system records during the current terminal session, use the **terminal history size** or **history size** command. The maximum number of commands is 256.

TIP   Although you can store the last 256 commands you entered, it is unwise to do so. These commands waste valuable memory resources and are flushed at the end of each executive session.

To recall commands in the history buffer beginning with the most recent command, press **Ctrl-p** or the **up-arrow** key (on some terminal settings). Repeat the key sequence to recall successively older commands.

To return to more recent commands in the history buffer after recalling commands, use **Ctrl-n** or the **down-arrow** key. Repeat the key sequence to recall successively more recent commands.

Table 9-2 contains a brief summary of the command history controls.

Table 9-2   *Navigating the Device Command History*

Key Sequence or Command	Functionality
Ctrl-p or **up arrow**	Last (previous) command recall
Ctrl-n or **down arrow**	More recent command recall
Router> **show history**	Shows command buffer contents
Router> **terminal history size** *lines*	Sets session command buffer size

Using CLI Help Features Example

Suppose you want to set the device clock. If you do not know the command, use context-sensitive help to check the syntax for setting the clock. If you intend to type the word *clock*, but mistype it as *clok*, the system performs a symbolic translation of the mistyped command as parsed by the Cisco IOS Software. IOS attempts to resolve an unknown command to a computer name to establish a Telnet session. If no command or computer name matches what you typed, an error message is returned.

You can use context-sensitive help to give you the command by typing just the first part, **cl** and a **?** without a space (in other words, **cl?**). The device then return the commands that start with the letters **cl**.

If you now type the correct command, **clock**, and press **Return**, the device gives you another error, % Incomplete command, meaning that you need to give the device more information. If you do not know what this information is, type a space and a **?** after the command (for example, **clock ?**). Help tells you that you need the keyword **set**.

After entering the **set** command, you can see that the device requires more information, such as the time in *hh*:*mm*:*ss* format. You can use the **?** character as an argument after any command string to see what options or requirements the device has for this string.

Example 9-4 documents the process of finding the correct **clock** command, as described in the preceding paragraphs.

Example 9-4 *Using Cisco IOS CLI Help to Resolve Command Problems*

```
Router# clok
Translating "CLOK"
% Unknown command or computer name, or unable to find computer address

Router# cl?
clear   clock

Router# clock
% Incomplete command.

Router# clock ?
set    set the time and date

Router# clock set
% Incomplete command.

Router# <Ctrl-P>clock set ?
hh:mm:ss Current Time
```

You can use last-command recall to retrieve the portion of the command you typed previously, so that you won't have to retype the command. Last-command recall occurs when you press **Ctrl-p** or use the **up arrow** (if supported by the terminal emulation program). This automatically repeats the previous command entry. Example 9-4 shows that after last-command recall, the administrator adds a space and a **?** to reveal the additional arguments.

Example 9-5 illustrates the command structure needed for setting the clock, continued from Example 9-4.

Example 9-5 *Setting the Router Clock*

```
Router# clock set 19:56:00
% Incomplete command.

Router# clock set 19:56:00 ?
<1-31>     Day of the month
MONTH    Month of the year

Router# clock set 19:56:00 04 8
                            ^
% Invalid input detected at the '^' marker

Router# clock set 19:56:00  04   August
% Incomplete command

Router# clock set 19:56:00 04 August ?
<1993-2035>    Year
```

Command prompting works as follows: When you see the Cisco IOS Software prompter indicating that the command entered is incomplete, enter the year using the correct syntax and press the **Return** key to execute the command.

Syntax checking uses the caret symbol (^) as an error location indicator. The caret symbol character appears at the point in the command string where you have entered an incorrect command, keyword, or argument. The error location indicator and interactive help system allow you to find and correct syntax errors easily.

Enhanced Editing Mode: Editing Key Functions

The user interface includes an enhanced editing mode that provides a set of editing key functions. Although enhanced editing mode is automatically enabled with the current software release, you can disable it and revert to the editing mode of previous software releases. You might also want to disable enhanced editing if you have written scripts that do not interact well when enhanced editing is enabled. Use the **no terminal editing** command at the privileged EXEC prompt to disable advanced editing features. To re-enable these features, use the **terminal editing** command.

The editing command set provides a horizontal scrolling feature for commands that extend beyond a single line on the screen. When the cursor reaches the right margin—69 characters by default—the command line shifts 10 spaces to the left. You cannot see the first 10 characters of the line, but you can scroll back and check the syntax at the beginning of the command.

Look at the following command entry:

```
Router>$ value for customers, employees, and partners
```

This command entry extends beyond one line. The dollar sign ($) indicates that the line has been scrolled to the left. Each time the cursor reaches the end of the line, the line is again shifted 10 spaces to the left. To scroll back, press **Ctrl-b** or the **left-arrow** key repeatedly until you are at the beginning of the command entry, or press **Ctrl-a** to return directly to the beginning of the line.

The key sequences listed in Table 9-3 are shortcuts or hot keys provided by the CLI to navigate the command line. The Ctrl and Esc key sequences are based on the key sequences used by the Emacs editor in the UNIX operating system. Use these features to move the cursor around on the command line for corrections and changes.

Table 9-3 *CLI Editing Key Sequences*

Command-Line Editing Key Sequence	Description
Ctrl-a	Moves the cursor to the beginning of the line.
Ctrl-e	Moves the cursor to the end of the line.
Ctrl-f	Moves the cursor forward one character.
Ctrl-b	Moves the cursor backward one character.
Esc-f	Moves the cursor forward one word.
Esc-b	Moves the cursor backward one word.
Ctrl-d	Deletes a single character.
Ctrl-k	Deletes everything to the right of the cursor.
Ctrl-x	Deletes everything to the left of the cursor.
Ctrl-w	Deletes a word.
Ctrl-r	Refreshes the command line and everything typed up to this point.
Backspace	Removes one character to the left of the cursor.
Tab	Completes a partially entered command if enough characters have been entered to make it unambiguous.

The Esc (Escape) key is not functional on all terminals.

After you understand how to use Cisco IOS and navigate the different modes, you are able to provide administration and configuration for the Cisco IOS devices and switches.

Cisco IOS Configuration Methods

The first method of configuration on a Cisco IOS device is the setup utility, which starts when no configuration exists. Setup allows a basic initial configuration to be created. The operation of the application is discussed in detail in the sections, "Starting a Cisco IOS Router" and "Starting a Cisco Catalyst IOS Switch" later in this chapter. For more complex and specific configurations, you use the command-line interface to enter terminal configuration mode.

From the privileged EXEC mode, you can enter global configuration mode with the **configure terminal** command. From the global configuration mode, you have access to the specific configuration modes, which include but are not limited to the following:

- **Interface**—Supports commands that configure operations on a per-interface basis
- **Subinterface**—Supports commands that configure multiple virtual interfaces on a single physical interface
- **Controller**—Supports commands that configure controllers (for example, E1 and T1 controllers)
- **Line**—Supports commands that configure the operation of a terminal line; for example, the console or the virtual terminal (vty) ports
- **Router**—Supports commands that configure an IP routing protocol
- **VLAN**—Supports commands that configure VLAN Trunking Protocol (VTP) parameters and VLAN parameters.

When you are in a subconfiguration mode, if you enter **exit**, the router backs out one level, eventually allowing you to log out. In general, enter **exit** from one of the specific configuration modes to return to global configuration mode. Press **Ctrl-Z** or enter the command **end** to leave configuration mode completely and return the router to the privileged EXEC mode.

In terminal configuration mode, you invoke an incremental compiler. Each configuration command entered is parsed as soon as you press the **Enter** key.

If no syntax errors occur, the command is executed and stored in the running configuration and is effective immediately.

Commands that affect the entire router are called *global commands*. The **hostname** and **enable password** commands are examples of global commands.

Commands that point to or indicate a process or interface that is to be configured are called *major commands*. When entered, major commands cause the CLI to enter a specific configuration mode. Major commands have no effect unless you immediately enter a subcommand that supplies the configuration entry. For example, the major command **interface serial 0** has no effect unless it is followed by a subcommand that tells what you want to do to that interface.

Understanding how to access and use the different user and configuration modes of the Cisco IOS device is critical in being able to operate and administer the device.

Basic Operation of the Cisco IOS Software Section Quiz

Use these practice questions to review what you learned in this section.

1 When you configure Catalyst switches from the user interface that runs on the console or a remote terminal, the Cisco IOS software provides a CLI called the _____.

A EXEC

B LOGIN

C ENABLE

D CONSOLE

2 What purpose does the Cisco IOS EXEC serve?

A Determines the switch IP address and default gateway

B Offers password security by encrypting Telnet passwords

C Provides a graphical user interface used to configure your switch

D Interprets the commands you enter and carries out the corresponding operations

3 What should you type to display a list of commands that begin with the letter *a* on a Catalyst switch?

A a?

B a ?

C help a

D help a*

4 What should you type to display the command syntax help so that you can see how to complete a command that begins with **show**?

A show?

B show ?

C help show

D help show*

5 Which Cisco IOS command takes you from the Router> prompt to the Router# prompt on a Cisco router?

A **user**

B **config**

C **enable**

D **privilege**

6 When the information displayed on a Cisco router is more than one page in length, what should you do to display the next page?

A Type **more**.

B Press any key.

C Press the **Spacebar**.

D Press the **Down-Arrow** key.

7 What does the "% Incomplete command" message mean on a Cisco router?

A You entered an invalid command parameter.

B You did not enter all of the keywords or values required by the command.

C You are running the Cisco IOS Software from Flash memory, not from RAM.

D You did not enter enough characters for the router to recognize the command.

8 What should you do if you receive a "% Ambiguous command" message on your Cisco router?

A Enter **help** and follow the instructions that appear on your screen.

B Enter a question mark (**?**) to display all of the commands or parameters that are available in this mode.

C Reenter the command followed by a question mark (**?**) with no space between the command and the question mark.

D Reenter the command followed by a question mark (**?**) with a space between the command and the question mark.

9 What does the Cisco IOS CLI do when you enter a command that is longer than allowed on a single line?

A The router truncates the command because commands longer than one line are not allowed.

B The router automatically scrolls the line to the left and uses a dollar sign ($) to indicate that the beginning of the line is elsewhere.

C The router automatically moves the cursor to the next line and uses a caret (^) symbol to indicate that the beginning of the line is elsewhere.

D The router automatically shortens the command to the smallest number of characters that still make the character string unique yet allow it to fit on one line.

10 What happens when you press the **Tab** key when working in the CLI?

A The current line is redisplayed.

B The cursor moves forward one word.

C The cursor moves to the end of the command line.

D The parser completes a partially entered command if you entered enough characters to make the command unambiguous.

11 Which tasks can you complete using the Cisco IOS command history feature? (Choose three.)

A Recall commands

B Set the history buffer size to 356

C Set the command history buffer size

D Delete the contents of the command buffer

E Display the contents of the command buffer

12 Which of the following recall commands displays what is in history buffer beginning with the most recent command? (Choose two.)

A **Ctrl-N**

B **Ctrl-P**

C **Up arrow**

D **show history**

E **Down arrow**

13 What happens when you start a Cisco IOS device that has no configuration in memory?

   A The device uses its default configuration.

   B The device prompts you to enter a minimum configuration.

   C The device obtains the configuration from its Flash memory.

   D The device uses a dialog called *enable* to prompt for the configuration.

14 Match each Cisco device startup action to its description.

   1 POST routine   **A** The device performs hardware checking routines

   2 System startup routine   **B** The device initiates the switch or router operating software.

   3 Application of software   **C** The device establishes the details needed for configuration   network operation.

15 If a network administrator is supporting a remote device, what is the preferred type of connection or configuration to permit the administrator to configure the device remotely?

   A Modem connection via the console port

   B Console connection via the console port

   C Modem connection via the auxiliary port

   D CD-ROM configuration with Cisco Fast Step

16 What are the two primary Cisco IOS EXEC modes?

   A User and root

   B User and enable

   C User and privileged

   D Normal and privileged

17 How do you enter commands into the Cisco IOS CLI?

    A Use a web interface to select commands from a list.

    B Type or paste entries within a console command mode.

    C Use the management feature to indicate the next command to enter.

    D Select commands from a menu provided by the Cisco IOS Software.

18 How do you know which command mode you are using on a Cisco device?

    A The command mode is indicated with a distinctive prompt.

    B The context-sensitive help feature indicates the command mode.

    C The command mode is displayed after you enter each command.

    D You see an error message if you are operating in the wrong command mode.

19 Which Cisco IOS command lists the commands that are available in the privileged EXEC mode?

    A **?**

    B **dir**

    C **list**

    D **help**

20 Which EXEC mode allows you to configure and debug a Cisco router?

    A User

    B Enable

    C Normal

    D Privileged

Booting a Cisco IOS Device

A Cisco IOS device goes through a startup procedure when you turn it on. When the startup is complete, you can access the device to configure the initial software settings and view the operational parameters. This section explains how the switches and routers start up and shows you how to verify their initial operation.

Recognizing the correct device startup is the first step in deploying an IOS device. The device must start successfully and have a default configuration to operate on the network.

Starting a Cisco Catalyst IOS Switch

The startup of a Catalyst switch requires that you verify the physical installation, power up the switch, and view the Cisco IOS Software output on the console. The initial startup of a Catalyst switch requires that you complete the following steps:

Step 1 Before you start the switch, verify the following:

— All network cable connections are secure.

— Your terminal is connected to the console port.

— Your console terminal application, such as HyperTerminal, is selected.

Step 2 Attach the power cable plug to the switch power supply socket.

The switch starts. Some Catalyst switches, including the Catalyst 2950, have no on/off switch on some.

Step 3 Observe the boot sequence:

— Look at the LEDs on the switch chassis.

— Observe the Cisco IOS software output text on the console.

NOTE This book focuses on the Catalyst 2950 series switches only. Switch information and configuration commands presented are specific to the Catalyst. Although most of the commands are platform independent, commands on your switch might differ somewhat. Hardware-specific items such as POST apply only to the Catalyst 2950.

The Catalyst 2950 series switches have several status LEDs that are generally lit in green when the switch is functioning normally but turn amber when a malfunction occurs.

The LED locations on the Catalyst 2950-12 and 2950-24 are shown Figure 9-1.

Table 9-4 explains the functions of the various switch LEDs.

Figure 9-1   *LEDs on a Catalyst 2950 Series Switch*

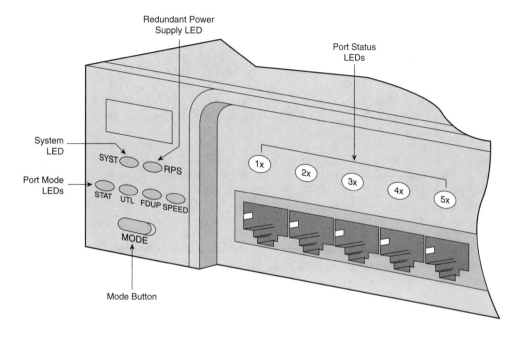

Table 9-4   *Catalyst 2950 Main LEDs*

Switch LED	Description
System LED	Off: System not powered up.
	Green: System powered and operational.
	Amber: System malfunction; one or more POST errors occurred.
Redundant power supply LED	Off: Redundant power supply is off or is not installed.
	Green: Redundant power supply is operational.
	Flashing green: Redundant power supply is connected but unavailable because it is providing power to another device.
	Amber: Redundant power supply is installed, not operational.
	Flashing amber: Internal power supply failed and redundant power supply is providing power to the switch.

Catalyst switch port LEDs have several modes of operation. The initial startup routines use LEDs to display POST status.

If the switch is up and running, press the **Mode** button, as shown in the figure, to toggle through other LED display modes. The three modes indicate the following:

- Port status
- Bandwidth utilization for the switch
- Full-duplex support
- Port Speed

The port LED display modes are indicated in Table 9-5, with information about the various LED colors or lighting.

Table 9-5   *LED Modes*

Port LED Display Mode	Description
Port status (STAT LED on)	Off: No link present.
	Green: Link present, no activity.
	Flashing green: Link present with traffic activity.
	Alternating green and amber: Link fault. Error frames can affect connectivity. Excessive collisions and cyclic redundancy check (CRC), alignment, and jabber errors are monitored for a link-fault indication.
	Amber: Port not forwarding because the port was disabled by management, suspended because of an address violation, or suspended by Spanning Tree Protocol (STP) because of network loops.
Bandwidth utilization (UTL LED on)	Green: Current bandwidth utilization displayed over the amber LED background on a logarithmic scale.
	Amber: Maximum backplane utilization since the switch was powered on.
	Green and amber: Depends on model as follows:
	• If all LEDs on Catalyst 2950-12, 2950-24, 2950C-24, and 2950T-24 switches are green, the switch is using 50 percent or more of the total bandwidth. If the far-right LED is off, the switch is using more than 25 but less than 50 percent of the total bandwidth, and so on. If only the far-left LED is green, the switch is using less than 0.0488 percent of the total bandwidth.
	• If all LEDs on Catalyst 2950G-12-EI switches are green, the switch is using 50 percent or more of the total bandwidth. If the LED for Gigabit Interface Converter (GBIC) module slot 2 is off, the switch is using more than 25 but less than 50 percent of the total bandwidth. If LEDs for both GBIC module slots are off, the switch is using less than 25 percent of the total bandwidth, and so on.

Table 9-5   *LED Modes (Continued)*

Port LED Display Mode	Description
Bandwidth utilization (UTL LED on)	• If all LEDs on Catalyst 2950G-24-EI and 2950G-24-EI-DC switches are green, the switch is using 50 percent or more of the total bandwidth. • If the LED for GBIC module slot 2 is off, the switch is using more than 25 but less than 50 percent of the total bandwidth. If LEDs for both GBIC module slots are off, the switch is using less than 25 percent of the total bandwidth, and so on. • If all LEDs on Catalyst 2950G-48-EI switches are green, the switch is using 50 percent or more of the total bandwidth. If the LED for the upper GBIC module slot is off, the switch is using more than 25 but less than 50 percent of the total bandwidth. If LEDs for both GBIC module slots are off, the switch is using less than 25 percent of the total bandwidth, and so on.
Full duplex (FDUP LED on)	Green: Ports configured in full-duplex mode. Off: Ports half duplex.
Speed (Speed LED on)	Green: Port speed set to 100 Mbps or operational at 10 Mbps. Off: Port speed set to auto or 10 Mpbs or operational at 10 Mbps.

The Catalyst POST is executed when the switch is powered up. The POST uses the switch port LEDs to indicate test progress and status.

Initially, all port LEDs are green. This condition indicates the start of the POST and that the LEDs are functioning properly. Each of the first 16 port LEDs (1x through 16x) is associated with one of the POST tests, as described in Table 9-6.

Table 9-6   *POST LED Status*

LED	Component Tested: Failure Type
LED 16x	Embedded control unit (ECU) dynamic random-access memory (DRAM): Fatal.
LED 15x	Not used.
LED 14x	Not used.
LED 13x	Not used.
LED 12x	Forwarding engine: Fatal.
LED 11x	Forwarding engine static random-access memory (SRAM): Fatal.

continues

Table 9-6   *POST LED Status (Continued)*

LED	Component Tested: Failure Type
LED 10x	Packet DRAM: Fatal.
LED 9x	ISLT application-specific integrated circuit (ASIC): Fatal.
LED 8x	Port control/status: Fatal.
LED 7x	System timer interrupt: Fatal.
LED 6x	Content-addressable memory (CAM) SRAM: Fatal.
LED 5x	Real-time clock: Nonfatal. If this test fails, the switch forwards packets. However, if the switch unexpectedly shuts down, it cannot restart itself automatically.
LED 4x	Console port: Nonfatal. If this test fails, you cannot access the management console through the console port. You can still use Telnet to access the management console.
LED 3x	CAM: Fatal.
LED 2x	Burned-in address: Nonfatal. If this test fails, the switch uses the default Ethernet address of the switch and begins forwarding packets.
LED 1x	Port loopback: Nonfatal. If this test fails, some functionality to one or more ports is lost. The switch disables any ports that failed this test, and the failure message on the Menu Console Logon screen indicates which ports did not pass this test. Connect only to ports that passed this test.

After each POST test, the LED for that test indicates the test results in the following manner:

- If the test completes without failure, the LED for that test turns off.
- If the test turns up a failure, the LED for that test turns amber and the system LED also turns amber.

On successful POST completion, the port LEDs blink and then turn off.

If fatal failures occur, as indicated in Table 9-6, the switch is not operational. The switch is still operational with nonfatal failures, but might have limited functionality.

During initial startup, if POST test failures are detected, they are reported to the console. If POST completes successfully, you can configure the switch.

If POST completes successfully on a Catalyst 2950 switch, you are prompted to enter the initial configuration for the switch. You can use an automatic setup program to assign switch IP information, host and cluster names, and passwords, and to create a default configuration for continued operation. Later, you can use CLI to customize your configuration. To run the setup program, access the switch from the PC terminal that you connected to the console port.

Complete the initial configuration by answering each question as it appears, as shown in Example 9-6.

Example 9-6 *Setup Dialog*

```
--- System Configuration Dialog ---

At any point you may enter a question mark '?' for help.
Use ctrl-c to abort configuration dialog at any prompt.
Default settings are in square brackets '[ ]'.
Continue with configuration dialog? [yes/no]: yes
Enter IP address: 172.16.1.101
Enter IP netmask: 255.255.255.0
Would you like to enter a default gateway address? [yes]: yes
IP address of the default gateway: 172.16.1.1
Enter a host name: SwitchA
Enter enable secret: secret_password
Would you like to configure a Telnet password? [yes] yes
Enter Telnet password: cisco
Would you like to enable as a cluster command switch? no

Enter cluster name: cls_name
```

After you enter the required settings, the setup program displays the configuration for you to confirm, as shown in Example 9-7.

Example 9-7 *Setup Output*

```
The following configuration command script was created:
ip subnet-zero
interface VLAN1
ip address 172.16.1.101 255.255.255.0
ip default-gateway 172.16.1.1
hostname host_name
enable secret 5 $1$M3pS$cXtAlkyR3/6Cn8/
line vty 0 15
password cisco
snmp community private rw
snmp community public ro
cluster enable cls_name
End
Use this configuration? [yes/no]: y
```

Enter **y** to load this script and complete the initial configuration using setup.

Starting a Cisco IOS Router

A Cisco router, like the switch, also goes through its startup when you turn the device on. When the startup is completed, you can configure the initial software configurations on the router using setup. This section explains how the router starts up and shows you how to verify its initial operation.

Recognizing the correct router startup is the first step in deploying a Cisco router. The router must start successfully and have a valid configuration to operate on the network.

The startup of a Cisco router requires that you verify the physical installation, power up the router, and view the Cisco IOS software output on the console. To start router operations, the router completes the following tasks:

1 Runs the POST to test the hardware

2 Finds and loads the Cisco IOS Software that the router uses for its operating system

3 Finds and applies the configuration statements about router-specific attributes, protocol functions, and interface addresses

When a Cisco router powers up, it performs a POST. During the POST, the router executes diagnostics to verify the basic operation of the CPU, memory, and interface circuitry.

After verifying the hardware functions, the router proceeds with software initialization, where it finds and loads the IOS image, and then finds and loads the configuration file, if one exists.

The initial startup of a Cisco router requires that you complete the following steps:

Step 1 Before you start the router, verify the following:

    — All network cable connections are secure.

    — Your terminal is connected to the console port.

    — Your console terminal application, such as HyperTerminal, is selected.

Step 2 Push the power switch to on.

Step 3 Observe the boot sequence and the Cisco IOS Software output on the console.

When the router starts up, it looks for a device configuration file. If it does not find one, the router executes a question-driven initial configuration routine, called *setup*.

After a router completes the POST and loads a Cisco IOS image, it looks for a device configuration file in its nonvolatile RAM (NVRAM). The router's NVRAM is a type of memory that retains its contents even when power is turned off. If the router has a configuration file in NVRAM, the user-mode prompt (hostname>) appears.

If no configuration file exists in NVRAM, the operating system executes a question-driven initial configuration routine referred to as the *system configuration dialog*. This special mode is also called the *setup dialog*.

Setup is not intended as the mode for entering complex protocol features in the router. You use setup to create a minimal configuration. Instead of setup, network administrators use various configuration-mode commands for most router configuration tasks.

The primary purpose of setup mode is to rapidly bring up a minimal-feature configuration for any router that cannot find its configuration from some other source.

Many of the prompts in the dialog of the setup command facility have default answers in square brackets ([ ]) following the question. Pressing the **Enter** key enables you to use the defaults.

When the setup dialog begins, you can choose not to continue with the system configuration by entering **No** at the prompt. To begin the initial configuration process, enter **Yes**.

You can press **Ctrl-c** to terminate the process at any time. **Ctrl-c** returns you to the user EXEC prompt (Router>) without making any configuration changes. If you want to start the dialog again, type the **setup** command at the privileged EXEC prompt (Router#**setup**).

Normally, you answer *no* to the basic management setup question illustrated in Example 9-8 so that you can enter extended setup and be able to configure the system interfaces.

Example 9-8 *System Configuration Dialog*

```
Router#setup


         --- System Configuration Dialog ---

Continue with configuration dialog? [yes/no]: y

At any point you may enter a question mark '?' for help.
Use ctrl-c to abort configuration dialog at any prompt.
Default settings are in square brackets '[]'.


Basic management setup configures only enough connectivity
for management of the system, extended setup will ask you
to configure each interface on the system

Would you like to enter basic management setup? [yes/no]: n
```

During setup, you are prompted for global parameters at the console. You use the configuration values you have determined for your router to enter the global parameters at the prompts. Example 9-9 shows the screen that prompts you for the initial global parameters.

Example 9-9 *Router Configuration: Initial Global Parameters*

```
Configuring global parameters:

  Enter host name [Router]:wg_ro_c

 The enable secret is a password used to protect access to
  privileged EXEC and configuration modes. This password, after
  entered, becomes encrypted in the configuration.
  Enter enable secret: cisco

  The enable password is used when you do not specify an
  enable secret password, with some older software versions, and
  some boot images.
  Enter enable password: sanfran

  The virtual terminal password is used to protect
  access to the router over a network interface.
  Enter virtual terminal password: sanjose
  Configure SNMP Network Management? [no]:
```

The first global parameter allows you to set the router host name. This host name precedes the Cisco IOS prompt in all configuration modes. The factory default router name is shown between the square brackets as [Router].

In the dialog box, the questions that immediately follow the system name are global parameters that set the various passwords used on the router.

You must enter an **enable secret** password. When you enter a string of password characters at the Enter enable secret prompt, the characters are processed by an MD5-based encryption algorithm, which can enhance the security of the password string. Whenever anyone lists the contents of the router configuration file, this **enable secret** password appears as a meaningless string of characters. Next, the **enable** password is entered into the configuration in plain text. The differences in these passwords are discussed in the section "Configuring a Router from the Command Line."

TIP

Setup recommends, but does not require, that the **enable** password be different from the **enable secret** password. If you choose the same password, this password is listed in plain text in the configuration file and could easily tip off anyone who might see this file.

NOTE

MD5 stands for message digest 5 and is defined by RFC 1321. MD5 is a one-way cryptographic algorithm used for encoding data.

As you continue through the setup dialog, you are prompted for additional global parameters at the console, as illustrated in Example 9-10. You use the configuration values you have determined for your router to enter the global parameters at the prompts.

Example 9-10 *Router Configuration: Initial Protocol Configurations*

```
Configure LAT? [yes]: n
  Configure AppleTalk? [no]:
  Configure DECnet? [no]:
  Configure IP? [yes]:
    Configure IGRP routing? [yes]: n
    Configure RIP routing? [no]:
  Configure CLNS? [no]:
  Configure IPX? [no]:
  Configure Vines? [no]:
  Configure XNS? [no]:
  Configure Apollo? [no]:
```

When you answer *yes* to a prompt, additional subordinate questions about that protocol might appear, as shown in Example 9-11.

Example 9-11 *Router Configuration: Additional Protocol Configurations*

```
BRI interface needs isdn switch-type to be configured
  Valid switch types are :
              [0]   none.........Only if you don't want to configure BRI.
              [1]   basic-1tr6....1TR6 switch type for Germany
              [2]   basic-5ess....AT&T 5ESS switch type for the US/Canada
              [3]   basic-dms100..Northern DMS-100 switch type for US/Canada
              [4]   basic-net3....NET3 switch type for UK and Europe
              [5]   basic-ni......National ISDN switch type
              [6]   basic-ts013...TS013 switch type for Australia
              [7]   ntt..........NTT switch type for Japan
              [8]   vn3..........VN3 and VN4 switch types for France
  Choose ISDN BRI Switch Type [2]:

Configuring interface parameters:

Do you want to configure BRI0 (BRI d-channel) interface? [no]:

Do you want to configure Ethernet0  interface? [no]: y
  Configure IP on this interface? [no]: y
    IP address for this interface: 10.1.1.33
    Subnet mask for this interface [255.0.0.0] : 255.255.255.0
    Class A network is 10.0.0.0, 24 subnet bits; mask is /24

Do you want to configure Serial0  interface? [no]:
```

You are prompted for parameters for each installed interface. Use the configuration values you have determined for your router interfaces to enter the interface-specific parameters at the prompts.

When you complete the configuration process for all installed interfaces on your router, the **setup** command presents the configuration command script that was created. Example 9-12 shows one example.

Example 9-12 *Router Configuration Command Script*

```
The following configuration command script was created:

hostname Router
enable secret 5 $1$/CCk$4r7zDwDNeqkxFO.kJxC3G0
enable password sanfran
line vty 0 4
password sanjose
no snmp-server
!
no appletalk routing
no decnet routing
ip routing
no clns routing
no ipx routing
no vines routing
no xns routing
no apollo routing
isdn switch-type  basic-5ess
interface BRI0
shutdown
no ip address
!
interface Ethernet0
no shutdown
ip address 10.1.1.31 255.255.255.0
no mop enabled
!
interface Serial0
shutdown
no ip address
!text omitted for brevity
end

[0] Go to the IOS command prompt without saving this config.
[1] Return back to the setup without saving this config.
[2] Save this configuration to nvram and exit.

Enter your selection [2]:
```

At this point, the router has not yet been configured, but you are presented with three options:

- **[0]**—Go to the EXEC prompt without saving or using the created configuration.

- **[1]**—Go back to the beginning of setup without saving the created configuration.

- **[2]**—Accept and use the created configuration, save it to NVRAM, and exit to privileged EXEC mode.

If you select option **[2]**, the router is configured with this script and the script is saved to NVRAM, allowing this script to be used the next time the router is restarted. After you have made this choice, your system is ready for use.

The script file generated by the **setup** command is additive. You can turn on features with **setup**, but you cannot turn them off. In addition, **setup** does not support many of the advanced features of the router or those features that require a more complex configuration.

After the device has booted and you have established a base configuration, you cannot use the IOS CLI to provide verification of operation and to enter more configuration parameters.

Booting a Cisco IOS Device Section Quiz

Use these practice questions to review what you learned in this section.

1 How should you power up a Catalyst 2950 switch?

  A Press the **Reset** button.

  B Turn the power switch to on.

  C Connect a Category 5 cable to another operating switch.

  D Attach the power cable plug to the switch power supply socket.

2 When you start the switch or router, what should you see on the console output?

  A Cisco IOS debug messages

  B The Diagnostic Console menu

  C Cisco IOS Software output text

  D A graphical picture showing the real-time LED's status

3 Which LED display modes of operation are used on a Catalyst switch? (Choose three.)

  A Port status

  B CPU utilization

  C Switch throughput

  D Full-duplex support

  E Bandwidth utilization

4 After a successful completion of the initial hardware testing, what do the port LEDs on a Catalyst switch do?

   A The LEDs remain green after the tests are complete.

   B The LEDs remain amber after the tests are complete.

   C The LEDs blink after the tests are complete and then turn off.

   D The LEDs blink after the tests are complete and then turn green.

5 When a Cisco router powers up, it performs a _____.

   A System configuration

   B Login and setup script

   C Software diagnostic test

   D Power-On Self-Test (POST)

6 Match each stage of a Catalyst switch LED POST to its description.

   1 Stage 1   **A** All port LEDs are green.

   2 Stage 2   **B** If no test fails, POST completes.

   3 Stage 3   **C** If a test fails, its LED turns amber.

   4 Stage 4   **D** System LED turns amber if any test fails.

   5 Stage 5   **E** Each LED turns off after its test completes.

   6 Stage 6   **F** On POST completion, LEDs blink and then turn off.

7 If POST completes successfully on the Catalyst 2950 switch, what happens next?

   A The switch shuts down.

   B The switch starts automatically.

   C The Menu Console Logon screen appears.

   D You are prompted to enter the initial configuration for the switch.

8 When the router starts up, which actions do the startup routines perform? (Choose three.)

   A Run POST.

   B Execute setup mode.

    C   Make sure that the router can reach other routers on the same network.

    D   Enter privileged EXEC mode so the network administrator can configure it.

    E   Find and load the Cisco IOS software that the router uses for its operating system.

    F   Find and apply the configuration statements about router-specific attributes, protocol functions, and interface addresses.

 9 Why would you use the *setup* dialog on a Cisco device?

    A   To bring up privileged EXEC mode

    B   To complete the initial configuration

    C   To enter complex protocol features in the router

    D   To create a test configuration file without saving it to NVRAM

Configuring a Switch from the Command Line

The Catalyst switch IOS Software has different configuration modes, including the global configuration mode and the interface configuration mode. This section explains how to complete the initial switch configuration for basic operation.

To configure global switch parameters like the switch host name or the switch IP address used for switch management purposes, use the global configuration mode. To configure a particular port (interface), use the interface configuration mode.

One of the first tasks in configuring your switch is to name it. Naming your switch helps you to better manage your network by being able to uniquely identify each switch within the network. The name of the switch is considered to be the host name and is the name displayed at the system prompt. You assign the switch name in global configuration mode. In Example 9-13, the switch name is set to **wg_sw_c**.

Example 9-13 *Setting the Switch Name*

```
Switch#config terminal
Switch(config)#hostname wg_sw_c
wg_sw_c(config)#
```

To configure the default IP address and subnet mask on the switch, use the **ip address** command at the VLAN 1 interface configuration mode. An IP address is required on a Layer 2 switch ONLY for management purposes. For example, an IP address must be assigned if you plan to use a Telnet connection, or if you plan to use the Simple Network

Management Protocol (SNMP) to manage the switch. Example 9-14 shows how to set the management address on a Catalyst 2950.

Example 9-14 *Setting the Switch Management Address*

```
wg_sw_c(config)#interface vlan 1
wg_sw_c(config-if)#ip address 172.16.1.101 255.255.255.0
wg_sw_c(config-if)#no shutdown
```

NOTE   The **no shutdown** command is required to activate the management address. A Layer 2 switch can have only one active management address any given time.

If you are going to Telnet to the switch from a different VLAN or subnet than the one it is addressed in, you need a default gateway. To configure a default gateway for your switch, use the **ip default-gateway** command. Enter the IP address of the next-hop router interface that is directly connected to the switch where a default gateway is being configured. The default gateway receives IP packets with unresolved destination IP addresses from the switch CPU. Example 9-15 shows how to configure the default gateway.

Example 9-15 *Setting a Default Gateway*

```
wg_sw_c(config-if)#exit
wg_sw_c(config)#ip default-gateway 172.16.101.1
```

After the default gateway is configured, the switch has connectivity to the remote networks with which a host needs to communicate.

NOTE   For a multilayer switch like a 4500, 6500, or 3550 running IOS Software that is configured to route with IP, you do not need to have a default gateway set if the device knows the route to the destination network.

After logging in to a Catalyst switch, you can verify the switch initial startup status using the following switch status commands:

- **show version**—Displays the configuration of the system hardware and the software version information.

- **show interfaces**—Displays statistics and status information of all the interfaces on the switch. Both the switch trunks and the switch line ports are considered interfaces. The resulting output varies, depending on the network for which an interface has been configured. Usually, you enter this command with the options *type* and *slot/number,* where *type* allows values such as Ethernet and Fast Ethernet, and *slot/number* indicates slot 0 and the port number on the selected interface (for example, e0/1).

- **show running-configuration**—Displays the active configuration of the device including the interface IDs.
- **show interfaces status**—Displays the interface ID, status, name, VLAN, and duplex in an easy-to-read table format
- **show ip**—Displays the IP address, subnet mask, and default gateway settings on the switch.

Example 9-16 shows the output from a **show version** command.

Example 9-16 *Switch* **show version** *Command*

```
wg_sw_c#show version
Cisco Internetwork Operating System Software
IOS (tm) C2950 Software (C2950-I6Q4L2-M), Version 12.1(11)EA1, RELEASE SOFTWARE
(fc1)
Copyright (c) 1986-2002 by cisco Systems, Inc.
Compiled Wed 28-Aug-02 10:25 by antonino
Image text-base: 0x80010000, data-base: 0x80528000

ROM: Bootstrap program is CALHOUN boot loader

wg_sw_c uptime is 2 minutes
System returned to ROM by power-on
System image file is "flash:/c2950-i6q4l2-mz.121-11.EA1.bin"

cisco WS-C2950-12 (RC32300) processor (revision G0) wit
00:02:28: %SYS-5-CONFIG_I: Configured from console by consoleh 20402K bytes of
memory.
Processor board ID FHK0646W0HR
Last reset from system-reset
Running Standard Image
12 FastEthernet/IEEE 802.3 interface(s)

32K bytes of flash-simulated non-volatile configuration memory.
Base ethernet MAC Address: 00:0B:5F:21:3C:40
Motherboard assembly number: 73-5782-11
Power supply part number: 34-0965-01
Motherboard serial number: FOC06440KTJ
Power supply serial number: PHI063906A6
Model revision number: G0
Motherboard revision number: A0
Model number: WS-C2950-12
System serial number: FHK0646W0HR
Configuration register is 0xF

wg_sw_c#
```

Table 9-7 describes the key output fields from the **show version** command.

Table 9-7 **show version** *Command Fields*

Output	Description
C2950 Software	This shows the hardware platform.
Version	Information identifying the software by name and version number. Always specify the complete version number when reporting a possible software problem. In the example, the switch is running Cisco IOS version 12.1(11)EA1.
Switch uptime	Current days and time since the system was last booted. In the example, the switch uptime is 2 minutes.

The **show interfaces** command displays physical layer status and statistics information on the network interfaces of the switch. Example 9-17 shows the output for a **show interfaces** command.

Example 9-17 show interfaces *Output*

```
wg_sw_c#show interface Fastethernet 0/1
FastEthernet0/1 is down, line protocol is down
  Hardware is Fast Ethernet, address is 000b.5f21.3c41 (bia 000b.5f21.3c41)
  MTU 1500 bytes, BW 10000 Kbit, DLY 1000 usec,
     reliability 255/255, txload 1/255, rxload 1/255
  Encapsulation ARPA, loopback not set
  Keepalive set (10 sec)
  Auto-duplex, Auto-speed
  input flow-control is off, output flow-control is off
  ARP type: ARPA, ARP Timeout 04:00:00
  Last input never, output 00:09:58, output hang never
  Last clearing of "show interface" counters never
  Input queue: 0/75/0/0 (size/max/drops/flushes); Total output drops: 0
  Queueing strategy: fifo
  Output queue :0/40 (size/max)
  5 minute input rate 0 bits/sec, 0 packets/sec
  5 minute output rate 0 bits/sec, 0 packets/sec
     1 packets input, 64 bytes, 0 no buffer
     Received 0 broadcasts, 0 runts, 0 giants, 0 throttles
     0 input errors, 0 CRC, 0 frame, 0 overrun, 0 ignored
     0 watchdog, 0 multicast, 0 pause input
     0 input packets with dribble condition detected
     1 packets output, 64 bytes, 0 underruns
     0 output errors, 0 collisions, 2 interface resets

wg_sw_c#
```

Table 9-8 shows some significant fields shown in Example 9-17 that are useful for checking on fundamental switch details.

Table 9-8   **show interfaces** *Command Fields*

Output	Description
Fast Ethernet 0/1 is down, line protocol is down	Indicates the current status of the interface. The possibilities are as follows: • administratively down—line protocol is down (interface is configured as **shutdown**). • down—line protocol is down (Interface problem, no physical connection, or device on other side is powered down). • up—line protocol is down (physical connection, but signaling is not working properly, for example, speed mismatch). • up—line protocol is up (working properly).
Hardware is Fast Ethernet	Shows the type of hardware interface.
Address is	Shows the Media Access Control (MAC) address that identifies the interface hardware.
MTU 1500 bytes	Shows the size of the maximum transmission unit (MTU) for this interface.
Auto-Duplex, Auto-Speed	Shows the speed and duplex for the interface.

Additional display from this command includes counters of the number and type of frames passing through the interface and any errors that have occurred.

The problem with the **show interfaces** command is that you have to go through many pages to see all the interface information. A more compact command for viewing output is the **show interfaces status** command used in Example 9-18.

Example 9-18 **show interfaces status** *Command*

```
wg_sw_c#show interfaces status

Port    Name            Status       Vlan    Duplex  Speed Type
Fa0/1                   notconnect   1         auto    auto 10/100BaseTX
Fa0/2                   notconnect   1         auto    auto 10/100BaseTX
Fa0/3                   connected    1       a-full   a-100 10/100BaseTX
Fa0/4                   notconnect   1         auto    auto 10/100BaseTX
Fa0/5                   notconnect   1         auto    auto 10/100BaseTX
Fa0/6                   notconnect   1         auto    auto 10/100BaseTX
Fa0/7                   notconnect   1         auto    auto 10/100BaseTX
Fa0/8                   notconnect   1         auto    auto 10/100BaseTX
Fa0/9                   notconnect   1         auto    auto 10/100BaseTX
Fa0/10                  notconnect   1         auto    auto 10/100BaseTX
Fa0/11                  notconnect   1         auto    auto 10/100BaseTX
Fa0/12                  notconnect   1         auto    auto 10/100BaseTX
wg_sw_c#
```

Notice in this command you can get a quick overview of all the interfaces; however, you do not get to see any counter information. You use the **show interfaces** and **show interfaces status** commands frequently while configuring and monitoring switches.

Use the **show ip interface brief** command to verify the IP address, and use the **show ip default** command to verify the default-gateway settings on the switch. Example 9-19 shows the output of these two commands.

Example 9-19 *Displaying Switch IP Configuration*

```
wg_sw_c#show ip interface brief
Interface              IP-Address      OK? Method Status                Protocol
Vlan1                  172.16.1.101    YES manual up                    up
FastEthernet0/1        unassigned      YES unset  down                  down
FastEthernet0/2        unassigned      YES unset  down                  down
FastEthernet0/3        unassigned      YES unset  up                    up
FastEthernet0/4        unassigned      YES unset  down                  down
FastEthernet0/5        unassigned      YES unset  down                  down
FastEthernet0/6        unassigned      YES unset  down                  down
FastEthernet0/7        unassigned      YES unset  down                  down
FastEthernet0/8        unassigned      YES unset  down                  down
FastEthernet0/9        unassigned      YES unset  down                  down
FastEthernet0/10       unassigned      YES unset  down                  down

wg_sw_c#show ip default
172.16.1.1
wg_sw_c#
```

Using the commands listed here, you should be able to move around a switch to provide basic configuration parameters and verification.

Configuring a Switch from the Command Line Section Quiz

Use these practice questions to review what you learned in this section.

1 Which Cisco IOS command displays the configuration of the system hardware and software version information on a Cisco device?

A **show version**

B **show interfaces**

C **show startup-config**

D **show running-config**

2 After you configure the IP address on an interface, how do you change the state from administratively down to up?

   A Enter **exit**.

   B Enter **shutdown**.

   C Enter **no shutdown**.

   D Enter **configure terminal**.

3 Which Cisco IOS command displays the interface bandwidth on a Cisco switch?

   A **show interfaces**

   B **show bandwidth**

   C **show interfaces bandwidth**

   D **show bandwidth interfaces**

4 Match each data-link protocol status to the message that appears with the **show interfaces** command.

1	Operational	**A**	Serial1 is up, line protocol is up.
2	Manually disabled	**B**	Serial 1 is up, line protocol is down.
3	Signaling problem	**C**	Serial1 is down, line protocol is down.
4	Physical connection problem	**D**	Serial1 is administratively down, line protocol is down.

Configuring a Router from the Command Line

The first method of router configuration presented was the setup utility. Setup allows a basic initial configuration to be created. For more complex and specific configurations, you can use the CLI to enter terminal configuration mode.

Recall that two variations of EXEC mode exist: user EXEC mode and privileged EXEC mode. From privileged EXEC mode, you can enter global configuration mode with the **configure terminal** command. From global configuration mode, you have access to specific configuration modes, which include the following:

- **Interface**—Supports commands that configure operations on a per-interface basis. The prompt for this configuration mode is as follows:

  ```
  Router(config-if)#
  ```

- **Subinterface**—Supports commands that configure multiple virtual (logical) interfaces on a single physical interface. The prompt for this configuration mode is as follows:

  ```
  Router(config-subif)#
  ```

- **Controller**—Supports commands that configure controllers (for example, E1 and T1 controllers). The prompt for this configuration mode is as follows:

  ```
  Router(config-controller)#
  ```

- **Line**—Supports commands that configure the operation of a terminal line. The prompt for this configuration mode is as follows:

  ```
  Router(config-line)#
  ```

- **Router**—Supports commands that configure an IP routing protocol. The prompt for this configuration mode is as follows:

  ```
  Router(config-router)#
  ```

Commands that affect the entire router are called *global commands*. The **hostname** and **enable password** commands are examples of global commands.

Commands that point to or indicate a process or interface that is to be configured are called *major commands*. When entered, major commands cause the CLI to enter a specific configuration mode. Major commands have no effect unless they are immediately followed by a subcommand that supplies the configuration entry. For example, the major command **interface serial 0** has no effect unless it is followed by a subcommand that says what you want to do to that interface.

The following are examples of major commands and the subcommands that go with them:

```
Router(config)#interface serial 0 (major command)
Router(config-if)#shutdown (subcommand)

Router(config-if)#line console 0 (major command)
Router(config-line)#password cisco (subcommand)

Router(config-line)#router rip (major command)
Router(config-router)#network 10.0.0.0 (subcommand)
```

Notice that entering a major command switches you from one configuration mode to another. However, you must know the syntax of the major command. The help function does not list major commands when in a subcommand configuration mode.

One of the first things you want to configure on your router is a name. Naming your router helps you better manage your network by being able to uniquely identify each router within the network. The name of the router is considered to be the host name and is the name displayed at the system prompt. If no name is configured, the default router name is *Router*. You assign the router name in global configuration mode. Example 9-20 demonstrates the process of naming the router.

Example 9-20 *Naming the Router*

```
Router(config)#hostname wg_ro_c
wg_ro_c(config)#
```

You can further identify your router by configuring a message-of-the-day banner to be displayed on all connected terminals. The banner is displayed at login and is useful for conveying security messages. When you enter the **banner motd** command, follow the command with one or more spaces and a delimiting character of your choice. In Example 9-21, the delimiting character is an ampersand (**&**). After you add the banner text, terminate the message with the same character and return to configuration mode. Press **Ctrl-c** to exit this mode without entering a message.

Example 9-21 *Configuring the Router's Message-of-the-Day Banner*

```
wg_ro_c(config)#banner motd  &
       Accounting Department
       You have entered a secured
       system. Authorized access
       only! &
```

You can also add a description of up to 80 characters in length to an interface to help you remember specific information about that interface, such as the network serviced by that interface's services. This description is meant solely as a comment to help identify how the interface is being used. The description appears in the output when you display the configuration information that exists in router memory and in a **show interfaces** command display. Example 9-22 demonstrates how to configure a router interface description.

Example 9-22 *Configuring the Router's Interface Description*

```
wg_ro_c(config)#interface ethernet 0
wg_ro_c(config-if)#description Engineering LAN, Bldg. 18
```

You can secure your router by using passwords to restrict access. Passwords can be established both on individual lines and to privileged EXEC mode. Passwords are case-sensitive.

Example 9-23 uses the **line console 0** command followed by the **login** and then the **password** subcommands to establish a login password for the console terminal. The purpose here is to establish the need for a user to log in to the console before gaining access to the router. **console 0** designates the router's console connection, and **login** prompts a user for a password before allowing console connectivity.

Example 9-23 *Configuring the Router's Console Password*

```
Router(config)#line console 0
Router(config-line)#login
Router(config-line)#password cisco
```

As demonstrated in Example 9-24, the **line vty 0 4** command followed by the **password** subcommand establishes a login password on incoming Telnet sessions.

Example 9-24 *Configuring the Router's Virtual Terminal Password*

```
Router(config)#line vty 0 4

Router(config-line)#password sanjose
```

NOTE   You do not have to enter the **login** command on the vty lines, because it is already there by default. This is why you cannot immediately Telnet to a router just by putting it on the network, assigning an IP address to the network interface, and enabling that interface. If you try to do so, you get the following message:

```
Password required, but none set.
```

This message occurs because login processing is already enabled on all the vty lines.

The **enable password** global command restricts access to privileged EXEC mode. Example 9-25 demonstrates how to configure the enable password. You can also assign an encrypted form of the enable password called the enable secret password. Just enter the **enable secret** command with the desired password at the global configuration mode prompt, as demonstrated in Example 9-26. If you configure both of these passwords, the enable secret password is used instead of the enable password.

Example 9-25 *Configuring the Router Enable Password*

```
Router(config)#enable password cisco
```

Example 9-26 *Configuring the Router Enable Secret Password*

```
Router(config)#enable secret sanfran
```

You can also add a further layer of security, which is particularly useful for passwords that are in configuration files stored on a TFTP server. Cisco provides a feature that allows you to use encrypted passwords. Passwords can be encrypted through the use of the **service password-encryption** command in global configuration mode. The encryption scheme used by this command is not as strong as the one used by the **enable secret** command.

To disable passwords, use the **no** form of the specific password command in global configuration mode, as shown in Example 9-27.

Example 9-27 *Disabling Passwords*

```
Router(config) #no enable secret sanfran
```

Additional Console Commands

Other useful console commands include the **exec-timeout 0 0** command. This command sets the timeout for the EXEC session to zero minutes and zero seconds. The purpose of this is to prevent the session from timing out and disconnecting you. You could also type the command **no exec-timeout** to achieve the same purpose. Example 9-28 demonstrates how to enter this command.

Example 9-28 *Preventing Console Session Timeout*

```
Router(config)#line console 0
Router(config-line)#exec-timeout 0 0
```

Although the **exec-timeout 0 0** command is useful in a classroom or laboratory environment, it is not wise to use it on a production device. The end result would be leaving the console port open indefinitely, thereby bypassing all security you might have set on that port.

The **logging synchronous** console line command is useful whenever console messages are being displayed at the same time that you are attempting to input EXEC or configuration commands. Instead of the console messages being intermingled with your input, your input is redisplayed on a single line at the finish of each console message that "interrupts" your input. This makes reading your input and the message much easier. Example 9-29 demonstrates how to enter this command.

Example 9-29 *Redisplaying Interrupted Console Input*

```
Router(config)#line console 0
Router(config-line)#logging synchronous
```

Configuring Router Interfaces

A router's main function is to relay packets from one network device to another. To do that, you must define the characteristics of the interfaces through which the packets are received and sent. These characteristics include, but are not limited to, the address of the port, the data encapsulation method, media type, bandwidth, and direct memory access buffering parameters.

Many features are enabled on a per-interface basis. Interface configuration mode commands modify the operation of Ethernet, Token Ring, FDDI, serial, HSSI, loopback, dialer, null, async, ATM, BRI, and tunnel interface types. When you issue the **interface** *type number* command at the Router(config)# prompt, you must define both the interface *type* and *number*. The number is assigned to each interface at the factory or by the physical location of the interface hardware in the router and is used to identify each interface. This identification is critical when you have multiple interfaces of the same type in a single router. Here are some examples of an interface type and number:

```
Router(config)#interface serial 0
Router(config)#interface ethernet 1
```

You specify an interface in Cisco 2600, 3600, 4000, 7000, and 7200 series routers (modular routers) by the physical slot in the router and the port number on the module in that slot. Here's an example:

```
Router(config)#interface ethernet 1/0
```

You define an interface in the Cisco 7000 and 7500 series routers with VIP cards by slot, port adapter (a module on the VIP card), and the port number on the port adapter. Here's an example:

```
Router(config)#interface ethernet 1/0/0
```

To configure an interface, select the appropriate interface type and location and enter the appropriate commands to modify the parameters. When you want to leave interface configuration mode and return to global configuration mode, type **exit** at the

Router(config-if)# prompt. The following steps illustrate the configuration of a serial interface on a Cisco router:

Step 1   Enter global configuration mode. As shown in the following command lines, you are configuring the interface from terminal mode:

```
Router#configure terminal
Router(config)#
```

Step 2   When in global configuration mode, you must identify the specific interface against which you will be issuing commands by entering the appropriate major command. As shown in the following command lines, the interface is serial 0.

```
Router(config)#interface serial 0
Router(config-if)#
```

Step 3   Enter the specified bandwidth for the interface. The **bandwidth** command overrides the default bandwidth that is displayed in the **show interfaces** command and is used by some routing protocols, such as IGRP. The default bandwidth for synchronous serial lines is T1 speed (1.544 Mbps). The bandwidth entered has no effect on the actual speed of the line. Instead, it is used to compute routing metrics and the load of the link. The following command lines show how to set the bandwidth for the router interface:

```
Router(config-if)#bandwidth 64
Router(config-if)#exit
Router(config)#exit
Router#
```

Step 4   In some environments (typically a laboratory), you might connect a data circuit-terminating equipment (DCE) cable to your router to simulate a carrier line. If a DCE cable is attached, issue the **clock rate** command with the desired speed. Be sure to type the complete clock speed. For example, a clock rate of 64,000 cannot be abbreviated as 64. To set the clock rate, you would issue the following command line:

```
Router(config-if)#clock rate 64000
Router(config-if)#
```

NOTE   Serial links have two sides. One side of the link is responsible for clocking and is called a DCE. The other side of the link is called the data terminal equipment (DTE). The DCE cable has a female connector, and the DTE has a male connector. In a production network, the DCE interface is provided by the service provider and is typically a connection to a channel service unit/data service unit (CSU/DSU). Routers are typically the DTE side of the serial interface. In environments where you want to simulate a serial connection, you can connect two routers back-to-back with a DTE and DCE cable. To simulate the environment, one of these devices must provide clocking. Clocking is the function of the router with the DCE cable. Clock rates that can be configured on serial interfaces are typically the following:

1,200; 2,400; 4,800; 9,600; 19,200; 38,400; 56,000; 64,000; 72,000; 125,000; 148,000; 500,000; 800,000; 1,000,000; 1,300,000; 2,000,000; and 4,000,000

However, this can vary with the type of serial interface you have in your router.

After you configure the router, you use **show** commands to verify the configuration changes.

The **show interfaces serial 0** command shown in Example 9-30 shows the changes issued in the initial serial interface configuration. Notice in the highlighted text that the interface is up and that the bandwidth, shown here as BW, is set to 64 Kbps.

Example 9-30 *Verifying Router Interface Configuration Changes with* **show interface**

```
Router#show interface serial 0
Serial0 is up, line protocol is up
  Hardware is HD64570
  Internet address is 10.140.4.2/24
  MTU 1500 bytes, BW 64 Kbit, DLY 20000 usec, rely 255/255, load 1/255
  Encapsulation HDLC, loopback not set, keepalive set (10 sec)
  Last input 00:00:09, output 00:00:04, output hang never
  Last clearing of "show interface" counters never
  Input queue: 0/75/0 (size/max/drops); Total output drops: 0
  Queueing strategy: weighted fair
  Output queue: 0/1000/64/0 (size/max total/threshold/drops)
    Conversations  0/1/256 (active/max active/max total)
    Reserved Conversations 0/0 (allocated/max allocated)
  5 minute input rate 0 bits/sec, 0 packets/sec
  5 minute output rate 0 bits/sec, 0 packets/sec
(output omitted)
```

You might need to set the media type on an Ethernet interface. Ethernet interfaces have different types of physical connections. For example, you might have an attachment unit interface (AUI) option and a 10BASE-T connector, as in the case of a Cisco 4000 series router. This router series has both of these physical connectors on a network interface module. The default connector is an AUI. Some routers might autosense the connection, but some might require that you select the connector in the configuration. Example 9-31 demonstrates how you would set the media type on an Ethernet interface.

Example 9-31 *Setting the Router's Ethernet Interface Media Type*

```
Router(config)#interface ethernet 2
Router(config-if)#media-type 10baset
```

You might need to disable an interface. This function is useful when you need to perform maintenance on a particular network segment. You might also choose to do this to isolate a network problem.

As shown in Example 9-32, the **shutdown** command administratively disables an interface. As demonstrated in Example 9-33, you use the **no shutdown** command in interface mode to reenable the interface.

Example 9-32 *Administratively Disabling a Router Interface*

```
Router#configure terminal
Router(config)#interface serial 0
Router(config-if)#shutdown
%LINK-5-CHANGED: Interface Serial0, changed state to administratively down
%LINEPROTO-5

5-UPDOWN: Line protocol on Interface Serial0, changed state to downd
```

Example 9-33 *Enabling a Router Interface That Is Administratively Shut Down*

```
Router#configure terminal
Router(config)#interface serial 0
Router(config-if)#no shutdown
%LINK-3-UPDOWN:  Interface Seria0, changed state to up
%LINEPROTO-5-UPDOWN:

 Line P

Protocol on Interface Serial0, changed state to up
```

TIP	Whenever you first configure an interface, unless in setup mode, you must use the **no shutdown** command to administratively enable the interface before it can be used to transmit packets.

The **show interfaces** command displays statistics for the network interfaces on the router, as demonstrated in Example 9-34.

Example 9-34 *Displaying Statistics for Router Interfaces*

```
Router#show interfaces
Ethernet0 is up, line protocol is up
  Hardware is Lance, address is 00e0.1e5d.ae2f (bia 00e0.1e5d.ae2f)
  Internet address is 10.1.1.11/24
  MTU 1500 bytes, BW 10000 Kbit, DLY 1000 usec, rely 255/255, load 1/255
  Encapsulation ARPA, loopback not set, keepalive set (10 sec)
  ARP type: ARPA, ARP Timeout 04:00:00
  Last input 00:00:07, output 00:00:08, output hang never
```

Example 9-34 *Displaying Statistics for Router Interfaces (Continued)*

```
Last clearing of "show interface" counters never
Queueing strategy: fifo
Output queue 0/40, 0 drops; input queue 0/75, 0 drops
5 minute input rate 0 bits/sec, 0 packets/sec
5 minute output rate 0 bits/sec, 0 packets/sec
   81833 packets input, 27556491 bytes, 0 no buffer
   Received 42308 broadcasts, 0 runts, 0 giants, 0 throttles
   1 input errors, 0 CRC, 0 frame, 0 overrun, 1 ignored, 0 abort
   0 input packets with dribble condition detected
   55794 packets output, 3929696 bytes, 0 underruns
   0 output errors, 0 collisions, 1 interface resets
   0 babbles, 0 late collision, 4 deferred
   0 lost carrier, 0 no carrier
   0 output buffer failures, 0 output buffers swapped out
```

Table 9-9 describes the significant **show interfaces** output fields.

Table 9-9   **show interfaces** *Output Fields*

Output	Description
Ethernet…is {up | down| administratively down}	Indicates whether the interface hardware is currently active and whether it has been taken down by an administrator.
line protocol is {up | down}	Indicates whether the software processes that handle the line protocol consider the interface usable (that is, whether keepalives are successful). If the interface misses three consecutive keepalives, the line protocol is marked as down.
Hardware	Hardware type (for example, MCI Ethernet, SCI, LANCE) and physical address.
Internet address	IP address followed by a subnet mask indicator.
MTU	Maximum transmission unit of the interface.
BW	Bandwidth of the interface in kilobits per second. The bandwidth parameter is used to compute routing metrics.
DLY	Delay of the interface in microseconds.
Rely	Reliability of the interface as a fraction of 255 (255/255 is 100 percent reliability), calculated as an exponential average over 5 minutes.
Load	Load on the interface as a fraction of 255 (255/255 is completely saturated), calculated as an exponential average over 5 minutes.
Encapsulation	Layer 2 encapsulation method assigned to the interface.

continues

Table 9-9   **show interfaces** *Output Fields (Continued)*

Output	Description
Loopback	Indicates whether loopback is set on the interface.
Keepalive	Indicates whether keepalives are set.
ARP type	Type of Address Resolution Protocol assigned.
Last input	Number of hours, minutes, and seconds since the last packet was successfully received by an interface. Useful for knowing when a dead interface failed.
Output	Number of hours, minutes, and seconds since the last packet was successfully transmitted by an interface. Useful for knowing when a dead interface failed.
Last clearing	Time at which the counters that measure cumulative statistics shown in this report (such as the number of bytes transmitted and received) were last reset to zero. Note that variables that might affect routing (for example, load and reliability) are not cleared when the counters are cleared. *** indicates that the elapsed time is too large to be displayed.
Output queue, input queue, drops	Number of packets in output and input queues. Each number is followed by a slash, the maximum size of the queue, and the number of packets dropped because of a full queue.
5 minute input rate, 5 minute output rate	Average number of bits and packets transmitted per second in the last 5 minutes. The 5 minute input and output rates should be used only as an approximation of traffic per second during a given minute period. These rates are exponentially weighted averages with a time constant of 5 minutes. A period of four time constants must pass before the average will be within 2 percent of the instantaneous rate of a uniform stream of traffic over that period.
packets input	Total number of error-free packets received by the system.
bytes input	Total number of bytes, including data and MAC encapsulation, in the error-free packets received by the system.
no buffer	Number of received packets discarded because no buffer space was available for the interface. Compare this with "ignored" count. Broadcast storms on Ethernet are often responsible for no input buffer events.

Table 9-9   **show interfaces** *Output Fields (Continued)*

Output	Description
Received... broadcasts	Total number of broadcast or multicast packets received by the interface. The number of broadcasts should be kept as low as practicable. An approximate threshold is less than 20 percent of the total number of input packets.
Runts	Number of packets that are discarded because they are smaller than the minimum packet size. For example, any Ethernet packet that is less than 64 bytes is considered a runt. Runts are usually caused by collisions. More than one runt per million bytes received should be investigated.
Giants	Number of packets that are discarded because they exceed the maximum packet size. For example, any Ethernet packet that is greater than 1518 bytes is considered a giant.

Once you have configured and verified the settings on your switch or router, you then need to save the parameters to be used each time the device reloads with the command **copy running-configuration startup-configuration**.

Configuring a Router from the Command Line Section Quiz

Use these practice questions to review what you learned in this section.

1 What should you do if you make an error during the system configuration dialog on a Cisco router?

A Type **Ctrl-C** to abort the process and start over.

B Use the **Page Up** key to go back and correct the error.

C Type **Ctrl-Q** to abort the process and return to the beginning.

D Use **Ctrl-P** or the **Up Arrow** to repeat the last command and make any corrections.

2 Which Cisco IOS command assigns the device name?

A **hostname** *hostname*

B **banner motd** *message*

C **hostname interface description**

D **description interface description**

3 What must you configure to ensure that anyone accessing your router from the console port is prompted for a password?

A The **password** command

B The **enable password** command

C The **login** command and the **password** command

D The **login required** command and the **password** command

4 Which Cisco IOS command configures Ethernet port 1 on a fixed port router?

A **Ethernet interface 1**

B **interface Ethernet 1**

C **Ethernet interface 0/1**

D **interface Ethernet 0/1**

5 Which Cisco IOS command do you use to bring up an interface on a Cisco router that is "administratively down"?

A **admin up**

B **shutdown**

C **no shutdown**

D **no admin shutdown**

Managing Configuration Changes

After logging into a Cisco IOS device, you can verify the initial startup status using the commands **show running-config** and **show startup-config**. You can then save configuration parameters by using the **copy running-configuration startup-configuration** command. This section describes the router status commands.

A Cisco IOS device has three primary types of memory:

- **RAM**—Stores routing tables, fast switching cache, running configuration, and so on
- **NVRAM**—Used for writable permanent storage of the startup configuration
- **Flash**—Memory cards that provide permanent storage of the Cisco IOS Software image, backup configurations, and any other files

The **show startup-config** command displays the saved configuration in NVRAM. The **show running-config** command displays the current (running) configuration in RAM. Example 9-35 shows the output of a **show running-config**.

Example 9-35 show running-config *Command*

```
g_sw_c#show running-configuration
Building configuration...

Current configuration : 921 bytes
!
version 12.1
no service pad
service timestamps debug uptime
service timestamps log uptime
no service password-encryption
!
hostname wg_sw_c
!
enable secret 5 $1$JY1/$4Mo5/WHMt/XqXowakvfpS1
!
ip subnet-zero
!
spanning-tree extend system-id
!
!
interface FastEthernet0/1
 no ip address
!
interface FastEthernet0/2
 no ip address
 --More--
```

The **Building configuration. . .** output indicates that the running configuration is being extracted from system RAM and converted into text to be displayed to the user.

After the running configuration is built from RAM, the **Current configuration:** message appears to indicate that this is the current configuration running in RAM.

The first line of the **show startup-config** command output indicates the amount of NVRAM used to store the configuration; for example, **Using 1359 out of 32762 bytes** indicates that the total size of the NVRAM is 32762 bytes and the current configuration stored in NVRAM takes up 1359 bytes. Example 9-36 shows the output from a **show startup-config** command.

Example 9-36 *show startup-config Command*

```
wg_sw_c#show startup-configuration
Using 921 out of 32768 bytes
!
version 12.1
no service pad
service timestamps debug uptime
service timestamps log uptime
no service password-encryption
!
hostname wg_sw_c
!
enable secret 5 $1$JY1/$4Mo5/WHMt/XqXowakvfpS1
!
ip subnet-zero
!
spanning-tree extend system-id
!
!
interface FastEthernet0/1
 no ip address
!
interface FastEthernet0/2
 no ip address
!
 --More--
```

After you have made configuration changes, you must save the active configuration to NVRAM if you want the router to use these changes the next time it is restarted.

To save your configuration to NVRAM, you enter the command **copy running-configuration startup-configuration**. (Use **write memory** or **write** in pre-Software Release 10.3.) If you do not save your configuration changes, they are lost if the router is powered off or reloaded. Example 9-37 shows how to copy the router's current configuration to NVRAM.

Example 9-37 *Copying the IOS Device's Current Configuration to NVRAM*

```
wg_ro_c#
wg_ro_c#copy running-config startup-config
Destination filename [startup-config]?
Building configuration...

wg_ro_c#
```

Managing Configuration Changes Section Quiz

Use these practice questions to review what you learned in this section.

1 Which Cisco IOS command saves the current configuration to be the starting configuration of the router?

   A **configure memory**

   B **configure terminal**

   C **copy startup-config running-config**

   D **copy running-config startup-config**

2 What information does the **show startup-config** command display?

   A Saved configuration in RAM

   B Running configuration in RAM

   C Saved configuration in NVRAM

   D Running configuration in NVRAM

3 Which Cisco IOS command displays the current active configuration settings on a Catalyst switch?

   A **show version**

   B **show interfaces**

   C **show startup-configuration**

   D **show running-configuration**

Chapter Summary

In this chapter, you explored the startup and initial configurations of Cisco Catalyst switches and Cisco routers. You learned how to maneuver through the EXEC mode of the switches and routers. You discovered help functions to aid in the use of Cisco IOS Software. You also explored the other modes and the syntax of the Cisco IOS and learned how to get a base configuration on a router using setup. As you perform advanced configurations on the routers and switches, you continue to use the basic functions and syntax learned here.

Chapter Review Questions

Use these review questions to test your knowledge of the concepts discussed in this chapter.

1 Access to the Cisco IOS CLI is generally referred to as _____.

   A A Telnet session

   B An EXEC session

   C A terminal session

   D A privileged session

2 Cisco IOS Software offers _____ features to ensure dependable access to networked resources.

   A Security

   B Reliability

   C Scalability

   D User interface

3 When a Cisco device starts up, it runs _____ to check its hardware.

   A Flash

   B RAM

   C POST

   D TFTP

4 When a Catalyst switch or Cisco router starts up, what is the first operation performed?

   A The device performs system startup routes.

   B The device performs hardware checking routines.

   C The device attempts to locate other devices on the network.

   D The device tries to find and apply software configuration settings.

5 Upon initial installation of a Cisco switch or router, the network administrator typically configures the networking devices from a _____.

A CD-ROM

B TFTP server

C Console terminal

D Modem connection

6 If a network administrator is supporting a remote device, the preferred method is to use a modem connection to the device's _____ for remote configuration.

A LAN port

B Uplink port

C Console port

D Auxiliary port

7 Which access level allows a person to access all router commands and can be password protected to allow only authorized individuals to access the router?

A User EXEC level

B Setup EXEC level

C Enable EXEC level

D Privileged EXEC level

8 How do you instruct a Cisco device to parse and execute an entered command?

A Click the **Send** key.

B Press the **Enter** key.

C Add a space at the end of the command.

D Wait 5 seconds after you enter a command.

9 Which CLI prompt indicates that you are working in privileged EXEC mode?

A Hostname#

B Hostname>

C Hostname-exec>

D Hostname-config

10 Which command would you enter in the privileged EXEC mode to list the command options?

A ?

B init

C help

D login

11 Match each step of the physical Catalyst switch startup process to its description.

1 Step 1   **A** Attach the power cable plug to the switch power supply socket.

2 Step 2   **B** Observe the boot sequence, including the Cisco IOS Software output text on the console.

3 Step 3   **C** Verify that all cable connections are secure, the terminal is connected to the console port, and the console terminal application is selected.

12 How do you start a Catalyst 2950 switch?

A Press the on/off switch.

B Power up the redundant power supply.

C Connect a network cable to another switch on the network.

D Attach the power cable plug to the switch power supply socket.

13 What color is the Catalyst 2950 switch redundant power supply LED if the redundant power supply is plugged in but not functioning correctly?

A   Green

B   Amber

C   Flashing green

D   Flashing amber

14 During a Catalyst switch POST test, what is the result of the console port test failing?

A   This is a fatal error, and you will not be able to access the switch.

B   This is a nonfatal error, but one or more ports will not be operational.

C   This is a nonfatal error, and you will be able to Telnet to the management console.

D   This is a nonfatal error, but the switch will not be able to restart itself automatically in case of a failure.

15 What should you type to display a list of commands that begin with the letter c on a Catalyst switch?

A   c?

B   c ?

C   help c

D   help c*

16 What should you type to display the command syntax help so that you can see how to complete a command that begins with **config**?

A   **config?**

B   **config ?**

C   **help config**

D   **help config***

17 Which configuration mode do you use to configure a particular port on a switch?

A User mode

B Global configuration mode

C Interface configuration mode

D Controller configuration mode

18 When you use the **show interfaces** command to display the status and statistics for the interfaces configured on a Catalyst switch, which output field indicates the MAC address that identifies the interface hardware?

A MTU 1500 bytes

B Hardware is . . . 10BASE-T

C Address is 0050.BD73.E2C1

D 802.1d STP State: Forwarding

19 Which **show** command requires that you have privileged EXEC mode access?

A **show ip**

B **show version**

C **show running**

D **show interfaces**

20 How should you power up a Cisco router?

A Press the **Reset** button.

B Turn the power switch to on.

C Connect the fiber cable to another router.

D Attach the power cable plug to the router power supply socket.

21 When you start a Cisco router, what should you see on the console?

   A Cisco IOS debug messages

   B The Diagnostic Console menu

   C Cisco IOS Software output text

   D A graphical picture showing the real-time LED's status

22 What is the primary purpose of setup mode on a Cisco router?

   A To display the current router configuration

   B To complete hardware and interface testing

   C To bring up a minimal feature configuration

   D To fully configure a Cisco router for IP routing

23 Which statement best describes what the user EXEC mode commands allow you to configure on a Cisco router?

   A You cannot configure anything; the user mode commands are used to display information.

   B The user EXEC mode allows you to perform global configuration tasks that affect the entire router.

   C The user EXEC mode commands allow you to enter a secret password so you can configure the router.

   D The user EXEC mode commands allow you to configure interfaces, subinterfaces, lines, and routers.

24 Which Cisco IOS command is used to return to user EXEC mode from the privileged EXEC mode?

   A **exit**

   B **quit**

   C **disable**

   D **userexec**

25 Match each type of help available with the Cisco IOS CLI to its description.

1 Context-sensitive help   **A** Provides a list of commands and the arguments associated with a specific command

2 Console error messages   **B** Allows recall of long or complex commands or entries for reentry, review, or correction

3 Command history buffer   **C** Identifies problems with router commands incorrectly entered so you can alter or correct

26 When you enter Cisco IOS commands on a router, which CLI editing key sequence redisplays a line?

A Ctrl-A

B Ctrl-F

C Ctrl-R

D Ctrl-W

27 What does the CLI editing key sequence **Ctrl-X** do?

A Erases everything to the left of the cursor

B Redisplays a line

C Deletes a single character

D Moves the cursor to the end of the line

28 Which Cisco IOS command sets the session command buffer size?

A set buffer

B show history

C history size line

D terminal history size *lines*

29 Which command returns to more recent commands in the history buffer after recalling commands?

A Ctrl-N

B Ctrl-P

C show history

D show terminal

30 What information does the **show running-config** command provide on a Cisco router?

A Current (running) configuration in RAM

B System hardware and names of configuration files

C Amount of NVRAM used to store the configuration

D Version of Cisco IOS software running on the router

31 Which Cisco IOS command displays the configuration of the system hardware and the software version information?

A **show version**

B **show interfaces**

C **show startup-config**

D **show running-config**

32 Match each router prompt to its configuration mode.

1 line

2 router

3 interface

4 controller

5 subinterface

A Router(config-if)#

B Router(config-line)#

C Router(config-subif)#

D Router(config-router)#

E Router(config-controller)#

33 If you enter a major command on a Cisco router, what happens?

A The router returns you to user EXEC mode.

B The router returns a list of possible commands.

C The router invokes a global configuration command.

D The router switches you from one configuration mode to another.

34 Which Cisco IOS command creates a message to be displayed upon router login?

A **hostname** *hostname*

B **banner motd** *message*

C **hostname interface description**

D **description interface description**

35 If both the **enable secret** and the **enable password** commands are configured on your router, how do you get to the # prompt?

  A Type in the configured enable secret password at the password prompt.

  B Type in the configured enable password at the password prompt.

  C Enter either the **enable secret** or the **enable password** command.

  D Enter both the **enable secret** and the **enable password** commands.

36 Which Cisco IOS command do you use to prevent a console session from timing out?

  A **no exec**

  B **no timeout**

  C **timeout 0 0**

  D **exec-timeout 0 0**

37 Which Cisco IOS command configures serial port in slot 0, port 1 on a modular router?

  A **serial 0/1 interface**

  B **interface serial 0 1**

  C **interface serial 0/1**

  D **serial 0 1 interface**

38 Which Cisco IOS command should you use to set the clock speed to 64 kbps on a serial interface on a Cisco router?

  A **clock rate 64**

  B **clock speed 64**

  C **clock rate 64000**

  D **clock speed 64000**

39 Which Cisco IOS commands correctly configure the IP address and subnet mask for Ethernet interface 1 in slot 1?

   A **interface FastEthernet 1 1**
       ip address 192.168.1.1 mask 255.255.255.0

   B **interface FastEthernet 1/1**
       ip address 192.168.1.1/24

   C **interface FastEthernet 1 1**
       ip address 192.168.1.1 255.255.255.0

   D **interface FastEthernet 1/1**
       ip address 192.168.1.1 255.255.255.0

40 What is a runt?

   A An Ethernet frame that has been discarded because it has a CRC error

   B An Ethernet frame that has been discarded because of an Ethernet collision

   C An Ethernet frame that has been discarded because it is smaller than the minimum Ethernet frame size

   D An Ethernet frame that has been ignored by the interface because the interface hardware ran low on internal buffers

41 A serial interface displays "Serial1 is up, line protocol is down". Which situations might cause this error? (Choose three.)

   A The clock rate has not been set.

   B The interface has been manually disabled.

   C No cable is attached to the serial interface.

   D No keepalives are coming in on the interface.

   E The encapsulation type on the other end is different than on your end.

Upon completion of this chapter, you will be able to perform the following tasks:

- Determine names and addresses of neighboring devices, given a Cisco switch in an operational environment

- Use CDP to obtain information remotely, given an operational switch and router

- Use information gathered using CDP, Telnet, and Cisco IOS commands to create a simple network map of your environment, given operational Cisco network devices

- Move configuration files between system components and network file servers, given an operational Cisco router

CHAPTER 10

Managing Your Network Environment

This chapter extends the network perspective by looking beyond the standalone device. In this chapter, you access and gather information about neighboring devices. You also gather information about remote devices—devices beyond your immediate neighbor. To help understand the topology of your network, you document the network, noting information you gathered using the Cisco-proprietary utility Cisco Discovery Protocol (CDP) and the IP utility Telnet.

In this chapter, you learn the processes and the procedures to perform configuration management. You learn where configuration files can reside, and you apply the commands to save and restore configuration files. You create and restore a backup software image using Trivial File Transfer Protocol (TFTP), Cisco IOS **copy**, and configurable boot-up options.

This chapter covers the management of a Cisco network device, including using CDP to build a network map and working with configuration file management and Cisco IOS image management.

Getting Information About Neighboring Devices

This section contains an overview of Cisco Discovery Protocol (CDP). CDP is a protocol- and media-independent tool used to aid in the management of Cisco devices. Table 10-1 shows the lower three layers of the OSI model. Notice that CDP is a Layer 2 implementation and that it works with multiple media types and protocol types.

Table 10-1 *TCDP Operates Across Multiple Protocol Suites and Media Types*

Upper-Layer Entry Addresses	TCP/IP	Novell IPX	AppleTalk	Others
Cisco Proprietary Data Link Protocol	CDP discovers and shows information about directly connected Cisco devices.			
Media Supporting SNAP	LANs	Frame Relay	ATM	Others

CDP is an information-gathering tool that enables you to access a summary of protocol and address information about other Cisco devices (regardless of which protocol suite they are running) that are directly connected to the device where you issue the command.

CDP runs over the data link layer, independent of the physical media to the upper-layer protocols. Because CDP operates at this level, two or more CDP devices that support different network layer protocols (for example, IP and Novell IPX) can learn about each other.

Physical media supporting the Subnetwork Access Protocol (SNAP) encapsulation connect CDP devices. These can include all LANs, Frame Relay and other WAN technologies, and ATM networks.

When a Cisco device boots up, CDP starts by default. Then, CDP can automatically discover neighboring Cisco devices running CDP, regardless of which protocol suite or suites are running.

NOTE   CDP runs on routers with Cisco IOS Release 10.3 or later and on Cisco switches and hubs.

Figure 10-1 is an example of how CDP exchanges information with its directly connected neighbors. You can display the results of this CDP information exchange on a console connected to a network device configured to run CDP on its interfaces.

Figure 10-1 *CDP Facilitates Information Exchange Between Neighboring Devices*

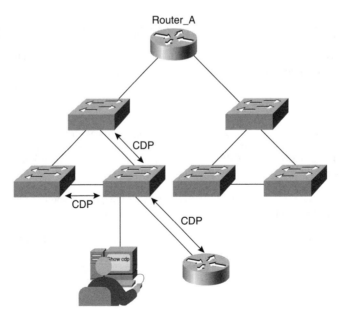

Displaying General Information About Neighboring Devices

You can use the **show cdp neighbors** command to display information about the devices directly connected to a switch or router and their associated Layer 3 addresses. Packets formed by CDP provide the following information about each CDP neighbor device:

- **Device identifiers**—For example, the switch's configured name and domain name (if any).
- **Address list**—Up to one address for each protocol supported.
- **Port identifier**—The name of the local and remote port (in the form of an ASCII character string, such as ethernet0).
- **Capabilities list**—Supported features. For example, the device acts as a source-route bridge and a router.
- **Platform**—The device's hardware platform; for example, Cisco 7000.

CDP version 2 (CDPv2) is the most recent release of the protocol and provides more intelligent device tracking features. These features include a reporting mechanism, which allows for more rapid error tracking, thereby reducing costly downtime. Reported error messages can be sent to the console or to a logging server and cover instances of mismatching native virtual LAN (VLAN) IDs (IEEE 802.1Q) on connecting ports and mismatching port duplex states between connecting devices.

Displaying CDP Information About a Device

Notice that Router_A in Figure 10-1 is not connected directly to the switch of the administrator's console. To obtain CDP information about this device, the administrator would need to Telnet to a switch directly connected to this target device.

You can view the CDP output via the **show cdp** command. CDP itself has several keywords that enable you to get different types of information and different levels of detail, as demonstrated in Example 10-1. CDP is designed and implemented as a simple, low-overhead protocol. A CDP packet can be as small as 80 octets, mostly made up of the ASCII strings that represent information such as the device name, protocol addressing information, port connectivity information, and device operating system information.

Example 10-1 **show cdp** *Keyword Options*

```
RouterA#show cdp ?
  entry      Information for specific neighbor entry
  interface  CDP interface status and configuration
  neighbors  CDP neighbor entries
  traffic    CDP statistics
  <cr>
RouterA(config)#no cdp run
RouterA(config)#interface serial0
RouterA(config-if)#no cdp enable
```

CDP functionality is enabled by default on all CDP compatible interfaces, but it can be disabled at the device level. To prevent other non-CDP-capable devices from getting information about your device, use the global configuration command **no cdp run**. This command disables the CDP protocol for the entire device. Use the **no cdp enable** command to disable CDP on a given interface. This would be useful to conserve bandwidth when connecting to a non-Cisco device. To re-enable CDP on an interface, use the **cdp enable** interface configuration command.

Although CDP frames are Layer 2 multicast, those frames are not forwarded by any Cisco switch. Two routers connected to a Cisco switch would show only the switch as a neighbor and not the other router. Disabling CDP on a switch would not allow it to forward packets from a router, only stop sending and receiving CDP on that port.

Displaying CDP Information About Neighboring Devices

Figure 10-2 shows an example of a router named RouterA. This figure is the basis for the output demonstrated in Example 10-2 through Example 10-11.

Figure 10-2 *CDP Neighbors*

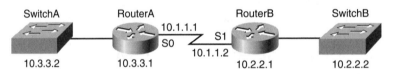

Running the **show cdp neighbors** command on RouterA results in the output shown in Example 10-2.

Example 10-2 show cdp neighbors *Command Output for RouterA in Figure 10-2*

```
RouterA#show cdp neighbors
Capability Codes: R - Router, T - Trans Bridge, B - Source Route Bridge
                  S - Switch, H - Host, I - IGMP, r - Repeater


Device ID          Local Intrfce   Holdtme   Capability  Platform  Port ID
RouterB            Ser 0           148          R        2522      Ser 1
SwitchA0050BD855780 Eth 0          167          T S      1900      2
```

| NOTE | SwitchA in Example 10-2 also provides its MAC address as part of the system name. |

For each local port, the display (as demonstrated in Example 10-2) shows the following:

- Neighbor device ID
- Local interface
- The holdtime value in seconds
- Neighbor device capability code
- Hardware platform of the neighbor
- Neighbor's remote port ID

The holdtime value indicates how long the receiving device should hold the CDP packet before discarding it.

The format of the **show cdp neighbors** output varies between types, but the available information is generally consistent across devices.

The **show cdp neighbors** command can be used on the Catalyst switch to display the CDP updates received on the local interfaces. Note that on a switch, the local interface is referred to as the *local port*.

Displaying Detailed CDP Information About Neighboring Devices

If you append the **detail** argument to the **show cdp neighbors** command, the resulting output includes additional information concerning the neighbor device. The output from the **show cdp neighbors detail** command is identical to that produced from the **show cdp entry** * command.

Use the CDP command **show cdp entry** [*router-name*] to display detailed information about neighbor devices. This command displays information about a specific neighbor when the neighbor's name is included in the command string. The name entered here is case-sensitive and can be discovered using the **show cdp** command. Use the CDP entry command variable * to display information about all neighbors, as demonstrated in Example 10-3.

Example 10-3 **show cdp entry** * *Command Output for RouterA*

```
RouterA#show cdp entry *
-------------------------
Device ID: RouterB
Entry address(es):
  IP address: 10.1.1.2
Platform: cisco 2522,  Capabilities: Router
Interface: Serial0,  Port ID (outgoing port): Serial1
Holdtime : 168 sec
```

continues

Example 10-3 **show cdp entry** * *Command Output for RouterA (Continued)*

```
Version :
Cisco Internetwork Operating System Software
IOS (tm) 2500 Software (C2500-JS-L), Version 12.0(3), RELEASE SOFTWARE (fci)
Copyright (c) 1986-1999 by Cisco Systems, Inc.
Compiled Mon 08-Feb-99 18:18 by phanguye
------------------------
Device ID: SwitchA0030805AB240
Entry address(es):
  IP address: 10.3.3.2
Platform: cisco 1900,  Capabilities: Trans-Bridge Switch
Interface: Ethernet0,  Port ID (outgoing port): 9
Holdtime : 147 sec


Version :
V8.01
```

The output from the **show cdp entry** command displays the following information:

- Neighbor device ID
- Layer 3 protocol information (for example, IP addresses)
- The device's platform
- The device's capabilities
- The local interface type and outgoing remote port ID
- The holdtime value in seconds
- IOS type and version

The output from the **show cdp entry** command includes all the Layer 3 addresses configured on neighbor device if configured (up to one Layer 3 address per protocol).

Displaying Information About Device Traffic

The **show cdp traffic** command displays information about interface traffic, as demonstrated in Example 10-4.

Example 10-4 **show cdp traffic** *Command Output for RouterA*

```
RouterA#show cdp traffic
CDP counters :
        Packets output: 56, Input: 38
        Hdr syntax: 0, Chksum error: 0, Encaps failed: 3
        No memory: 0, Invalid packet: 0, Fragmented: 0
```

The **show cdp traffic** command shows the number of CDP packets sent and received, as well as the number of errors for the following error conditions:

- Syntax error
- Checksum error
- Failed encapsulations
- Out-of-memory conditions
- Invalid packets
- Fragmented packets

Displaying Configuration Information and Interface Status for a Device

The **show cdp interface** command displays interface status and configuration information about the local device, as demonstrated in Example 10-5.

Example 10-5 show cdp interface *Command Output for RouterA*

```
RouterA#show cdp interface
BRI0 is administratively down, line protocol is down
  Encapsulation HDLC
  Sending CDP packets every 60 seconds
  Holdtime is 180 seconds
```

The **show cdp interface** command displays the following status fields:

- Administrative and protocol condition of the interface
- The line and data-link status of the interface
- Frequency at which CDP packets are sent (default is 60 seconds)
- Holdtime value, in seconds (default is 180 seconds)

CDP is limited to gathering information about immediate neighbors. Other tools are available for gathering information about remote devices, as described in the following section.

Creating a Network Map of the Environment

After you use CDP to discover the devices on the internetwork, you should document the network so you understand and can support it.

You can use topology documentation to validate design guidelines and to better understand the network for future design, change, or troubleshooting. Topology documentation should include both logical and physical documentation for these components:

- Connectivity
- Addressing

- Media types
- Devices
- Rack layouts
- Card assignments
- Cable routing
- Cable identification
- Termination points
- Power information
- Circuit identification information

Maintaining accurate network topology documentation is the key to successful configuration management. To create an environment where topology documentation maintenance can occur, the information must be available for updates. It is always a good practice to update topology documentation whenever a network change occurs.

Getting Information About Neighboring Devices Section Quiz

Use these practice questions to review what you learned in this section.

1 Which statements accurately describe CDP? (Choose two.)

   A CDP runs over the data link layer.

   B CDP runs over the application layer.

   C CDP automatically discovers all neighboring devices.

   D CDP automatically discovers neighboring CDP devices.

   E CDP automatically discovers information about remote devices.

2 Which network layer protocol must two CDP devices run to learn about each other?

   A IP

   B IPX

   C AppleTalk

   D The network layer protocol is unimportant to CDP

3 A CDP device learns information about _____.

   A All directly connected devices

   B All directly connected IP devices

   C All directly connected CDP devices

   D All devices on the local network segment

4 Which pieces of information does a CDP packet include? (Choose two.)

   A Link speed

   B Port identifier

   C Capabilities list

   D MAC address list

   E Destination address

5 Which command disables CDP on a specific interface?

   A **no cdp run**

   B **no cdp enable**

   C **no cdp interface** *if-id*

   D **interface** *if-id* **no cdp**

6 What does the command **no cdp run** do?

   A Disables CDP for the entire device

   B Disables CDP for a specific interface

   C Disables CDP for a specific time period

   D Disables CDP for all interfaces of a specific type

7 Which Cisco IOS command produces the same result as **show cdp entry** *?

   A **show cdp traffic**

   B **show cdp neighbors**

   C **show cdp interface all**

   D **show cdp neighbors detail**

8 If the letters *R* and *B* appear in the Capabilities column in the output of the **show cdp neighbors** command, it indicates that the specified device is acting as both a _____ and a _____.

   A Router; switch

   B Repeater; switch

   C Router; source route bridge

   D Repeater; source route bridge

9 Which Cisco IOS commands display a holdtime value? (Choose three.)

   A **cdp enable**

   B **show cdp entry**

   C **show cdp traffic**

   D **show cdp interface**

   E **show cdp neighbor**s

   F **interface** *if-id* **no cdp**

10 What information is included in the output of the command **show cdp traffic**?

   A Remote port ID

   B Holdtime value

   C Number of CDP packets sent

   D Frequency at which CDP packets are sent

11 Which CDP commands can you use to display the network layer address information of the CDP neighbor? (Choose two.)

   A **cdp enable**

   B **show cdp entry**

   C **show cdp traffic**

   D **show cdp interface**

12 How often should you update your network map?

   A Yearly

   B Weekly

   C Monthly

   D Whenever the network topology changes

13 Which pieces of information should you include in a network map? (Choose three.)

   A Addressing

   B Rack layouts

   C Serial numbers

   D Performance data

   E Cable identification

Getting Information About Remote Devices

This section contains an introduction to Telnet concepts. The Cisco CDP protocol provides information about devices directly connected to the device initiating the **cdp** command. This helps you find out about directly connected CDP-capable devices. To get information about remote devices — those not directly connected to the device initiating the command — you need to use Telnet.

Establishing a Telnet Session to a Remote Device

One way to learn about a remote network device is to connect to it using the Telnet application. Telnet is a virtual terminal protocol that is part of the TCP/IP protocol suite. Telnet allows remote connections to the EXEC process from one device to one or more other remote devices.

You can see slight variations when you use Telnet on Cisco routers compared to using it on most Catalyst switches. To open a Telnet connection from a Catalyst switch, use the **telnet** command before the target IP address or host name. With Cisco IOS Software, you do not have to enter the **telnet** command to establish your Telnet connection. If you prefer, you can just enter the IP address or host name of the target device. Example 10-6 demonstrates the use of the **telnet** command to establish a Telnet connection with a remote Catalyst switch.

Example 10-6 telnet *Command Establishes a Connection with a Remote Device*

```
RouterA#telnet 10.2.2.2

Trying 10.2.2.2 ... Open

- - - - - - - - - - - - - - - - - - - - - - - - - - - - - - - - - - - - - - - - -

Catalyst 1900 Management Console

Copyright (c) Cisco Systems, Inc.   1993-1998

All rights reserved.

Enterprise Edition Software

Ethernet Address:       00-90-86-73-33-40

PCA Number:             73-2239-06

PCA Serial Number:      FAA02359H8K

Model Number:           WS-C19210-EN

System Serial Number:   FAA0237X0FQ

.

.

SwitchB>
```

Verifying and Displaying Active Telnet Sessions

For both router and switch targets, a successful Telnet connection is indicated by a prompt for console login. Use the EXEC user mode prompt as a way to make sure which device is active on your console.

To verify your Telnet connectivity, you should use the **show sessions** command, as demonstrated in Example 10-7.

Example 10-7 show sessions *Command Verifies Telnet Connectivity*

```
RouterA#show sessions
Conn Host            Address        Byte   Idle Conn Name
   1 10.2.2.2        10.2.2.2          0      1 10.2.2.2
*  2 10.3.3.2        10.3.3.2          0      0 10.3.3.2
```

The output of the **show sessions** command displays a list of hosts to which you have established Telnet connectivity. Information in the **show sessions** output displays the host name, the IP address, the byte count, the amount of time the device has been idle, and the connection name assigned to the session. If you have multiple sessions in progress, the asterisk (*) helps by indicating which was your last session and to which session you return if you press the Enter key.

Use the **show user** command to show whether the console port is active, and to list all active Telnet sessions, with the IP address or IP alias of the originating host, on the local device, as demonstrated in Example 10-8.

Example 10-8 **show user** *Command Lists Active Telnet Sessions and Verifies Console Port Activity*

```
RouterA#show user
    Line    User      Host(s)             Idle Location
*  0 con 0            10.2.2.2            3
                      10.3.3.2            2
   11 vty 0           idle                1 10.2.2.2
```

In the **show user** output, the line **con** represents the local console, and **vty** represents a remote connection. If multiple users exist, the asterisk (*) denotes the current terminal session user.

TIP   Although they aren't documented, most versions of Cisco IOS support the UNIX commands **who** and **where**. The **who** command is equivalent to the IOS **show users** command, and the **where** command is the equivalent of the IOS **show sessions** command.

Suspending, Re-Establishing, and Ending Active Telnet Sessions

Assume that you have an established Telnet session from RouterA to RouterB. To suspend a Telnet session and escape from the remote target system back to your local switch or router, press the keys **Ctrl-Shift-6** at the same time, release the key sequence, and then press the character **x**, as demonstrated in Example 10-9. The prompt of the local system indicates that our Telnet session has been suspended. A suspended Telnet session is one you have left open, but are not currently using. You would be able to return to this session later.

Example 10-9 *Suspending and Resuming an Active Telnet Session*

```
RouterB#<Ctrl-Shift-6>x
RouterA#show session
Conn Host              Address          Byte  Idle Conn Name
  1 10.1.1.2           10.1.1.2           0     1 10.1.1.2
RouterA#resume 1
RouterB#
```

You can re-establish a suspended Telnet session in several ways:

- Press the **Enter** key followed by a **Ctrl-R** to return to the previous device prompt.
- Type the **resume** command if you have only one session. (Typing **resume** without a *sessionnumber* takes you back to the last active session.)
- Use the **show sessions** command to find the session number, as demonstrated in Example 10-9.
- Use the **resume** *sessionnumber* command to reconnect to a specific Telnet session, as shown in Example 10-9.

Just as you have more than one way of resuming a connection, you can end a Telnet session on a Cisco device using one of the following methods:

- Enter the **exit** or **logout** EXEC command while on the remote device. This logs you out of the Telnet session of the remote device and returns you to the EXEC process of the local device. If you open a Telnet session to a device, from that device Telnet to a second device, and you suspend the connection, you return to the executive process of the original device.

- Another way to end a Telnet session from the local device is to use the **disconnect** EXEC command while on the local device, as demonstrated in Example 10-10. If you have multiple sessions, you can disconnect from a single session using the **disconnect** [*sessionname*] [*sessionnumber*] command from the local device.

Example 10-10 *Using the* **disconnect** *Command to End a Telnet Session Opened by the Local Device*

```
RouterA#disconnect
Closing connection to 10.3.3.2 [confirm]
```

- If you suspect a Telnet session from a remote user is causing bandwidth or other types of problems, ask the user to close the session. Alternatively, you can terminate the session from your EXEC prompt. To close a Telnet session from a foreign host, use the **clear line** command, as demonstrated in Example 10-11. At the other end of the connection, the user gets a notice that the connection was "closed by a foreign host." To determine which line to clear, use the **show users** command, illustrated in Example 10-8, to determine from where the connection is coming.

Example 10-11 *Using the* **clear line** *Command to End a Telnet Session Opened by a Remote Device*

```
RouterA#clear line 11
[confirm]
 [OK]
```

Documenting the Network with the ping and traceroute Commands

This section contains an overview of documenting the network. Using CDP and Telnet helps you compile relevant device information about your immediate and remote networks. This information is useful to help you create and maintain a network topology map. Other tools that you can use to help understand your network topology include the **ping** command and the **traceroute** command.

The **ping** command verifies connectivity. The term originates from the practice in which naval vessels send out sonar pings to locate or verify other vessels or obstructions. The **ping** command also tells you the minimum, average, and maximum times it takes for ping packets to find the specified system and return. This gives you an idea of the reliability of the path to the specified system. Example 10-12 shows output from a **ping** command.

Example 10-12 *Use the* **ping** *Command to Verify Device Connectivity to the Network*

```
Router#ping 10.1.1.10
Type escape sequence to abort.
Sending 5, 100-byte ICMP Echos to 10.1.1.10, timeout is 2 seconds:
!!!!!
Success rate is 100 percent (5/5), round-trip min/avg/max = 4/4/4 ms
```

Table 10-2 lists the possible output characters from the **ping** facility.

Table 10-2 *Output Characters for* **ping** *Command*

Character	Description
!	Indicates receipt of a reply
.	Indicates the no reply received within the allotted time
U	Indicates a destination unreachable error protocol data unit (PDU) was received
Q	Indicates source quench (destination too busy)
M	Could not fragment
?	Unknown packet type
&	Packet lifetime exceeded
N	Indicates network unreachable

Use the **traceroute** command to see the outgoing routes that packets take between devices, as shown in Example 10-13.

Example 10-13 *Use the* **trace** *Command to Display Packet Routes Between Devices*

```
Router#traceroute 10.1.1.10

Type escape sequence to abort.
Tracing the route to 10.1.1.10

  1 10.3.4.1 4 msec 4 msec 4 msec
  1 10.4.1.1  4 msec 4 msec 4 msec
  1 10.5.1.1 4 msec 4 msec 4 msec
  1 10.1.1.10 4 msec 4 msec 4 msec

Router#
```

The **traceroute** command shows the actual routes the packets take between devices. The device sends out a sequence of User Datagram Protocol (UDP) datagrams to an invalid port address at the remote host. Three datagrams are sent, each with a Time-To-Live (TTL) field value set to 1. The TTL value of 1 causes the datagram to time out as soon as it hits the first router in the path. This router then responds with an Internet Control Message Protocol (ICMP) Time Exceeded Message (TEM) indicating that the datagram has expired.

Another three UDP messages are then sent, each with the TTL value set to 2, which causes the second router to return ICMP TEMs. This process continues until the packets actually reach the other destination. Because these datagrams are trying to access an invalid port at the destination host, ICMP Port Unreachable messages are received, indicating an unreachable port. This event signals the **traceroute** program that it is finished. The purpose behind this is to record the source of each ICMP TEM to provide a trace of the path the packet took to reach the destination.

Table 10-3 lists the characters that can appear in the **trace** command output.

Table 10-3   *Characters for the* **trace** *Command*

Character	Description
nn msec	For each node, the round-trip time in milliseconds for the specified number of probes
*	The probe timed out
A	Administratively prohibited (for example, access list)
Q	Source quench (destination too busy)
I	User interrupted test
U	Port unreachable
H	Host unreachable
N	Network unreachable
P	Protocol unreachable
T	Timeout
?	Unknown packet type

NOTE   Because IP domain name lookup is enabled by default, the router attempts to reconcile each IP address to a name, which can cause the **traceroute** command to take some time.

Getting Information About Remote Devices Section Quiz

Use these practice questions to review what you learned in this section.

1 Which Cisco IOS command opens a Telnet connection from a Cisco router to a device with the IP address 10.1.1.1?

A **open 10.1.1.**1

B **telnet 10.1.1.1**

C **10.1.1.1 telnet**

D **10.1.1.1 connec**t

2 You use the **show users** command to display all active Telnet sessions and to determine if _____.

A Telnet is enabled

B The console is active

C The remote port is active

D Telnet is enabled on a remote device

3 Which key sequence suspends a Telnet session?

A **<Ctrl-Alt-6>x**

B **<Ctrl-Shift-x>6**

C **<Ctrl-Shift-6>x**

D **<Ctrl-Shift-9>x**

4 Which actions continue a suspended Telnet session? (Choose two.)

A Pressing the **Esc** key

B Pressing the **Enter** key

C Pressing **<Ctrl-Shift-6>x**

D Entering the **resume** command

E Entering the **reconnect** command

5 Which commands end a Telnet session when entered on the remote device? (Choose two.)

   A **exit**

   B **logout**

   C **clear line**

   D **disconnect**

6 Which command ends an incoming Telnet session from a remote device?

   A **exit**

   B **logout**

   C **clear line**

   D **disconnect**

7 Which pieces of information are displayed as the result of the **ping** command? (Choose three.)

   A Failure rate

   B Success rate

   C Median round-trip time

   D Average round-trip time

   E Minimum round-trip time

8 What does the **ping** command verify?

   A Bandwidth

   B Connectivity

   C Functionality

   D Bit error rate

Router Booting Sequence and Verification Commands

This section covers in more detail the events that occur during router initialization than were covered in Chapter 9, "Operating and Configuring Cisco IOS Devices." Included are commands to control and verify router operation.

Router Booting Sequence

The sequence of events that occurs during the power up or the booting of a router or switch is important to understand. Knowledge of this sequence can help you accomplish operational tasks and troubleshoot router problems.

When power is initially applied to a router, the following events occur in the order shown:

1 **Power-On Self-Test (POST)**—This event is a series of hardware tests to verify that all the router's components are functional. During this test, the router also determines what hardware is present. POST executes from microcode resident in the system ROM.

2 **Load and run bootstrap code**—Bootstrap code performs subsequent events, such as finding the Cisco IOS software, loading it, and then running it. After the IOS Software is loaded and running, the bootstrap code is not used until the next time the router is reloaded or power-cycled.

3 **Find the IOS Software**—The bootstrap code determines where the IOS Software to be run is located. The Flash memory is the normal place where the IOS image is found. The configuration register and configuration file in NVRAM help determine where the IOS images are and what image file should be used.

4 **Load the IOS Software**—After the bootstrap code has found the proper image, it loads that image into RAM and starts the IOS running. Some routers (such as the 2500 series) do not load the IOS image into RAM, but execute it directly from Flash memory.

5 **Find the configuration**—The default is to look in NVRAM for a valid configuration. A parameter can be set to have the router attempt to locate a configuration file from another location, such as a TFTP server.

6 **Load the configuration**—The desired configuration for the router is loaded and executed. If no configuration exists or is being ignored, the router enters the setup utility or attempts an Autoinstall. Autoinstall is attempted if a router is connected to a functioning serial link and can resolve an address through a process of SLARP (Serial Line Address Resolution Protocol).

7 **Run**—The router is now running the configured Cisco IOS Software.

Router Components

The following list describes the major components of a router (most are hardware):

- **RAM**—Random-access memory contains the software and data structures that allow the router to function. The principal software running in RAM is the Cisco IOS image and the running configuration. Some routers, such as the 2500 series, run IOS from Flash and not RAM.

- **ROM**—Read-only memory contains microcode for basic functions to start and maintain the router. rxboot is also contained in ROM.

- **Flash memory**—Flash is used primarily to contain the IOS Software image. Some routers run the IOS image directly from Flash and do not need to transfer it to RAM.

- **NVRAM**—Nonvolatile random-access memory is used mainly to store the configuration. NVRAM uses a battery to maintain the data when power is removed from the router.

- **Configuration register**—The configuration register controls how the router boots up.

- **Interfaces**—The physical connections to the external world for the router. These interfaces include the following types:

  — Ethernet and Fast Ethernet

  — Asynchronous and synchronous serial

  — Token Ring

  — Fiber Distributed Data Interface (FDDI)

  — Asynchronous Transfer Mode (ATM)

  — Console and auxiliary ports

ROM Microcode

The four major areas of microcode that are contained in ROM are as follows:

- **Bootstrap code**—The code used to bring the router up during initialization. It reads the configuration register to determine how to boot and then, if instructed to do so, loads the Cisco IOS Software.

- **Power-On Self-Test code**—The microcode used to test the basic functionality of the router hardware and to determine what components are present.

- **ROM monitor**—A low-level operating system normally used for manufacturing testing and troubleshooting.

- **A "partial" or "mini" IOS**—A subset of the IOS. This partial IOS can be used to load a new software image into Flash memory and to perform some other maintenance operations. It does not support IP routing and most other routing functions. Sometimes, this subset of the IOS is referred to as *rxboot* code or the *bootloader*.

The bootstrap code has the responsibility of locating the IOS Software. Here is the sequence of events it follows to find the image:

1 Check the boot field of the configuration register. The boot field is the lower 4 bits of the configuration register. It specifies how the router is to boot. These bits can point to Flash for the IOS image, and then the saved configuration (if one exists) is searched for commands that tell the router how to boot. The field can indicate that the router should load the rxboot image, or it can specify that no IOS is to be loaded and to just start the ROM monitor image. The rest of the configuration register bits perform other functions as well, such as selecting console baud rate and choosing whether to use the configuration in NVRAM.

   For example, a configuration register value of 0x2102 (the 0x indicates that the digits that follow are in hexadecimal notation) has a boot field value of 0x2. (The far-right digit in the register value is 2, and it represents the lower 4 bits of the register.)

2 If the configuration register boot field value is from 0x2 to 0xF, the bootstrap code parses any configuration in NVRAM for **boot system** commands that specify the name and location of the IOS image to load. Several **boot system** commands can be in sequence to provide a fault-tolerant boot-up plan.

   The **boot system** command is a global configuration command that allows you to specify the source of the IOS Software image to load. Some of the syntax options available include the following:

   — **boot system flash** [*filename*]

   — **boot system rom**

   — **boot system tftp** [*filename*][*server-address*]

3 If no **boot system** commands exist in the configuration, the router defaults to loading the first file in Flash memory and running it.

4 If no valid file is found in Flash, the router attempts a netboot using the boot field value as a pointer for the name of the file to request to be downloaded.

NOTE netboot is a seldom-used method of loading an IOS Software image. If netboot fails, and the configuration register is set to the default settings, the router boots the rxboot file from ROM.

---

5 If no rxboot (mini-IOS) file exists, or if it is corrupted, the router boots the ROM monitor (ROMMON) from ROM.

The flowchart shown in Figure 10-3 displays the sequence of events that occur during router boot.

Before you alter the configuration register, you should determine how the router is currently loading the software image. Use the **show version** command to obtain the current configuration register value, as illustrated in Example 10-14. The last line of the display from the **show version** command contains the configuration register value.

Figure 10-3 *Router Boot Flowchart*

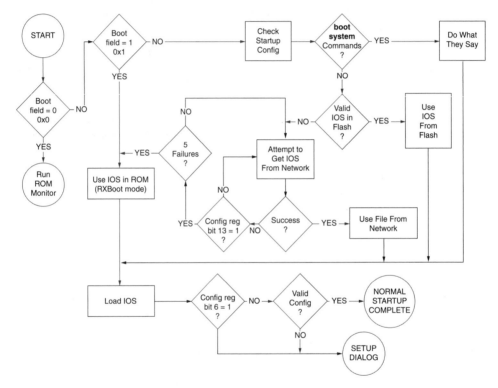

Example 10-14 *Use* **show version** *to Display Current Router Configuration Register Value*

```
wg_ro_a#show version
Cisco Internetwork Operating System Software
IOS (tm) 2500 Software (C2500-JS-L), Version 12.0(3), RELEASE SOFTWARE (fc1)
Copyright (c) 1986-1999 by cisco Systems, Inc.
Compiled Mon 08-Feb-99 18:18 by phanguye
Image text-base: 0x03050C84, data-base: 0x00001000
```

Example 10-14 *Use* **show version** *to Display Current Router Configuration Register Value (Continued)*

```
ROM: System Bootstrap, Version 11.0(10c), SOFTWARE

BOOTFLASH: 3000 Bootstrap Software (IGS-BOOT-R), Version 11.0(10c),

 RELEASE SOFTWARE (fc1)


wg_ro_a uptime is 20 minutes

System restarted by reload

System image file is "flash:c2500-js-l_120-3.bin"


--More--


Configuration register is 0x2102
```

If you are in ROM monitor mode, use the **o** or the **config-register** command to list the configuration register setting. The command to use is processor- and platform-dependent. You can determine which command to use by using a **?** at the rommon> prompt.

You can change the default configuration register setting with the global configuration mode command **config-register**, as demonstrated in Example 10-15.

Example 10-15 *Use the* **config-register** *Command to Change the Router Default Configuration Register Setting*

```
Router#configure terminal

Router(config)#config-register 0x2102

[Ctrl-Z]

Router#reload
```

NOTE   Configuration parameters changed in configuration mode are dynamic and do not require a reload. This is not the case for the **config-register** command. This change alters a memory stack of the router and requires a reload before the value is set. Because this value is checked only during the boot process, it is not critical to reload the router immediately after changing the register.

The configuration register is a 16-bit register. The lowest 4 bits of the configuration register (bits 3, 2, 1, and 0) form the boot field. A hexadecimal number is used as the argument to set the value of the configuration register.

When changing the boot field, follow these guidelines:

- Set the boot field to 0 (0x0) to enter ROM monitor mode automatically upon next reboot. This value sets the boot field bits to 0-0-0-0. The router displays the > or the rommon> prompt in this mode. You can boot manually using the **b** or **reset** command.

- Set the boot field to 1 (0x1) to configure the system to boot automatically from ROM. This value sets the boot field bits to 0-0-0-1. The router displays the Router(boot)> prompt in this mode.

- Set the boot field to any value from 2 to F (0x2 to 0xF) to configure the system to use the **boot system** commands in NVRAM. This is the default. These values set the boot field bits to 0-0-1-0 through 1-1-1-1. 0x2 is the default setting.

Use the **show version** command to verify your changes in the boot field setting, as demonstrated previously in Example 10-14.

WARNING   When you use the **config-register** command, you set all 16 bits of the configuration register. Be careful to change only the bits that you are trying to change (the boot field, for example) and leave the other bits as they were. Remember that the other configuration register bits perform functions that include the selection of console baud rate and whether to use the configuration in NVRAM.

When the specified IOS image file is located, the image is normally loaded into RAM to run. Some routers, including the Cisco 2500 series, do not have an architecture that would accommodate the IOS image, system tables, and system buffers in RAM, and therefore run (execute the IOS software) directly from Flash memory.

If the image is to be loaded from Flash into RAM, it must first be decompressed. The files are compressed in Flash memory to save space. The IOS image file starts after it is decompressed into RAM. Figure 10-4 illustrates this process.

Figure 10-4 *Router Boot Flowchart*

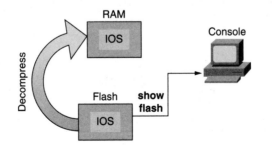

The **show flash** command displays the contents of Flash memory, which includes the image filenames and sizes, as shown in Example 10-16.

Example 10-16 show flash *Command Displays Flash Memory Contents*

```
wg_ro_a#show flash


System flash directory:
File  Length   Name/status
  1   10084696  c2500-js-l_120-3.bin
[10084760 bytes used, 6692456 available, 16777216 total]
16384K bytes of processor board System flash (Read ONLY)
```

Loading/Running the Router Configuration

After the IOS is loaded and started, the router must be configured to be useful. If you have an existing configuration in NVRAM, it is executed. If you have no configuration in NVRAM, the router either commences Autoinstall or enter the setup utility. Figure 10-5 illustrates this process.

Figure 10-5 *Loading Configuration Parameters into RAM*

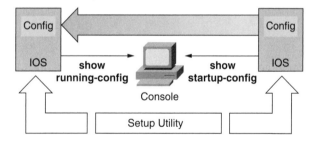

Autoinstall attempts to download a configuration from a TFTP server. Autoinstall requires a connection to the network and a previously configured TFTP server to respond to the download request.

Setup is a utility that prompts a user at the console for specific configuration information to create a basic initial configuration on the router that is to be copied into both RAM (running configuration) and NVRAM (startup configuration) upon acceptance of the script created by the utility, as shown in Figure 10-5.

The **show running-config** and **show startup-config** commands are among the most-used Cisco IOS Software EXEC commands because they allow an administrator to see the current running configuration in RAM on the router or the startup configuration commands in NVRAM that the router uses on the next restart. Example 10-17 and Example 10-18 demonstrate some sample output for the **show running-config** and **show startup-config** commands, respectively.

Example 10-17 **show running-config** *Command Displays the Current Router Configuration Running in RAM*

```
wg_ro_c#show running-config
Building configuration...


Current configuration:
!
version 12.0
!
      -- More --
```

Example 10-18 **show startup-config** *Command Displays the Router Configuration Saved in NVRAM*

```
wg_ro_c#show startup-config
Using 1359 out of 32762 bytes
!
version 12.0
!
      -- More --
```

You know that you are looking at the active configuration file when you see the words **Current configuration** at the top of the display, as highlighted in Example 10-17.

You know that you are looking at the stored configuration file when you see a message at the top telling you how much nonvolatile memory has been used, as highlighted in Example 10-18.

Managing Router Configurations with copy Commands

In addition to using either Autoinstall or the Setup utility to load or create a configuration, several other sources for configurations exist.

The IOS **copy** commands move configurations from one component or device to another, as illustrated in Figure 10-6.

Figure 10-6 *IOS* **copy** *Commands Move Configurations Between Routers/Router Components*

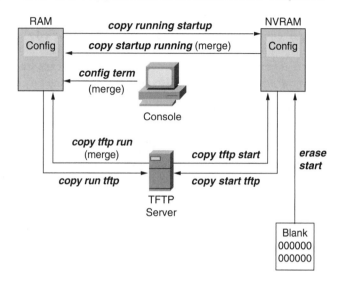

The syntax of the **copy** command requires that the first argument indicate the source (from where the configuration is to be copied) and then the destination (to where the configuration is to be copied). For example, in the command **copy running-configuration tftp** (**copy run tftp**), the running configuration in RAM is to be copied to a TFTP server.

You can copy a running configuration to NVRAM to be saved with the **copy running-configuration startup-configuration** (**copy running startup**) command. This command is used any time you make a configuration change and want to save it. Going the other way, you can copy the saved configuration in NVRAM back into RAM with **copy startup-configuration running-configuration** (**copy startup running**). Note that the commands can be abbreviated.

Analogous commands exist for copies between a TFTP server and either NVRAM or RAM.

NOTE   When a configuration is copied into RAM from any source, the configuration merges with, or overlays, any existing configuration in RAM rather than overwriting it. New configuration parameters are added, and changes to existing parameters overwrite the old parameters. RAM configuration commands for which there are no corresponding commands in NVRAM are untouched.

Configurations are created interactively from the console (or remote terminal) with the **configure terminal** (**config t**) command.

Commands entered from configuration mode or files copied into a running configuration are merged with the existing information. If a file is copied into NVRAM, it is a complete overwrite. If you need to delete the NVRAM file, the **erase startup-configuration** command writes 0s into NVRAM and thereby deletes the saved configuration.

TFTP servers can be used to store configurations in a central place. These devices must be set up and configured before the upload. The upload process allows centralized management and updates of configuration files.

The **copy running-config tftp** command allows you to upload and save your current configuration to a TFTP server. You are required to supply the TFTP server's address or name and to specify a filename for your uploaded configuration, as demonstrated in Example 10-19.

Example 10-19 **copy running-config tftp** *Command Uploads and Saves the Local Router Configuration to a TFTP Server*

```
wg_ro_a#copy running-config tftp
Address or name of remote host []? 10.1.1.1
Destination filename [running-config]? wgroa.cfg
.!!
1684 bytes copied in 13.300 secs (129 bytes/sec)
```

In the display, the series of exclamation marks shows the progress of the upload.

The **copy tftp running-config** command downloads a configuration file from the TFTP server to running memory. Again, you must specify the address or name of the TFTP server and the filename of the configuration you want to download. Remember that this is a merge process, not an overwrite. Example 10-20 demonstrates sample output from the **copy tftp running-config** command.

Example 10-20 **copy tftp running-config** *Command Downloads a Configuration File from a TFTP Server to Active Router Configuration*

```
wg_ro_a#copy tftp running-config
Address or name of remote host []? 10.1.1.1
Source filename []? wgroa.cfg
Destination filename [running-config]?
Accessing tftp://10.1.1.1/wgroa.cfg...
Loading wgroa.cfg from 10.1.1.1 (via Ethernet0): !
[OK - 1684/3072 bytes]


1684 bytes copied in 17.692 secs (99 bytes/sec)
```

Router Booting Sequence and Verification Commands Section Quiz

Use these practice questions to review what you learned in this section.

1 The router IOS is usually found in _____, and the saved configuration file (startup-config) is usually found in _____.

    A Flash memory; RAM

    B RAM; Flash memory

    C Flash memory; ROM

    D Flash memory; NVRAM

    E NVRAM; Flash memory

2 Which stage of router bootup occurs first?

    A Load IOS

    B Load bootstrap

    C Find configuration

    D Load configuration

3 Which router component is used primarily to contain the Cisco IOS Software image?

    A RAM

    B NVRAM

    C Flash memory

    D Configuration register

4 Which component tests the basic functionality of the router hardware and determines which components are present?

    A POST

    B Bootstrap

    C Mini-IOS

    D ROM monitor

5 When a Cisco router starts up, where does it look to find the Cisco IOS Software, by default, if the saved configuration file in NVRAM does not contain boot system commands?

A ROM

B RAM

C NVRAM

D Flash memory

6 During the boot process, which of the following describes where the device boots from if the boot field value is 0x2?

A Runs ROM monitor

B Loads IOS from ROM

C Loads first IOS file from Flash memory

D Parses the NVRAM configuration

7 Which Cisco IOS command displays the current value of the configuration register?

A **show config**

B **show version**

C **show startup-config**

D **show config-register**

8 If the configuration register value is 0x2100, what does the router do the next time it boots?

A Loads IOS from ROM

B Loads IOS from flash memory

C Runs ROM monitor automatically

D Checks startup config for the boot system commands

Cisco IOS File System and Devices

The Cisco IOS File System (IFS) feature provides a single interface to all the file systems that a router uses, including the following:

- Flash memory file systems
- Network file systems (TFTP, RCP, and FTP)
- Any other endpoint for reading or writing data (such as NVRAM, the running configuration, ROM, raw system memory, system bundled microcode, Xmodem, Flash load helper log, modems, and BRI MUX interfaces)

For a complete description of the IFS commands, refer to the "Cisco IOS File System Commands" chapter of the *Configuration Fundamentals Command Reference*. You can find it on your hardware documentation CD-ROM or at the Cisco website (http://www.cisco.com).

One key feature of the IFS is the use of the Universal Resource Locator (URL) convention to specify files on network devices and the network. For example, the command to copy from NVRAM to a TFTP server would be as follows:

```
Switch#copy startup-configuration tftp://172.16.100.15/config.txt
```

172.16.100.15 is the IP address of the TFTP server, and **config.txt** is the name of the file to be saved.

Table 10-4 lists some commonly used URL prefixes for Cisco network devices.

Table 10-4   *Commonly Used IFS URL Prefixes*

Prefix	Description
bootflash:	Boot Flash memory.
flash:	Flash memory. This prefix is available on all platforms. For platforms that do not have a device named **flash:**, the **flash:** prefix is aliased to **slot0:**. Therefore, you can use the **flash:** prefix to refer to the main Flash memory storage area on all platforms.
flh:	Flash load helper log files.
ftp:	File Transfer Protocol (FTP) network server.
nvram:	NVRAM.
rcp:	Remote Copy Protocol (RCP) network server.
slot0:	First PCMCIA Flash memory card.
slot1:	Second PCMCIA Flash memory card.
system:	Contains the system memory, including the running configuration in RAM.
tftp:	Trivial File Transfer Protocol (TFTP) network server.

Moving and Managing Router Configuration Files

With Cisco IOS Release 12.0, commands used to copy and transfer configuration and system files have changed to conform to IFS specifications. The old commands continue to perform their normal functions in the current release, but support for these commands might cease in a future release.

NOTE   Commands presented in this book were the most commonly used formats at the time of publication.

Table 10-5 lists the old and new commands used for configuration file movement and management.

Table 10-5   *Configuration File Commands*

Old Commands	New Commands
N/A **copy rcp running-config** **copy tftp running-config or configure network** (pre-Cisco IOS Release 10.3)	**copy ftp: system:running-config** **copy rcp: system:running-config** **copy tftp: system:running-config**
N/A **copy rcp startup-config** **copy tftp startup-config or configure overwrite-network** (pre-Cisco IOS Release 10.3)	**copy ftp: nvram:startup-config** **copy rcp: nvram:startup-config** **copy tftp: nvram:startup-config**
show startup-config or show configuration (pre-Cisco IOS Release 10.3)	**more nvram:startup-config**
erase startup-config or write erase (pre-Cisco IOS Release 10.3)	**erase nvram:**
copy running-config startup-config or write memory (pre-Cisco IOS Release 10.3)	**copy system:running-config nvram:startup-config**
N/A **copy running-config rcp** **copy running-config tftp or write network** (pre-Cisco IOS Release 10.3)	**copy system:running-config ftp:** **copy system:running-config rcp:** **copy system:running-config tftp:**
show running-config or write terminal (pre-IOS Cisco Release 10.3)	**more system:running-config**

Managing IOS Images

This section contains an introduction to managing IOS images. As your network grows, you might want to store your Cisco IOS Software and configuration files on a central server. This allows you to control the number and revision level of software images and configuration files you must maintain. In this section, you learn how to create and load a backup software image in case you lose the software image in the router.

Production internetworks usually span wide areas and contain multiple routers. For any network, it is always prudent to retain a backup copy of your Cisco IOS Software image in case the system image in your router becomes corrupted.

Widely distributed routers need a source or backup location for software images. Using a network server allows image and configuration uploads and downloads over the network. The network server can be another router, a workstation, or a host system.

Before you copy software from Flash memory in the router to the network server, you should perform the following tasks:

Step 1 Check to make sure that you have access to the network server.

Step 2 Verify that the server has sufficient room to accommodate the Cisco IOS Software image.

Step 3 Check the filename requirements.

Step 4 Create the destination file to receive the upload if required. This step is network server operating system-dependent.

The **show flash** command is an important tool for gathering information about your router memory and image file. With the **show flash** command, you can determine the following:

- Total amount of memory on your router

- Amount of memory available

- Name of the system image file used by the router

- Size of the system image file stored in Flash

Example 10-21 demonstrates how to use the **show flash** command to gather router memory and image file information to verify that you have room on the server for the IOS image.

Example 10-21 show flash *Command Displays Router Memory and Image File Information*

```
wg_ro_a#show flash


System flash directory:
File  Length   Name/status
  1   10084696  c2500-js-l_120-3.bin


[10084760 bytes used, 6692456 available, 16777216 total]
16384K bytes of processor board System flash (Read ONLY)
```

The name of the Cisco IOS image file contains multiple parts, each with a specific meaning. For example, the filename c2500-js-l_120-3.bin (shown in Example 10-21) contains the following information:

- The first part of the image name identifies the platform on which the image runs. In this example, the platform is Cisco 2500 series router.

- The second part of the name identifies the special capabilities of the image file. A letter or series of letters identifies the features supported in that image. In this example, the j indicates that this is an enterprise image, and the s indicates that it contains extended capabilities.

- The third part of the name specifies where the image runs and if the file is compressed. In this example, l indicates that the file can be relocated and is not compressed.

- The fourth part of the name indicates the version number. In this example, the version number is 120-3.

- The final part of the name is the file extension. The .bin extension indicates that this file is a binary executable file.

The Cisco IOS Software naming conventions, field meaning, image content, and other details are subject to change. Refer to your sales representative, distribution channel, or the Cisco website for updated details.

Backing Up Your IOS Image File

You create a software backup image file by copying the image file from a router to a network server. To copy the current system image file from the router to the network server, you would use the **copy flash tftp** command in privileged EXEC mode, as demonstrated in Example 10-22

Example 10-22 *Using the* **copy flash tftp** *Command to Back Up Current Image Files Prior to Updating Flash*

```
wg_ro_a#copy flash tftp

Source filename []? c2500-js-l_120-3.bin

Address or name of remote host []? 10.1.1.1

Destination filename [c2500-js-l_120-3.bin]?

!!!!!!!!!!!!!!!!!!!!!!!!!!!!!!!!!!!!!!!!!!!!!!!!!!!!!!!!!!!!!!!!!!!

<output omitted>

10084696 bytes copied in 709.228 secs (14223 bytes/sec)

wg_ro_a#
```

The **copy tftp flash** command requires you to enter the IP address of the remote host and the name of the source and destination system image file, as demonstrated in Example 10-23.

Example 10-23 copy tftp flash *Command Copies the IOS Image File to the Network Server*

```
wg_ro_a#copy tftp flash

Address or name of remote host [10.1.1.1]?

Source filename []? c2500-js-l_120-3.bin

Destination filename [c2500-js-l_120-3.bin]?

Accessing tftp://10.1.1.1/c2500-js-l_120-3.bin...

Erase flash: before copying? [confirm]

Erasing the flash filesystem will remove all files! Continue? [confirm]

Erasing device... eeeee (output omitted) ...erased

Erase of flash: complete

Loading c2500-js-l_120-3.bin from 10.1.1.1 (via Ethernet0): !!!!!!!!!!!!!!!!!!!!

(output omitted)

[OK - 10084696/20168704 bytes]

Verifying checksum...  OK (0x9AA0)

10084696 bytes copied in 309.108 secs (32636 bytes/sec)

wg_ro_a#
```

Loading a New IOS Image File from the Network Server

You load a new system image file on your router if the existing image file has become damaged or if you are upgrading your system to a newer software version. You download the new image from the network server using the following command:

```
Router#copy tftp flash
```

The **copy tftp flash** command prompts you for the IP address of the remote host and the name of the source and destination system image file. Enter the appropriate filename of the update image as it appears on the server.

After you confirm your entries, the procedure asks if you want to erase Flash. Erasing Flash makes room for the new image. You should perform this task if you have insufficient Flash memory for more than one Cisco IOS image.

If no free Flash memory space is available, or if the Flash memory has never been written to, the erase routine is required before new files can be copied. The system informs you of these conditions and prompts you for a response.

Each exclamation point (!) means that one User Datagram Protocol (UDP) segment has been successfully transferred. Example 10-24 shows the complete syntax for copying a new image from the TFTP server into Flash memory. Note that the image file is erased from Flash memory before the new image is loaded. The output also displays a message that the image already exists.

Example 10-24 copy tftp flash *Command Copies an IOS Image File from the Network Server to the Router*

```
wg_ro_a#copy tftp flash
Address or name of remote host [10.1.1.1]?
Source filename []? c2500-js-l_120-3.bin
Destination filename [c2500-js-l_120-3.bin]?
Accessing tftp://10.1.1.1/c2500-js-l_120-3.bin...
Erase flash: before copying? [confirm]
Erasing the flash filesystem will remove all files! Continue? [confirm]
Erasing device... eeeee (output omitted) ...erased
Erase of flash: complete
Loading c2500-js-l_120-3.bin from 10.1.1.1 (via Ethernet0): !!!!!!!!!!!!!!!!!!!!!!
(output omitted)
[OK - 10084696/20168704 bytes]
Verifying checksum...  OK (0x9AA0)
10084696 bytes copied in 309.108 secs (32636 bytes/sec)
wg_ro_a#
```

Executing Adds, Moves, and Changes

You might occasionally need to move network equipment from one location to another, remove equipment from the network, or change the configuration to meet new network requirements. The process is referred to as *adds, moves, and changes*. This topic explains how to complete adds, moves, and changes for Cisco routers on the network.

To add equipment to the network, complete the following steps:

Step 1 Determine the IP address to be used for management purposes. Select an IP address that is assigned to a loopback interface, because a loopback interface is always operational an usually available if one physical interface is active.

Step 2 Configure administrative access for the console, auxiliary, and virtual terminal (vty) interfaces, as appropriate.

Step 3 Configure passwords for privileged EXEC mode for the device. For privileged EXEC mode on a router, use the **enable secret** command so that the password displayed in the configuration is encrypted.

Step 4 Configure the network management access to the device. If your site uses Simple Network Management Protocol (SNMP) to manage network devices, configure the appropriate SNMP parameters on the router.

Step 5 Determine the IP address to assign to each interface. Typically, each interface requires an IP address for routing. Make sure you have the correct network mask for the assigned address.

Step 6 Configure the new device with the appropriate configuration to meet the network requirements. The specific configuration depends on the network requirements.

When completing a move, complete the following task:

- Determine what to do with obsolete equipment. If it is to be put on the shelf for spares or placed in a lab, you should erase the configuration after you complete the following tasks:
  - Determine which devices connect to the equipment being moved.
  - Determine if the move and reconfiguration affects the current security policy.
  - Determine if this device plays a role in the network that no other devices play. For example, is a modem attached, and if so, will it be moved to another device? Does this device also act as a TFTP server for Cisco IOS images? If so, what will replace it?
  - Review the facility considerations of the new location. Is there sufficient power and cooling? Do you have rack space for your new equipment? How is the wiring closet accessed? Is it secure from passersby?
  - After the move and reconfiguration, test network connectivity.

Configuration changes are a regular part of any network maintenance plan and might reflect changes in network topology, security policy, and preferred routes, as well as changes in routing protocols.

To change the hardware, complete the following tasks:

- Power down the equipment when doing upgrades. Many Cisco routers support hot-swapping, called *online insertion and removal (OIR)*. Check the latest release notes for your specific chassis to see if you need to power down the device before you add new hardware.
- Have the appropriate modules available before scheduling the upgrade.
- Read the hardware installation manual and verify that you have the necessary antistatic mat and grounding cable to prevent static discharges from ruining new equipment. Some new hardware modules might require a minimum version of IOS to operate. Check the requirements of your system before physically upgrading.
- Verify your organization's policies and plans to make sure the hardware change conforms.

If you are upgrading the Cisco IOS Software, review the release notes prior to installation. Evaluate the following questions:

- Does the new version support all of the features you are currently using? Does it support the features you plan on adding in the future?

- Does your platform have sufficient Flash memory to hold the new image? Does your platform have sufficient RAM to support the feature set?

Using debug on Operational Cisco Devices

The **show** and **debug** commands are troubleshooting tools built in to Cisco IOS Software. The **show** command displays static information, while the **debug** command displays dynamic data and events. This section compares the **show** and **debug** commands and describes guidelines for using **debug** commands.

The functions of the **show** and **debug** commands are as follows:

- **show commands**—Snapshot problems with interfaces, media, or network performance

- **debug commands**—Check the flow of protocol traffic for problems, protocol bugs, or misconfigurations

Table 10-6 describes the major differences between the **show** and **debug** commands.

Table 10-6   **show** *and* **debug** *Commands*

Command	Description
show	Provides a static collection of information about the status of a network device, neighboring devices, and network performance. Use **show** commands when you are gathering facts for isolating problems in an internetwork, including problems with interfaces, nodes, media, servers, clients, or applications.
debug	Provides a flow of information about the traffic being seen (or not seen) on an interface, error messages generated by nodes on the network, protocol-specific diagnostic packets, and other useful troubleshooting data. Use **debug** when you want to see process operations on the router or network to determine if events or packets are working properly.

Use **debug** commands to isolate problems, not to monitor normal network operation. Because the high overhead of **debug** commands can disrupt router operation, you should use **debug** commands only when you are looking for specific types of traffic or problems and have narrowed your problems to a likely subset of causes.

Some considerations when using **debug** commands are as follows:

- Be aware that the **debug** commands might generate too much data that is of little use for a specific problem. You normally need to have knowledge of the protocol(s) being debugged to properly interpret the debug outputs.

- Because the high CPU overhead of **debug** commands can disrupt network device operation, you should use **debug** commands only when you are looking for specific types of traffic or problems and have narrowed your problems to a likely subset of causes.

- When using the **debug** troubleshooting tools, be aware that output formats vary with each protocol. Some generate a single line of output per packet, whereas others generate multiple lines of output per packet.

- If running **debug** from a Telnet connection, you must enter the command **terminal monitor** to see the output on the telnet privileged EXEC session.

- Use of **debug** commands is suggested for obtaining information about network traffic and router status. Use these commands with great care.

- If you are unsure about the impact of a **debug** command, check the Cisco website for details or consult with a technical support representative.

You should use three commands if you plan to use a **debug** command for troubleshooting. Table 10-7 describes the use of these commands.

Table 10-7   *Complementary Commands for* **debug**

Command	Description
service timestamps	Use this command to add a time stamp to a **debug** or log message. This feature can provide valuable information about when debug elements occurred and the duration of time between events.
show processes	Displays the CPU utilization for each process. This data can influence your decision about using a **debug** command, if it indicates that the production system is already too heavily used for adding a **debug** command.
no debug all or **undebug all**	Disables all **debug** commands. This command can free up system resources after you finish debug.

Because the problem condition is an abnormal situation, you might be willing to temporarily trade off switching efficiency for the opportunity to rapidly diagnose and correct the problem. To effectively use debugging tools, you need to know about the following:

- The impact your troubleshooting tool has on router performance
- The most selective and focused use of the diagnostic tool

- How to minimize the impact of your troubleshooting in other processes competing for resources on the network device

- How to stop the troubleshooting tool when you are finished diagnosing so that the router can resume its most efficient switching.

It is one thing to use **debug** to troubleshoot a lab network that lacks end user application traffic. It is another thing to use **debug** on a production network that users depend on for data flow. Without proper precautions, the impact of a broadly focused **debug** could make matters worse.

With the proper, selective, and temporary use of these tools, you can easily obtain potentially useful information without needing a protocol analyzer or other third-party tool.

The following are some guidelines for using **debug** commands:

- Ideally, it is best to use **debug** commands during periods of lower network traffic and fewer users. Debugging during these periods reduces the effect these commands have on other users on the system.

- When you interpret the information you need from the **debug** command and undo the debug (and any other related configuration setting if any), the router can resume its faster switching and you can resume your problem-solving, create a better targeted action plan, and be better able to take the action that fixes the network problem.

All **debug** commands are entered in privileged EXEC mode, and most **debug** commands take no arguments.

WARNING   Do not use the **debug all** command because this can cause a system crash.

To list and see a brief description of all the debugging command options, enter the **debug ?** command in privileged EXEC mode.

By default, the network server sends the output from **debug** commands and system error messages to the console. You can use syslog to monitor debug messages rather than using the console port. To redirect debugging output, use the **logging** command options within configuration mode. Possible destinations include the console, virtual terminals, internal buffer, and UNIX hosts running a Syslog server. The Syslog format is compatible with 4.3 Berkeley Standard Distribution (BSD) UNIX and its derivatives. Syslog is also available for Windows products.

Cisco IOS File System and Devices Section Quiz

Use these practice questions to review what you learned in this section.

1 What is the Cisco IOS 12.0 IFS name for the running-config file?

A running-config

B RAM:running-config

C system:running-config

D memory:running-config

2 Which Cisco IOS command(s), starting in Cisco IOS Release 12.0, deletes the startup configuration?

A **erase nvram:**

B **delete nvram:**

C **erase startup-config**

D **delete startup-config**

3 Which Cisco IOS command creates a backup copy of the IOS image file on a TFTP server?

A **copy ios tftp**

B **copy tftp flash**

C **copy flash tftp**

D **backup flash tftp**

4 Which command displays the size of the IOS image file in Flash memory?

A **show flash**

B **show flash size**

C **show file size flash**

D **show flash memory**

5 For which reasons would you copy configuration files from a TFTP, RCP, or FTP server to the running configuration or startup configuration of a router? (Choose three.)

   A To restore a backed-up configuration file

   B To use the configuration file for another router

   C To identify the device to other devices on the network

   D To institute a common security policy across the network

   E To load the same configuration commands onto all the routers in your network

6 Which Cisco IOS command merges a configuration file from a TFTP server into the current configuration?

   A **copy startup running**

   B **copy tftp startup-config**

   C **copy running-config tftp**

   D **copy tftp running-config**

7 What does the **copy running startup** command do?

   A Copies the configuration in RAM to NVRAM

   B Copies the configuration in NVRAM to RAM

   C Merges the configuration in RAM with the configuration in NVRAM

   D Downloads a configuration file from a TFTP server to running memory

8 When adding new equipment to the network, what is the final step you should take?

   A Determine the IP address to assign to each interface.

   B Configure passwords for privileged EXEC mode for the device.

   C Configure administrative access for the console, auxiliary, and vty interfaces.

   D Configure the new device with the appropriate configuration to meet the network requirements.

9 When you make a hardware change to your router, should you power down the device?

A Never

B Always

C Does not matter

D Depends on whether the Cisco device supports OIR

10 Which type of Cisco IOS command should you use to create a snapshot of network conditions to troubleshoot problems with interfaces, media, or network performance?

A **debug** commands

B **trace** commands

C **show** commands

D **config** commands

11 Which type of Cisco IOS command should you use to view a process operating on a router or the network for troubleshooting purposes?

A **trace** commands

B **show** commands

C **config** commands

D **debug** commands

Chapter Summary

In this chapter, you learned commands that help you determine names and addresses of neighboring devices. You also learned how to use CDP to obtain information remotely, given an operational switch and router. You also saw how to use information gathered using CDP, Telnet, and Cisco IOS commands to create a simple network map of their environment, given operational Cisco network devices. Finally, this chapter discussed how to move configuration files between system components and network file servers, given an operational Cisco router.

Chapter Review Questions

Use these review questions to test your knowledge of the concepts discussed in this chapter.

1 Which statements are true of CDP? (Choose two.)

  A It is a proprietary protocol.

  B It is an open protocol standard.

  C It discovers information about connected Cisco devices.

  D It discovers information about all devices on the network.

2 When is CDP started?

  A When the Cisco device boots

  B When you enter a **debug** command

  C When you enter the command **cdp enable**

  D When the configuration of the device changes

3 How could you obtain CDP information about a nondirectly connected remote device?

  A Use the command **show cdp neighbors** *address.*

  B Use the command **show cdp neighbors** *hostname.*

  C Use Telnet to access a Cisco device connected to the target device.

  D It is not possible to obtain CDP information about a remote device.

4 Which pieces of information are included in a CDP update packet? (Choose two.)

  A Platform

  B Routing updates

  C Device identifiers

  D MAC address list

5 Which command disables CDP on the device as a whole?

A **no run cdp**

B **no cdp run**

C **no cdp enable**

D **no cdp execute**

6 What does the command **cdp enable** do?

A Disables CDP on a specific interface

B Enables CDP on the device as a whole

C Enables CDP on an individual interface

D Enables CDP on a specific type of interface

7 Which Cisco IOS command produces the same result as **show cdp neighbors detail**?

A **show cdp traffic**

B **show cdp entry ***

C **show cdp neighbors**

D **show cdp interface all**

8 What keyword do you add to the **show cdp neighbors** command to obtain additional information in the output?

A **full**

B **detail**

C **verbose**

D **complete**

9 Which Cisco IOS command displays the frequency at which packets are sent?

A **show cdp entry**

B **show cdp traffic**

C **show cdp interface**

D **show cdp neighbors**

10 What information is included in the output of the command **show cdp interface**?

   A Remote port ID

   B Remote device ID

   C Encapsulation type

   D Number of CDP packets sent

11 Which command displays the device platform of a directly connected device?

   A **show cdp entry**

   B **show cdp traffic**

   C **show cdp interface**

   D **show cdp platform**

12 Which command displays CDP packets checksum errors?

   A **show cdp entry**

   B **show cdp traffic**

   C **show cdp interface**

   D **show cdp neighbors**

13 Which statements identify the primary uses of a network map? (Choose three.)

   A Modifies network design

   B Creates a software inventory

   C Tracks changes to the topology

   D Troubleshoots network problems

   E Tracks changes in protocol configurations

14 Which Cisco IOS commands open a Telnet session from a router to a device with the host name switch123 and the IP address 10.1.1.2? (Choose two.)

   A **open 10.1.1.2**

   B **telnet 10.1.1.2**

   C **open switch123**

D **10.1.1.2 connect**

E **telnet switch123**

F **switch123 connect**

15 Which Cisco IOS command displays a list that includes all Telnet sessions currently connected to other devices?

A **show logins**

B **show telnet**

C **show sessions**

D **show connections**

16 What does an asterisk (*) mean in the output of the **show sessions** command?

A Identifies the most recent Telnet session

B Identifies a Telnet session that has been suspended

C Identifies the Telnet session that has been idle longest

D Identifies a Telnet session that is experiencing a problem

17 What does the command **resume 3** do?

A Continues the last three suspended Telnet sessions

B Continues the most recently suspended Telnet session

C Continues the suspended Telnet session with the session id of 3

D Makes three attempts to resume the most recently suspended Telnet session

18 What does the key sequence **<Ctrl-Shift-6>x** do?

A Closes the current Telnet session

B Suspends the current Telnet session

C Resumes the Telnet session with session ID 6

D Suspends the Telnet session with session ID 6

19 When you have multiple active Telnet sessions and enter the command **resume**, which Telnet session is continued?

A The most recent session.

B The session idle the longest.

c A session chosen at random.

D None—The **resume** command requires a session id number argument.

20 At what level of the Cisco CLI do you execute the **disconnect** command?

A Privileged EXEC mode

B Global configuration mode

c Interface configuration mode

D Virtual terminal (vty) configuration mode

21 What does the command **clear line** do?

A Closes the current Telnet session

B Closes all active Telnet connections

c Reconnects the current Telnet session

D Closes a Telnet session from a foreign host

22 Which pieces of information are displayed as the result of the **ping** command? (Choose three.)

A Packets lost

B Bit error rate

c Source address

D Maximum round-trip time

E Size of the ICMP echo packets

23 Which Cisco IOS command would you use to display the path a packet takes to a specific destination?

A **ping**

B **trace**

C show path

D show sessions

24 Which stage during a Cisco router bootup occurs last?

A POST

B Find and load IOS

C Find and load bootstrap

D Find and load configuration

25 Which stage of the Cisco router bootup process verifies that all router components are operational?

A POST

B Find IOS

C Find bootstrap

D Find configuration

26 Which Cisco router component is used primarily to store the startup configuration?

A RAM

B ROM

C NVRAM

D Flash memory

E Configuration register

27 The _____ is a low-level operating system normally used for manufacturing testing and troubleshooting.

A POST

B Bootstrap

C Partial-IOS

D ROM monitor (ROMMON)

28 During the Cisco router boot process, what does the router do if the boot field value is 0x2?

A Runs ROM monitor

B Loads IOS from Flash memory

C Loads IOS subset from ROM

D Checks the startup configuration file for boot system commands

29 What happens if the router cannot find a valid startup configuration file in NVRAM during router bootup?

A The router enters setup mode.

B The router attempts to restart.

C The router runs ROM monitor.

D The router performs a shutdown.

30 On most routers, the IOS Software is loaded into _____ to run, but on some it is run directly from _____.

A RAM; NVRAM

B RAM; Flash memory

C Flash memory; RAM

D NVRAM; Flash memory

31 From the ROM monitor, which should you enter to determine the current value of the configuration register?

A o

B v

C **show version**

D **show config-register**

32 The command **show startup-config** displays the configuration in which location?

A ROM

B RAM

C NVRAM

D Flash memory

33 Which bits of the configuration register value make up the boot field?

A Lowest octet

B Highest octet

C Lowest 4 bits

D Highest 4 bits

34 Which Cisco IOS command downloads a copy of the IOS image file from a TFTP server?

A **copy ios tftp**

B **copy tftp flash**

C **copy flash tftp**

D **backup flash tftp**

35 Given the system image file c2500-js-l_120-3.bin, which part of the name indicates the platform?

A l

B js

C 120-3

D c2500

36 Which Cisco mIOS command displays the amount of Flash memory available on your router?

A **show flash**

B **show nvram**

C **show memory**

D **show running-config**

37 Where is the IOS device's running configuration always stored?

A Flash

B RAM

C NVRAM

D Bootflash

38 Which Cisco IOS command merges a configuration file from NVRAM into the configuration in RAM?

A copy startup running

B copy running-config tftp

C copy startup-config RAM

D copy NVRAM running-config

39 What does the **copy tftp startup** command do?

A Copies the configuration in NVRAM to a TFTP server

B Downloads a configuration file from a file TFTP to RAM

C Downloads a configuration file from a TFTP server to NVRAM

D Merges the configuration in RAM with the configuration file on a TFTP server

40 When you copy a configuration from another source into RAM, what happens to the existing configuration?

A It is overwritten.

B It is retained in its current state.

C It is merged with the new configuration, with the existing configuration taking precedence.

D It is merged with the new configuration, with the new configuration taking precedence.

41 You should use **debug** commands to _____ problems, not to monitor normal network operation.

A Test

B Repair

C Isolate

D Duplicate

42 Why must you be careful when using **debug** commands?

A Because **debug** commands are destructive

B Because **debug** commands open up security holes

C Because **debug** commands prevent normal traffic processing

D Because **debug** commands can negatively impact performance

43 Which Cisco IOS command adds a time stamp to a debug or log message?

A **timestamps debug**

B **debug timestamps**

C **service timestamps**

D **service debug timestamps**

44 Which action can lead to software reload on a Cisco device?

A Disabling a **debug** privileged EXEC command on a heavily used production router

B Enabling a **debug** privileged EXEC command on a heavily used production router

C Enabling a **debug** privileged EXEC command on a lightly used production router

D Disabling a **debug** privileged EXEC command on a lightly used production router

45 Which Cisco IOS command enables a Telnet session to receive console messages?

A **terminal monitor**

B **terminal debug monitor**

C **terminal debug messages**

D **terminal console messages**

46 It is best to use **debug** commands during periods of _____ network traffic and _____ users.

A Lower; more

B Lower; fewer

C Higher; more

D Higher; fewer

PART IV

Appendixes

Answers to the Chapter Review Questions and Quizzes

Chapter 1

Network Computing Basics Section Quiz

1 Match each of the following definitions with the appropriate word. (Choose the best answer.)

  B A silicon based CPU

  G Read-write memory that is lost when the power turned off

  F The main part of a PC, including the chassis, microprocessor, main memory, bus and ports

  I A printed circuit board that adds capabilities to a computer

2 A laptop has the same main components as a PC, but they are typically smaller in size.

  A. True

3 Which of the following are true statements about a NIC?

  A. A NIC is an expansion card.

  C. A NIC requires an IRQ to request CPU services.

  E. A NIC can use DMA architecture to directly access the system memory without using the CPU.

Internetworking Fundamentals Section Quiz

1 Match each of the following definitions with the appropriate word. (Choose the best answer.)

  G A set of rules by which computers communicate

  E A high-speed network confined to a limited geographic region

  B Devices used to connect cable segments, or subnets, into a larger internetwork

  I The layout or physical shape of a network

2 Which of the following are network applications?

B. E-mail

C. FTP

F. Web browser

3 All corporate internetworks use the same components regardless of their business structure.

B. False

Principles of Data Communication Section Quiz

1 Match the layer of the OSI model with the appropriate function.

 E Synchronizes dialogue between the presentation layers of the two host and manages their data exchange.

 A Defines the maximum transmission distance and data rates for a network.

 C Provides connectivity and path selection between two hosts systems.

 G Establishes, maintains, and terminates connectivity between devices.

2 For peer-to-peer communications, which of the following statements are true?

A. Between systems, the headers at each layer communicate information from peer-to-peer.

C. The name of the encapsulated information at a particular layer of the OSI model is called a PDU.

E. The physical address of a device is located in the Layer 2 PDU.

Computer Numbering Systems Section Quiz

1 Which of the following value expressions are true? (Choose all that apply.)

A. 2000 kBps > 2 Mbps

B. 9000 kbps > 1 kBps

C. 8000 kBps = 8 MBps

D. 200 kbps < 2000 kBps

2 Which of the following characters express hexadecimal values?

A. A

D. F

E. C

3 Given the binary number 11110100111010101010010101, which of the following would be the hexadecimal equivalent?

E. 0xF4EA95

Chapter 1 Review Questions

1 The _____ is a signal that informs a CPU that an event that needs its attention has occurred.

D. IRQ

2 What computer component allows the computer to communicate with the network?

B. NIC

3 Today, what are the common measurements for the speed of a computer microprocessor? (Choose two.)

C. MHz

E. GHz

4 Convert the decimal number 240 into binary.

A. 11110000

5 What is the binary number 10111001 in decimal?

B. 185

6 Which of the following is an application-layer protocol?

E. All of the above

7 What organization created the OSI reference model?

B. ISO

8 An e-mail message is sent from Host A to Host B on a LAN. To send this message, the data must be encapsulated. Which of the following best describes the first step of data encapsulation?

D. The user data is sent from an application to the application layer.

Chapter 2

Network Topology Section Quiz

1 Which of the following correctly describes networking topology?

   A. The network topology defines the way in which the computers, printers, network devices, and other devices are connected.

2 Which of the following statements best describes the bus topology?

   B. All of its nodes connect directly to one physical link

3 Which topology has all its nodes connected directly to one center point and has no other connections between nodes?

   C. Star

4 What is the primary purpose of the second ring in a dual-ring network?

   C. Redundancy

5 In a complete, full-mesh topology, every node

   A. Is linked directly to every other node

Functions of Internetwork Devices Section Quiz

1 Multiport repeaters can provide a simple solution for which of the following problems?

   D. No single cable connecting all devices

2 What is one disadvantage of using a hub?

   B. A hub cannot filter network traffic.

3 Which of the following is true concerning bridges and their forwarding decisions?

   C. Bridges operate at OSI Layer 2 and use MAC addresses to make decisions.

4 Which of the following is true concerning the function of switches?

   B. Switches combine the connectivity of a hub with the traffic regulation of a bridge.

5 What does a router do?

   A. A router matches information in the routing table with the destination IP address of the data and sends incoming data to the correct next hop device or host.

6 Which of the following statements is true?

   D. All of the above

7 What are the functions of AAA servers?

D. All of the above

Chapter 2 Review Questions

1 In a star topology, what happens when a cable between a device and the central device fails?

C. The device at the end of the cable becomes disconnected.

2 The rings in a dual-ring topology operate in different directions.

A. True

3 Which three functions are defined by the Cisco hierarchical model?

B. Distribution layer

C. Core layer

F. Access layer

4 Which of the following is a characteristic of a hub?

C. They are used as network concentration points.

5 What universally unique identifier does each network device have at Layer 2?

C. MAC address

6 Which of the following does a router forward?

C. Layer 3 datagrams

7 What does DSLAM stand for?

B. Digital subscriber line access multiplexer

8 Which of the following characteristics do firewalls have? (Select all that apply.)

A. Software-based

B. Hardware-based

C. Filter traffic

9 Which OSI layer defines an address that consists of a network portion and a node portion?

C. Layer 3

10 Which OSI layer defines a flat address space?

B. Layer 2

Chapter 3

LANs Overview Section Quiz

1 Which of the following is *not* one of the recognized IEEE sublayers?

B. Data Link Control

2 What is the name of the access control method used by Ethernet?

B. CSMA/CD

3 Fast Ethernet supports up to what transfer rate?

C. 100 Mbps

4 Identify two Gigabit Ethernet cable specifications.

C. 1000BASE-CX

D. 1000BASE-LX

WANs Overview Section Quiz

1 Which of the following statements best describes a WAN?

A. Connects LANs that are separated by a large geographic area

2 What is a group of networks that are networked to each other called?

A. An internetwork

3 A CSU/DSU is generally used as what type of equipment?

D. DCE

4 DCE and DTE equipment is found at which layer of the OSI reference model?

C. Physical

5 Which physical layer standard is used primarily in Europe and Japan?

C. X.21

6 Which data link layer has been replaced by PPP?

B. SLIP

Service Networks Section Quiz

1 Which of the following is *not* one of the features of a SAN?

D. SANs minimize the system and data availability.

2 Which of the following does *not* correctly describe the features of CNs?

C. The CN was designed to accelerate the delivery of information over the MAN infrastructure.

3 What service offers secure, reliable connectivity over a shared public network infrastructure?

B. Virtual private network

4 What links enterprise customer headquarters, remote offices, and branch offices to an internal network over a shared infrastructure?

B. Intranet VPNs

5 What is the name for the part of the company's LAN that is made available to select parties such as employees, customers, or partners?

B. The extranet

Chapter 3 Review Questions

1 Why did the IEEE create LLC?

D. To meet the need to have part of the data link layer function independently of existing technologies

2 What happens in the event of a collision on an Ethernet segment?

B. Initially, the data is lost but is resent using a backoff algorithm.

3 Which is the IEEE standard for Fast Ethernet?

C. 802.3u

4 What is the transmission medium for 1000BASE-SX?

D. Short-wave laser over multimode fiber.

5 Which statement is *not true about a Cisco GBIC?*

A. A 1000BASE-LX/LH interface has the ability to go up to 20 kilometers over single-mode fiber.

6 What is the largest component of the Internet commonly referred to as?

B. The Internet backbone

7 Select all correct attributes of a WAN.

B. WAN users must subscribe to services.

D. It can transport data, voice, and video.

8 The WAN path between DTEs is known as what?

   D. All of the above

9 Which two aspects of CNs make them better than traditional transmission over the Internet? (Choose two.)

   A. They bypass potential sources of congestion by distributing the load across a collection of content engines.

   C. They locate content engines near the audience.

10 What is the name given to a private network that is constructed within a public network infrastructure?

   D. VPN

11 What type of VPN links regional and remote offices to the headquarters' internal network?

   B. Intranet VPN

12 An extranet is the extension of two or more intranet strategies with a secure interaction between participant enterprises and their respective intranets.

   A. True

Chapter 4

Cabling and Infrastructure Section Quiz

1 What is the maximum cable length for STP?

   C. 100 m

2 What is an advantage that coaxial cable has over STP or UTP?

   C. It can run for a longer distance unboosted.

3 A _____ fiber-optic cable transmits multiple streams of LED-generated light.

   A. Multimode

4 Wireless communication uses which of the following to transmit data between devices on a LAN?

   A. Radio frequencies

5 What is one advantage of using fiber-optic cable in networks?

   D. It is capable of higher data rates than either coaxial or twisted-pair cable.

LAN Cabling Options Section Quiz

1 Which of the following is an 802.3u specification?

C. 100BASE-TX

2 Which of the following is a more appropriate choice for Ethernet connectivity?

C. Fast Ethernet as a link between the access layer and distribution layer devices to support the aggregate traffic from each Ethernet segment on the access link

3 Which standard body created the cables and connector specification used to support Ethernet implementation?

C. EIA/TIA

4 Which of the following statements does *not* correctly describe a media connector?

A. RJ-45 connectors are 8-pin connectors that resemble telephone jacks.

5 For which of the following would you *not* need to provide a crossover cable?

B. Connecting routers to switches

WAN Cabling Section Review

1 Which of the following is *not* a physical WAN implementation?

C. Frame Relay

2 What type of data transmission method is used by a WAN?

B. Serial

3 Which of the following media interconnects the ISDN BRI port to the service-provider device?

A. UTP straight-through

4 What type of connector is used for DSL connection?

B. RJ-11

5 What type of connector connects a router and cable system?

C. F-Type

6 What type of cable connects a terminal and a console port?

B. Rollover

Chapter 4 Review Questions

1 What is the maximum cable length for Thinnet coaxial cable?

B. 185 meters

2 What are the transmission rates of wireless communication?

B. 9 kbps–54 Mbps

3 At which layer of the OSI model do the cabling aspects of a LAN exist?

D. Physical

4 Which of the following are *not* optical GBICs?

B. High-frequency wavelength (1000BASE-FX/HX)

5 How is serial transmission different from parallel transmission? (Select two.)

B. They use different connectors.

C. Serial transmission sends data 1 bit at a time, and parallel transmission sends several bits at one time.

6 Typically, a router is _____.

A. A DTE device

7 If you are using an ISDN device that has an interface marked *BRI S/T, what does this imply?*

C. The device does not have an NT1 built in.

Chapter 5

Shared Ethernet Technologies Section Quiz

1 What is the maximum distance for thin Ethernet without using a repeater?

A. 185 meters

2 Which statements describe a feature of a hub? (Choose three.)

A. All resources are shared.

C. A hub implements physical layer functionality.

F. A hub transmits all bits to all devices on a segment.

3 Which behavior best describes a unicast transmission?

B. A frame is sent from one point to another point.

4 Which behavior best describes a broadcast transmission?

D. A frame is sent from one point to all other points.

5 Which behavior best describes a multicast transmission?

E. A frame is sent simultaneously to a specific group of devices.

6 What term describes the results of two or more stations on a network trying to transmit simultaneously on a shared network segment?

B. Collision

7 Which condition is a likely cause of network congestion?

D. Bandwidth-intensive applications

Bridged and Switched Ethernet Section Quiz

1 Which characteristics best describe a LAN switch? (Choose two.)

B. Functionally resembles a multiport bridge

D. Code is optimized and embedded in hardware

2 Which statements describe a feature of a switch? (Choose three.)

B. Builds and maintains a MAC address table

C. Interconnects multiple LAN segments

E. Filters frames based on the destination address

3 Which of the following functionalities of a switch differentiate it from a bridge? (Choose four.)

B. Enables full-duplex communication

C. Creates dedicated segments per user

F. Handles multiple simultaneous conversations

G. Translates speeds between different rate segments

4 Which statements accurately describe the two forwarding methods used by switches? (Choose two.)

B. Store-and-forward switching performs error checking.

E. Cut-through switching does not wait to receive the whole frame before forwarding it to the destination.

5 Which switch type provides switched connections between ports of unlike bandwidths?

D. Store-and-forward switch

6 Which functionality best fits a Layer 2 switch?

D. Forwards frames based on MAC addresses

7 Number the frame forwarding sequence in the correct order of occurrence for a switch receiving a frame that has an unknown source address.

4, 1, 5, 2, 6, 3

8 In which of the following conditions would a bridging loop most likely occur?

E. A redundant bridged network without the Spanning Tree Protocol

9 The Spanning Tree Protocol performs which of the following?

D. Detects and breaks loops by placing some connections is a standby mode

Virtual LAN Section Quiz

1 Which characteristic best describes a VLAN?

E. Devices are geographically in the same place but communicate virtually as if they are in different broadcast domains.

2 Which statements are benefits of adding a VLAN? (Choose two.)

A. Managing broadcasts reduces traffic load.

B. Flooding of a packet is limited to the switch ports that belong to a VLAN.

3 Which of these components is used as the entry point into the VLAN?

C. Switch port

4 Which method can dynamically establish VLAN membership?

A. MAC address

5 Which device provides communication between broadcast domains?

E. Switch

Chapter 5 Review Questions

1 Using a hub to interconnect devices has the same results as having the network devices on one Ethernet 10BASE2 segment.

A. True

2 Congestion causes which effects? (Choose two.)

B. Lower reliability and low traffic rates

D. Slower response times, longer file transfers, and network delays

3 What type of traffic can cause the most overhead on an Ethernet network?

C. Broadcast

4   Which statements best describe a bridge? (Choose two.)

   C. Forwards data packets from one network segment to another

   E. Addresses the problem of too much traffic on a segment or a network

5   At what layer of the OSI model do switches operate?

   D. Data link layer

6   Which best describes a network segment?

   A. A section of the network to which a group of devices share the same physical media

7   Which statement is not a characteristic of LAN switching?

   C. Forwards packets based on IP addresses

8   What features do store-and-forward mode allow the switch to perform? (Choose two.)

   B. Error checking

   D. Full receipt of all bits before forwarding the frame

9   Which switching method looks at the destination address of the frame and then forwards the frame without waiting to receive the entire frame?

   A. Cut-through

10 What are the functions of the Spanning Tree Protocol? (Choose two.)

   A. Manages the topologies within a switched or bridged network

   D. Transparently reconfigures bridges and switches to avoid the creation of loops

11 What is the only switching method supported by bridges?

   D. Store-and-forward

12 What function of a Cisco switch allows a user to create separate broadcast domains?

   A. VLAN

13 Identify the benefits of using a VLAN. (Choose two.)

   C. Easier implementation of segmentation

   D. Increased number of broadcast domains

14 What device is needed to pass a packet between VLANs?

   C. Router

15 Which statement pertaining to VLANs is false for Cisco switches?

   B. VLANs can be defined according to port groups, users, or protocols.

16 VLANs can be created according to which category? (Choose all that apply.)

A. Ports

B. Groups

C. MAC addresses

D. Functional teams

E. Users sharing an application

17 What is the result of segmenting a switch into multiple VLANS? (Choose two.)

C. The amount of broadcast traffic is limited.

Chapter 6

IP Internet Layer Overview Section Quiz

1 Which of the following protocols operates at the TCP/IP network layer? (Choose two.)

B. ARP

D. ICMP

2 Which statements best describe a function of IP? (Choose three.)

B. Is an unreliable, best-effort delivery method

C. Uses datagrams to carry information through the network

D. Addresses each packet with the source and destination address

3 Which statements best describe a function of ICMP? (Choose three.)

C. Announces when a device is unreachable on the network

E. Generates messages to slow down network traffic from the source

F. Uses the echo function to send a packet on a round trip between two devices

4 Which statement best describes a function of ARP?

B. Maps an IP address to a MAC address

5 Which statement best describes a function of RARP?

C. Maps a given MAC address to an IP address

6 Which statement best describes a function of DHCP?

D. Dynamically assigns addresses across the network

7 Which of the following are fields in the IP datagram? (Choose three.)

   C. Total length

   D. Time-To-Live

   F. Source IP address

8 Which statement best describes the function of a Protocol field in an IP diagram?

   C. Identifies a transport-layer protocol

Transport Layer Section Quiz

1 Which statement best describes a network protocol?

   D. A standard set of rules and conventions that determine how computers communicate with each other across networks

2 Which statement best describes the TCP/IP protocol stack?

   B. A suite of protocols that allows for data transmission across a multitude of networks

3 Which statements best describe characteristics of TCP? (Choose four.)

   A. TCP is a transport layer protocol.

   D. TCP numbers segments so that the destination can reorder received segments.

   E. A checksum technique verifies that data is not corrupted.

   G. TCP provides a synchronization method between end systems to manage flows and adapt to congestion in the network.

4 Which descriptions best define the differences between TCP and UDP? (Choose two.)

   D. TCP uses failed acknowledgements to alert the sender of lost segments.

   E. UDP offers applications direct access to the datagram service of the IP layer.

5 Which applications are members of the TCP/IP protocol stack? (Choose two.)

   B. FTP

   E. TFTP

6 Place the steps for establishing a connection with a peer system in the correct order.

   — After all synchronization has occurred, a connection is established.

   — One machine initiates a connection that is accepted by the other.

   — The sending application informs the operating system that a connection is to be initiated.

   — Protocol software modules in the two operating systems communicate by sending messages across the network.

   3, 2, 4, 1

7 Which names correctly identify the encapsulation term at the transport layer? (Choose two.)

B. Packet

C. Segment

8 Which terms identify a component of the TCP header? (Choose three.)

C. Window

D. Checksum

G. Sequence number

9 Which terms identify a component of the UDP header? (Choose two.)

B. Length

D. Checksum

10 Which statement best describes window size?

D. The number of octets that can be transmitted while awaiting an acknowledgment

11 Select the statement that correctly orders the steps to establish a TCP connection.

C. SYN=1, SYN=1 ACK=1, SYN=0 ACK=1

12 Which statement best describes positive acknowledgment?

B. Positive acknowledgment requires a recipient to send back an acknowledgment message when the recipient receives data.

13 Which statements correctly identify a characteristic of a port? (Choose two.)

A. Port numbers identify the upper-layer protocol.

C. Well-known ports are assigned numbers below 1024.

Chapter 6 Review Questions

1 Which protocols reside at the network layer? (Choose two.)

A. IP

E. ICMP

2 Which functions are true about IP? (Choose three.)

A. Routes datagrams

B. Forwards packets

D. Provides best-effort delivery

3 Which statement best describes a function of the IP protocol?

C. It fragments and reassembles packets transparently.

4 Identify the primary function of the ICMP protocol.

D. Generates IP control messages

5 What is the primary reason people use the ICMP protocol?

A. To test connectivity

6 What is the purpose of an ARP?

E. To associate an IP address to a MAC address

7 Which of the following statements best describes the role of RARP in an IP network?

C. RARP resolves a MAC address to an IP address.

8 Which of the following are *not* fields in an IP packet? (Choose three.)

A. Flags

C. Protocol

E. Header checksum

9 What is the purpose of the Protocol field in an IP header?

A. Indicates the type of transport packet being carried

10 Which functions best describe a communication protocol? (Choose two.)

D. The format a message must take

E. The way in which computers exchange messages

11 Which terms correctly correlate TCP/IP layers to OSI model layers? (Choose three.)

A. Internet; Network

C. Transport; Transport

E. Network Access; Physical-Data Link

12 Which of the following are primary duties of Layer 4 TCP? (Choose two.)

A. Provides end-to-end control

C. Acknowledges and sequences segments

13 What TCP characteristics are *not* found in UDP? (Choose three.)

A. Connections

B. Flow control

E. Fragment-free

14 Which application is supported by TCP?

C. FTP

15 Which statement indicates the correct sequence of events in establishing a TCP connection?

D. 1) The sending application informs the operating system that a connection is to be initiated.

2) One machine initiates a connection that is to be accepted by the other.

16 In TCP communication, when can a data transfer begin?

A. After all synchronization has occurred

17 How is data formatted at the transport layer?

D. Segments

18 Which components are found in a TCP header? (Choose three.)

B. Window

D. Checksum

E. Destination port

19 Which components are found in a UDP header? (Choose two.)

A. Length

E. Destination port

20 What flow control method does TCP implement?

D. Windowing

21 What does the ACK refer to in a TCP acknowledgment?

B. The number of the byte expected next

22 What will the ACK bit of the first segment of the three-way handshake most likely be?

B. 0

23 Which description best defines port numbers?

B. A numbering system to label the connections between devices

24 Which statements are characteristics of port numbers? (Choose two.)

D. The well-known ports cover the range of possible port numbers from 0 through 1023.

E. Communicating hosts specify an assigned application number in each data transmission.

Chapter 7

IP Network Addressing Section Quiz

1 The IP address consists of two parts: _____ and _____.

   A. Network portion and host portion

2 How many bits are in an IP address?

   B. 32

3 In a Class B address, which of the octets are the host address portion and are assigned locally?

   D. The third and fourth octets are assigned locally.

4 The following address is of which class? 172.16.128.17

   B. Class B

5 Which of the following is true of a broadcast address?

   C. A broadcast address is an address that has all 1s in the host field.

6 Which are private IP addresses? (Choose two.)

   A. 10.215.34.124

   C. 172.17.10.10

7 What percentage of the total IPv4 address allocation is made up of Class A addresses?

   B. 50

8 How many bits are there in an IPv6 address?

   D. 128

9 Which of the following is a feature of CIDR?

   D. Route aggregation

IP Subnetting Section Quiz

1 Originally, the Internet used how many levels of hierarchy addressing?

   A. Two

2 What is the function of a subnet mask?

   A. To determine which part of the IP address is the network or subnetwork part and which part is the host part

3 What is the practical maximum number of host bits you can borrow from a Class A address for subnetting?

B. 22

4 List the steps for determining a subnetwork number in order.

3, 1, 2, 4

5 How many octets does a Class A network have in the host field?

A. 3

6 Using 6 subnet bits, how many usable subnets are created?

C. 62

7 How many host addresses can be used in a Class C network?

B. 254

8 What is the maximum number of bits that can be borrowed to create a useable subnet for a Class C network?

C. 6

Routing Basics Section Quiz

1 Which term best describes the operation of a router in evaluating available routes to a destination and establishing the preferred handling of a packet?

B. Path determination

2 Which best describes a routed protocol?

A. Provides enough information in its network layer address to allow a packet to be forwarded from host to host

3 Which of the following statements about the path determination process is *not* correct?

C. Dynamic routing occurs when information is configured onto each router by the network administrator.

4 Which of the following contains routing information that helps a router in determining the routing path?

C. Routing table

5 Which of the following are goals for routing protocols? (Choose three.)

A. Optimization

C. Simplicity

D. Rapid convergence

6 Which of the following is not a routing metric?

C. Length

Routing Protocols Section Quiz

1 Which of the following is an example of an EGP?

C. BGP

2 What are IGPs used for?

D. To deliver routing information within a single autonomous system

3 Which best describes a distance vector protocol?

A. It determines the direction and distance to any network in the internetwork.

4 Which of the following best describes link-state algorithms?

C. They recreate the exact topology of the entire internetwork.

5 In the IP RIP routing protocol, how often are periodic routing updates sent?

A. Every 30 seconds

6 By default, which of the following is a routing metric used by IGRP?

A. Bandwidth and delay

7 Which of the following is *not* a basic component of EIGRP?

A. Routes only for IP

8 Which of the following is *not* a feature of OSPF?

C. Selects paths based on hop count

9 BGP is an example of which type of protocol?

C. Routing protocol

Chapter 7 Review Questions

1 Host addresses can be dynamically assigned.

A. True

2 What network address is reserved for loopback testing?

C. 127.0.0.0

3 What is the translation of private addresses to public addresses referred to as?

D. NAT

4 Which is the IP protocol that is being implemented to increase the number of network addresses available?

C. IPv6

5 How many host addresses are available if the IP subnet address is 206.15.8.0/20?

C. 4094

6 Which of the following is a benefit from subnetting a network? (Choose two.)

A. Better traffic control

B. Better performance

7 If you were going to borrow four bits to create a subnet mask for a Class B address, what would the subnet mask be?

C. 255.255.240.0

8 How many subnets could be created if six bits are borrowed?

D. 62

9 What are the key functions of a router? (Choose all that apply.)

A. Maintain routing tables

B. Use routing tables to determine the optimal path for network traffic

C. Determine where to forward a packet of data

D. Add necessary framing for an interface

10 What happens in the third step of the encapsulation/de-encapsulation process?

C. The packet is re-encapsulated in the data link layer frame for the selected interface and transmitted.

11 What are some informational items contained in a routing table? (Choose two.)

A. Destination/next-hop associations

B. Routing metric

12 Which of the following is *not* a routing protocol?

C. IP

13 A router compares the destination network address to a routing table to select a path.

A. True

14 For a Cisco router, which of the following is used by the Cisco IOS to help measure delay?

B. Bandwidth

15 What do routers use to exchange data?

B. Routing protocols

16 What do link-state protocols propagate when a network change occurs?

 B. LSA

17 When using RIP, what is the hop-count limitation?

 C. 15

18 Which of the following are benefits of IGRP when compared to RIP? (Choose two.)

 A. Higher hop-count limitation

 C. Versatility for handling complex networks

19 Which of the following is *not* true about EIGRP?

 D. It has more overhead than IGRP.

20 Which is *not* true about OSPF?

 C. It sends updates to neighbors every 30 seconds.

Chapter 8

WAN Technology Basics Section Quiz

1 Which of the following best describes a WAN?

 A. Connects LANs that are separated by a large geographic area

2 Which of the following is an example of a circuit-switching protocol?

 A. ISDN

3 Which of the following phrases describes a packet-switching protocol?

 A. A switching method in which users share common carrier resources for data transmission

4 A leased line is a _____ link that provides a single, preestablished WAN communication path from the customer to a remote network.

 A. Point-to-point

5 How many DS0s can be bundled to get a DS1/T1 line?

 A. 24

6 Which of the following is a type of physical-layer multiplexing? (Choose all that apply.)

 A. TDM

 B. FDM

 C. WDM

WAN Access Technologies Section Quiz

1 Which protocol does PPP use for establishing and maintaining point-to-point connections?

B. LCP

2 Which is the default encapsulation type for serial interfaces on a Cisco router?

B. HDLC

3 Which of the following statements pertaining to ISDN is false?

D. The total bit rate of the ISDN BRI is 2.533 Mbps.

4 Which of the following media is used by DSL to transport data?

B. Existing twisted-pair telephone lines

5 What are the two basic types of DSL technology?

C. Asymmetric DSL and symmetric DSL

6 Which of the following standards organizations and industries have contributed to the evolution of DSL? (Choose all that apply.)

A. ANSI

B. ITU-T

E. ETSI

7 Which of the following is *not* one of the benefits of DSL?

C. ADSL stations can be up to 18,000 feet from the CO.

8 How does Frame Relay handle multiple conversations on the same physical connection?

A. Frame Relay multiplexes the circuits.

9 Which of the following is *not* true about ATM technology?

D. ATM cells are always a fixed length of 35 bytes, whereas the sizes of frames and packets vary.

10 Name the family of very high-speed physical layer technologies that offers a series of data rates with special designations implemented at different transmission rates ranging from 51.84 Mbps to 40 Gbps.

C. SONET

Modem Section Quiz

1 Which of the following is true of analog modems?

D. All of the above are true.

2 Which of the following cable standards allows a 56 kbps downstream data transmission rate?

D. V.90

3 Which of the following media are used by a cable modem to transport data?

A. Existing coaxial cable TV lines

4 Which of the following best describes upstream?

A. Data flowing from the user to the network

5 Which of the following is an advantage of cable modem?

C. Coaxial cable wiring offers greater bandwidth using broadband for more applications to the home network.

Chapter 8 Review Questions

1 ISDN is an example of a circuit-switched WAN technology.

A. True

2 Which of the following are true about a point-to-point link? (Choose three.)

A. It is a single, pre-established WAN communications path from the customer premises through a carrier network.

B. It is usually leased from a carrier and thus is often called a leased line.

C. It is generally priced based on bandwidth required and distance between the two connected points.

3 Which of the following statements are true about bandwidth? (Choose three.)

A. Bandwidth refers to the speed at which data is transferred over the communication link.

C. A T1 line is the same as a DS1 line.

D. 28 DS1s can be bundled to get a DS3 line.

4 Which of the following is *not* a type of multiplexing?

B. ATM

5 Which of the following is *not* true regarding permanent virtual circuits (PVCs)?

B. Data communication across a PVC requires call setup and termination states.

6 What is the size of the ATM payload?

A. 48 bytes

7 What is the aggregate speed of the B channels for ISDN BRI?

C. 128 kbps

8 Which of the following is data-link encapsulation for a WAN? (Choose all that apply)

A. High-Level Data Link Control (HDLC)

C. Point-to-Point Protocol (PPP)

E. Frame Relay

9 Which of the following is *not* a symmetrical standard for DSL?

D. ADSL

10 Which of the following protocols do *not* operate at Layer 2?

D. IP

11 DSL service can be added incrementally as more users subscribe.

A. True

12 Which was the first true worldwide standard for modems that allowed 2400 bits per second (bps) at 600 baud?

E. V.22bis

13 Which of the following statements about cable modems are true? (Choose three.)

A. Cable modems use the same coaxial lines that transmit cable television.

B. Cable modem access provides speeds that are superior to leased lines.

C. Cable modems provide a full-time connection.

Chapter 9

Basic Operation of the Cisco IOS Software Section Quiz

1 When you configure Catalyst switches from the user interface that runs on the console or a remote terminal, the Cisco IOS Software provides a CLI called the _____.

A. EXEC

2 What purpose does the Cisco IOS EXEC serve?

D. Interprets the commands you enter and carries out the corresponding operations

3 What should you type to display a list of commands that begin with the letter *a* on a Catalyst switch?

A. a?

4 What should you type to display the command syntax help so that you can see how to complete a command that begins with *show?*

B. show ?

5   Which Cisco IOS command takes you from the Router> prompt to the Router# prompt on a Cisco router?

C. enable

6   When the information displayed on a Cisco router is more than one page in length, what should you do to display the next page?

C. Press the Space bar.

7   What does the % Incomplete command message mean on a Cisco router?

B. You did not enter all of the keywords or values required by the command.

8   What should you do if you receive a % Ambiguous command message on your Cisco router?

C. Reenter the command followed by a question mark (?) with no space between the command and the question mark.

9   What does the Cisco IOS CLI do when you enter a command that is longer than allowed on a single line?

B. The router automatically scrolls the line to the left and uses a dollar sign ($) to indicate that the beginning of the line is elsewhere.

10 What happens when you press the Tab key when working in the CLI?

D. The parser completes a partially entered command if you entered enough characters to make the command unambiguous.

11 Which tasks can you complete using the Cisco IOS command history feature? (Choose three.)

A. Recall commands

C. Set the command history buffer size

E. Display the contents of the command buffer

12 Which of the following recall commands displays what is in history buffer beginning with the most recent command? (Choose two.)

B. Ctrl-P

C. Up arrow

13 What happens when you start a Cisco IOS device that has no configuration in memory?

B. The device prompts you to enter a minimum configuration.

14 Match each Cisco device startup action to its description.

1-A, 2-B, 3-C

15 If a network administrator is supporting a remote device, what is the preferred type of connection or configuration to permit the administrator to configure the device remotely?

C. Modem connection via the auxiliary port

16 What are the two primary Cisco IOS EXEC modes?

C. User and privileged

17 How do you enter commands into the Cisco IOS CLI?

B. Type or paste entries within a console command mode.

18 How do you know which command mode you are using on a Cisco device?

A. The command mode is indicated with a distinctive prompt.

19 Which Cisco IOS command lists the commands that are available in the privileged EXEC mode?

A. ?

20 Which EXEC mode allows you to configure and debug a Cisco router?

D. Privileged

Booting a Cisco IOS Device Section Quiz

1 How should you power up a Catalyst 2950 switch?

D. Attach the power cable plug to the switch power supply socket.

2 When you start the switch or router, what should you see on the console output?

C. Cisco IOS Software output text

3 Which LED display modes of operation are used on a Catalyst switch? (Choose three.)

A. Port status

D. Full-duplex support

E. Bandwidth utilization

4 After a successful completion of the initial hardware testing, what do the port LEDs on a Catalyst switch do?

C. The LEDs blink after the tests are complete and then turn off.

5 When a Cisco router powers up, it performs a _____.

D. Power-On Self-Test (POST)

6 Match each stage of a Catalyst switch LED POST to its description.

1-A, 2-E, 3-C, 4-D, 5-B, 6-F

7 If POST completes successfully on the Catalyst 2950 switch, what happens next?

D. You are prompted to enter the initial configuration for the switch.

8 When the router starts up, which actions do the startup routines perform? (Choose three.)

A. Run POST.

E. Find and load the Cisco IOS software that the router uses for its operating system.

F. Find and apply the configuration statements about router-specific attributes, protocol functions, and interface addresses.

9 Why would you use the setup dialog on a Cisco device?

B. To complete the initial configuration

Configuring a Switch from the Command Line Section Quiz

1 Which Cisco IOS command displays the configuration of the system hardware and software version information on a Cisco device?

A. show version

2 After you configure the IP address on an interface, how do you change the state from administratively down to up?

C. Enter no shutdown.

3 Which Cisco IOS command displays the interface bandwidth on a Cisco switch?

A. show interfaces

4 Match each data-link protocol status to the message that appears with the show interfaces command.

1-A, 2-D, 3-B, 4-C

Configuring a Router from the Command Line Section Quiz

1 What should you do if you make an error during the system configuration dialog on a Cisco router?

A. Type Ctrl-C to abort the process and start over.

2 Which Cisco IOS command assigns the device name?

A. hostname hostname

3 What must you configure to ensure that anyone accessing your router from the console port is prompted for a password?

C. The login command and the password command

4 Which Cisco IOS command configures Ethernet port 1 on a fixed port router?

B. interface Ethernet 1

5 Which Cisco IOS command do you use to bring up an interface on a Cisco router that is "administratively down"?

C. no shutdown

Managing Configuration Changes Section Quiz

1 Which Cisco IOS command saves the current configuration to be the starting configuration of the router?

D. copy running-config startup-config

2 What information does the show startup-config command display?

C. Saved configuration in NVRAM

3 Which Cisco IOS command displays the current active configuration settings on a Catalyst switch?

D. show running-configuration

Chapter 9 Review Questions

1 Access to the Cisco IOS CLI is generally referred to as _____.

B. An EXEC session

2 Cisco IOS Software offers _____ features to assure dependable access to networked resources.

B. Reliability

3 When a Cisco device starts up, it runs _____ to check its hardware.

C. POST

4 When a Catalyst switch or Cisco router starts up, what is the first operation performed?

B. The device performs hardware checking routines.

5 Upon initial installation of a Cisco switch or router, the network administrator typically configures the networking devices from a _____.

C. Console terminal

6 If a network administrator is supporting a remote device, the preferred method is to use a modem connection to the device's _____ for remote configuration.

D. Auxiliary port

7   Which access level allows a person to access all router commands and can be password protected to allow only authorized individuals to access the router?

   D. Privileged EXEC level

8   How do you instruct a Cisco device to parse and execute an entered command?

   B. Press the Enter key.

9   Which CLI prompt indicates that you are working in privileged EXEC mode?

   A. Hostname#

10 Which command would you enter in the privileged EXEC mode to list the command options?

   A. ?

11 Match each step of the physical Catalyst switch startup process to its description.

   1-C, 2-A, 3-B

12 How do you start a Catalyst 2950 switch?

   D. Attach the power cable plug to the switch power supply socket.

13 What color is the Catalyst 2950 switch redundant power supply LED if the redundant power supply is plugged in but not functioning correctly?

   B. Amber

14 During a Catalyst switch POST test, what is the result of the console port test failing?

   B. This is a nonfatal error, but one or more ports will not be operational.

15 What should you type to display a list of commands that begin with the letter *c* on a Catalyst switch?

   A. c?

16 What should you type to display the command syntax help so that you can see how to complete a command that begins with config?

   B. config ?

17 Which configuration mode do you use to configure a particular port on a switch?

   C. Interface configuration mode

18 When you use the **show interfaces** command to display the status and statistics for the interfaces configured on a Catalyst switch, which output field indicates the MAC address that identifies the interface hardware?

   C. Address is 0050.BD73.E2C1

19 Which show command requires that you have privileged EXEC mode access?

   C. show running

20 How should you power up a Cisco router?

B. Turn the power switch to on.

21 When you start a Cisco router, what should you see on the console?

C. Cisco IOS Software output text

22 What is the primary purpose of setup mode on a Cisco router?

C. To bring up a minimal feature configuration

23 Which statement best describes what the user EXEC mode commands allow you to configure on a Cisco router?

A. You cannot configure anything; the user mode commands are used to display information.

24 Which Cisco IOS command is used to return to user EXEC mode from the privileged EXEC mode?

C. disable

25 Match each type of help available with the Cisco IOS CLI to its description.

1-A, 2-C, 3-B

26 When you enter Cisco IOS commands on a router, which CLI editing key sequence redisplays a line?

C. Ctrl-R

27 What does the CLI editing key sequence Ctrl-X do?

A. Erases everything to the left of the cursor

28 Which Cisco IOS command sets the session command buffer size?

D. terminal history size lines

29 Which command returns to more recent commands in the history buffer after recalling commands?

A. Ctrl-N

30 What information does the show running-config command provide on a Cisco router?

A. Current (running) configuration in RAM

31 Which Cisco IOS command displays the configuration of the system hardware and the software version information?

A. show version

32 Match each router prompt to its configuration mode.

1-B, 2-D, 3-A, 4-E, 5-C

33 If you enter a major command on a Cisco router, what happens?

D. The router switches you from one configuration mode to another.

34 Which Cisco IOS command creates a message to be displayed upon router login?

B. banner motd message

35 If both the enable secret and the enable password commands are configured on your router, how do you get to the # prompt?

A. Type in the configured enable secret password at the password prompt.

36 Which Cisco IOS command do you use to prevent a console session from timing out?

D. exec-timeout 0 0

37 Which Cisco IOS command configures serial port in slot 0, port 1 on a modular router?

C. interface serial 0/1

38 Which Cisco IOS command should you use to set the clock speed to 64 kbps on a serial interface on a Cisco router?

C. clock rate 64000

39 Which Cisco IOS commands correctly configure the IP address and subnet mask for Ethernet interface 1 in slot 1?

D. interface FastEthernet 1/1
    ip address 192.168.1.1 255.255.255.0

40 What is a runt?

C. An Ethernet frame that has been discarded because it is smaller than the minimum Ethernet frame size

41 A serial interface displays **Serial1 is up, line protocol is down**. Which situations might cause this error? (Choose three.)

A. The clock rate has not been set.

D. No keepalives are coming in on the interface.

E. The encapsulation type on the other end is different than on your end.

Chapter 10

Getting Information About Neighboring Devices Section Quiz

1 Which statements accurately describe CDP? (Choose two.)

A. CDP runs over the data link layer.

D. CDP automatically discovers neighboring CDP devices.

2 Which network layer protocol must two CDP devices run to learn about each other?

D. The network-layer protocol is unimportant to CDP

3 A CDP device learns information about _____.

C. All directly connected CDP devices

4 Which pieces of information does a CDP packet include? (Choose two.)

B. Port identifier

C. Capabilities list

5 Which command disables CDP on a specific interface?

B. no cdp enable

6 What does the command no cdp run do?

A. Disables CDP for the entire device

7 Which Cisco IOS command produces the same result as **show cdp entry ***?

D. show cdp neighbors detail

8 If the letters R and B appear in the Capabilities column in the output of the **show cdp neighbors** command, it indicates that the specified device is acting as both a _____ and a _____.

C. Router; source route bridge

9 Which Cisco IOS commands display a holdtime value? (Choose three.)

B. show cdp entry

D. show cdp interface

E. show cdp neighbors

10 What information is included in the output of the command **show cdp traffic**?

C. Number of CDP packets sent

11 Which CDP commands can you use to display the network layer address information of the CDP neighbor? (Choose two.)

B. show cdp entry

D. show cdp interface

12 How often should you update your network map?

D. Whenever the network topology changes

13 Which pieces of information should you include in a network map? (Choose three.)

A. Addressing

B. Rack layouts

E. Cable identification

Getting Information about Remote Devices Section Quiz

1 Which Cisco IOS command opens a Telnet connection from a Cisco router to a device with the IP address 10.1.1.1?

B. telnet 10.1.1.1

2 You use the **show users** command to display all active Telnet sessions and to determine if _____.

B. The console is active.

3 Which key sequence suspends a Telnet session?

C. <Ctrl-Shift-6>x

4 Which actions continue a suspended Telnet session? (Choose two.)

B. Pressing the Enter key

D. Entering the resume command

5 Which commands end a Telnet session when entered on the remote device? (Choose two.)

A. exit

B. logout

6 Which command ends an incoming Telnet session from a remote device?

C. clear line

7 Which pieces of information are displayed as the result of the **ping** command? (Choose three.)

B. Success rate

D. Average round-trip time

E. Minimum round-trip time

8 What does the **ping** command verify?

B. Connectivity

Router Booting Sequence and Verification Commands Section Quiz

1 The router IOS is usually found in _____, and the saved configuration file (startup-config) is usually found in _____.

D. Flash memory; NVRAM

2 Which stage of router bootup occurs first?

B. Load bootstrap

3 Which router component is used primarily to contain the Cisco IOS software image?

C. Flash memory

4 Which component tests the basic functionality of the router hardware and determines which components are present?

A. POST

5 When a Cisco router starts up, where does it look to find the Cisco IOS Software, by default, if the saved configuration file in NVRAM does not contain boot system commands?

D. Flash memory

6 During the boot process, which of the following describes where the device boots from if the boot field value is 0x2?

D. Parses the NVRAM configuration

7 Which Cisco IOS command displays the current value of the configuration register?

B. show version

8 If the configuration register value is 0x2100, what does the router do the next time it boots?

C. Runs ROM monitor automatically

Cisco IOS File System and Devices Section Quiz

1 What is the Cisco IOS 12.0 IFS name for the running-config file?

C. system:running-config

2 Which Cisco IOS command(s), starting in Cisco IOS Release 12.0, deletes the startup configuration?

A. erase nvram:

C. erase startup-config

3 Which Cisco IOS command creates a backup copy of the IOS image file on a TFTP server?

C. copy flash tftp

4 Which command displays the size of the IOS image file in Flash memory?

A. show flash

5 For which reasons would you copy configuration files from a TFTP, RCP, or FTP server to the running configuration or startup configuration of a router? (Choose three.)

A. To restore a backed-up configuration file

B. To use the configuration file for another router

E. To load the same configuration commands onto all the routers in your network

6 Which Cisco IOS command merges a configuration file from a TFTP server into the current configuration?

D. copy tftp running-config

7 What does the copy running startup command do?

A. Copies the configuration in RAM to NVRAM

8 When adding new equipment to the network, what is the final step you should take?

D. Configure the new device with the appropriate configuration to meet the network requirements.

9 When you make a hardware change to your router, should you power down the device?

D. Depends on whether the Cisco device supports OIR

10 Which type of Cisco IOS command should you use to create a snapshot of network conditions to troubleshoot problems with interfaces, media, or network performance?

C. show commands

11 Which type of Cisco IOS command should you use to view a process operating on a router or the network for troubleshooting purposes?

D. debug commands

Chapter 10 Review Questions

1 Which statements are true of CDP? (Choose two.)

   A. It is a proprietary protocol.

   C. It discovers information about connected Cisco devices.

2 When is CDP started?

   A. When the Cisco device boots

3 How could you obtain CDP information about a nondirectly connected remote device?

   C. Use Telnet to access a Cisco device connected to the target device.

4 Which pieces of information are included in a CDP update packet? (Choose two.)

   A. Platform

   C. Device identifiers

5 Which command disables CDP on the device as a whole?

   B. no cdp run

6 What does the command **cdp enable** do?

   C. Enables CDP on an individual interface

7 Which Cisco IOS command produces the same result as **show cdp neighbors detail**?

   B. show cdp entry *

8 What keyword do you add to the **show cdp neighbors** command to obtain additional information in the output?

   B. detail

9 Which Cisco IOS command displays the frequency at which packets are sent?

   C. show cdp interface

10 What information is included in the output of the command **show cdp interface**?

   C. Encapsulation type

11 Which command displays the device platform of a directly connected device?

   A. show cdp entry

12 Which command displays CDP packets checksum errors?

   B. show cdp traffic

13 Which statements identify the primary uses of a network map? (Choose three.)

A. Modifies network design

C. Tracks changes to the topology

D. Troubleshoots network problems

14 Which Cisco IOS commands open a Telnet session from a router to a device with the host name switch123 and the IP address 10.1.1.2? (Choose two.)

B. telnet 10.1.1.2

E. telnet switch123

15 Which Cisco IOS command displays a list that includes all Telnet sessions currently connected to other devices?

C. show sessions

16 What does an asterisk (*) mean in the output of the **show sessions** command?

A. Identifies the most recent Telnet session

17 What does the command resume 3 do?

C. Continues the suspended Telnet session with the session id of 3

18 What does the key sequence **<Ctrl-Shift-6>x** do?

B. Suspends the current Telnet session

19 When you have multiple active Telnet sessions and enter the command **resume**, which Telnet session is continued?

A. The most recent session.

20 At what level of the Cisco CLI do you execute the **disconnect** command?

A. Privileged EXEC mode

21 What does the command **clear line** do?

D. Closes a Telnet session from a foreign host

22 Which pieces of information are displayed as the result of the **ping** command? (Choose three.)

A. Packets lost

D. Maximum round-trip time

E. Size of the ICMP echo packets

23 Which Cisco IOS command would you use to display the path a packet takes to a specific destination?

B. trace

24 Which stage during a Cisco router bootup occurs last?

D. Find and load configuration

25 Which stage of the Cisco router bootup process verifies that all router components are operational?

A. POST

26 Which Cisco router component is used primarily to store the startup configuration?

C. NVRAM

27 The _____ is a low-level operating system normally used for manufacturing testing and troubleshooting.

D. ROM monitor (ROMMON)

28 During the Cisco router boot process, what does the router do if the boot field value is 0x2?

D. Checks the startup configuration file for boot system commands

29 What happens if the router cannot find a valid startup configuration file in NVRAM during router bootup?

A. The router enters setup mode.

30 On most routers, the IOS software is loaded into _____ to run, but on some it is run directly from _____.

B. RAM; Flash memory

31 From the ROM monitor, which should you enter to determine the current value of the configuration register?

A. o

32 The command **show startup-config** displays the configuration in which location?

C. NVRAM

33 Which bits of the configuration register value make up the boot field?

C. Lowest four bits

34 Which Cisco IOS command downloads a copy of the IOS image file from a TFTP server?

B. copy tftp flash

35 Given the system image file c2500-js-l_120-3.bin, which part of the name indicates the platform?

D. c2500

36 Which Cisco IOS command displays the amount of Flash memory available on your router?

A. show flash

37 Where is the IOS device's running configuration always stored?

B. RAM

38 Which Cisco IOS command merges a configuration file from NVRAM into the configuration in RAM?

A. copy startup running

39 What does the **copy tftp startup** command do?

C. Downloads a configuration file from a TFTP server to NVRAM

40 When you copy a configuration from another source into RAM, what happens to the existing configuration?

D. It is merged with the new configuration, with the new configuration taking precedence.

41 You should use **debug** commands to _____ problems, not to monitor normal network operation.

C. Isolate

42 Why must you be careful when using **debug** commands?

D. Because debug commands can negatively impact performance

43 Which Cisco IOS command adds a timestamp to a debug or log message?

C. service timestamps

44 Which action can lead to software reload on a Cisco device?

B. Enabling a debug privileged EXEC command on a heavily used production router

45 Which Cisco IOS command enables a Telnet session to receive console messages?

A. Terminal monitor

46 It is best to use **debug** commands during periods of _____ network traffic and _____ users.

B. Lower; fewer

GLOSSARY

A

algorithm. A well-defined rule or process for arriving at a solution to a problem. In networking, algorithms commonly are used to determine the best route for traffic from a particular source to a particular destination.

ANSI. American National Standards Institute. A voluntary organization composed of corporate, government, and other members that coordinates standards-related activities, approves U.S. standards, and develops positions for the United States in international standards organizations. ANSI helps develop international and U.S. standards relating to, among other things, communications and networking. ANSI is a member of the IEC and the ISO.

ARP. Address Resolution Protocol. An Internet protocol used to map an IP address to a MAC address. Defined in RFC 826.

ARPA. Advanced Research Projects Agency. Research and development organization that is part of the U.S. Department of Defense (DoD). ARPA is responsible for numerous technological advances in communications and networking. ARPA evolved into DARPA and then back into ARPA again (in 1994).

ASIC. application-specific integrated circuit. An integrated circuit that has been programmed to perform a specific application at a high rate of speed. These circuits are used heavily in Layer 2 and Layer 3 switches.

asynchronous transmission. A term describing digital signals that are transmitted without precise clocking. Such signals generally have different frequencies and phase relationships. Asynchronous transmissions usually encapsulate individual characters between control bits (called start and stop bits) that designate the beginning and the end of each character.

ATM. Asynchronous Transfer Mode. The international standard for cell relay in which multiple service types (such as voice, video, or data) are conveyed in fixed-length (53-byte) cells. Fixed-length cells allow cell processing to occur in hardware, thereby reducing transit delays. ATM is designed to take advantage of high-speed transmission media, such as E3, SONET, and T3.

AUI. attachment unit interface. IEEE 802.3 interface between a media attachment unit (MAU) and a network interface card (NIC). The term AUI also can refer to the rear panel port to which an AUI cable might attach. Also called *transceiver cable*.

authentication. In security, the verification of the identity of a person or a process.

autonomous system. Sometimes abbreviated as *AS*. 1. A collection of networks under a common administration sharing a common interior routing strategy; for example, Enhanced Interior Gateway Routing Protocol (EIGRP) or Interior Gateway Routing Protocol (IGRP). 2. A collection of networks expressed as a common system to one or more external networks as used by Border Gateway Protocol (BGP). These external autonomous systems are subdivided by areas, and each autonomous system must be assigned a unique 16-bit number by the Internet Assigned Numbers Authority (IANA).

B

backplane. The internal connections between ports or interfaces on a switch or router usually in the form of several buses.

Bellman-Ford-Moore algorithm. The algorithm used by Routing Information Protocol (RIP) to choose the best routing path.

BIA. burned-in MAC address. An identifier hardcoded into a network device by the manufacturer.

binary. A numbering system characterized by ones and zeros (1 = on, 0 = off).

BPDU. bridge protocol data unit. A Spanning Tree Protocol hello packet that is sent out at configurable intervals to exchange information among bridges in the network.

bridge. A device that connects and passes packets between two network segments that use the same communications protocol. Bridges operate at the data link layer (Layer 2) of the OSI reference model. In general, a bridge filters, forwards, or floods an incoming frame based on the MAC address of that frame.

broadcast. A data packet that is sent to all nodes on a network. Broadcasts are identified by a broadcast address.

broadcast domain. A set of all devices that receive broadcast frames originating from any device within the set. Broadcast domains typically are bounded by routers because routers do not forward broadcast frames.

buffer. A storage area used for handling data in transit. Buffers are used in internetworking to compensate for differences in processing speed between network devices. Bursts of data can be stored in buffers until they can be handled by slower processing devices. Also called a *packet buffer.*

bus. A signaling path made up of wires or other media that allow electronic signals to be sent from one part of a device to another.

C

canonical. Addresses that are sent on the wire with the least significant or low order bit first. Ethernet addresses are canonical. For each byte of the Ethernet address the last bit of the byte is sent first.

CCITT. Consultative Committee for International Telegraph and Telephone. An international organization responsible for the development of communications standards. Now called the ITU-T.

CDP. Cisco Discovery Protocol. A media- and protocol-independent device-discovery protocol that runs on Cisco-manufactured equipment, including routers, access servers, bridges, and switches. Using CDP, a device can advertise its existence to other devices and receive information about other devices on the same LAN or on the remote side of a WAN. Runs on all media that support Subnetwork Access Protocol (SNAP) encapsulation, including LANs, Frame Relay, and ATM media.

cell. The basic data unit for ATM switching and multiplexing. Cells contain identifiers that specify the data stream to which they belong. Each cell consists of a 5-byte header and 48 bytes of payload.

Cisco IOS Software. Cisco operating system software that provides common functionality, scalability, and security for all Cisco products. Cisco IOS Software allows centralized, integrated, and automated installation and management of internetworks while ensuring support for a wide variety of protocols, media, services, and platforms.

coaxial cable. A cable consisting of a hollow outer cylindrical conductor that surrounds a single inner wire conductor. Two types of coaxial cable currently are used in LANs: 50-ohm cable, which is used for digital signaling, and 75-ohm cable, which is used for analog signaling and high-speed digital signaling.

collision domain. In Ethernet, the network area within which frames that have collided are propagated. Repeaters and hubs propagate collisions; LAN switches, bridges, and routers do not.

compression. The running of a data set through an algorithm that reduces the space required to store, or the bandwidth required to transmit, the data set.

convergence. The speed and capability of a group of internetworking devices running a specific routing protocol to agree on the topology of an internetwork after a change in that topology.

CoS. class of service. An indication of how an upper-layer protocol requires a lower-layer protocol to treat its messages. In Systems Network Architecture (SNA) subarea routing, CoS definitions are used by subarea nodes to determine the optimal route to establish a given session. A CoS definition comprises a virtual route number and a transmission priority field. Also called *ToS*.

CPU. central processing unit. The main processor for a computing device. The CPU runs instructions from the operating system to perform device functions.

CRC. cyclic redundancy check. An error-checking technique in which the frame recipient calculates a remainder by dividing frame contents by a prime binary divisor and compares the calculated remainder to a value stored in the frame by the sending node.

D

daemon. A program that is not invoked explicitly but lies dormant waiting for some condition(s) to occur.

DDR. dial-on-demand routing. Technique whereby a router can automatically initiate and close a circuit-switched session as transmitting stations demand. The router spoofs keepalives so that end stations treat the session as active. DDR permits routing over ISDN or telephone lines using an ISDN terminal adapter or modem.

debug. An application used by Cisco IOS devices that displays output for operations being performed by the device. The debug application is extremely processor intensive and can disrupt network service if not used carefully.

DEC. Digital Equipment Corporation. An early internetworking company that pioneered many of the components used in today's networks. Most notably, the first version of Spanning Tree Protocol was developed at DEC, and they were one of three manufactures who developed the AUI connector for Ethernet.

DECnet. (Standards and Specifications) A group of communications products (including a protocol suite) developed and supported by Digital Equipment Corporation. DECnet/OSI (also called DECnet Phase V) is the most recent iteration and supports both OSI protocols and proprietary digital protocols. Phase IV Prime supports inherent MAC addresses that allow DECnet nodes to coexist with systems running other protocols that have MAC address restrictions.

delay. The time between the initiation of a transaction by a sender and the first response received by the sender. Also, the time required to move a packet from source to destination over a given path.

Dijkstra's algorithm. An algorithm developed by Dr. Edsger Dijkstra that calculates routes given a link- and a nodal-state topology database. This algorithm is also known as the SPF algorithm.

Dot1Q. A Cisco abbreviation for the IEEE standard 802.1Q that specifies standards for bridged virtual LANs (VLANs).

E

EIA/TIA. Electronic Industries Alliance/Telecommunications Industry Alliance. A group that specifies electrical transmission standards. The EIA and the TIA have developed numerous well-known communications standards, including EIA/TIA-232 and EIA/TIA-449.

encapsulation. The wrapping of data in a particular protocol header. For example, Ethernet data is wrapped in a specific Ethernet header before network transit. Also, when bridging dissimilar networks, the entire frame from one network is simply placed in the header used by the data link layer protocol of the other network.

encrypt. The process of applying a specific algorithm to data to alter the appearance of the data, making it incomprehensible to those who are not authorized to see the information.

Ethernet. A baseband LAN specification invented by Xerox Corporation and developed jointly by Xerox, Intel, and Digital Equipment Corporation. Ethernet networks use CSMA/CD and run over a variety of cable types at 10 Mbps. Ethernet is similar to the IEEE 802.3 series of standards.

expansion card. A card that is installed into a computer to provide access to communication device or to provide input/output.

expansion slot. A slot in a computer for the installation of cards that provide additional services such as communications or input/output devices.

F

FCS. frame check sequence. Extra characters added to a frame for error control purposes. Used in High-Level Data Link Control (HDLC), Frame Relay, and other data link layer protocols.

FDDI. Fiber Distributed Data Interface. A LAN standard, defined by ANSI X3T9.5, specifying a 100 Mbps token-passing network using fiber-optic cable, with transmission distances of up to 2 km. FDDI uses a dual-ring architecture to provide redundancy.

filtering. The process by which a network device screens traffic for certain characteristics such as address, protocol, or application. When a particular characteristic matches, the traffic is not relayed beyond the filtering process.

firewall. A filtering device that is designated as a buffer between any connected public network and private network. A firewall uses rules and lists to filter traffic to ensure the security of the private network.

Flash. A special type of electrically erasable programmable read-only memory (EEPROM) that can be erased and reprogrammed in blocks instead of 1 byte at a time. Many modern PCs have their BIOS stored on a Flash memory chip so that it can be updated easily if necessary. Such a BIOS is sometimes called a *Flash BIOS*. Flash memory is also popular in modems because it enables the modem manufacturer to support new protocols as they become standardized.

flooding. A traffic-passing technique used by switches and bridges in which traffic received on an interface is sent out through all the interfaces of that device except the interface on which the information was received originally.

flush. A process used by switches to remove aged out entries from the MAC address table.

forwarding. The process by which a network device screens traffic for certain characteristics such as address, protocol, or application. When a particular characteristic matches, the traffic is then relayed to the appropriate port based on these characteristics

forwarding table. A dynamic table built by Layer 2 switches that relates a device MAC address to a port on the switch so that the filtering and forwarding processes can take place.

FRAD. Frame Relay access device. Any network device that provides a connection between a LAN and a Frame Relay WAN.

frame. A logical grouping of information sent as a data link layer unit over a transmission medium. Often refers to the header and the trailer, used for synchronization and error control, that surround the user data contained in the unit. The terms *cell, datagram, message, packet,* and *segment* also describe logical information groupings at various layers of the OSI reference model and in various technology circles.

Frame Relay. An industry-standard, switched data link layer protocol that handles multiple virtual circuits using HDLC encapsulation between connected devices. Frame Relay is more efficient than X.25, the protocol for which it generally is considered a replacement.

G–H

global configuration mode. The main configuration mode for a Cisco IOS device that configures parameters common to the device or move to other configuration modes.

hexadecimal. A numbering system used in computers and networking that consists of 16 characters, 10 digits, and 5 letters. This numbering system is used to specify Layer 2 Media Access Control addresses.

holddown. A state into which a route is placed so that routers neither advertise the route nor accept advertisements about the route for a specific length of time (the holddown period). Holddown flushes bad information about a route from all routers in the network. A route typically is placed in holddown when a link in that route fails.

hub. In Ethernet, a multiport repeater that acts as the center of a star topology network.

I

IANA. Internet Assigned Numbers Authority. An organization operated under the auspices of the ISOC as a part of the IAB. The IANA delegates authority for IP address space allocation and domain name assignment to the InterNIC and other organizations. IANA also maintains a database of assigned protocol identifiers used in the TCP/IP stack, including autonomous system numbers.

IEEE. Institute of Electrical and Electronic Engineers. A professional organization that develops communications and network standards, among other activities.

infrastructures. The foundational building blocks of internetworking systems. Infrastructures include wiring and networking devices that are interconnected to form a computer internetwork.

interface configuration mode. A sub-configuration mode of the Cisco IOS that configures attributes of physical or virtual interfaces on a given device.

internetwork. A collection of physical networks that are interconnected via internetworking devices like routers and switches.

IPX. Internetwork Packet Exchange. A Novell NetWare network layer (Layer 3) protocol used for transferring data from servers to workstations. IPX is similar to IP and XNS.

ISDN. Integrated Services Digital Network. A communication protocol offered by telephone companies that permits telephone networks to carry data, voice, and other source traffic.

ISL. Inter-Switch Link. A Cisco proprietary protocol that maintains VLAN information as traffic flows between switches and routers.

ITU-T. International Telecommunications Union-Telecommunications Standards Section. An international body that develops worldwide standards for telecommunications technologies. The ITU-T carries out the functions of the former CCITT.

L

LAN. local-area network. A high-speed, low-error data network covering a relatively small geographic area (up to a few thousand meters). LANs connect workstations, peripherals, terminals, and other devices in a single building or in another geographically limited area. LAN standards specify cabling and signaling at the physical and data link layers of the OSI model. Ethernet, FDDI, and Token Ring are widely used LAN technologies.

latency. The delay between the time a device receives a frame and the time that frame is forwarded out the destination port.

Layer 2 switch. An internetworking device that uses specialized hardware to provide high-speed connectivity using Layer 2 MAC addressing for forwarding frames between segments.

Layer 3 switch. An internetworking device that uses specialized hardware to provide high-speed connectivity using Layer 3 network addressing for forwarding packets between networks.

Layer 4 switch. An internetworking device that uses specialized hardware to provide high-speed connectivity using Layer 4 protocol and port information along with either Layer 2 MAC or Layer 3 network addressing for forwarding frames between segments.

Linux. A public domain version operating system that runs on Reduced Instruction Set Computer (RISC) and Intel-based processors based on the UNIX operating system.

LLC. logical link control (TCP/IP). The higher of the two data link layer sublayers defined by the IEEE. The LLC sublayer handles error control, flow control, framing, and MAC-sublayer addressing. The most prevalent LLC protocol is IEEE 802.2, which includes both connectionless and connection-oriented variants.

loop. A route where packets never reach their destination, but simply cycle repeatedly through a constant series of network nodes.

M

MAC. Media Access Control. The lower of the two sublayers of the data link layer defined by the IEEE. The MAC sublayer handles access to shared media, such as whether token passing or contention is used.

MAN. metropolitan-area network. A network that spans a metropolitan area. Generally, a MAN spans a larger geographic area than a local-area network (LAN), but a smaller geographic area than a wide-area network (WAN).

mapping. A process in networking that links a Layer 2 address to a Layer 3 address.

MD5. Message digest algorithm 5. A one-way hashing algorithm that produces a 128-bit hash. Both MD5 and Secure Hash Algorithm (SHA) are variations on MD4 and are designed to strengthen the security of the MD4 hashing algorithm. Cisco uses hashes for authentication within the IPSec framework. Also used for message authentication in Simple Network Management Protocol (SNMP) v2. MD5 verifies the integrity of the communication, authenticates the origin, and checks for timeliness.

media. Plural of medium. Various physical environments through which transmission signals pass. Common network media include twisted-pair, coaxial, and fiber-optic cable, and the atmosphere (through which microwave, laser, and infrared transmission occurs). Sometimes called *physical media*.

media contention. In Ethernet or other shared media networks, this is what occurs when devices are forced to wait for other devices to finish transmitting before transmitting their own data. Media contention causes latency in shared media networks.

motherboard. A printed circuit board that houses the CPU, RAM, and expansion slots for a personal computer.

MTU. maximum transmission unit. The maximum packet size, in bytes, that a particular interface can handle.

multiplexing. A process that allows multiple logical signals to be transmitted simultaneously across a single physical channel.

N

NBMA. nonbroadcast multiaccess. A term describing a multiaccess network that either does not support broadcasting (such as X.25) or in which broadcasting is not feasible (for example, a Switched Multimegabit Data Service [SMDS] broadcast).

neighbor (router). In Open Shortest Path First (OSPF), two routers that have interfaces to a common network. On multiaccess networks, neighbors are discovered dynamically by the OSPF Hello protocol.

next hop. The next Layer 3 addressed interface for an internetwork path.

NIC. 1. network interface card. A board or chipset that provides network communication capabilities to and from a computer system. Also called an *adapter*. 2. Network Information Center. An organization whose functions have been assumed by the IANA.

non-canonical. Addresses that are sent on the wire with the most significant or high-order bit first. Token Ring addresses are non-canonical. For each byte of the Token Ring address, the first bit of the byte is sent first.

NVRAM. nonvolatile RAM. A type of random-access memory (RAM) that retains its contents when a unit is powered off.

O–Q

octet. A term meaning 8 bits in a row. In networking, the term *octet* often is used (rather than byte) because some machine architectures employ bytes that are not 8 bits in a row.

OSI. Open System Interconnection. An international standardization program created by International Organization for Standardization (ISO) and ITU-T to develop data networking standards that facilitate multivendor equipment interoperability.

PDU. protocol data unit. An OSI term used to describe a unit of data from a particular layer of the OSI model.

POP. point of presence. In OSS, a physical location where an interexchange carrier has equipment installed to interconnect with a *local exchange carrier (LEC)*.

POTS. plain old telephone service. A general term referring to the variety of telephone networks and services in place worldwide. Sometimes called *Public Switched Telephone Network (PSTN)*.

preamble. The beginning of an Ethernet frame that indicates to other devices on the segment that data is being transmitted.

printed circuit board (PCB). A multilayer circuit board on which chips are placed to create computer components.

privileged EXEC mode. A mode used to view and modify the operational and configurational parameters for a Cisco IOS device. This mode is also used to access global configuration mode.

proprietary. Refers to information (or other property) that is owned by an individual or an organization and for which the use is restricted by that entity.

protocol. A formal description of a set of rules and conventions that govern how devices on a network exchange information.

PSTN. Public Switched Telephone Network. A general term referring to the variety of telephone networks and services in place worldwide. Sometimes called *POTS*.

PTT. Post, Telephone, and Telegraph. A government agency that provides telephone services. PTTs exist in most areas outside of North America and provide both local and long-distance telephone services.

public domain. Computer software that has been written to be shared for free with everyone. These program and operating systems are free for anyone to use and/or altere, but cannot be resold or copyrighted by anyone.

QoS. quality of service. A measure of performance for a transmission system that reflects its transmission quality and service availability.

queue. 1. An ordered list of elements waiting to be processed. 2. A backlog of packets waiting to be forwarded over a router interface.

R

RADIUS. Remote Authentication Dial-In User Service. A database that provides a number of authentication services including authenticating modem and ISDN connections and tracking user connection time.

RAM. random-access memory. A type of volatile memory that can be read and written by a microprocessor.

RFC. Request For Comments. A document series used as the primary means for communicating information about the Internet. Some RFCs are designated by the Internet Architecture Board (IAB) as Internet standards. Most RFCs document protocol specifications, such as Telnet and File Transfer Protocol (FTP), but some are humorous or historical. RFCs are available online from numerous sources.

ROM. read-only memory. A type of nonvolatile memory that can be read, but not written, by the microprocessor.

ROMMON. read-only memory monitor. This is a command-line interface used to allow direct interaction with the processor involved in system startup.

router. A network layer device that uses one or more metrics to determine the optimal path along which network traffic should be forwarded. Routers forward packets from one network to another based on network layer information.

S

SAID. Security Association ID. A value used in IEEE 802.10 FDDI frames for security purposes.

segment. 1. A section of a network that is bounded by bridges, routers, or switches. 2. In a LAN using a bus topology, a segment is a continuous electrical circuit that often is connected to other such segments with repeaters. 3. A term used in the TCP specification to describe a single transport layer unit of information.

segmenting. In networking, this is the process of dividing large networks or groups of users into smaller more manageable groups.

serial port. A port on a router that allows synchronous or asynchronous transmissions where bits are transmitted sequentially over a single channel.

service provider. A company or corporation the provides and sells internetwork services and connections between geographical disperse locations.

signaling. 1. A process of sending a transmission signal over a physical medium for the purposes of communication. 2. The sending of call information across a telephone connection. This information can be transmitted by many techniques, such as opening and closing a loop to stop and start the flow of DC loop current (used to indicate on-hook and off-hook state and to transmit dial-pulsing of digits), sending of ringing voltage to alert the other side of an incoming call, sending digit information in the form of dual-tone multifrequency (DTMF) or multifrequency (MF) tones, or sending call state information on a digital service 0 (DS0) timeslot by using robbed bits.

SNAP. Subnetwork Access Protocol. An Internet protocol that operates between a network entity in the subnetwork and a network entity in the end system. SNAP specifies a standard method of encapsulating IP datagrams and Address Resolution Protocol (ARP) messages on IEEE networks. The SNAP entity in the end system makes use of the services of the subnetwork and performs three key functions: data transfer, connection management, and quality of service (QoS) selection.

SONET. Synchronous Optical Network. A standard format for transporting a wide range of digital telecommunications services over optical fiber. SONET is characterized by standard line rates, optical interfaces, and signal formats. SONET is a high-speed synchronous network specification developed by Bellcore and designed to run on optical fiber. STS-1 is the basic building block of SONET. Approved as an international standard in 1988.

SPF. Shortest path first is an algorithm developed by Dr. Edsger Dijkstra used by link state protocols like OSPF and Intermediate System-to-Intermediate System (IS-IS) to determine the best route through a network system.

subnet. 1. In IP networks, a network sharing a particular subnet address. Subnetworks are networks arbitrarily segmented by a network administrator in order to provide a multilevel, hierarchical routing structure while shielding the subnetwork from the addressing complexity of attached networks. Sometimes called a *subnet*. 2. In Open System Interconnection (OSI) networks, a collection of end systems and intermediate systems under the control of a single administrative domain and using a single network access protocol.

supernet. An aggregation of IP network addresses advertised as a single classless network address. For example, given four Class C IP networks, 192.0.8.0, 192.0.9.0, 192.0.10.0, and 192.0.11.0, each having the intrinsic network mask of 255.255.255.0, you can advertise the address 192.0.8.0 with a subnet mask of 255.255.252.0.

switch. 1. A network device that filters, forwards, and floods frames based on the destination address of each frame. The switch operates at the data link layer of the Open System Interconnection (OSI) reference model. 2. A general term applied to an electronic or mechanical device that allows a connection to be established as necessary and terminated when a session to support no longer exists. 3. In telephony, a general term for any device, such as a private branch exchange (PBX), that connects individual phones to phone lines.

switch fabric. The internal connections between the ports of a switch used to transmit data between end devices connected to these ports.

synchronous transmission. A term describing digital signals that are transmitted with precise clocking. Such signals have the same frequency, with flags that designate the beginning and the end of each character.

T

TACACS. Terminal Access Controller Access Control System. An authentication protocol, developed by the Defense Data Network (DDN) community, that provides remote access authentication and related services, such as event logging. User passwords are administered in a central database rather than in individual routers, providing an easily scalable network security solution.

tag. Identification information, including a number plus other information. Used in switches to identify a frames originating VLAN between two switches.

TCP/IP. Transmission Control Protocol/Internet Protocol. A common name for the suite of protocols developed by the U.S. Department of Defense in the 1970s to support the construction of worldwide internetworks. TCP and IP are the two best-known protocols in the suite.

Telnet. The standard terminal emulation protocol in the TCP/IP protocol stack. Telnet is used for remote terminal connection, enabling users to log in to remote systems and use resources as if they were connected to a local system. Telnet is defined in RFC 854.

TFTP. Trivial File Transfer Protocol. A simplified version of FTP that allows files to be transferred from one computer to another over a network, usually without the use of client authentication (for example, username and password).

Token Ring. A token-passing LAN developed and supported by IBM. Token Ring runs at 4 or 16 megabits per second (Mbps) over a ring topology.

topology. A physical arrangement of network nodes and media within an enterprise networking structure.

trunk. 1. A physical and logical connection between two switches across which network traffic travels. A backbone is composed of a number of trunks. 2. A telephone company connection between two central offices (COs) or between a CO and a private branch exchange (PBX).

trunking. The Cisco term used to describe marking Layer 2 VLAN identifiers on ISL or IEEE 802.1Q links between network devices.

tunneling. An architecture that is designed to provide the services necessary to implement any standard point-to-point encapsulation scheme.

twisted pair. Physical medium consisting of two insulated wires twisted around one another to decrease electromagnetic interference.

U–Z

UNIX. An operating system developed in 1969 at Bell Laboratories. UNIX has gone through several iterations since its inception, which include UNIX 4.3 BSD (Berkeley Standard Distribution), developed at the University of California at Berkeley, and UNIX System V, Release 4.0, developed by AT&T.

WAN. wide-area network. A data communications network that serves users across a broad geographic area and often uses transmission devices provided by common carriers. Frame Relay, SMDS, and X.25 are examples of WANs.

Xmodem. An asynchronous transfer protocol. This protocol can be used to recover lost operating systems for Cisco devices.

INDEX

Symbols

$ (dollar sign), scroll line indicator, 325
> (greater than symbol), CLI prompt, 318

Numerics

10BASE2, 57
10BASE5, 57
10BASE-T, 58
100BASE-F, 58
100BASE-T, 58

A

AAA servers, 78
abbreviating commands, 321
access layer (hierarchical network model), 50
access points, 127
access technologies, 293
    ATM, 301
    DSL, 296–299
    Frame Relay, 299–300
    HDLC, 294–295
    ISDN, 295–296
    PPP, 293–294
    SONET, 302–303
access VPNs, 110
accounting, 79
acknowledgment process, TCP three-way
   handshakes, 210
address classes, 229–231
address space, calculating, 249–250
addresses, network layer, 70–71
adds, moves, and changes, 412–414
administratively disabling routers, 358
ADSL (asymmetric DSL), 297
analog modems, 305
APNIC (Asia Pacific Network Information Centre),
   236
application layer
    OSI model, 34
    TCP/IP protocol stack, 40
applications. *See also* network applications
    TCP/IP, 202
ARIN (American Registry for Internet Numbers),
   229, 236
ARP (Address Resolution Protocol), 258
    local ARP, 192
    messages, 193
ARP cache, 192

B

backbone layer, 51
backoff algorithms, 61
backplane components, 10
backup IOS images, 409–411
balanced hybrid routing protocols, 268–269
    EIGRP, 271
bandwidth, 73, 143
    on Ethernet LANs, 159
    on point-to-point WAN connections, 288
base 16 numbering system, 22
    converting to binary, 23–26
    converting to decimal, 23–24
best path selection, 267
BGP (Border Gateway Protocol), 272
binary numbering system, 14
    converting to decimal, 20
    converting to hexadecimal, 25
bits, 14–15
    tokens, 54
boot field, router configuration, 400
boot system command, 397
boot system flash command, 397
boot system rom command, 397
boot system tftp command, 397
booting Cisco IOS devices, 332
    Catalyst switches, 332–337
    Cisco routers, 337–343, 395
bootloader, 396
bootstrap code, 395, 397
branch offices, 48
BRI (Basic Rate Interface), 296
bridging, 67, 162–163
    frame forwarding decision process, 67
    transparent, 67
broadcast addresses, 157, 232, 247–248
    local broadcasts, 233

ASICs (application-specific integrated circuits), 66
assigning
    IP addresses, 233
    name to Catalyst switch, 345
    name to Cisco routers, 352
asynchronous router connections, 148–149
ATM (Asynchronous Transfer Mode), 301
    virtual circuits, 302
AUIs (attachment unit interfaces), 133, 357
authentication, 79
authentication phase (PPP), 294
authorization, 79
Autoinstall utility, 401
autonomous systems, 264
auxiliary connections, 149

M

T

U

V

W

X–Z

☐ **YES!** I'm requesting a **free** subscription to *Packet*™ magazine.

☐ No. I'm not interested at this time.

☐ Mr.
☐ Ms.

First Name (Please Print) _____ Last Name _____

Title/Position (Required) _____

Company (Required) _____

Address _____

City _____ State/Province _____

Zip/Postal Code _____ Country _____

Telephone (Include country and area codes) _____ Fax _____

E-mail _____

Signature (Required) _____ Date _____

☐ I would like to receive additional information on Cisco's services and products by e-mail.

1. Do you or your company:
- A ☐ Use Cisco products
- B ☐ Resell Cisco products
- C ☐ Both
- D ☐ Neither

2. Your organization's relationship to Cisco Systems:
- A ☐ Customer/End User
- B ☐ Prospective Customer
- C ☐ Cisco Reseller
- D ☐ Cisco Distributor
- E ☐ Integrator
- F ☐ Non-Authorized Reseller
- G ☐ Cisco Training Partner
- I ☐ Cisco OEM
- J ☐ Consultant
- K ☐ Other (specify): _____

3. How many people does your entire company employ?
- A ☐ More than 10,000
- B ☐ 5,000 to 9,999
- C ☐ 1,000 to 4,999
- D ☐ 500 to 999
- E ☐ 250 to 499
- F ☐ 100 to 249
- G ☐ Fewer than 100

4. Is your company a Service Provider?
- A ☐ Yes
- B ☐ No

5. Your involvement in network equipment purchases:
- A ☐ Recommend
- B ☐ Approve
- C ☐ Neither

6. Your personal involvement in networking:
- A ☐ Entire enterprise at all sites
- B ☐ Departments or network segments at more than one site
- C ☐ Single department or network segment
- F ☐ Public network
- D ☐ No involvement
- E ☐ Other (specify): _____

7. Your Industry:
- A ☐ Aerospace
- B ☐ Agriculture/Mining/Construction
- C ☐ Banking/Finance
- D ☐ Chemical/Pharmaceutical
- E ☐ Consultant
- F ☐ Computer/Systems/Electronics
- G ☐ Education (K–12)
- U ☐ Education (College/Univ.)
- H ☐ Government—Federal
- I ☐ Government—State
- J ☐ Government—Local
- K ☐ Health Care
- L ☐ Telecommunications
- M ☐ Utilities/Transportation
- N ☐ Other (specify): _____

CPRESS

Packet magazine serves as the premier publication linking customers to Cisco Systems, Inc. Delivering complete coverage of cutting-edge networking trends and innovations, *Packet* is a magazine for technical, hands-on users. It delivers industry-specific information for enterprise, service provider, and small and midsized business market segments. A toolchest for planners and decision makers, *Packet* contains a vast array of practical information, boasting sample configurations, real-life customer examples, and tips on getting the most from your Cisco Systems' investments. Simply put, *Packet* magazine is straight talk straight from the worldwide leader in networking for the Internet, Cisco Systems, Inc.

We hope you'll take advantage of this useful resource. I look forward to hearing from you!

Cecelia Glover
Packet Circulation Manager
packet@external.cisco.com
www.cisco.com/go/packet